Robert Peckham is a cultural his
Royal Historical Society. The foun
promotes the integration of the humanities with the sciences and technology, he was previously Professor of History and M.B. Lee Endowed Professor in the Humanities and Medicine at the University of Hong Kong. He has held fellowships at Cambridge, Oxford, LSE and King's College London. He lives in New York.

Praise for *Fear*

'This exceptional and thought-provoking book sheds light on the intricate position fear occupies in the unavoidable realities of politics and our spiritual existence' Ai Weiwei

'Peckham's mapping of fear across centuries of thought offers an opportunity to reflect on a persistent political geography of anxiety' *Lancet*

'Brilliant and breathtakingly wide-ranging ... as Peckham shows in gripping and beautifully written detail, fear isn't just the stock in trade of wicked despots; in some circumstances it can be turned to positive effect. Could it, now, be that fear is our friend? Read Peckham and judge for yourself'
Simon Schama

'His book ... illuminates the many ways in which fear has shaped human behaviour over the past 700 years, from which readers can draw lessons for the present' *Economist*

'We all know what fear is, but who amongst us have considered its history? Peckham is fear's astute historian-translator in this big, brave, honest, and learned book ... gripping as well as uncomfortable reading, that shows us the stakes when fear and freedom are twinned' Alison Bashford

'An ambitious deep dive into history' *Irish Independent*

'Robert Peckham's deeply informed and lucidly staged anatomy of fear is a remarkable achievement. Peckham shapes a fundamentally transformative account of the sociology of fear – and of fear as a constitutive element of modern sociality itself. A groundbreaking study' Mark Seltzer

'Clear and engaging ... readers keen to grasp a better understanding of the history of the world will be entranced by Peckham's ability to communicate complex political, religious, economic, artistic, medical, military, technological and cultural trends' *BBC History Magazine*

'Fascinating, compelling and erudite. I have written quite a lot about fear and the brain, but learned so much about fear itself from this book' Joseph LeDoux

FEAR

An Alternative History of the World

ROBERT PECKHAM

Profile Books

This paperback edition first published in 2024

First published in Great Britain in 2023 by
Profile Books Ltd
29 Cloth Fair
London
EC1A 7JQ
www.profilebooks.com

3 5 7 9 10 8 6 4 2

Typeset in Berling Nova Text by MacGuru Ltd
Printed and bound in Great Britain by
CPI Group (UK) Ltd, Croydon CR0 4YY

Extract on p. ix from 'Greeting an Intoxicating Spring' by
Ai Qing printed with the kind permission of Ai Weiwei.

A CIP catalogue record for this book is available from the British Library.

ISBN 978 1 78816 725 3
eISBN 978 1 78283 813 5

For Alexander

Contents

'Can there be hope where fear is?'
Cervantes, *Don Quixote* (1605)

'Finally, we live without fear'
Ai Qing, 'Greeting an Intoxicating Spring' (1979)

Illustrations

Shoes of victims of Auschwitz at the Auschwitz-Birkenau State Museum, Oświęcim, Poland. Photo by Kallerna (2019). Reproduced under Creative Commons Attribution 4.0 International licence.

George Tooker, *The Subway*, 1950. Whitney Museum of American Art, New York. © Estate of George Tooker. Courtesy DC Moore Gallery, New York.

Cover art of *Atomic War!* #1 (November 1952). Published by Ace Comics.

Preface

I began writing this book in Hong Kong as Beijing cracked down on freedom in the name of security. Months of tear gas, rubber bullets and water cannon couldn't crush dissent, but a pandemic turned out to be the ultimate anti-protest weapon, one that the city's chief executive, Carrie Lam, deployed ruthlessly to stifle opposition. When I resigned from my professorship at the University of Hong Kong in the summer of 2021, friends were being hounded by the authorities, news agencies shut down and opposition leaders jailed. Fear stalked a city that a few years before had buzzed with optimism.[1]

At the height of the protests in 2019, pro-democracy graffiti sprung up across Hong Kong, with walkways and underpasses plastered with posters, colourful post-it notes and catchy pop-art images. One of the messages that moved me most was 'Freedom from Fear'; it was daubed on the glass pane of a bus shelter close to the Hong Kong Polytechnic University, where riot police had besieged students, shattering any illusion of academic immunity. Amid the violence, here was Franklin Delano Roosevelt's 1941 credo, later embedded in the preamble to the UN's Universal Declaration of Human Rights, resurrected by an anonymous protester seventy-eight years later.

Freedom from Fear is also the title of a painting by the American artist Norman Rockwell, published in the *Saturday Evening Post* in 1943 to illustrate Roosevelt's four 'essential human freedoms' doctrine – freedom of speech, freedom of worship and freedom from want and fear. In the picture, two children are shown asleep in bed, while their solicitous mother leans in to adjust the sheets and their father looks on, spectacles and folded newspaper in hand. It's a quaint scene of domestic bliss, except that the father is clearly pensive, shadows loom over the group and a doll lies ominously discarded on the floor. We can just make out the newspaper headline: 'Bombings Kill' and 'Horror Hit'.

Rockwell's painting was printed with an essay by the Pulitzer Prize-winning poet and novelist Stephen Vincent Benét. 'Since our nation began,' Benét wrote, 'men and women have come here for just that freedom – freedom from the fear that lies at the heart of every unjust law, of every tyrannical exercise of power by one man over another man.'[2] While the image reaffirms the values embodied in the nuclear family, it is also a call to action, a reminder to American citizens that violence will wreck their peaceful way of life unless they step up to defend it.[3]

When, how and why did fear come to be shackled to tyranny and invoked in opposition to freedom, even as it is marshalled in support of this very cause? Answering these questions involves grappling with the long history of fear's exploitation as a tool of power, and a means of both asserting and challenging authority.

There's also the issue of how we characterise 'power', a notoriously tricky word to pin down because it is everywhere and ever shifting – like water, Bruce Lee might have said. We could define it as the ability or capacity to act, as legal and political authority, as the control or influence one has over others, as mental or moral strength, and, of course, there is the power of physical force.[4] Many aspects of these distinct but overlapping notions are discussed in this book, whether in relation to religious institutions, the state, machines or ideas. Fear becomes a lens for reconsidering what power is and how it works, just as the study of power gives us new perspectives on fear.

The argument I make is that many of our assumptions about the relationship between fear, power and freedom are simplistic and even plain wrong. Fear isn't always inimical to freedom but may be its corollary, an integral facet of empowerment. Fear has generative potential, even when it appears as a desperate invocation graffitied on a bus shelter. It can be harnessed to change the world, creating new possibilities, even as it forecloses others.

In the chapters that follow, we'll consider the kinds of fear associated with different historical phenomena: natural disasters, pandemics, revolutions, technologies, financial crashes, wars and dictatorships. The book moves from pre-Reformation Europe to twenty-first-century China, from the Black Death to contemporary eco-panics, and will show how fear in one domain can spill over into another, to the extent that it is constantly being redistributed across political, social and technological systems. This 'liquid fear' eludes confinement, evidence of a fugitive property that it shares with freedom.[5]

The book is more than a 'Greatest Hits' compilation of historical fears, though. I'm interested in what fear has meant to individuals and societies in the past, as well as how events have shaped what we think about fear and its uses. On a more practical level, I'll argue that an historical awareness of how fear has been conscripted to serve power may help us avoid being exploited by it in the future. It's not, to use that hoary chestnut of an adage, that those who forget the past are doomed to repeat it; rather, history can be a potent antidote to the fallacies of fear.

Of course, history can also be a focus for fear – and not just in autocracies. In democratic societies around the world it has become central to splenetic debates about race, gender, sexuality, class and culture. Fear is intrinsic to this polarised politics where history is viewed in moral terms, either as a means of extolling traditional values or as grounds for a public reckoning with unexpiated injustices. Both viewpoints preclude any possibility of reconciliation or real change: in the first case, we're given a nostalgic roll call of triumphs, transformations and progressive freedoms; in the second, a relentless recitation of misdeeds. Is it any wonder that hope feels brittle when it's clamped between a contested past and an impossible future?

And what about fear in history? Dynasties rise and fall;

religions are created, reform and break apart; modern states are born; profits are had, and markets implode; the world is made and unmade – and all, in part, because of fear and its offshoot, panic. Yet if you look up 'fear' in the index of most history books, it's doubtful you'll find it. Like the background noise in a film, it's part of the atmospherics. Something that happens incidentally, the almost inaudible soundtrack of real life.

Given its modern-day pervasiveness, it seems perplexing that fear in the past is often downplayed, consigned to a side-show of big events, perhaps because it is hard to discern, too diffused through life to be winkled out as an object in itself. As the poet Louise Glück writes, 'panic is a synonym for being'; it just *is*.[6] It's the ever-presence but elusiveness of fear that makes it so thorny, but also hard to resist. How do we evade the effects of an emotion that we can never fully grasp?

Meanwhile, when historians look back at the past, they tend to project modern fears onto earlier times. The great Dutch historian Johan Huizinga, writing shortly after the First World War, saw fear as a characteristic of the late Middle Ages. 'So violent and motley was life,' he wrote, 'that it bore the mixed smell of blood and of roses.' These words probably tell us as much about the fear that hung over war-ravaged Europe in 1919 as they do about the fourteenth and fifteenth centuries.[7]

Likewise, when the German physician Justus Hecker dwelt on the terror of the fourteenth-century plague in his book *The Black Death*, published in 1832, he did so against the backdrop of a devastating cholera pandemic that was sweeping Europe. As thousands died, draconian quarantine measures were imposed and civil disturbances broke out, while rumours swirled that doctors, in collusion with government officials, were deliberately killing off the poor. As Hecker put it, 'the voice of nature was silenced by fear and horror'.[8]

Although recent world events have given urgency to the writing of this book, its genesis goes back decades to my student days backpacking across Pakistan in the late 1980s. It was 22 January 1988, to be precise, and I'd hitched a ride from Peshawar across the border into Afghanistan, along with thousands of Pashtun mourners, to attend the funeral of Abdul Ghaffar Khan, otherwise known as Bacha Khan. Together with Gandhi, Nehru and Jinnah – the architects of modern India and Pakistan – Khan, a pacifist, had been a prominent figure in the anti-colonial struggle for Indian independence. However, because he'd opposed the partition of India and rejected the North-West Frontier Province's incorporation into Pakistan in 1947, he'd been sidelined and for a time imprisoned and placed under house arrest in Peshawar. His last wish was to be buried in the grounds of his house in Jalalabad, where he'd lived in self-imposed exile during the 1960s and 1970s.

We left at dawn and drove through the Khyber Pass to Jalalabad, past Soviet checkpoints, tanks and truck-mounted rocket launchers. The Soviet–Afghan War was ongoing, but both sides, Soviets and Mujahideen – Islamicist anti-Soviet guerrilla fighters backed at that time by the United States – had declared a ceasefire for Bacha Khan's burial.

When we reached the city, we parked beside a row of battered buses in a crowded plot a five-minute walk from the Khan family compound. By then, thousands of mourners had converged on the modest cluster of buildings, among them the Afghan president and the vice-president of India, as verses from the Quran were recited over a glitchy megaphone.

Boom. Suddenly, just as the twenty-one-gun salute began, the crowd was jolted by a loud blast that came from the direction of the parking lot. For perhaps thirty seconds, the ceremony continued uneasily. But then came another explosion, louder this time, and people began to scatter. Jalalabad was under attack.

Moments before, the crowd had been respectfully unified in grief, but now it fractured. People kicked and elbowed each other, desperate to escape. Five of the buses had been bombed, with at least eight people killed and many more injured by flying debris. Vans and cars across from ours had been written off. People were dazed, wondering how they would get home. Some were sobbing. Fights broke out and guns were pointed.[9]

As we sped along the main road back to Peshawar, stranded mourners tried to wave us down. Long-bearded Afghans in combat jackets and white shalwar kameez squatted on the roadside. We didn't stop. The driver cursed. The security guard in the back, high on pungent hash, fingered his AK-47 fretfully. Panic, which made us human, also made us cruel.

This memory of fear has lodged in my mind as an awakening, the sudden appreciation of life's full possibilities at the very moment life felt endangered. Robert Burton, author of the seventeenth-century medical compendium *The Anatomy of Melancholy*, understood how fear and sorrow are both 'cause and symptom' of each other, while C. S. Lewis wrote of the 'same fluttering in the stomach, the same restlessness, the yawning'.[10] In retrospect, fear and grief come to seem like agents of a moral lesson, teaching us how to live when we think we're going to die.

Experiences of fear, as I'll show in this book, often go hand in hand with attempts to explain how it works. My ordeal in Jalalabad was no exception, leading me on a search to understand the nature of fear and the panic it can trigger. How was it that I'd become complicit in a violence which was motored by a compulsion to get away, that in our rush for self-preservation, none of us in the crowd that day recognised any humanity other than our own? Were we following some pre-coded plot line of panic that we'd unconsciously assembled and internalised from media reports and movies? Was this panic even *real*? All of us at Bacha Khan's wake – his 'Red Shirt' Pashtun followers, Afghan officials, journalists, visiting dignitaries, Soviet troops and bystanders – were part of the explosion we were running from.

Afterwards, when my travelling companions and I talked through our experience, it was evident that the panic had had similar effects on us all. It had both strengthened and diminished our self-awareness. In the general mayhem, we'd experienced an acute sense of isolation; the threat of terror had heightened our consciousness of ourselves as individuals set apart from the anonymity of the stampeding crowd. And yet the panic had also eroded our sense of self, sucking us into the collective flight from terror.[11]

In *Crowds and Power*, first published in German in 1960 but more widely publicised after its author, Elias Canetti, won the Nobel Prize in Literature in 1981, a fire in a crowded theatre is used to illustrate how panic works on a crowd.[12] Along with contagion, fire is a common analogy for the spread of panic. Like fire, panic *rages*, a striking metaphor that associates both fear and fire with anger. Although the individuals inside the theatre are united by a common fear, there isn't space to act in unison. The crowd, which not long before has been joined in enjoyment of a performance, suddenly and violently breaks apart.

'Only one or two persons can get through each exit at a time,' Canetti writes, 'and thus the energy of flight turns into an energy of struggle to push others back.' This is the paradox of panic: it's a form of collective fear that shatters the collective. In the panicking crowd, everyone fends for themselves: 'Each man sees the door through which he must pass; and he sees himself alone in it, sharply cut off from all the others.'[13] The French statesman and political philosopher Alexis de Tocqueville – one of the most astute commentators on modern fear – observed how it acts upon people 'as a mechanical pressure might upon very hard bodies, which are compelled to adhere to one another so long as the pressure continues, but which separate so soon as it is relaxed'.[14] As the cultural critic Susan Sontag put it, 'Fear binds people together. And fear disperses them.'[15]

'It is strange to observe how strongly for the person struggling with it the crowd assumes the character of fire,' Canetti tells us. 'The people he pushes away are like burning objects to him; their touch is hostile, and on every part of his body; and it terrifies him.' As we fled from Bacha Khan's burial place in Jalalabad, we were all alight, individually and collectively 'tainted with the general hostility of fire'.[16]

Our panic had an imagined cause: fear of death extrapolated from the sound of bomb blasts. One neurobiological interpretation might be that in the face of a presumed threat, a hardwired emergency response system had kicked in, short-circuiting the 'thinking' part of our brains. Panic was the outcome of a synaptic communiqué.

Or was it that some primitive instinct had showed its rump? Like many of his contemporaries, the early twentieth-century Scottish psychologist William McDougall thought that panic was the relic of a feral past. 'The panic,' he wrote, 'is the crudest and simplest example of collective mental life.'[17] It's an idea that has been remarkably enduring: our basic urges may have been tamed by civilisation, but they've never been wholly dispelled. A related version of this theory crops up in histories that view fear as the first stage in a process of human advancement that leads to modern enlightenment, a transformative arc that's often imagined in terms of a child's maturation to adulthood. As human societies evolve, primordial fear is banished to the edges of rational life, although it continues to break out periodically to disrupt our inexorable development.

In all such fear theories, panic is the convulsion of a hardwired reflex that shatters dreams of human progress. This is what the Dutch primatologist Frans de Waal calls the 'veneer theory', the belief that civilisation is a layer of culture that humans impose upon their animal selves. Essentially, we make morality to keep a lid on our basic biology. But all it takes is a violent shake-up – a bomb blast, for instance – and the mask slips to reveal the inner ape.[18] Panic is what lurks beneath and threatens to pierce the thin skin of human cultivation. Our lives have a higher purpose until an elemental ferocity rips the script and we're back where we began.

Except that wasn't how we experienced it, and nor is it how I remember it. The panic belonged to a specific moment: the afternoon of Friday, 22 January 1988, in Jalalabad. Buried within the specificity of that moment was an expansive history that linked me to Bacha Khan, Indian nationalism, British colonialism, imperial geopolitics and post-colonial struggle – the bitter seeds of what thirteen years later would become George W. Bush's 'war on terror', as America's erstwhile allies, the Mujahideen, transmogrified into the new enemy, part of Bush's nefarious 'axis of evil'.[19] The panic that day, so fleeting and fatal, accommodated all of these. It was biological, but it was more than biology: it was scripted, and it was improvised; it had deep roots in history, and it had a long future yet to play out.

It was also part of a political calculation; the chaos had been planned. After the bombing, Afghan officials placed responsibility on the US-funded Mujahideen but the guerrillas denied involvement. On their side, Pakistani government sources accused Afghan police operatives of trying to undermine the Pakistani state, which had guaranteed the safety of Bacha Khan's mourners.[20] Whatever party was to blame, the bombing had been designed to trigger panic in order to frustrate any possibility of political accommodation; it had helped to perpetuate a climate of mutual fear in which sectarian violence could thrive; and it had linked the backyard theatre of Bacha Khan's funeral with an emerging theatre of global war.

I make two arguments in this book. The first is that different political regimes are enabled by the production of different kinds of fear, just as counter-fears, often unforeseen, disrupt the smooth operation of those regimes, sometimes shattering them, but often creating a pressure on them to evolve. Viewed like this, fear isn't just the tool and nemesis of power; it's also the reactive agent that can force change. Power resembles technology in that there's no steady accumulation, but components of one power regime recombine to create a new system. Elements of what came to be called 'feudal' kingship recombined to produce absolutism, components of which in turn formed the building blocks of the modern state. 'We can say that technology creates itself out of itself,' the economist W. Brian Arthur has said. The same holds true for power that 'bootstraps itself upward' through the reassimilation of pre-existing constituents, creating itself out of itself. And if we stick with this analogy, fear is the catalyst that makes this 'recombinatory evolution' possible.[21]

Tracing the history of fear can help us rethink assumptions about the nature of power, freedom, egalitarianism and market capitalism. We've been taught to think that fear is antithetical to democratic systems; in contrast to fear-dependent autocracies, where the repressive state uses terror to subdue its citizens, democracies, we're told, protect us from coercive infringements on our lives. This is the book's second claim. It is a mistake to assume that modern freedoms have been won by the abrogation of fear from political life. On the contrary, as we'll see, state-sponsored fear has played a crucial role, not only in the ascent of modern freedom but also in the emergence of the economic order on which it has been built.

Prologue

Is This Fear We're Feeling?

In Marshall Heights, a neighbourhood of south-east Washington, DC, residents live with the ever-present threat of gun crime. 'Fear,' proclaimed a 2021 report in the *Washington Post* about the district, 'is part of everyday life.'[1]

In Hong Kong, a national security law was introduced in June 2020 to quell anti-government protest. Vaguely defined activities from 'subversion' to 'collusion with foreign forces' are classified as crimes that may lead to life imprisonment. 'If they can induce fear in you, that's the cheapest way to control you and the most effective way,' the newspaper publisher and pro-democracy campaigner Jimmy Lai told the BBC before he was hauled off to jail. 'To live your life in fear is worse than losing your freedom,' observed the Chinese artist and activist Ai Weiwei, now living in self-imposed exile in Portugal.[2]

Meanwhile, Russian T-64 tanks and SU-27 fighter aircraft were blasting their way across Ukraine. 'I'm in Kyiv, and it is terrifying,' a Ukrainian journalist told the world as she woke to bombs and sirens. 'I felt fear crawling in my guts,' she wrote, 'as if someone, maybe Mr Putin himself, had grabbed my heart and squeezed it.'[3] 'We are not afraid of anything or anyone,' Ukraine's defiant president, Volodymyr Zelensky, declared in a video press conference from his bunker in the besieged capital, as violence unspooled across the country.

And since March 2020, when the World Health Organization (WHO) declared that a rapidly spreading coronavirus had become pandemic, much of the world has been in the grips of *coronaphobia*, 'a new emerging phobia specific to Covid-19'.[4]

It isn't just gun crime, autocratic rule, war and viral disease that generate fear. It's terrorism, cyberattacks, government conspiracies, immigrants, economic ruin, climate change and much more. In 2022 a US survey listed corrupt government officials, loved ones dying or falling sick, a nuclear attack by Russia, the United States' involvement in a world war, financial and economic collapse, pollution and biological warfare among the nation's top ten fears.[5]

As the philosopher Brian Massumi writes, 'naturalized fear, ambient fear, ineradicable atmospheric fright', has become the ubiquitous, 'discomfiting affective Muzak' that may well be remembered as 'a trademark' of our age.[6] Novel technologies, it's argued – above all the rise of the internet, along with a 24/7 news cycle – have created new vectors for distant terrors to cross borders with unprecedented speed. After 9/11, the 2008 financial crisis and the Covid-19 pandemic, we're more fearful than we've ever been.[7]

Perhaps we should attribute a portion of these fears to the so-called 'probability neglect', which is when a potential risk triggers such an intense emotional response in us that we confuse possibility with probability and overlook the fact that it's unlikely to occur. According to the 'loss aversion' hypothesis developed in behavioural economics to explain decision-making and risk, we tend to be more concerned about avoiding losses than we are about making gains, more fearful of things going wrong than we are hopeful of things going right.[8]

While some fears may arise from credible threats, others appear exaggerated, even imaginary. You could argue that there's a dissonance between proliferating fears and evidence that the early twenty-first century is arguably the safest era in history, with rising life expectancy and a marked fall in extreme poverty and war, even though glaring inequalities and violence persist in many parts of the world.[9] In 2022 the World Bank declared that global progress in reducing poverty had stalled, with over 700 million people living below the extreme poverty line, the majority in sub-Saharan Africa.[10] Viewed from the ruins of Homs or Aleppo, or the Ukrainian port city of Mariupol, the world doesn't look so bright. Or from neighbourhoods of Detroit, St Louis and Memphis, for that matter, which are often ranked among America's deadliest cities.

In this book I'll argue that fear is a means to power, and that it's stoked by those who stand to gain from it, whether they're politicians, religious movements, media organisations, tech companies, big pharma or financial institutions.[11] But more than that, the condemnation of fear-for-profit is itself a political stratagem, as when those who campaigned for the UK to leave the European Union in the 2016 Brexit referendum accused their opponents of instigating 'Project Fear'. At the same time, the long history of fear-for-profit raises an important secondary question: how do we break free of this exploitative cycle? And if we were to succeed, what would happen to all the public-spirited interventions that rely on the strategic use of fear to influence our behaviour? Don't we need fear to take our problems seriously?

Although it may serve as a means of control, fear's protean properties make it difficult to manage. As we'll see in subsequent discussions of nineteenth- and early twentieth-century technology and financial crashes, fear and a disposition to panic were understood by many contemporary commentators as inherent facets of an industrialising world where new freedoms brought new risks.

But first, what is this fear we're talking about? The word, after all, covers a disconcertingly vast spectrum of experience. It describes an emotional state and is used as a shorthand for complex psychological and physiological processes. It's a net so large that it ensnares the mass event and the individual experience. Our lexicon of fear branches into such a variety of not-quite-equivalents that it's easy to get lost in definitions: anxiety, angst, terror, dread, horror, panic, hysteria and so forth.

'Fear is the anticipation of pain,' wrote the psychologist Granville Stanley Hall in the late 1890s, echoing Aristotle, who famously defined fear 'as a pain or disturbance due to a mental picture of some destructive or painful evil in the future'.[12] Hall, the inaugural president of the American Psychological Association, set about classifying different kinds of fear, based on feedback from a questionnaire he'd sent to 748 participants in one of the first ever public surveys on the subject. He was flummoxed by the plethora of phobias he uncovered: fears of wind, thunder, meteors, darkness, fire, water, solitude, guns, dirt, mechanical vehicles, dogs, cats, snakes, spiders, bugs and beetles, the sight of blood, strangers, disease, death, ghosts, witches and sin, to name a few.

Hall's aim wasn't to get rid of fear, which he considered necessary to human progress: 'fears', he wrote 'are the roots of so many of the strongest intellectual interests'. Instead, he wanted to understand where fears came from and what function they performed. The problem was, with so many kinds of fear, where should he begin?[13]

An elevator-pitch definition of fear might be a neurobiological process to keep us alive. The language we use seems to point to an instinct for self-preservation. The English noun 'terror', for example, shares an ancient root with the word 'tremble', while 'horror' and 'anxiety' derive from Latin verbs meaning to bristle and to tighten or asphyxiate, suggesting physiological responses to some perceived threat. Despite the received wisdom that we ought to overcome, conquer or resist fear, the fact is that it's a survival mechanism, shielding us from harm.[14] The nature of that mechanism, however, is debated.

It was Charles Darwin who popularised the idea that emotions are innate mental states that we express via a repertoire of facial actions and behaviours, some of which are instinctive and others acquired.[15] Contemporary neuroscientists have tended to go along with this theory, identifying bundles of cells in two almond-shaped regions of the brain, called the amygdalae, that act as epicentres of an emergency detection system. A cluster of neurons there decode external stimuli that indicate threats, sparking physiological responses – perspiration, increased heart rate, shortness of breath – and reflex behaviours, including fight or flight.

In recent years, however, this explanation has been challenged, and some scientists now believe that fear can't be localised in this way. What we call 'fear' may not be part of a specific neurological circuit after all but is probably distributed across different functions of the brain. And while the amygdalae appear to have an important role in threat memories, evidence has indicated that it's possible to experience fear even when they are damaged.[16]

It turns out, then, that there's little scientific consensus about how fear is produced or, for that matter, what it is. In fact, as early as 1884, the philosopher and psychologist William James had challenged the assumption that fear is an automatic response to an external threat. While common sense tells us that when we meet a bear we're frightened and run, he hypothesised that it's only in hindsight that we register our subjective response as 'fear'. 'My thesis,' he wrote, 'is that the bodily changes follow directly the PERCEPTION of the exciting fact, and that our feeling of the same changes as they occur IS the emotion.'[17]

The neuroscientist Joseph LeDoux at New York University's Emotional Brain Institute agrees that the feeling is the emotion, but, contrary to James, argues that bodily responses are not an essential ingredient.[18] He says that we should regard fear as distinct from the expression of defensive behaviours triggered by external stimuli. They often go together because they are both elicited by the same stimulus but have different effects in the brain. As LeDoux writes, 'Fear, anxiety, and other emotions are, in my view, just what people have always thought they were – conscious feelings.' In other words, fear belongs to our 'emotional consciousness' and, like all our emotions, it's a cognitive construction, a mental model of the situation that not only determines how we feel but also allows for a novel, consciousness-based decision-making and behavioural control process.[19]

But how should we differentiate fear from the other terms with which it overlaps? Although 'fear' and 'anxiety' can't be understood apart from one another, from his research LeDoux concludes that 'different brain mechanisms are engaged when the state is triggered by an objective and present threat as opposed to an uncertain event that may or may not occur in the future'.[20] This isn't just armchair posturing. Failure to recognise the difference between subjective fear and its objective correlated responses, LeDoux suggests, accounts for the failure of medications that have been developed to treat mental illness by testing their effects on animals.[21]

It's easy to become over-fixated on terminology, to the extent that a history of fear might end up becoming little more than a hair-splitting exercise in semantics. Perhaps this is the point at which we ought to resurrect the Austrian-born philosopher Ludwig Wittgenstein's notion of semantic 'family resemblances'. Words, he suggested, don't capture the essence of some external object or idea, but exist in relation to a network of other words with similar meanings. Viewed from this perspective, fear is part of a family comprised of many words with strong resemblances, such as anxiety, terror, fright, panic, hysteria, paranoia and so forth.[22] It may be that fear's power lies precisely in its murkiness, ambiguity and durability as an emotion, behaviour, idea and tool.

Over-emphasising neurobiological arguments also minimises the issue of how emotions have been defined in history, and the differences in how they've been experienced and understood. Our hardwired capacity to detect and respond to an imminent threat is related to but distinct from the fear that's generated by the neocortex, the part of the human brain associated with higher cognitive functioning. In the latter case, fear is assembled in a process of categorisation, where previous experiences are pulled together and compared. To assess a potential threat, we draw on a repository of past experiences. Fear is shaped by our previous encounters; through our ancestry, upbringing and membership of a given community, we're socially primed to experience it in specific ways.

As soon as we recognise that fear has this acquired social and cultural dimension, we concede the possibility that it may be unlearned, and our responses modulated. 'Fears are educated into us, and can, if we wish, be educated out,' the American psychiatrist Karl Menninger wrote in 1927.[23] Understood like this, fear is personal, tribal and adaptive. In contrast to the core biological threat-detection-and-response function, it is contingent and acquired. It is also central to how societies are organised and regulated, and it is manifest in distinct ways at different times and in different cultures. That's why, if we are to grasp the nature of fear, we need to understand its histories and the local contexts in which it arises.

If we approach fear in this way, as a composite cultural and neuroscientific phenomenon, we begin to see that it is in many instances a response to uncertainty. In LeDoux's compelling formulation, anxiety is 'the price we pay for our ability to imagine the future'.[24] In effect, fear and anxiety pull us in two directions: they draw on the past to forewarn of a possible future.

Capturing the fear of uncertainty and manipulating its twin hope have long been the basis of power. Writing in 1605, the English philosopher and statesman Sir Francis Bacon enumerated the political benefits to be had from playing off the 'predominant affections of fear and hope' against each other in order to keep a lid on rival factions within the state.[25] Bacon's contemporary the English scholar and clergyman Robert Burton used a striking metaphor from siege warfare when he described fear and hope as the Devil's 'two battering-Cannons and principal Engines, with their objects, reward and punishment'.[26]

Fear isn't necessarily a top-down affair driven by the political elite; it can also derive from bottom-up populist concerns which are fuelled by charismatic, autocratic-leaning 'anti-establishment' leaders and their parties. Political fears are now coming from two directions: from those anxious about the consequences of disruptive populism and from populist movements distrustful of the media and state institutions, such as Donald Trump's Make America Great Again brand of American Republicanism, or Viktor Orbán's Civic Alliance in Hungary. 'Anger and fear is what gets people to the polls,' Trump's former chief strategist, Steve Bannon, insists.[27]

Neither is fear necessarily despotic or tyrannical. It can be beneficial, working as a social glue and a check on power. Likewise, it may be integral to freedom. In his book *The Concept of Anxiety*, published in 1844, the Danish philosopher and theologian Søren Kierkegaard argued that an individual's capacity to make free choices may induce paralysing anxiety, even terror. He asks us to imagine that we're at the top of a cliff, gazing down at the ground far below. While we recoil in horror at the prospect of falling into this 'yawning abyss', we also feel a terrifying compulsion to throw ourselves off the edge simply because we can. Our very freedom to choose, Kierkegaard suggests, creates frightful possibilities, a mind-crushing vertigo that he calls the 'dizziness of freedom'. Fear and freedom turn out to be inseparable, not antithetical.[28]

At the same time, the political, religious and social systems we live within – whether democratic or totalitarian, secular or theocratic, liberal or illiberal – are the outcome of struggles to corral, instrumentalise and neutralise fear. British abolitionists in the late eighteenth century dramatised the terror of slavery as a means of ending it, while democratic states have used fear to galvanise collective action. The medieval Church, absolute monarchies, colonial states and liberal democracies have all recognised the power of fear and developed strategies for co-opting it to their cause. In many ways, the modern world was made by fear.

*

This book traces the history of roughly 700 years of fear. The story begins in the fourteenth century, when the Catholic Church's monopoly on fear in western Europe was challenged by a series of catastrophic events, including a devastating plague. By the seventeenth century, European states had been forged out of political and religious strife. Soon they began to carve out empires in the Americas, Asia and Africa, exporting Western assumptions about fear and its management around the globe. This traffic in fear was far from unidirectional, though, since European exposure to non-Western societies provided a comparative framework for reflecting on fear at home, along with a new appreciation of the ways that culture shaped the human 'passions'.

Modernising processes distributed power and fear in new ways. By the nineteenth century, bureaucratisation had effected far-reaching social transformations. A rising professional class began to flex its muscles; as societies became more urban and industrialised, power dispersed. In factories, workers became dependent on the vagaries of the market and the logic of supply and demand. The wealth and influence of financiers and industrial leaders, along with a vocal bourgeoisie, forced the political establishment to accommodate their interests. Concurrently, the rise of the 'masses' and the spectre of popular dissent created a dynamic that challenged this accommodation. It is the tension between these forces – the citizen and the state, the individual and the mass, nation-building and globalisation – and the entanglement of fears they produced that we'll explore. The capitalisation of fear, particularly in the late nineteenth century and the twentieth, is the focus of the second half of the book.

Today, while centralised states continue to form the organisational basis for national economies and societies, corporations have exploited new technology to create global communities of users that cut across state boundaries. The possibilities and vulnerabilities created by this technological convergence pose a growing challenge for state authorities, particularly in the management of fear.

Although I'll argue that power depends on fear, I'll also trace the unforeseen consequences that have stemmed from attempts to manipulate it: how the abolition of one fear invariably gives rise to other countervailing fears; how terror arises out of efforts to suppress the despotic use of fear; how fear is summoned as justification for political or social change; and how fears are marketed to us by businesses that trade on our hopes. Fear is integral to the booming 'happiness market' that sells us positivity with the veiled threat of everlasting misery. 'Every saving invention and every intellectual advance,' Martin Luther King once remarked, 'has behind it as a part of its motivation the desire to avoid or escape some dreaded thing.'[29]

Historians, philosophers and political scientists have tended to write about fear as if it were either a cultural or a political phenomenon, as if culture can somehow be unhitched from politics, or politics removed from the social world that shapes it.[30] And the emphasis for the most part has been on the corrosive nature of the emotions in public life, with fear viewed as a pernicious influence that feeds on ignorance and perpetuates inequalities and discrimination. 'Fear,' wrote the poet and cultural critic bell hooks, 'is the primary force upholding structures of domination.'[31]

In the 1940s the American historian Arthur Schlesinger cautioned that fear was disabling democratic processes. Industrialisation and unregulated capitalism, buttressed by technology and science, had created 'a terrifying problem of adjustment', which risked driving disaffected citizens into the arms of totalitarianism. As he put it, 'fear and want' were undermining democracy, providing an ideal climate for communism to take seed.[32]

The German-Jewish psychoanalyst and philosopher Erich Fromm, who fled to the United States in 1934 after the Nazis were elected to power, argued that, while democracy may have set people free, it had created societies in which individuals felt 'powerless and alone, anxious and insecure'. It was in order to escape from this alienating freedom that they willingly submitted to authoritarian rule. Democracy, he argued, had produced the social and psychological conditions within which Nazi ideology could thrive.[33]

Schlesinger and Fromm weren't alone in grappling with the problem of fear and freedom during and in the aftermath of the Second World War, as Stalin intensified his repression in the Soviet Union. Among other books, George Orwell's *Nineteen Eighty-Four* appeared in 1949 and Hannah Arendt's *The Origins of Totalitarianism* in 1951. In different ways, these writers contended with the nature of political fear, totalitarian terror and the threats that they posed to the liberal order.

'Power based on love,' Mahatma Gandhi said in 1925, 'is a thousand times more effective and permanent than the one derived from fear of punishment.'[34] But while democratic leaders like Gandhi and Martin Luther King may have cultivated love to promote their causes, from the late twentieth century the emphasis has been on less positive political emotions. Writing in the 1990s, following the dissolution of the Soviet Union, the start of war in Afghanistan and genocide in Bosnia and Rwanda, the Canadian writer and politician Michael Ignatieff warned: 'In the twentieth century, the idea of human universality rests less on hope than on fear, less on optimism about the human capacity for good than on dread of human capacity for evil, less on a vision of man as maker of his history than of man the wolf toward his own kind.'[35]

'Convinced that we lack moral or political principles to bind us together,' writes the American political scientist Corey Robin, 'we savor the experience of being afraid, as many writers did after 9/11, for only fear, we believe, can turn us from isolated men and women into a united people.' According to Robin, this politics of fear is sapping our belief in universal values – justice and equality, among them – that undergird democratic institutions, ultimately weakening their legitimacy, as well as our faith in them. When we succumb to fear in this way, we unwittingly oblige the self-serving interests pushing it, which is another reason, he says, that 'fear is not, and cannot, be a foundation of moral and political argument'.[36]

But not everyone sees it this way. Another line of reasoning holds that fear keeps us alert to potential infractions on our rights and attentive to the state's repressive instincts.[37] And the biggest threats to our freedom may come from within, often from the exorbitant measures implemented to protect that freedom. In his inaugural presidential address, delivered in March 1933 during the Great Depression – best known for the slogan 'The only thing we have to fear is fear itself' – President Roosevelt declared his intention of asking Congress 'for the one remaining instrument to meet the crisis – broad Executive power to wage a war against the emergency, as great as the power that would be given to me if we were in fact invaded by a foreign foe'.[38] Roosevelt is rightly remembered today for the ambitious New Deal measures he took to meet the crisis, but the point is that fear can be used to justify dangerous states of exception anywhere, even by progressive reformers.[39]

These quarrels over the uses and abuses of fear reflect different ideas about what freedom is and how it has been understood historically. It's been argued that our modern conception of freedom arose in the course of the nineteenth century as a counter-revolutionary reaction by an elite to 'fears that the newly enfranchised masses would use state power for economic redistribution'. Freedom was espoused as a safeguard against the dangers of democratic extremes and as a means of warding off the economic threat posed by popular power.[40] But is the longing for freedom innate in humans, regardless of culture? Does freedom mean freedom from others meddling in our lives, or freedom to shape our own destinies? Is it 'the absence of external pressure or is it also the *presence* of something – and if so, of what'?[41] Is it negative or positive: freedom *from* some putative threat, or freedom to *do* as we wish?[42] And are we really ever free if we depend on the will of another, simply because there is always a possibility of interference?[43]

While debates such as these may have become more heated over the last decade, they are hardly new. In the nineteenth century, as education expanded and industrial societies democratised, many commentators noted the complex relationship between freedom, equality and fear. Tocqueville, who studied America's political system in the early 1830s, wrote about his fears and hopes for the 'great democratic revolution'. The second volume of his monumental *Democracy in America* highlights the unsettling contradictions that democracy produces. Citizens in democratic states, he reflects, are haunted by a 'fear of anarchy [that] holds them constantly in suspense and always ready to throw out their freedom at the first disorder'. In this circular conundrum, the end leads back to the beginning: freedom creates equality which generates fear which jeopardises freedom.

Like Kierkegaard's 'dizziness of freedom', Tocqueville describes how citizens, ever fearful of the possibility of lawlessness, 'dread their free will; they are afraid of themselves'. But he also notes that fear may function as a crucial defence against despotism. 'Let us therefore have that salutary fear of the future that makes one watchful and combative,' he concludes, 'and not that sort of soft and idle terror that wears hearts down and enervates them.'[44]

The problem with polarised arguments about fear and liberalism is that they imply a zero-sum game – you either hustle for fear or you don't. But why should an adherence to the principles of freedom and justice preclude recognising the positively charged nature of fear, which isn't only mobilised to uphold the status quo but may challenge authority in ways that effect favourable change? The history of fear, I'd suggest, is more hopeful than many accounts would have us believe.

Besides, most discussions of political fear stress its perturbing, antagonistic nature, omitting just how integral it has been to the creation of political rights and liberties. While freedom may imply freedom from some potential threat, the fear of loss, I'll argue, is inseparable from the hope that must drive any commitment to social justice. We would do well to reflect on the seventeenth-century philosopher Baruch Spinoza's claim that 'There is no hope unmingled with fear, and no fear unmingled with hope.'[45]

'Fear of losing power corrupts those who wield it and fear of the scourge of power corrupts those who are subject to it,' the Myanmar politician Aung San Suu Kyi has written. 'It is not easy for a people conditioned by fear' to free themselves from its 'enervating miasma' – and yet it has never been more important, as we enter an era of insidious, mediatised fear.[46] A better understanding of the history of fear may be a first step towards rethinking the role that it plays, not only in shaping institutions of power but also in our understanding of freedom and its possibilities.

1
The Great Pestilence

Modern humans and our ancestors have probably been fearful for millions of years. It may well be that our emotional responses have their origins in a deep evolutionary past, and that many of our phobias – of snakes, spiders and darkness – are responses to the risks faced by our hunter-gatherer progenitors, which remain embedded in our neural circuitry. As the evolutionary biologist Gordon Orians has suggested, we're haunted by ghosts of habitats and predators past. 'The typical objects of fears and phobias pose little danger in modern societies,' he writes, 'yet our fear and avoidance of the feared object persists.'[1]

Darwin reckoned that all humans share emotional expressions and behaviours, which he called 'the language of the emotions', inferring from his research that 'fear was expressed from an extremely remote period, in almost the same manner as it now is by man'.[2] The American psychologist Paul Ekman likewise believes that human emotions are universal and that we're programmed to recognise facial expressions associated with anger, disgust, happiness, sadness, surprise and fear – although many scientists argue that emotional experiences are personalised and differ between cultures.[3]

Fear may be present in the paintings etched on cave walls by our Palaeolithic forebears, in the megafauna that overshadow the timorous stick men hunters that hang back on the margins and in those ominous 'therianthropes', half human and half non-human animal beings with beak, snout and tail discovered in 2017–18 on the island of Sulawesi, Indonesia – rock art dating back at least 43,900 years – which must have appeared particularly terrifying when viewed by the flickering light of a fire torch or grease lamp.[4]

By the time *Homo sapiens* began to domesticate plants and animals, and settled in villages and cities during the Neolithic period some 12,000 years ago, the threat of predatory beasts had been superseded by other fears: political tyranny, inter-community violence, droughts, blights, famine and disease. In Jared Diamond's dismal assessment, the agricultural revolution may have been 'the worst mistake in the history of the human race'.[5]

The British archaeologist Ian Hodder, who oversaw excavations of the 9,000-year-old Neolithic settlement at Çatal Hüyük in south-central Turkey, has suggested that the images of fearful creatures that adorn the walls of houses there – including a painting of vultures with seemingly human legs lunging at a headless human figure – functioned as a way of domesticating fears of the wild.[6] Fear and faith interlocked in these new societies, working to ensure an increasingly hierarchical social and political order, and an economic system reliant on new divisions of labour.

The earliest forms of writing appeared in Mesopotamia around 3400 BCE. While the first cuneiform records – signs inscribed on clay tablets and other artefacts – consist of lists used for administrative and accounting purposes, the Babylonian epic of Gilgamesh, probably composed from the second millennium BCE, tells of the multiple fears that haunt the citizens of Uruk, a powerful Sumer city state on the Euphrates: fear of death and the underworld where the dead dwell in darkness; of the wilderness beyond civilisation and the end of the world patrolled by half human-scorpion monsters; and the tyrannical behaviour of the unreformed young Gilgamesh, Uruk's mythical ruler.

According to the controversial Axial Age hypothesis proposed by the German philosopher Karl Jaspers in the 1940s, new religious and philosophical systems emerged independently across Eurasia during the first millennium BCE, forming a new civilisational 'axis'.[7] The Analects of Confucius, the Upanishads and Bhagavadgita, the teachings of Buddha, the Hebrew prophets and the Greek philosophers – all emphasised the importance of self-reflection and self-discipline. Written language, in conjunction with prayer, meditation and argumentation, became a crucial social and psychological tool.[8] Together, these innovations not only transformed how humans understood the world but ultimately shaped their behaviour, creating a new capacity for managing thoughts and feelings, fear among them.

Fear certainly had its political uses in antiquity. The ancient Greeks had different words to convey fear, including *deos*, which derives from the root word 'two' and suggests that fear occurs when a person is 'in two minds', and *phobos*, which is etymologically linked to the verb 'to run'.[9] Writing in the fifth century BCE, Thucydides claimed that the Peloponnesian War was caused by Sparta's fear, or *phobos*, of Athens's growing power.[10] Meanwhile, the word *ekplexis* denoted terrified astonishment. Finally, panic, or *phobos panikos*, was associated with the half-goat and half-human god Pan, a deity of the Arcadian woods and mountains, whose scream was said to spark panic in all who heard it.[11]

In early imperial China, between the fourth century BCE and the third century CE, fear of the gods shaped the conventions that governed social relations, status and class. Fear at the prospect of divine retribution for a transgression acted as a form of social control and a check on destabilising worldly ambitions, whether from refractory subjects or rulers tempted to overreach the accepted limits of their power.[12]

Let's be clear, then. It's not as if humans suddenly developed a new propensity for fear and an awareness of its uses in fourteenth-century western Europe. So what happened in the fourteenth century that changed the nature of fear? The short answer is that a series of catastrophic events primed western Europe for profound social and political transformations, which a century and a half later would lead to the globalisation of fear. Reeling from the impact of famine and pandemic, the unity of the Catholic Church was challenged and then fragmented amid the bloodshed of religious and political conflict. A politics of fear that had been honed in war-torn Europe was mobilised to subdue the Americas, Asia and Africa. This exportation of Western fear was central to the making of the modern world.

Pieter Bruegel the Elder's painting *The Triumph of Death* offers clues about the nature of these transformations. Completed in the early 1560s, it depicts a legion of skeletons slaughtering the living and herding them through what appears to be a trapdoor to Hell. In the foreground, Death rides a skeletal mare and wields a scythe. An infernal landscape stretches into the horizon, devoid of vegetation and scarred by violence; victims hang from dead trees or are wracked on torture wheels; fires smoulder, and smoke drifts towards a shipwreck-littered coastline.

What's striking is the intensity and authenticity of the emotional world Bruegel conjures. We can hear the blood-curdling screams of these men and women, and feel their desperation to escape. Panic is visceral and sudden, a spontaneous response to the fear of excruciating pain and death, as well as the prospect of divine judgement. The crowd scenes are made up of numerous vignettes that focus on individual fears, whether a king's fear of losing his power or a parent's fear of losing her child. In effect, Bruegel provides a sixteenth-century anatomy of fear, breaking it down for us in a world that's being torn apart. Death, the great equaliser, has reduced the king to the level of a scavenging dog. The painting shows us human fallibility and the terror of God's retribution, but it also gives us an urgently contemporary perspective on mass violence.

In Bruegel's homeland, the Low Countries, fear was ever-present in the 1560s, as Philip II of Spain, who'd inherited the territory from his father, the Habsburg emperor Charles V, cracked down on his Protestant subjects. The violence of the Inquisition would lead to full-blown war from 1568, rumbling on until Spain's grudging recognition of the Dutch Republic in 1648. Godevaert van Haecht, an artisan from Antwerp, recorded how people panic-bought weapons to defend their homes; the word 'fear' pervades his chronicle for the years between 1565 and 1574.[13] Here we have, in other words, two integral fears: fear of God and fear that comes with the suppression of freedom and faith. Added to this are the terrifying spectres of plague and famine that stalked sixteenth-century Europe.

To get a measure of the scale of upheaval shown in Bruegel's hellscape, it's worth comparing it to another, earlier depiction of the world: the lavishly illustrated vellum prayer book known as the *Très Riches Heures*, probably begun around 1412 by Paul, Herman and Jean Limbourg for the Duc de Berry, son of the king of France. Consisting of 206 pages, with numerous miniature paintings, the book is a devotional guide organised around prescribed periods of daily prayer. The manuscript contains readings from the Gospels, prayers to the Virgin, psalms and a calendar of liturgical days. At the front there's a twelve-scene cycle known as the 'Labours of the Months', which depicts the changing seasons and associated activities: peasants toiling on the land and aristocrats going about their business against a vista of medieval castles and grand interiors. Arching above these everyday scenes are the Heavens, painted in brilliant blue lapis lazuli with golden zodiac signs.

In contrast to the chaos of Bruegel's *The Triumph of Death*, this is a hierarchical world depicted as profoundly ordered and locked in a single, universal time. There's no overt fear or panic in this divinely ordained universe. Take the depiction of the month of October. Only the presence of a scarecrow with a bow and arrow and the looming castle in the background suggest that social cohesion is ensured by the ubiquitous threat of force. Here we have an ideal, pyramidal social system with God at the pinnacle and, working down from the king, the nobles, knights, freemen, villeins – feudal tenants – and serfs. It's an intricate edifice knitted together by reciprocal obligations, by rights bestowed in return for oaths of fealty and service in kind.

As the art critic Erwin Panofsky suggested, the sumptuous illustrations in the *Très Riches Heures* may reflect an attempt to reassert social distinctions at a time when 'the ruling class of an aging society' was threatened by competition from 'younger forces rising against it'.[14] Nonetheless, something clearly happened between 1412 and 1562 that replaced the idealised view of the Duc de Berry's prayer book with the spectacle of fear and panic so vividly dramatised in Bruegel's painting. It's not that fear and panic were suddenly invented; it's just that by the mid-sixteenth century they had acquired a new visibility in everyday life.

The Reformation and the break-up of Christendom changed how fear was understood, providing lessons for how it might be exploited as the basis for new institutions of belief and novel forms of centralised power. But before we turn to the causes and consequences of these transformations, we should rewind to a time before disaster struck. What place did fear have in this world?

The great Gothic cathedrals of the twelfth, thirteenth and early fourteenth centuries dominated the medieval landscape. These buildings weren't just professions of faith; they were emblems of wealth, ingenuity and confidence. Among the many innovations of the thirteenth century were the mechanical clock, new methods of glassmaking and the spread of paper-mill technology, which had been introduced into southern Europe from the Arab world in the twelfth century. Banking boomed with trade and industry, and Italian cities emerged as hubs of international finance. Many of the great universities were founded and thrived as intellectual centres, such as those in Cambridge, Coimbra, Montpellier, Padua, Salamanca, Siena and Valladolid. All of this was powered by economic expansion. As populations grew, the extraction of natural resources intensified, from mining to the felling of forests for timber and large-scale land clearance for farming. Some historians speak of an 'agricultural revolution', suggesting that technological breakthroughs had transformational effects and led to a steep rise in productivity. Among them was the introduction of the heavy-wheeled ploughshare, which saved labour and enabled the cultivation of fertile land in northern Europe, whose dense, unyielding clay soils had previously been difficult to till.[15]

Prosperity didn't put an end to fear, which remained a feature of life. People feared famine, disease, war, Satan and his minions, the wrath of God, the apocalypse and damnation.[16] Fear hovered in the corners of the everyday, like demons in the marginalia of illuminated manuscripts. In the fourteenth-century compilation of devotional texts known as *The Neville of Hornby Hours*, fallen angels are shown as horned creatures with cloven hooves tumbling downwards towards Hell. The demons depicted have all the animal characteristics of the Greek goat god Pan, who was progressively demonised in the post-classical period. It wasn't only his appearance – hooves, tail and horns – but his violent desires, unbridled sexuality and musical passions. Like Pan, the Devil tempts humans to sin, estranging them from their true nature and inducing manic behaviour – in a word, panic.[17]

Fear was linked to the unknown, and monsters tended to congregate on the shadowy outlands of the world. In *The Visions of the Knight Tondal*, a popular twelfth-century tale, a knight encounters an assortment of ghoulish monsters as he travels through Hell to Paradise, guided by an angel. The sole surviving illuminated copy of the text, in the collection of the Getty Museum, depicts tortured sinners writhing in agony inside the fiery maw of Hell, which is kept ajar by two demonic giants.

The best-known trek through the underworld, however, occurs in the *Divine Comedy*, completed in 1320. Having woken to find himself lost in the middle of a dark wood, the poet Dante spies a sunlit hill ahead and his terror subsides: but not for long, because soon his path is blocked by a leopard, lion and ferocious she-wolf that force him back, 'all tears and attrition', into the darkness. So begins a descent into the Inferno that turns out to be a journey through fear, which both shatters any lingering complacency and reaffirms God's omniscience.[18]

Fear isn't just a literary theme, and neither are these diabolical monsters always allegorical abstractions. It was thought that satanic agents saturated the physical world, communicating through birdsong and leaving menacing signs of their presence for those who could decipher them. One thirteenth-century Cistercian abbot claimed that people were surrounded by swarms of invisible demons that floated in the air like motes of dust.[19]

Church doctrine and ritual nurtured and directed this fear, recruiting it to the cause of faith, while countering despair with assurances of an afterlife and hope of redemption. In his influential *Summa Theologiae*, written between 1266 and 1273, the theologian Thomas Aquinas considers the objects, causes and effects of fear. He asks whether fear is necessarily evil and answers that, because it is 'natural to man' and a fundamental condition of being human, it isn't intrinsically good or bad. 'Now fear is born of love,' he reflects, citing St Augustine, 'since man fears the loss of what he loves.' Fearlessness, Aquinas suggests, ought to be regarded as a vice since fear of God is a prerequisite for loving Him: 'God can and ought to be feared.'[20]

Fear had other benefits; it could awaken sinners to God's grace and act as a deterrent against propensities for evil.[21] In his treatise *On Morals*, the theologian William of Auvergne, bishop of Paris from 1228 to 1249, reflects on the nine virtues – Faith, Fear, Hope, Charity, Piety, Zeal, Poverty, Humility and Patience – which are personified and given a platform to persuade the reader of their value. 'I am the doorkeeper and guardian of the human heart,' proclaims Fear, who like all the other virtues is portrayed as a woman. Fear is a motivator, protector and torturer;

she is a scarecrow to keep away 'the birds of flighty, vain, impure, and harmful thoughts', a balm to heal 'the wounds of carnal and worldly desires', and a schoolteacher who is cruel to be kind, using Hell as a rod to teach and chastise God's children.[22]

Material power underpinned the Church's spiritual influence, and in the late twelfth century it hit on the idea of trading fear for profit by granting full or partial remission of sin with the cash payment of an indulgence. If you had the means, you could reduce the time you'd have to spend in Purgatory. But the Church also used fear, intimidation and outright force to eliminate dissent. Christian sects who challenged orthodoxies, such as the Cathars and Waldensians in southern France, were branded heretics who were in league with Satan and brutally suppressed. 'Human life is constant fear,' declared Innocent III, the most formidable of medieval popes and the architect of the twenty-year campaign against the Cathars, as well as the sponsor of the disastrous Fourth Crusade, which set out to seize Jerusalem from its Muslim rulers in 1202 but ended up further dividing Christendom.[23]

Then came the first of two major disasters. Between 1315 and 1322 famine ravaged the continent, killing up to 10 per cent of the urban population in northern Europe, and far more in some areas.[24] People panicked when hunger was compounded by sickness. According to one witness, 'the bodies of paupers, dead of starvation, littered the streets', and the stink of decay was overpowering.[25] Contemporaneous accounts describe people hoarding what food they could find, foraging for roots and nuts, and eating wild grasses and bark to survive. The more sensationalist reports describe people devouring horses and dogs, feeding on the carcasses of dead cattle and bird shit. Chroniclers provide anecdotal evidence of infanticide and cannibalism. Prisoners purportedly ate their fellow inmates in jail; parents and children consumed each other. Criminals were seized from the gallows and corpses exhumed from cemeteries. Inequality increased and crime exploded: extortion, robbery, assault and murder.[26]

Perhaps unsurprisingly, death, sin and redemption loom large as themes in devotional art at this time. *The Triumph of Death*, a fresco in the Campo Santo, the cemetery building beside Pisa Cathedral, is thought to have been painted in the 1330s. Fear is at the core of this vast mural comprised of numerous chilling scenes, including one showing three open caskets with snakes writhing over decomposing bodies. Although the fresco suggests social resilience – the show goes on despite the calamity – it also depicts a society overwhelmed by death. While a group of noblewomen make music in a peaceful grove, a terrifying white-haired witch hurtles towards them with a scythe. This may well be the depiction of a society reeling from the impact of famine, but what's certain is that across much of western Europe famine aggravated social tensions and exposed new stress points. The consequences were to become evident a decade later, when a second catastrophe struck: plague.

By late 1346 reports had begun to reach Christendom of a devastating disease in the East. It was said that earthquakes, tempests, hail, fire and brimstones presaged the contagion. Venomous beasts – serpents, scorpions and 'pestilential worms' – had fallen from the sky.[27] Gabriel de Mussis, a notary from Piacenza in northern Italy, claimed that Mongol soldiers besieging the Genoese port city of Caffa (present-day Feodosia) on the Black Sea had catapulted infected corpses over the walls in an act of biological warfare. In October 1347 twelve Genoese galleys landed at Messina in Sicily, bringing the disease with them from Crimea.[28]

Although there is little direct evidence that rodents were implicated in the plague's spread, it's long been thought that infection spread via rats – hosts of the plague flea – that fed off the grain stored in the holds, or from flea-infected bales of cloth and fur pelts traded by the Genoese. While some historians have noted striking epidemiological differences between the fourteenth-century plague and the rat-borne plague pandemic of the late nineteenth century, recent scientific research, including genetic corroboration from a fourteenth-century burial pit in London's East Smithfield, has confirmed that the disease was bubonic plague caused by the *Yersinia pestis* bacterium.[29] It's likely that the plague spread through Central Eurasia with the Mongol invasions of the thirteenth century and that the outbreaks in the following century were the result of spillover events from these new plague reservoirs.[30]

So lethal was the plague, claimed the Sicilian chronicler Michele da Piazza, that anyone who came into fleeting contact with infected persons or their belongings was doomed. The inhabitants of Messina decamped to the countryside, expanding the circle of infection further.[31] 'The plague frightened and killed,' wrote the Arab historian Ibn al-Wardi, a first-hand witness to the widespread panic triggered by the plague's arrival in the Middle East, including the devastation of his home city, Aleppo, in 1348.[32] The poet Petrarch lamented that the plague 'trampled and destroyed the entire world'. 'Everywhere we see sorrow, on all sides we see terror,' he wrote. How would future generations comprehend what it was like to live at a time when 'dwellings were emptied, cities abandoned', and bodies dumped unceremoniously in fields? Petrarch worried too about the fate of those he loved. 'Free me from these fears as soon as possible by a letter from you, my dear brother, if you still live,' he enjoined his Flemish friend Lodewijk Heyligen. His patron, Cardinal Giovanni Colonna, succumbed to the disease, while his brother Gerardo, a Carthusian monk, was the sole survivor of his monastery in the south of France.[33]

The most famous description of the plague occurs in the introduction to Giovanni Boccaccio's collection of stories *The Decameron*, begun around 1349 and completed by 1353. A former banker and lawyer, Boccaccio was a thirty-four-year-old bachelor living in Florence when the epidemic struck. He tells us that over a few months 100,000 people perished, a figure that may not be far off the mark. The pestilence, he writes, 'was spread by the slightest contact between the sick and the healthy just as a fire will catch dry or oily materials when they are placed right beside it'. Plague victims – and Boccaccio's father and stepmother were among them – apparently woke up 'perfectly healthy, dined in the morning with their families, companions, and friends, only to have supper that evening with their ancestors in the next world'.[34]

All such accounts need to be treated with circumspection and in some cases outright scepticism. When the Sienese chronicler Agnolo di Tura tells us that people thought it was the end of the world and that he buried five of his own children, should we take him at face value?[35] Read side by side, many accounts sound indistinguishable. Boccaccio's description of the plague is indebted to Thucydides and functions as a literary framing device for the subsequent tales. Petrarch's letters, for all their pathos, were hardly spontaneous outpourings but carefully crafted literary works modelled on the letters of the Roman philosopher Cicero. The issue of literary indebtedness raises the question of how real the fear and panic really were. Are the descriptions of social collapse and mass hysteria overblown? After all, the chroniclers reporting on the plague are in many cases the same ones who would have us believe that toads fell from the Heavens as portents of the disaster.

An analysis of last wills and testaments in Bologna in 1348 suggests that social ties proved resilient and trust didn't vanish overnight. Even at the peak of the crisis, family, friends and neighbours were witnessing the wills of plague victims.[36] But how reliable are these records? The historian Samuel Cohn has pointed out that they account for only 5 per cent of those who died of the plague in that year. What happened to all the others? Were people dying too fast to prepare for their end?[37] It seems disingenuous to play down the magnitude of a pandemic that contemporaries described as 'The Great Pestilence' or 'The

Great Mortality', and which much later came to be known as the 'Black Death' – a disaster that may have wiped out half of Europe in just three years.

Looking back from the 1380s, the Florentine chronicler Baldassarre Bonaiuti describes how the dead were thrown into large communal pits, with hundreds of bodies stacked on top of one another, separated by a shallow covering of earth, 'just as one makes lasagne with layers of pasta and cheese'.[38] In a conservative estimate, 25 million people died between 1347 and 1351, but the figure may have been much higher, perhaps double this number. In some parts of the western Mediterranean as many as 60 per cent or more of the population may have perished, and it would take well over a century for population levels to recover.[39]

In the earliest known medical tract on the plague, written in April 1348, weeks before the pandemic reached his home town of Lleida in western Catalonia, the physician Jacme d'Agramont compared the destructive nature of plague fear to the terror caused by an approaching fire. 'Everyday experience,' he observed, 'shows us that when a dwelling catches on fire all the neighbors become afraid, and the nearer they live, the more frightened they become.' D'Agramont's purpose in writing was to allay some of the 'doubts and fears' caused by the impending contagion.[40]

Although the effects and responses to the plague varied greatly across Europe, North Africa, the Middle East and Central Asia, the scale of mortality created political, economic and psychological shocks that would irrevocably change western Europe. 'The fear was such that nobody knew what to do,' one chronicler reported.[41] Fear, untethered from conventional religious observance, unleashed a powerful destabilising force that affected every aspect of life. The French historian Jean Delumeau has claimed that the plague, among other psychological shocks, produced 'morbid fantasies' that contributed to the rise of a collective European insecurity, which was to last until the eighteenth century. In this pessimistic mindset, obsessed with guilt and shame, dangers were seen to lurk everywhere.[42]

While some historians have questioned the plague's long-term effects, it is generally agreed that the pandemic's first wave in Europe triggered 'wild and unsanctioned displays of emotion'.[43] First and foremost, fear of the deadly disease prompted flight from infected cities and towns, particularly in urbanised regions such as central and northern Italy. Even though some municipal authorities attempted to prevent people from leaving their homes by imposing fines or placing guards at city gates, many sought to escape. Echoing the description of the Great Plague of Athens in Thucydides' *History of the Peloponnesian War*, Boccaccio tells us that 'respect for the reverend authority of the laws, both divine and human', evaporated. When citizens stepped in to help bury their dead neighbours, they did so not out of charity but because they feared catching the disease. In *The Decameron* a group of seven young women and three young men flee from plague-infested, crime-riven Florence to spend a fortnight in the countryside. The spectacle of so much death and destruction, not to mention the ever-present stench of decay, 'caused all sorts of fears and fantasies in those who remained alive'. The poor weren't so lucky, according to Boccaccio; left without help, they died 'more like animals than human beings'.[44]

The mystery of the disease's origins and the distinctive 'buboes', or swollen lymph glands that accompanied infection, amplified those fears. What caused the disease? No one knew. The medical faculty of the University of Paris prepared a report for King Philip VI of France in which the pandemic was attributed to astrological influences: a celestial constellation had precipitated noxious vapours. To ward off this poisonous miasma, the report advised staying away from fetid marshland and any place with stagnant water; it also recommended fumigations to purify the air with agarwood or, for those rich enough to afford them, amber resin and musk.[45]

If some people reacted with panicked flight, others opted for self-imposed isolation and barricaded themselves inside their homes. Still others did the opposite and, sticking their fingers up at decorum, revelled in 'life's pleasures'. Loss of propriety in pursuit of self-indulgent gratification seems to have been one characteristic of this plague panic.[46]

But panic as a response to plague could take more aggressive forms. Before the pandemic struck, Siena had been a flourishing republic ruled by a mercantile oligarchy. However, during and after the plague the city council struggled to deal with the economic and social fallout, including a dramatic population decline and an uptick in violence. As in many other places, new legislation was introduced to restore order, but it was too little too late, and it was in this atmosphere of heightened tension that a rebellion overthrew the government in 1355. The plague may not have caused regime change directly, but it had created conditions propitious for it.[47]

There was a similar intensification of factional hatreds in Marseille. Instead of resolving social tensions, acrimonious court cases aggravated them, encouraging extrajudicial retribution.[48] Another manifestation of social precarity and turbulence was an emphasis on castle-building, evidence of a need for security in a world where unruly tenants, the wandering poor and opportunistic mercenaries challenged the status quo.[49]

Fear in response to plague perpetuated stereotypes, with minority groups – Jews, Muslims, paupers, lepers and foreigners – targeted as malevolent carriers of contagion. Meanwhile, authorities capitalised on 'localised threats', turning them into a universal menace that created the basis for anxieties that could be more systematically exploited.[50] Scapegoating minority communities was one way of legitimising power. While rulers might fear for their souls and bequeath the Church substantial sums for masses to be sung for them after their death, they could also rule through fearmongering.[51]

In 1348 rumours began to circulate in northern Spain and

southern France that Jews were poisoning the wells to kill off Christians, leading to anti-Jewish riots and massacres in parts of Catalonia and Languedoc.[52] Local factors affected the form that this persecution took. In the Iberian territories of the Crown of Aragon, a long history of anti-Jewish violence – manifest in the stoning of Jewish properties during the Holy Week riots – fed into plague fears.[53] In Savoy, Jews were formally tried, with confessions extracted under torture. On St Valentine's Day in 1349 two thousand Jews were publicly burned to death in Strasbourg. While non-Jews, including the city's mayor, tried to intervene, others were only too eager to join in the killing spree.[54]

Many historians have argued that this antisemitic hysteria percolated upwards from the people; it was spontaneous and peasant-led, triggered by the shock of mass death and resentment at the role of Jews as moneylenders. In the words of the Italian historian Carlo Ginzburg, an obsession with Jewish conspiracies formed 'a thick sediment in the popular mentality'.[55] Others, however, have pointed to evidence that indicates the opposite: that the massacres were, in fact, driven by members of the elite.[56] The bishop of Strasbourg, who was instrumental in the pogrom there, was heavily in debt to Jewish creditors, so scapegoating Jews and inciting violence against them benefited him personally.[57] Pope Clement VI himself recognised that vested interests were fuelling the atrocities and reissued a decree affirming the Church's protection of the Jews. Some Christians, he declared, were 'chasing after their own profit and are blinded by greed in getting rid of the Jews, because they owe great sums of money to them'.[58]

Popular reactions to plague challenged and undermined secular and religious authorities, but it wasn't just the populace that panicked. The elite were fearful of labour shortages as a result of the population collapse; peasants, yeomen and artisans meanwhile found themselves in a strengthened position to negotiate their wages and began to demonstrate new social aspirations. As the French labour law of 1354 puts it, peasants were 'working whenever it pleased them and spending the rest of their time in taverns playing games and enjoying themselves'. In reaction to such presumptions and to deal with the dramatic fall in tax revenue, rulers in many parts of Europe hiked taxes and brought in emergency measures to curb wages, fix prices and limit freedom of movement.[59]

The effects of the plague played into a host of local political, economic and social grievances, and from the mid-1350s to the 1380s there was an upsurge in popular revolts across Europe: the Jacquerie uprising in northern France in 1358, the Ciompi Revolt in Florence in 1378 and the Peasants' Revolt in England in 1381.[60] Dissenting voices and heretical movements faced up to authority in new ways, the best-known radical sect being the 'flagellant' confraternities that roamed the countryside of northern and central Europe, beating themselves in frenzied displays of public penance.[61]

To counter disruptive fear and the antisocial panic it gave rise to, the Church adopted two main approaches. The first was a crackdown on dissent. While fear of plague tested the establishment, it also provided an opportunity for secular and religious institutions to reassert their power. The other Church response was a vigorous promotion of its credo as an antidote to breakdown and a route to salvation. Having been pummelled by disaster, people were susceptible to political and spiritual influences, and panic could be exploited. Plague fear, for example, could be channelled into spiritual renewal. From this perspective the message of much plague art, with its emphasis on death, should be understood not just as a reflection of prevalent fears but also a means of redirecting them towards new forms of devotion. Fear was to be assiduously nurtured.

This celebration of fear took many forms. The *danse macabre* was a reminder of the evanescence of life. The best-known and earliest visual record of the motif is a mural from the 1420s in the cemetery of Les Saints Innocents in Paris, which was destroyed in the seventeenth century and is known to us today only from prints and literary descriptions. A ghoulish iconography of dancing skeletons, it was a means of inculcating devotion through fear of death and divine judgement. This was also an aim of cadaver monuments, sculpted effigies known as *transi* (from the Latin for 'to pass away'), where the deceased were represented as recumbent skeletons or decomposing bodies. Such graphic depictions of death instilled obedience by reminding viewers of the transience of earthly life and the terrifying punishment that awaited sinners.

In the long run, however, such strategies for controlling fear didn't work. Through the fifteenth century sectarianism flourished, and the Church struggled to keep order. Tensions that had long been present were exacerbated. In a celebrated decree of 1302 Pope Boniface VIII had declared the spiritual and temporal supremacy of the pope, a claim that was soon challenged by King Philip IV of France, who defended his right to tax the French clergy. As a result of the ensuing power struggle, the papacy moved from Rome to Avignon between 1309 to 1377, a period known as the 'Babylonian Captivity'; and from 1378 to 1417 it was divided among allegiances with two rival claimants, a state of affairs now referred to as the Western Schism. Although the Council of Constance between 1414 and 1418 finally resolved the controversy with the election of Pope Martin V, the damage had been done.

For a thousand years the Catholic Church had enjoyed a monopoly on fear, which it exploited to channel belief. Religious depictions emphasised the terrors of Purgatory and Hell. Fear was an incentive for devotion, embedded in doctrine and the sacramental rituals that shaped daily life. But the multiple shocks – social, psychological, political and economic – produced by plague between 1347 and 1351 contributed to a loosening of the Church's grip. The fear that it had harnessed so effectively was now up for grabs and competing interests, among them those of radical reformist movements and centralising states, began to claim it for their cause.

2

A New Age of Fear

In the religious and political upheaval of the sixteenth century, which saw the authority of the Catholic Church challenged across northern and central Europe, fear was transformed. In some places – parts of northern Germany, Scandinavia, the Netherlands and England – the Catholic Church was overthrown, and new Protestant communities arose that professed their loyalty to the state. In 1520 Martin Luther, a crucial figure in the Reformation, urged German princes in the Holy Roman Empire – a loose confederation of mainly German-speaking territories under the overlordship, or suzerainty, of an emperor – to take up the cause of reform in their lands, insisting that the Church was wrong in claiming jurisdiction over temporal power.[1] For these rulers, there were clear benefits to championing reform; it enhanced their influence and wealth at the expense of the Church and emperor, while also helping to instil obedience in their subjects.[2]

State control of religious institutions wasn't confined to Protestant territories. Elsewhere, in Spain, France and areas of eastern Europe, Catholicism was reaffirmed, often through coercion. To ward off the Protestant threat the Church was forced to rely on the intervention of local princes. As a consequence, in these places too religion became a facet of state power. The tools that the Church had developed to promote a common faith – fear among them – were progressively absorbed into the machinery of government.

But fear also moved in another direction. Luther may have

appealed to secular rulers, but he insisted on a believer's personal relationship with God. Individuals, he argued, were the subjects of two kingdoms: an outer, temporal order and an inner, spiritual one.[3] According to the doctrine of *sola scriptura*, 'by scripture alone', the Bible was a source of infallible authority, far preferable to the dubious precepts handed down by tradition, Church councils, theologians and popes. Belief in Purgatory, for example, which was key to the selling of indulgences, had no basis in Scripture. Remission from punishment for sins couldn't be bought, salvation had to be worked for and meditation was a crucial spiritual exercise that involved 'repeating and comparing oral speech and literal words of the book, reading and rereading them with diligent attention and reflection'.[4]

It's the simultaneous propagandising and individualisation of fear during the Reformation, as well as its ambiguous role as a tool of governance and a force for liberation, that we'll now explore, beginning with a discussion of how books of political philosophy and works of literature grappled with the experience of fear, its place in society and its relationship with faith and power.

It is often forgotten that the Renaissance, the explosion of Western art and culture that took place from the late fourteenth century, unfolded amid political turmoil and extreme violence.[5] The great nineteenth-century Swiss historian Jacob Burckhardt, to whom we owe the idea of the Renaissance as a period of radical transition from the Middle Ages to the modern world, emphasised the period's fearful 'spirit of doubt' as well as its 'vicious tendency', born of what he called 'the worst features of an unbridled egotism'.[6] Bruegel's apocalyptic vision *The Triumph of Death* is one take on this turbulence; *The Book of Miracles*, an illuminated manuscript produced in around 1550 in the Swabian city of Augsburg, is another. There, biblical catastrophism converges with the horrors of war and the devastation caused by a fatal flood, swarms of locusts and human-devouring monsters.[7]

In a letter written in the early 1480s to his patron Ludovico Sforza, ruler of Milan, Leonardo da Vinci described the ingenious 'war machines' that he was developing to cause 'great terror to the enemy': catapults, portable mortars, cannons, firebombs and armoured vehicles.[8] Although gunpowder had reached Europe from Asia in the thirteenth century, by the fifteenth century the use of artillery had transformed the nature of warfare. So much, then, for the new post-plague 'humanism' that championed human values and civic virtues and drew its inspiration from Classical antiquity. 'Fear arises sooner than anything else,' da Vinci jotted in his notebook. 'Just as courage imperils life, fear protects it.'[9]

In fact, the states that emerged from the plague in the late fourteenth and early fifteenth centuries were founded on a new sort of politics, with a contract between the sovereign ruler and his subjects that posited the intrinsic violence of human nature and the consequent need for new disciplinary strategies for keeping that violence in check. According to one study of the French reformer John Calvin and his followers, the Reformation precipitated a 'disciplinary revolution' in places such as the Netherlands and Brandenburg-Prussia that would serve as a template for the world. A new infrastructure of governance and social control developed in these places, which had its roots in the promotion of religious discipline. 'What steam did for the modern economy,' the historical sociologist Philip Gorski observes, 'discipline did for the modern polity.'[10] Fear lay at the heart of this new political compact.

In 1516 Desiderius Erasmus, the Dutch philosopher, theologian and scholar, condemned the savagery of war and stressed the value of love over fear. 'The tyrant strives to be feared, the king to be loved,' he wrote.[11] Many of his contemporaries took the opposite view. Three years earlier, Niccolò Machiavelli had given eloquent expression to the political merits of fear. As its second chancellor, he had led important diplomatic missions for the Florentine republic and been charged with organising the city's militia. When the ruling Medici family was reinstated in 1512 after eighteen years in exile, however, Machiavelli's associations with the old regime made him persona non grata, and he was dismissed from office. A few months later he was imprisoned for his alleged involvement in a plot to overthrow the new administration and tortured for a confession using the infamous *strappado* technique, in which a prisoner is suspended by a rope from a pulley with his hands tied behind his back.[12] It was after these tribulations that Machiavelli withdrew to his country house in Sant'Andrea in Percussina and wrote *The Prince*, a treatise on power dedicated to Florence's new ruler, Lorenzo di Piero de' Medici, no doubt as a gesture of pragmatic ingratiation.

Political crisis in Florence had encouraged Machiavelli to think about how to counter the tendency that institutions seemed to have for corruption and gradual obsolescence. Conceived as an introduction to politics and a primer for aspiring rulers, his book argues that the successful leader needs to anticipate rebellion and push back against divisive forces within the state by inculcating fear in the population. 'One can make this generalization about men,' he writes: 'they are ungrateful, fickle, liars, and deceivers, they shun danger and are greedy for profit.' Is it 'better to be loved than feared, or the reverse'? he asks, before answering his own question: 'it is far better to be feared than loved if you cannot be both.'[13] According to Machiavelli, only fear and the threat of violence can hold society together. If it is in his interest to do so, it is perfectly reasonable for the prince to 'act in defiance of good faith, of charity, of kindness, of religion'.[14] What was new about this formulation wasn't so much the idea of fear as a political expedient, reflecting cynical assumptions about human nature, as its brazen promotion as a tool for acquiring and retaining power.

Machiavelli's *The Prince* was one of many works concerned with the battle to control fear that was being waged across sixteenth-century Europe. In the same year that Erasmus had commented on the tyrannical use of fear, his good friend Sir Thomas More – philosopher, lawyer and later lord high chancellor of England – published the book *Utopia*, in which an imaginary island republic becomes a vehicle for critiquing contemporary political institutions and showing up the dangers of religious sectarianism, civil strife and social inequity. In many respects, More's Utopia is an extraordinarily liberal society, notwithstanding its reliance on slaves for 'all the rough and dirty work' and the state's constant surveillance of its citizens to ensure discipline.[15] It is a representative democracy, ruled by an elected prince; there is no private property or money, and the sick are treated in public hospitals. Fear, however, plays an important role in More's fictional commonwealth. While citizens of Utopia enjoy religious freedom, fear of God's judgement is viewed as indispensable; atheists who are fearless can't hold public office. As More puts it, 'if you're not afraid of anything but prosecution, and have no hopes of anything after you're dead, you'll always be trying to evade or break the laws of your country, in order to gain your own private ends'.[16]

The social order in Utopia, it turns out, relies on the right sort of fear being balanced with the right kind of fearlessness. While religious fear is viewed as motivational, fear of starvation and basic material wants are considered unacceptable because they destabilise society. At the time More was writing, spiritual and material fears had become dangerously out of kilter across Europe, dislocating this delicate equilibrium. The dystopian world of modern panic had been born, along with a counterbalancing drive to engineer a new kind of state to contain it.

This new thinking about the uses and misuses of different types of fear came into being at precisely the moment that the unity of Christendom was under threat. Across Europe the authority of the Catholic Church was being contested by dissenters and advocates of reform. In 1517 Luther wrote his *Ninety-Five Theses*, a list of grievances against the papacy that precipitated a theological quarrel which soon morphed into a radical breakaway movement. Among his gripes with Rome was the sale of indulgences, which by the mid-fifteenth century were being issued as small printed forms, promissory notes that resembled blank cheques with spaces left for the purchaser's name and the date of purchase. In a creative, money-generating ruse operated by the Church from 1476, it was even possible to buy them for deceased family members.

It wasn't long before other demands were being made by rival Protestant factions, including those led by Calvin and Ulrich Zwingli in Switzerland.[17] 'I sadly fear that the gospel may involve us in a deadly war,' Erasmus wrote in 1529. A year later he predicted that 'the long war of words and pamphlets will soon be waged with halberds and cannons'.[18]

By then violence had already broken out. The Peasants' War in western and southern Germany, energised by the Protestant challenge to the Catholic Church and led by the preacher Thomas Müntzer, had been defeated, with perhaps as many as 100,000 peasants slaughtered. Müntzer himself was captured, tortured and executed in 1525. And in the years following the publication of *Utopia*, More's patron Henry VIII broke with Rome and consolidated his power as head of a newly established Church of England. More, a devout Catholic, was found guilty of treason and beheaded in July 1535. It was to prevent the spread of this Protestant heresy that Pope Paul III created the Supreme Sacred Congregation of the Roman and Universal Inquisition in 1542, with a brief to prosecute those accused of heretical crimes.

The remarkable speed with which Catholic Europe fragmented was due in part to a new technology that was transforming communication in the Western world, with far-reaching consequences for the Church's management of fear: the printing press, designed by Johann Gutenberg in the 1440s. Movable-type printing had been invented centuries earlier in China, but the publication of Gutenberg's Latin translation of the Bible in the 1450s, the first 'mass-produced' publication in the West, heralded a new age of printing. Although the dissemination of handwritten manuscripts would continue well into the seventeenth century, it was Luther who was to demonstrate just how important print technology could be as a weapon of attack and self-promotion, and a means of instilling fear of God's judgement, which he argued was fundamental to faith. As he declared in his *Small Catechism* of 1529 – an exposition of doctrines written for the edification of lay people and children – 'We are to fear, love, and trust God above all things.'[19]

Luther himself was wracked by fear of death and attributed his religious vocation to a terrifying experience he'd had in July 1505; caught in a thunderstorm, he'd vowed to become a monk if he survived the ordeal. According to Luther, lack of fear leads to pride, while filial fear of God, as opposed to servile fear, is a precondition for grace and resembles a child's fear of their parents; in both instances fear is mixed with love and constitutes a form of reverence.[20] However, he also inveighed against the Catholic Church's shameless abuse of fear, reserving particular opprobrium for the unscrupulous methods of the Dominican friar Johann Tetzel, who terrified his congregations into buying indulgences by conjuring visions of their dead parents wailing for mercy in Purgatory.[21] What was egregious about such behaviour was the way it exploited fear for money and muddied the water between absolution and the remission of punishment for sins.

Print culture was used by Luther to condemn these practices and promote his own beliefs. Pamphlets were relatively cheap and quick to produce, and they were also a way of reaching a much larger audience of readers and listeners. One of Luther's tactics was to undermine the papacy by exposing it to vituperative satire, which could neutralise fear and undercut authority. Text was combined with vivid cartoons – many of them by Luther's friend the artist Lucas Cranach – which drew on familiar, burlesque and often salacious elements in

German folk culture. Rome is a brothel; cardinals extrude from the Devil's backside; the pope, imagined as the Antichrist, sits astride a pig while holding a pile of steaming shit. Exploiting popular prejudice, Luther accused the papacy of conspiring with the Jews, revealing a disturbing antisemitism that would inspire Hitler and the Nazis in the twentieth century.[22]

While Luther's radical theology may have promoted subjective experience and freedom from corrupt Catholic Church strictures, it also stressed original sin. Salvation was only possible through God's grace, a doctrine known as 'justification by faith alone'. As Luther's friend the German scholar and reformer Philip Melanchthon expressed it in Article IV of the Augsburg Confession (1530), 'we cannot obtain forgiveness of sin and righteousness before God by our own merits, works, or satisfactions' – but only by God's grace. In other words, spiritual freedom went hand in hand with capitulation to divine authority. Erich Fromm would later argue, controversially, that the legacy of this fundamental ambiguity – the simultaneous emphasis on freedom from and submission to authority in the theology of Luther and Calvin – characterised democratic systems as they developed in western Europe and helped to explain the rise of twentieth-century authoritarianism.[23]

The fervour ignited by religious conflict, the adherence to new orthodoxies and the fear of God's wrath encouraged the demonisation of dissenters, as well as mass uprisings and violence. Fearmongering was a feature of the period, with minority communities, notably of Jews and Muslims, persecuted. Faith and the threat of heresy were understood as a spiritual conflict that necessitated vigilance against temptation, alongside efforts to root out demonic conspiracies. Although witch-hunting manifested as a rash of local panics, the theological idea was fear on a grand scale: an existential threat to Christendom posed by heterodoxy and disobedience.

German-speaking territories in central Europe may have

been the heartland of witch scares in the sixteenth and seventeenth centuries, but they were a pan-European phenomenon, 'a livid symptom of social and political turmoil'.[24] The southern German states are good examples of how the flipside of fear was rage: an intense confessional struggle between different politico-religious identities. There, witch-hunting was a poisonous by-product of the most vicious struggles between the forces of the Reformation and those of the Counter-Reformation, the Catholic Church's fight back against the Protestant threat.

In Scotland, particularly in the Lowlands dominated by the God-fearing Calvinist kirk, fear of witches also led to panic, with James VI playing a key role as a self-professed demonologist who in 1597 published *Daemonologie*, a treatise intended to prove the existence of witches and make the case for their persecution.[25] As far away as the remote frontiers of the New World, in the plantations of Massachusetts, fear of witchery would lead to the denunciation and trial of those accused of practising the Devil's art to cause sickness and death.[26] Folk healers, soothsayers and those who were thought to possess powers of prophesy and divination had for centuries roamed the European countryside selling their services. Although these practices would continue into the nineteenth century, in the wake of violent confessional conflict they were increasingly condemned as a threat to the Christian community.[27]

The Catholic Church had frequently denounced the dangers of witchcraft. A papal bull issued by Pope Innocent VIII in 1484 extended the authority of the Inquisition to punish those who, in league with 'devils, incubi and succubi', perpetrated the 'foulest abominations'.[28] A few years after this decree, the treatise *Malleus Maleficarum*, or 'Hammer of Witches', written by the Dominican inquisitor Heinrich Kramer, provided instructions on how to identify, capture, torture, try and execute witches. Although the Church hadn't previously been engaged in the large-scale persecution of witches, a witch-hunt hysteria now began a spiralling cycle of violence, fuelled by the printing press. While Kramer may have been a disreputable authority, and there is little evidence, as is sometimes suggested, that the *Malleus Maleficarum* was much used, in the two centuries after its first publication in 1486 it was frequently reprinted and allegedly sold more copies than any other book except for the Bible.[29]

Protestants also participated in witch-hunts. Luther condemned popular superstitions and magic, and expressly authorised the execution of witches. In Geneva, Calvin introduced 'a new reign of terror' in 1545, urging the city's magistrates 'to extirpate the race of witches'.[30] Witch trials yielded the greatest benefit in places where religious tensions were the most intense – although that tended to be illusory, since witch-hunts exacerbated rather than resolved the social and economic chaos which had caused them in the first place. In the new climate of religious conflict, Church authorities used popular fear to extend their influence and recruit new followers to their cause by demonstrating their prowess in hunting down, capturing and destroying witches.[31]

Witch scares were also linked to the centralisation of state functions that was key to the rise of the modern state. The trial and public execution of witches reflected an expansion of government into areas that had previously been outside its remit, although it was also a means of shoring up state authority against the threat of competing beliefs.[32] Despite this, it is important not to overemphasise the scale of these scares or the extent to which they were connected and politically directed. Witch panics were sporadic and scattered in nature; they were also rare and short-lived, and most places never had them. When they did occur, they were most often impelled by popular fears, which reflected wider concerns. Bitter religious and political strife, along with the social upheaval caused by war, created an environment of suspicion within which fear of heresy festered.[33]

This was a world where deeply embedded traditions had

begun to collide with a new understanding of the natural world, where the boundaries between what we'd now call magic, religion and science remained fluid, even as fundamental religious precepts were being challenged. Kepler, Copernicus and Galileo were applying new models to explain planetary motion, overturning the prevailing geocentric view of the cosmos in which the sun and the planets revolved around the Earth. Although there was no sudden rupture with the past, this new thinking took place at a time when institutions strove to impose order and reaffirm threatened orthodoxies. Galileo, after all, was hauled before the Inquisition and found 'vehemently suspect of heresy' in 1633.[34] Fear and violence were symptoms of the profound structural changes taking place: the birth pangs, one might say, of modernity.

Despite these interdictions, the dissemination of pamphlets and books written in the vernacular, rather than in Latin – including translations of Classical authors – helped to forge new communities grounded in shared faith, culture and experience.[35] As we've seen, Luther and Calvin were also promoting a contemplative spirituality that encouraged self-examination through the close reading of Scripture, and fear was an important feature of this new introspection. Writing during the Peasants' War in the 1520s, one German Anabaptist – a member of a radical Christian sect that rejected civil and ecclesiastic authorities, refusing to pay tithes or swear oaths – observed that the human 'spirit of fear' was quite different from the true 'fear of God', which led to an 'anxious questioning, to an examination of oneself and of God in all things'.[36]

These new techniques of spiritual self-discipline were encouraged by the printing press, and it was at this time that treatises began to circulate proffering practical and moral guidance. While passions were intrinsic to human nature, disciplining them was viewed as essential to self-knowledge and often framed as a therapeutic exercise. When it came to rulers, the importance of controlling and manipulating fear was crucial to their power.[37]

Advice books on etiquette and the cultivation of civility may not have been new, but they gained a new audience in an age of religious dissension and war. There was a politics to the task of disciplining the passions and commending polite behaviour. In 1530 Erasmus published a handbook on good manners for children, which was reprinted numerous times and widely translated. 'Although the external appearance of the body proceeds from a well-ordered mind,' he advised, 'an otherwise upright and educated man, if taught carelessly, is sometimes lacking in social grace.' Some things weren't permissible in public, such as wiping your nose with your hand, yawning without covering your mouth, hunching your shoulders, licking your fingers or urinating indiscreetly. While Erasmus condemned the use of 'fear and terror' in education, he emphasised the importance of exploiting the threat of shame as a means of motivating students.[38]

Machiavelli had been concerned with the ruler's authority, and Thomas More had grappled with philosophical issues around statecraft. But as the sixteenth century progressed, books and pamphlets began to open up a confessional arena that promoted the experience of the individual. It was a shift in emphasis that was also evident in art, as artists such as Bruegel began to register a sensitivity to everyday experience.

This new confessional style was manifest in the writings of the French philosopher Michel de Montaigne, author of three books of essays which became bestsellers when they were published in 1580 and 1588. In them he touched on everything from pain and memory loss to education – and, above all, fear. 'The thing I fear most is fear,' he wrote in his essay 'Of Fear', since 'it exceeds all other disorders in intensity'. For Montaigne, different scales of fear exist in a continuum that ranges from personal fear to the collective 'panic terrors' that trigger armies, cities and nations to self-destruct.[39]

The *Essays* were written with a background of violent religious strife in south-west France, where he lived. In 1562 Catholics clashed with Protestants in Toulouse, leaving several thousand dead. Before long, France exploded into a full-blown civil war. As Jean Delumeau has observed, given the threats facing Europe at this time, one wouldn't think there was much occasion for self-examination. On the contrary, however, what Delumeau calls a siege mentality 'was accompanied by an oppressive feeling of guilt, an unprecedented movement toward introspection, and the development of a new moral conscience'. 'A global anxiety, broken up into "labelled" fears,' he wrote, 'discovered a new foe in each of the inhabitants of the besieged city, and a new fear – the fear of one's self.'[40]

Montaigne's philosophical project hinged on finding ways to manage this fear, which, as he told his readers, can control us and alienate us from ourselves. But if we succeed in harnessing and converting its energy, fear may also help us to live more fully. In discussing his own life with such apparent openness, Montaigne projected an informal image of himself with which his readers could readily identify. He wrote frankly, for example, about the agony he experienced while passing kidney stones, and how this gave heightened intensity to his life between attacks. For him, abrupt relief from pain was a reminder of the transience of life and the ever-presence of death. Montaigne's intimate and affable tone, along with his preoccupation with the everyday, encouraged his readers to reflect on their own experiences. 'He who fears he will suffer, already suffers from his fear,' he observed in his essay 'Of Experience'. 'I shall be in plenty of time when I feel the pain, without prolonging it by the pain of fear.'[41]

An important influence on Montaigne's thinking was the first-century Stoic philosopher, dramatist and statesman Seneca, who had sought to develop a practical philosophy that enabled his readers to cope with their fears. Our lives, Seneca claimed, are suspended between fearful memories and the dread of an unpredictable future, 'tormented alike by what is past and what is to come'. 'Widely different though they are,' he reflected, fear and hope 'march in unison like a prisoner and the escort he is handcuffed to'. The challenge was to live fully in the present, free of fear and expectations.[42]

Other early modern writers showed a similar interest in fear. Robert Burton's cult book *The Anatomy of Melancholy*, first published in 1621, was an encyclopaedic self-help reference work and manual for those suffering from melancholia. Today, we're likely to think of melancholia as an antiquated term for depression, but in the sixteenth and seventeenth centuries its main symptom and cause were believed to be debilitating fear. The word derives from the Greek for 'black bile', one of the four vital bodily fluids, or 'humours', that were thought to influence the health of the body and its emotions, along with blood, phlegm and yellow bile. Melancholia was an excess of black bile that caused 'a commotion of the mind' or 'a perpetual anguish of the soul'.[43]

Although Burton describes himself as 'a loose, plain, rude writer', *The Anatomy of Melancholy* eruditely encompasses everything from the Classics to the latest medical tracts. Despite this breadth of learning, Burton stresses that the book was originally conceived as an antidote to his own funk. Its contents, he tells us, were designed 'to help and medicinally work upon the whole body'.[44]

Burton insists that, while fear is triggered by the prospect of an imminent danger, it can also originate from an imagined threat. He provides numerous tragi-comic examples of fantasy fears with damaging physical effects. An Italian baker who's convinced he's made of butter is so terrified of melting that he won't go near his oven or sit in the sun. Sometimes, Burton advises, extreme fantasies can be fatal. A man meets someone he believes is infected with the plague and dies from the shock, even though his fear is groundless. Or a man who has successfully negotiated a narrow plank across a stream in the dark dies of fright when he subsequently realises the danger he had put himself in.[45]

Like Montaigne, Burton thinks of fear as a continuum that extends from individual trauma to the terrors that grip communities. As an example, he takes a devastating earthquake that struck Bologna in December 1504. Among those who experienced the event was the humanist Filippo Beroaldo. When the city began to shake, 'people thought the world was at an end', Beroaldo wrote, and some inhabitants, including his servant Fulco Argelanus, became 'so grievously terrified' that they went mad. Collective terror, Burton suggests, intersects with an individual's progressive trauma that culminates in suicide.

The causes of melancholia don't only lie in the body, but are also in the mind, aggravated by environmental factors. These are melancholic times, Burton reminds us; the backdrop to his writing is a deluge of 'rumours of war, plagues, fires, inundations, thefts, murders, massacres, meteors, comets, spectrums, prodigies, apparitions, of towns taken, cities besieged in France, Germany, Turkey, Persia, Poland, etc., daily musters and preparations, and such-like, which these tempestuous times afford'.[46]

While seventeenth-century philosophical and medical treatises sought to anatomise fear and instruct readers on how best to cope with it, other writers were creating fiction that explored the nature of fear and its relationship with power. Shakespeare's *Macbeth*, first performed in 1606 in front of King James – the monarch whose treatise on witchcraft may have influenced the playwright – tracks the corrupting effects of power and the ambiguous role of fear as a destructive, moral and motivational force. 'A play both about fear and consumed by fear,' observes the literary scholar Allison Hobgood, 'it narrates and performs the symptomatic process of fear engendering illness and death.'[47]

The play opens with the appearance of three witches on a bleak Scottish moor. When this demonic trio prophesy that

Macbeth, a successful general, will become king, they awaken murderous desires in him. Egged on by his ambitious wife, he overcomes his fear, murders King Duncan and seizes the throne. But he's soon tormented by fresh doubts, and in his paranoia he becomes increasingly tyrannical. Violence escalates and Scotland descends into civil war.

What's striking in the play is the tension that Shakespeare pinpoints between the corrosive influence of fear, which leads to violence, and fear as a moral force, which puts a brake on Macbeth's urge to act upon his vicious fantasies. So long as he experiences the latter kind of fear, we know that Macbeth hasn't relinquished his humanity. But by the climax of the play, he has lost all capacity for moral fear and instead succumbs to full-blown paranoia. His disposition at this point is similar to the state of mind that Burton ascribes to melancholia in which 'suspicion follows fear and sorrow at heels, arising out of the same fountain'.[48] 'The mind I sway by, and the heart I bear,' Macbeth declares in the play's final act, 'Shall never sag with doubt, nor shake with fear.'[49] This is the moment we realise that, in his determination not to feel fear, Macbeth has irrevocably left a moral universe.

While Shakespeare was writing *Macbeth*, the Spanish novelist, playwright and poet Miguel de Cervantes had just published the first volume of *Don Quixote*, a novel that delves into the psychology of fear. The book follows the exploits of an impoverished aristocrat from the plains of La Mancha in central Spain whose chivalric idealism jars in a world of cruel pragmatism and wanton violence where fear is the order of the day.

In his prologue Cervantes asserts that his novel will present the reader with 'a sincere and uncomplicated' history – no easy feat, since Spain during the Inquisition could be a dangerous place to speak your mind. In 1492 the Jews had been expelled from the country by King Ferdinand and Queen Isabella, just as the conquest of the New World began. Silver and gold may have poured in from the Americas, and art and literature may have flourished at home, but this 'Golden Age', to which Don Quixote alludes facetiously, was a time of violence and institutionalised fear.[50] From the 1560s, as we've seen, Philip II had moved against his Protestant subjects in the Low Countries. In the face of the growing threat of the Ottoman Empire in the Mediterranean, anyone with a Muslim background was viewed with suspicion. Between 1609 and 1614 a policy of ethnic cleansing was formally adopted and the *moriscos* – Muslim converts to Christianity – were driven out.

Far from being just a comic romp, this is a tale of terror and loss in which Cervantes draws on his own experience: fighting against the Ottomans at the naval Battle of Lepanto off the coast of Greece in 1571, where he was shot and maimed; captured by Barbary pirates and enslaved for five years in Algiers; excommunicated by the Church in Spain and imprisoned for embezzling funds.

In one scene of the novel, intended as a satire on the Inquisition's censorship, a bigoted cleric scours Don Quixote's library for offending books to burn.[51] The crackpot knight isn't the only character whose worldview is blinkered by ideological assumptions – everyone in this rapacious society looks at the world through the narrow prism of their fear. When he spies two flocks of sheep on a plain, Don Quixote is convinced they are opposing armies drawing up for battle. After his squire, Sancho Panza, protests that they are really sheep, the knight replies that fear is keeping Sancho 'from seeing or hearing properly, because one of the effects of fear is to cloud the senses and make things appear other than they are'.[52]

By the turn of the sixteenth and seventeenth centuries, then, fear was being experienced and examined in novel ways. Human 'passions' and 'affections' were understood as intrinsically political. As Francis Bacon noted in 1605, affections were feelings that had to be kept in check by reason. The English writer Thomas Wright, a contemporary of Bacon's, likewise stressed the recalcitrant quality of passions, which could all too easily unsettle reason – just as rebels might challenge the authority of their king, or rival factions might disrupt the operations of the state. And Robert Burton noted how fear tyrannises, working to shatter the peace. These were metaphors of conflict that spoke to the turbulence of the post-Reformation period. Even the word 'emotion', introduced into English at the beginning of the seventeenth century through translations from the French, didn't just connote an excited mental state and strong feelings; it continued to signify political agitation and civil unrest. The frontispiece to the English translation of a book on the use of the passions by the French priest and philosopher Jean-François Senault, published in 1649, depicts their subjugation – Fear and Hope among them – imagined as manacled supplicants arraigned before the court of Reason.[53]

Meanwhile, the 'panic fears' produced by religious strife, war, famine and disease were creating new opportunities that states exploited for political ends as they consolidated. These proto nation-states – recognisable antecedents of countries in modern-day Europe – were in part brought into being by print culture. Books, pamphlets and newspapers played an important role in the manufacture of these new collective identities by promoting a standardised vernacular that in turn helped to override regional differences and catalysed a sense of national identity.[54]

Printing also helped to forge a new sense of the self by facilitating individual study and the sharing of experience. The emphasis on a direct engagement with sacred texts encouraged personal responsibility, rather than a reliance on institutional authority. Individuals could read about the fear of others and identify with them, meaning that private fears were amplified and collective fears personalised.[55]

But while books and pamphlets helped to train readers on how to master their fears, they could also encourage the spread of misinformation, discord and heresy. Calvin railed against the 'confused forest' of bad books being published, as did the Swiss physician and philologist Conrad Gessner, who in 1545 complained about the 'harmful abundance of books'.[56] By the end of the seventeenth century some readers felt lost in the glut of information.[57] In 1680 the philosopher and mathematician Gottfried Leibniz warned that 'disorder will become nearly insurmountable', given the 'horrible mass of books which keeps on growing'.[58]

It's this uneasy relationship between information and power, the individual and the collective, the state and the citizen, and the nation and the state, that the absolute rulers of seventeenth- and eighteenth-century Europe would claim to resolve, promising to restore order to a world in turmoil with the cultivation of salutary terror.

3

Theatre of Power

Violence during the Reformation and Counter-Reformation – the Catholic Church's fight back against the Protestant threat – became a justification for rulers to ratchet up state power and extend the reach of the law, particularly during and after the Thirty Years' War, which began in 1618 and decimated the population of central Europe. Catholic states in the Holy Roman Empire had joined forces in 1609 to create a military alliance known as the Catholic League. The brutal destruction of the Protestant city of Magdeburg by League forces in May 1631 became an enduring emblem of the horrors of a conflict in which perhaps 8 million people died from war, famine and disease.[1] 'May God have mercy upon us,' wrote one eyewitness to the violence, 'for this was a spectacle that has not seen its like in horror and cruelty in many hundred years, for it was beyond all measure.'[2] In a series of eighteen poignant small etchings entitled *The Miseries and Misfortunes of War*, published in 1633, the French artist Jacques Callot captured the savagery of the conflict with depictions of torture, rape and gruesome public executions. Marauding soldiers are shown ransacking a farm and convent, and burning a village.

One way in which this chaos could be managed was by cultivating another kind of fear: that of the absolute monarch and the state institutions he embodied. In the 1570s, during the turmoil of the French wars of religion, the jurist and political philosopher Jean Bodin had argued for the importance of a strong monarch to reassert order. Sovereignty, according to

Bodin in his *Six Books of the Republic*, is the 'absolute and perpetual power' of the state, vested in a ruler whose authority hinges on a complex arrangement of counterbalancing fears and affections. The king, who is accountable to God alone, upholds law and order in his realm by pacifying his enemies with terror and using fear to ensure the compliance of his subjects at home. However, this salutary fear has to be carefully calibrated: too much of it may fuel resentment, and too little may encourage defiance. The difference between a king and a tyrant, Bodin suggested, is that while the former cultivates his subjects' love alongside fear, the latter depends on fear alone. Consequently, while the king enjoys peace and security, the tyrant rules with the constant threat of insubordination. And yet Bodin insists that love and fear are closely connected, since to love someone is to live in dread of offending them.[3]

A later proponent of absolutism was the theologian and bishop Jacques-Bénigne Bossuet, who served as court preacher to Louis XIV and tutor to his eldest son and heir. In his book *Politics Drawn from the Very Words of Holy Scripture*, published posthumously in 1709, Bossuet developed the doctrine of the divine right of kings, arguing that all power derives from God and the sovereign rules through divine dispensation. According to this doctrine, fear is an effective political tool for countering a natural human propensity for indulgence and pride. And while kings ought to inspire terror in their enemies and fear in their subjects, this is entirely compatible with justice and love. 'The people must fear the prince,' Bossuet wrote, 'but if the prince fears the people, all is lost.' Finally, although they are vested with absolute power, rulers can't exercise that power arbitrarily, but only for the public good and 'with fear and circumspection, as a thing that comes from God'.[4]

Perhaps the best-known – and certainly the most influential – contribution to the debate on fear and sovereignty, however, is *Leviathan*, the political treatise published in 1651 by the English philosopher Thomas Hobbes, who was born, as he himself recognised, in fearful times. When news reached England in April 1588 that Philip II of Spain was readying an armada to invade and restore Catholicism, Hobbes's mother went into premature labour from the shock. He would later quip that she gave birth to twins: 'me and fear'.[5] However apocryphal this story may be, fear was to become one of his main philosophical concerns.

Because there is much about the world that is inexplicable, Hobbes said, humans are prone to 'perpetual fear' of the unknown – and, in particular, fear of death – which is readily exploited by religions as a strategy 'to keep the people in obedience' in order to ensure the status quo. Hobbes himself was to be a casualty of this fear when, in 1666, he was accused of promoting atheism in his work, which was denounced in the House of Commons as a possible cause of the plague and the Great Fire of London. After several bishops 'made a motion to have the good old gentleman burn't for a heretic', reports his contemporary the antiquarian and biographer John Aubrey, Hobbes feared that his papers would be searched for incriminating evidence and destroyed some of his writings.[6]

Appetites and aversions define human nature, Hobbes claimed, and above all a 'restless' desire for power. Paradoxically, it is because all men are born equal that they are locked in an endless conflict for dominance, 'a condition of War of every one against every one'. However, if fear can be dangerous, generating doubt and mistrust that incite rancour and division, it may also have its uses. It is a passion closely associated with curiosity and the pursuit of knowledge. 'Anxiety for the future time,' Hobbes wrote, 'disposeth men to inquire into the causes of things: because the knowledge of them, maketh men the better able to order the present to their best advantage.'[7] Fear also motivates us to act out of self-interest; the prospect of some future mishap spurs us to take precautionary measures. 'On going to bed, men lock their doors,' Hobbes declared. '[When] going on a journey, they arm themselves because they are afraid of robbers.

Countries guard their frontiers with fortresses, their cities with walls, through fear of neighbouring countries.' Foresight and prudence arise out of fear, which can therefore be understood as a fundamental requirement for security.[8]

These views were to influence Hobbes's younger contemporary the English philosopher and physician John Locke, whose liberal ideas – formulated against the backdrop of further political turmoil in England during the 1680s – were in turn to influence later thinkers such as Voltaire and Rousseau. Fear is an implicit link between Locke's theory of knowledge and his political philosophy, including the argument he makes for religious toleration and the importance he attaches to the social contract between the citizen and civil government. In an essay on courage and fear in children's education, Locke reflects on how 'Fear is a Passion, that, if rightly governed, has its Use.' Courage that overcomes fear can be disadvantageous, Locke maintained, since 'Fear was given us as a Monitor to quicken our Industry, and keep us upon our Guard against the Approaches of Evil.' What is needed, he insisted, is a balance: 'so much Fear as should keep us awake, and excite our Attention, Industry and Vigour; but not disturb the calm Use of our Reason, nor hinder the Execution of what that dictates'.[9]

But of all Hobbes's arguments it is the claims he makes about the role of fear in the relationship between the sovereign and his subjects that have proved most influential. Strife characterises our natural state, he tells us, because humans are selfish, always looking to their own interests. In one of his best-known formulations he described this antisocial existence as one of 'continual fear, and danger of violent death', where life is 'solitary, poor, nasty, brutish, and short'. It's not, as is often claimed, that Hobbes believed humans to be inherently evil. Rather, he thought that the qualities that ensured self-survival were precisely those that drove competition, ultimately militating against cooperation. The only way to minimise discord and ensure peace in society is if individuals renounce some of their freedom and enter into a social contract that vests authority in a strong ruler who is able to 'over-awe them all': 'a Common Power, to keep them in awe, and to direct their actions to the Common Benefit'. Fear of intra-communal conflict has to be counterbalanced by the greater fear of the sovereign ruler. 'The Obligation of Subjects to the Sovereign, is understood to last as long, and no longer, than the power lasteth, by which he is able to protect them,' Hobbes asserted. The name he gave to this new body politic was the 'Leviathan', after the sea monster in the Bible.[10]

The iconic frontispiece to the first edition of *Leviathan* depicts a colossal figure wearing a crown and holding a sword and crosier, symbols of earthly and religious power. The arms and torso of this giant are comprised of hundreds of miniature figures all turned towards him, and above the image is a quotation in Latin from the Book of Job: 'There is no power on earth to be compared with him.' Only fear can contain fear; if it causes war, it can also function as a tool for peace, since 'fear is the basis both of man's most urgent plight and of his only possible escape'.[11]

These arguments in *Leviathan* reflect an important current of mid-seventeenth-century thought that drew on the religious conflict and political tumult of the preceding decades.[12] Central to the English Civil War, fought between royalists and parliamentarians from 1642, was the issue of religious toleration, the impartiality of the law and arguments about the relative power wielded by the king and Parliament. In 1640, with the country drifting towards war, Hobbes had fled to Paris, fearing that his royalist sympathies would get him into trouble with Parliament; he would spend the next eleven years in exile. On 27 January 1649, King Charles I was found guilty of high treason and a few days later he was executed in front of the Banqueting House in Whitehall wearing 'two heavy shirts, lest he should shiver and seem afraid'.[13] A parliamentary republic was inaugurated, which soon transformed into an authoritarian protectorate under Oliver Cromwell. Hobbes's theories, then, weren't merely the fashionable topics of drawing-room discussion; they made important contributions to philosophical debates about power, fear and political order.

By the mid-seventeenth century monarchies in many parts of Europe were explicitly claiming ownership of fear and building its management into the heart of their political calculus. In France, during Louis XIV's long reign from 1643 to 1715, fear not only helped to produce an aura of inviolability around the king but was central to the operations of the French state. It wasn't simply the terror of brute force and military aggression. It was calculated fearmongering, reliant on access to information and requiring a small but functional bureaucracy. It was fear confected through ceremony, resting on an elaborate choreography of kingship and driven by new institutional processes – a centralisation of power that was spectacularly embodied in the Palace of Versailles.

It's hard not to be impressed by the grandeur of Versailles today, even as you negotiate the tourist coaches and tour groups. The monumental buildings and gardens were designed to convey authority and prestige, summing up an ideal of royal governance and a broader geopolitical vision. The palace was a fitting edifice for a ruler who was known as the 'Sun King'.[14] As courtiers strolled through the magnificent grounds, marvelling at the ingenuity of its design, the French military were busy building fortress cities to consolidate and defend the expanding territories of the state.[15]

Versailles was an embodiment of power devised to produce fear and awe. Visiting dignitaries had to cross a series of courtyards, climb flights of stairs and pass through antechambers lined with guards before they reached the 'Apollo Salon', where Louis sat on a silver throne raised on a dais between two massive silver torch lamps.[16] Not surprisingly, many foreign ambassadors were quivering wrecks by the time they reached him.

The elaborate etiquette that governed behaviour at Versailles was a means of control that operated through the manipulation of fear. As the Duc de Saint-Simon put it, 'The Court was yet another device to sustain the King's policy of despotism.' 'The awe inspired by his appearance,' he concluded, 'was such that wherever he might be, his presence imposed silence and a degree of fear.'[17]

Versailles would later serve as an architectural blueprint for other authoritarian polities. When Albert Speer designed the monumental new Reich Chancellery for Adolf Hitler in Berlin, he drew inspiration from Versailles. Visitors passed through the main entranceway to a central courtyard, up external steps flanked by two neoclassical sculptures into an internal reception hall, and through 17-feet-high double doors into a ballroom, a domed hall and a marble gallery modelled on the Hall of Mirrors. Hitler was delighted with the plan, commenting that the long walk would give dignitaries 'a sense of the power and dimensions of the German Reich'.[18]

Fear of unrest in Paris and childhood memories of a coup staged against the regency of his mother in 1648, followed by five years of civil war, had influenced Louis's decision to move his court out of the capital. Although in his memoirs he brushed aside any talk of 'fear, hate and vengeance' that his youthful experience of war may have inspired in him, it was a disavowal that spoke volumes.[19]

Some 20 kilometres south-west of Paris, the new palace was planned as an alternative seat of government where the king could keep a watchful eye over the nobility. Once at court, nobles were ensnared in elaborate rituals devised to inculcate a permanent state of anxiety. While they could lobby the king for preferment, they could also be manipulated through control of access to his person – a process epitomised by the ritual that saw courtiers competing to attend to the monarch's early-morning and evening ablutions.

A centralised model of kingship demanded a new disciplinary apparatus to foster obedience and regulate behaviour, inaugurating what the French historian Robert Muchembled has called a 'policed society'.[20] It was no coincidence that an honour code and highly ritualised court etiquette emerged at the same time as the military drill arose as a training procedure for a professional army. A common analogy used by contemporaries was that of the court as a finely tuned machine organised with clock-like precision around the king.[21]

The apparent frippery of court entertainments at Versailles belied their serious political intent. Far from being distractions from the serious business of power, performances of ballets and plays were vehicles for promoting the monarchical order. Louis himself conceded as much when he wrote, 'The people over whom we reign, unable to grasp the true nature of things, have a tendency to base their judgements on external appearances.'[22] There are echoes here of Machiavelli's advice to the prince on the importance of appearances. 'Everyone sees what you appear to be, few experience what you really are,' he had noted. 'The common people are always impressed by appearances and results.'[23]

Grand balls and elaborate dances were opportunities for the king to display his magnificence. In 1653, at the age of fourteen, he had appeared on stage as Apollo in a performance of the *Ballet de la nuit*; refulgent in a golden costume bedecked with suns and a crown of flames, he was the rising sun restoring order out of chaos.[24] Even clothes acquired political meaning at court, with strict rules of precedence determining who could wear what when.[25] Fear informed court pageantry and daily formalities. Prescriptions on how to eat, talk, walk and dance kept courtiers in line, with the ever-present threat that they might be stripped of their privileges if rules of comportment were infringed. An Academy of Royal Dance, established in 1661, was charged with overseeing the implementation of new dancing protocols; instructors were required to obtain teaching licences, with hefty fines imposed if there was any deviation from the standards set out by the academy. In what was tantamount to censorship, all new dances were reviewed by a board of academicians before they could be taught or performed.[26]

Scrupulous attention was also paid to the pedigree of those at court. In 1661 the king issued a declaration against 'usurpers of nobility' – fake aristocrats who were 'prejudicial to the honour of the true nobility'. Clerks were appointed to check proof of title, a policy that created considerable fear in those whose lineage was being investigated. If genealogical claims couldn't be attested, or evidence of impropriety was discovered, entitlements could be revoked and those found guilty demoted to 'commoners' and banished from court.[27] All of this was part of a system that used fear as a means of exercising royal power.

While nobles were coaxed to Versailles, officials were dispatched to the provinces. Under the direction of Jean-Baptiste Colbert, the king's chief adviser and finance minister from 1665, these provincial functionaries were instrumental in extending royal authority across the country. Their loyalty could be counted on since they owed their status to the king's largesse. Louis stood at the apex of the system; although he never actually made the memorable statement for which he is credited – *l'État, c'est moi*, 'I am the state' – Bossuet wrote of Louis that 'the whole of the state is embodied in him'.[28]

A Royal Academy of Painting and Sculpture was founded in 1648, under the directorship of the artist Charles Le Brun. Other royal academies served to reinforce heroic stereotypes of the enlightened ruler through his patronage of music, architecture and the sciences. The Académie des Inscriptions, established in 1663 as a committee of the Académie Française, was charged with designing inscriptions for medallions and advising on art works that exalted the king.[29] In the so-called 'statue campaign', launched in 1685, plans were drawn up to erect equestrian statues of the king in public squares across the country.[30] Medallions and statuary were manufactured in bulk, which is why auction houses and online antique marketplaces today have a seemingly endless supply of Louis XIV memorabilia.

Promotion of the royal person went hand in hand with the policing of books, pamphlets and gazettes for seditious and libellous content, an information crackdown overseen by Colbert and the lieutenant-general of police, Gabriel Nicolas de la Reynie.[31] Censorship helped to ensure conformity, but it also reflected a deep-seated fear of subversion. A decree of 1685 stipulated that prints had to be approved by authorities before they could be published, and in 1694 those responsible for printing a drawing that caricatured a statue of the king in the Place des Victoires in Paris were executed. Instead of depicting an omnipotent monarch glorified by shackled slaves, the cartoon showed an enslaved monarch, subservient to his mistresses and wife.[32]

Louis XIV's absolutism involved more than court ritual and propaganda, however; it also entailed the prospect of arbitrary force.[33] In tandem with a concentration of authority came a clampdown on religious independence. Absolute power required the centralisation of the monarchy in order to realise a policy of 'internal pacification and external aggression'.[34] Fear could be used to suppress those within and intimidate those without.

With the 'Declaration of the Clergy of France', a document approved by a general assembly of French clergy convened by the king in 1681, the French Catholic Church was effectively brought under his control. At the same time, in Louis's drive to consolidate and extend his domestic power, all forms of religious dissent were suppressed. From 1661 Jansenism – a Catholic reformist movement named after the Dutch theologian Cornelius Jansen, which counted many influential aristocrats and intellectuals among its followers – was condemned, and in 1710 the Abbey of Port-Royal des Champs, a Jansenist centre, was demolished.

But it was France's sizeable Protestant minority, the Huguenots, who were particular targets of violence. The Edict of Nantes, promulgated by Louis's grandfather Henri IV in 1598, had granted the Protestant community considerable religious and civil freedoms. In 1685 Louis formally revoked this policy of toleration and a new lexicon of terror gained traction: the word 'extermination' was commonly employed to describe the butchering of a population en masse, while 'refugee' was used for the first time of a person fleeing terror.[35]

The persecution of Protestants began with restrictions on travel, employment, education and worship. Interfaith marriages were forbidden, and Protestant churches were destroyed. Soon the violence escalated. Among the most notorious tactics adopted was the billeting of the king's unruly dragoons in Protestant households with a licence to harass the occupants.

First-hand accounts of the terror triggered shock and outrage across Protestant Europe. Jean Migault's description of his persecution in Poitou conveys the gathering storm and the gut-wrenching terror of a world turned upside down. Migault details the implosion of a community as terror and panic take hold and neighbours turn on one another. As law and order break down, vigilantes patrol the streets, houses are ransacked and families, stripped of their possessions, flee into the countryside.[36] The king's suppression of the Huguenots would lead to the War of the Camisards from 1702, in which hundreds of Protestant villages in the Cévennes and Vaunage regions of southern France were targeted in concerted terror campaigns.[37]

It wasn't only in France that Louis XIV sought to enhance his authority. In the same year that the Edict of Nantes was revoked, a royal decree was passed – later known as the *Code Noir* – consisting of sixty articles regulating slave labour in France's Caribbean colonies. While the torture of slaves was forbidden and freed slaves were to enjoy 'the same rights, privileges and immunities as those enjoyed by freeborn persons', the enslaved were required to convert to Roman Catholicism. Punitive measures were also to be put in place to ensure discipline, including branding runaways with the fleur-de-lys, an emblem of royal power, and the beating of slaves with rods or straps whenever their masters saw fit. As chattels, slaves were obliged to seek their masters' permission if they wished to marry, and any offspring they produced were to be the property of the mother's owner.[38]

And then there were the military campaigns, notably against the Habsburgs. Four major wars were fought between 1667 and 1713, in which period the French standing army became the largest in Europe. Brutal tactics were adopted, and in the 1672 campaign against the Dutch, French troops 'unleashed a reign of terror'.[39] Although the king notionally condemned the practice of terrorising local populations, the tactic was widely used and caused anti-French sentiment across Europe.[40] In the German-speaking lands of the Habsburg Empire, pamphleteers stoked fears of Louis's military conquest and religious persecution, kindling worries that Louis was building a 'Universal Monarchy', and leading to a remarkably unified anti-French coalition.[41] In a withering attack on Louis's expansionist ambitions, Gottfried Leibniz portrayed the king as an invidious tyrant who ruled by 'Fire and Sword'.[42] The king was an evil machinator, like Machiavelli, as ruthless as Attila the Hun, and as debauched as the infamous Roman emperor Nero.[43] Books and pamphlets reviled the 'infernal barbarities' he'd inflicted on other European states and the way he'd squelched ancient freedoms, leaving the French to endure a 'harshness unknown to all people who live under Christian princes'.[44]

In the early 1690s the archbishop and theologian François Fénelon had written an anonymous letter to Louis containing a scathing rebuke of the despotic king. 'The whole of France,' he wrote, 'has been reduced to nothing more than a big hospital, desolate and empty of provisions.' The king took advice from corrupt ministers who were fearful of speaking the truth lest it displeased him. He had tyrannised the Church and waged illegitimate wars, which had ravaged Europe for twenty years. And all of this violence had been paid for by bleeding the country dry. The people who had once loved him now despised him, and 'sedition is breaking out everywhere'.[45]

Fénelon described a political world that operated through different kinds of fear. There was the fear that the sycophantic ministers had of displeasing the king, the fear that the king's despotism produced and the king's own fear of confronting the truth. 'Kings who dream only of being feared, and of browbeating their subjects to make them more submissive, are the scourges of the human race,' Fénelon would later write in his bestselling novel *The Adventures of Telemachus, Son of Ulysses* (1699). 'They are feared as they want to be; but they are hated, detested; and they have more to fear from their subjects than their subjects have to fear from them.'[46]

In the decades after Louis's death in 1715, criticism of absolutism increased. In 1748 the political philosopher Charles Louis de Secondat – better known as Montesquieu – distinguished despotism from republicanism and monarchy as a political system in which a single leader governs according to his wants and whims, 'without rule or law'. Terror is the presiding principle of despotic government, rather than virtue and honour, and it has a stultifying effect, overwhelming a citizen's courage and extinguishing 'even the slightest feeling of ambition'.[47] To uphold civic virtue and avoid the despot's monopoly on power requires constant vigilance, Montesquieu argued, as well as the separation of judicial, legislative and executive functions.

And yet, despite the outward projection of royal power as regulated and efficient, Louis's court was riven by rivalries and intrigues. 'Not even Louis XIV, for all the fear and awe he inspired, was in total control,' remarks his modern biographer.[48] In the 1670s, during the so-called 'Affair of the Poisons', courtiers began to fall sick at Versailles and evidence of a plot was uncovered involving satanic rituals and poisoning. Even after the alleged perpetrators were apprehended, tortured and executed, the king was believed to be at risk; the Paris chief of police was warned, and a commission was set up to investigate. When the king's mistress was implicated, the court was left in disarray. Such scandals exposed the fragility of royal power.

Power also bred paranoia. 'Nothing is terrible except fear itself,' Francis Bacon had observed in 1623, and in an essay titled 'Of Empire' he had written about how the insidious nature of fear could poison the mind of a ruler. 'It is a miserable state of mind to have few things to desire and many things to fear,' he wrote, 'and yet that commonly is the case of kings.' Isolated amid their grandeur, rulers began to see 'perils and shadows' wherever they looked.[49]

Fear of the king could just as easily function as a destabilising force. The centralisation of power gave Louis reason to be fearful of political intrigues and discontent fomenting outside his trusted coterie. Because he symbolised the state, all of its failings could be laid at his door, and fear could quickly turn to resentment. The plots against him weren't all imaginary, either. While his reign saw protests and rebellions, fears and counter-fears produced instability that would have profound consequences seventy years later, when panic became a catalyst for revolution.[50]

In so far as he made royal power a form of dramatic spectacle, Louis ensured that authority rested on who controlled what was seen and how it was staged.[51] Social and technological transformations, however, made it harder to monopolise this 'performance of power'. The increasing influence of highly literate bourgeois mercantile and commercial classes, together with the rise of printing and the dissemination of slanderous pamphlets, broadsides, magazines, newspapers and books, meant that information was far more difficult to police, as was the border between public and private worlds.[52]

In 1792, some eighty years after Louis's death, the English writer Mary Wollstonecraft travelled to Paris, where she witnessed the intensifying terror of the French Revolution. On one occasion, crossing the Place de la Révolution – as the Place de la Concorde was then known – she was shocked by the sight of blood on the ground beneath the guillotine. In seeking to understand where this upsurge of violence had come from, she laid the blame on the 'character' of the French nation, which had been 'depraved by the inveterate despotism of ages'. Revolutionary terror, she suggested, had antecedents in the old regime.[53]

An aspect of French political culture that she singled out was its propensity for theatre. According to Wollstonecraft, the 'theatrical entertainments' at Louis XIV's court had originated out of an earlier 'feudal taste for tournaments and martial feats'. And from Versailles this theatrical politics had extended across the realm until the nation itself came to resemble 'a grand theatre', with wars promoted as 'theatrical exhibitions' to distract citizens from their real subjugation.[54] After the Revolution in 1789 the tables may have turned, but the strategies of power remained remarkably similar. Instead of the king and his court, Revolutionary demagogues and the National Convention now presided over elaborate show trials and public executions, including that of Louis's progeny, Louis XVI, who was condemned for high treason and guillotined in the Place de la Révolution on 21 January 1793, a month after Wollstonecraft's arrival in Paris. The spectacle of the king's ignominious death marked the continuation, not the end, of absolutist terror.

4

Colonising Panic

At some time in the mid-fifteenth century, perhaps fifty years before Machiavelli wrote *The Prince*, a teenage girl was led to her death near the summit of Mount Ampato, a dormant volcano in southern Peru. Her frozen remains were discovered there in 1995, along with those of three other children, remarkably well preserved in the thin, dry air of the Andes. Archaeologists surmised that she'd been sacrificed to the mountain spirits, or *apus*, possibly to appease them during the eruption of a neighbouring volcano.[1] What had the 'Ice Maiden', or Juanita, as she became known, been thinking as she was led to her death? As the Peruvian novelist Mario Vargas Llosa asked, 'Did Juanita feel fear, panic, in those final moments?'[2]

In the years after the discovery of Juanita, other sacrificial remains were found, intimating that the Inca ritual sacrifice of children, a practice known as *capacocha*, was commonplace. In 1996 a teenage girl nicknamed Sarita was discovered in Peru. And in 1999 yet another well-preserved body was found at the top of the Llullaillaco volcano in Argentina, close to the Chilean border. Andrew Wilson, one of the lead researchers conducting the excavation, noted that 'no outward signs of fear' were identifiable, while biochemical analysis of her hair indicated that she'd been drugged with coca leaves and alcohol. Along with the other children recovered at the site, she was sitting beside intact offerings, further evidence that she hadn't struggled.

Wilson and his colleagues concluded that these elaborate and logistically challenging ritual killings had been designed to impart fear. 'The placement of the *capacocha* children could act on two levels,' they wrote: '[first], that of a sophisticated belief system in which the existence of gods was not in doubt; and second, on a more atavistic level, as a successful operationalization of Machiavelli's insight that fear coupled with respect is the most effective tool of governance.'[3] According to this 'social control hypothesis', human sacrifices and violent cult ceremonies played an important role in consolidating social hierarchies and legitimising political authority, a suggestion that's been confirmed by evolutionary biologists and psychologists who argue that historically they've functioned as a means of coercing pliant populations.[4]

Like the Aztecs – a misnomer for the Mexica, the dominant, Nahuatl-speaking indigenous people of central Mexico – an Inca elite carved out an expansive empire by subduing and enslaving less powerful competitors. It's thought that around 100,000 ethnic Incas may have dominated a population of some 10 million, subjugating their rivals with fear.[5] Sacrifice and displays of ritual violence were features of their rule, just as they were for the Mayans and Mexica. However, while the use of fear as a political tool can hardly be regarded as a Western invention, it was Europeans who used it as a key facet of their overseas empire-building. At the same time they would justify their brutal conquests by dwelling on the 'orgies of violence' that they claimed were features of the 'uncivilised' societies they colonised.[6]

Christopher Columbus was the first European to make contact with the peoples of the Caribbean and Central and South America, in four expeditions between 1492 and 1504. Spain and Portugal soon dominated the Americas, their acquisitions sanctioned by a papal disposition that divided all territories west of the Cape Verde Islands between them. Spanish and Portuguese accounts of the conquest of the New World tend to contrast European exploits with the barbaric customs of the natives, with gruesome indigenous practices such as *capacocha* used to vindicate their colonisation. As the biographer of the Spanish conquistador Hernán Cortés wrote, Mexica society was ripe for a takeover: 'disloyalty seethed throughout the Empire only awaiting the propitious moment to throw off the supremacy of fear'. Although the Mexica had an organised religion, 'their deities were gloomy and ferocious, fear was the motive of worship', and they lived 'engulfed in a dreadful superstition' that kept them 'in a state of perpetual degradation'.[7]

In the Dutch artist Jan van der Straet's drawing from the 1580s *Allegory of America*, the Florentine explorer Amerigo Vespucci – the man who gave his name to America – is shown standing before a reclining native American woman who is naked apart from a loincloth, anklets and a feathered cap. In the distance three native cannibals roast a human leg on an open fire. In the foreground, a club rests against a tree trunk. While he holds a crucifix and astrolabe, Vespucci is shown wearing armour, with a sword half-concealed among the folds of his cloak, in anticipation of bloodshed to come. Amazement at the wonders of the New World is matched by apprehension about the danger that it conceals. Meanwhile, it's clear that Vespucci, bolstered by a fleet of warships and with God and science on his side, will be the victor in any future struggle.

Violence and fear were integral to the colonial project, but they didn't only play a role in the subjection of indigenous peoples and the conquest of their lands. A shared fear and hatred of native 'savages' in early North American settlements was a crucial factor in unifying the colonisers, who came from different regions of Europe, spoke different languages and professed different faiths. Ironically, as the historian Peter Silver has argued, it was fear of a common threat that helped to develop the principle of tolerance that would become a central tenet of an independent United States in 1776.[8]

While stock descriptions of natives as uncouth aggressors shouldn't come as a surprise in European accounts, not every chronicle was so biased. In 1552 the Dominican priest Bartolomé de las Casas published *A Brief Account of the Destruction of the Indies*, a searing indictment of Spanish rule in the Americas. Fear, according to Las Casas, was frequently deployed by the conquerors as a tool, with indigenous people put to the sword as a way of 'increasing and spreading terror throughout the land'. This terror incited revolts that were then used to justify further repression.[9]

The invading Westerners weren't just feared for their brutality and weaponry; they also came to be feared for the diseases they brought. Research has pointed to a decline of as much as 80 or 90 per cent in the indigenous populations of Central and South America following the conquests. Although many factors contributed to this fall, the arrival of new diseases was a major cause. Environmental circumstances, including the social havoc wrought by the colonisers, as well as a lack of immunity, made indigenous populations particularly susceptible to imported infections, such as smallpox, measles, malaria and yellow fever.[10] The Franciscan missionary Toribio de Benavente, known as Motolinía, begins his *History of the Indians of New Spain*, completed in 1541, with a biblical allegory about the 'ten terrible plagues' that visited the Mexica, including famine and an epidemic of smallpox. 'As the Indians did not know the remedy of the disease, they died in heaps, like bedbugs,' Motolinía wrote. 'In many places it happened that everyone in a house died, and as it was impossible to bury the great number of dead, they pulled down the houses over them, so that their homes became their tombs.'[11]

Just as the Mexica civilisation was being overwhelmed by the Spanish in 1521, the Portuguese explorer Ferdinand Magellan made landfall on an island in an archipelago across the Pacific. A few years later it would be named the 'Philippines' in honour of Prince Philip of Asturias, later King Philip II of Spain, the monarch who was responsible for the repression of Protestant communities in the Netherlands.

The extraction of silver by the Spanish in Central and South America from the mid-sixteenth century changed the global economy. Silver mined by enslaved natives in Mexico, Peru and Bolivia was transported from Acapulco in galleons – armed merchant ships – 9,000 miles across the Pacific, where it was used to buy luxury goods from China, Japan, India and South-East Asia: silk, porcelain, ivory, lacquerware, jade, cotton and spices. The galleon trade created a dynamic flow that connected Europe, the Americas, Asia and Africa for the first time.[12]

With their extensive trade networks linking Europe with Asia and the Americas, Mexico City and Manila in the Philippines have claims to be the first global cities. By the early eighteenth century Manila had grown to become a populous shipping hub. During the trading season Chinese junks and European ships docked from the Far East, and traders visited from India and Ceylon, Sumatra and the Moluccas. Despite its prosperity, however, significant shifts in global maritime power had begun to highlight the vulnerability of the Spanish colony's economy.[13] The British already dominated the Indian subcontinent through the East India Company, a joint-stock company with regional headquarters in Calcutta, but they had now begun to push eastward into new markets. In the same period independence movements in the Spanish Americas disrupted the galleon trade, which ceased altogether in 1815.

These changes were to have a major impact on the Philippine economy, fuelling discontent towards the colonial administration and heightening tensions between the Spanish, the Filipinos and the sizeable Chinese community. This was the context for the violent panic in Manila in 1820, triggered by an outbreak of cholera. At that time the cause of the disease was still unknown; its bacterial origins, along with the germ's transmission route via contaminated water and food, were only established several decades later. In 1817 an outbreak in Bengal in the Ganges delta had launched the first Asiatic cholera pandemic, with the disease spreading along trade routes to the

Middle East. It also moved eastward to China and Japan, and by late September 1820 it had reached Manila, bringing the port to a standstill.[14] While the sick were left unattended, carts piled with corpses rumbled through the streets, and in the Paco district of the city residents dug a new cemetery. It was reported that 15,000 Filipinos died in a fortnight, although the final tally was probably much higher. The French ship's surgeon Charles Benoît, who survived the epidemic and later adopted the name Carlos Luis after long service to the Spanish, called it 'a theatre of horror and desolation'.[15]

The authorities made some effort to manage the outbreak, discouraging residents from using water from the Pasig, a river that bisects the city. In the early days people stayed indoors, burning aromatic herbs and dousing their homes with vinegar.[16] An infusion of brandy and *cinchona* bark, which was known for its fever-quelling properties, was apparently distributed via street stalls, although the effects of this tonic were by all accounts 'a thousand times more pernicious than the disease it was intended to prevent'.[17] In any case, these measures evidently did little to appease public fear, and panic began to spread. Paul de la Gironière, a French doctor and entrepreneur caught up in the crisis, wrote, 'Next to the fright occasioned by the epidemic, quickly succeeded rage and despair.'[18]

Foreigners were blamed for the outbreak, and the mood in the city turned ugly. When some empty barrels were found floating in the Pasig, it was rumoured that they had been used to poison the water. The discovery of the decomposing corpse of a French sailor fed further speculation, with some suggesting that the body had been deliberately dumped as part of a plot to kill off the natives and take control of the Philippines.[19] Several foreigners had assisted in the relief work, among them the French surgeon Victor Godefroy, who had recently arrived in the Philippines. As he walked down the street near his lodgings in the district of Santa Cruz on the morning of 9 October, a few Filipinos shouted abuse at him. Soon a crowd gathered, accusing him of killing cholera patients who had died under his care. According to Gironière, he was struck in the face and pinned to the ground. When a vial of laudanum was discovered on his person, his assailants, convinced it was poison, administered it to a dog which reportedly dropped dead – proof of the man's villainy. Vindicated, the crowd went in search of other Europeans, while Victor was left for dead.[20]

At this point the governor sent a sergeant with a contingent of soldiers to keep the peace, but in the confusion the besieged foreigners mistook their protectors for aggressors and shot at them. Storming the house, the crowd of Filipinos butchered the occupants, including Victor's brother. Twenty-two-year-old Félix-François Godefroy had been one of three young naturalists dispatched to acquire new specimens for the Museum of Natural History in Paris. The cabinet of curiosities discovered in his room, which included tortoiseshells, Polynesian native weapons, skeletons of animals and humans, stuffed parrots, iguanas, monkeys and 'several snakes preserved in alcohol', was taken as evidence that sorcery was at play. It was believed that venom had been extracted from the snakes and thrown into the river, causing the epidemic.[21] A package of black powder wrapped in rice paper was presented as corroborating evidence.[22]

News of the attack spread rapidly through the increasingly jittery foreign community. The panic was intensifying, and armed Filipino rowdies now prowled the streets. In the portside district of Binondo, a crowd of several thousand assembled, armed with pikes, knives and bludgeons. David Nicoll, the young Scottish captain of the *Merope*, an East India Company vessel that had sailed from Bengal, was cornered in an alleyway. He tried to escape, but the mob soon caught up with him and stabbed him in the back, while other foreigners were butchered alongside him.

Although accounts of the massacre are confused and often contradictory, panic is invariably dramatised as a series of snapshots. We're offered glimpses of dining rooms, lodgings, backyards, teahouses and prisons during what became a deadly game of hide-and-seek. A protagonist hides under a bed or jumps through a window. Captain Warrington and Captain Balston of the East India Company ship *Edward Strettel* rush into the house of a Parsee merchant and escape via a sewer. A tavern run by a German is ransacked. Four Frenchmen have lodgings there, and one of them leaps through a window into the yard of an adjacent house, escaping under cover of darkness; the others are cut to pieces.[23]

The Chinese, however, suffered the biggest losses. Casualty estimates vary greatly according to different accounts, but over a two-day period perhaps thirty or so Europeans were murdered, along with some eighty Chinese who were accused of conspiring with them. Through all of this, the Spanish did little to intervene. Despite enjoying a reputation as a disciplinarian, Mariano Fernández de Folgueras, governor-general of the Philippines, waited in the wings with his troops. The authorities' inaction suggested, at least to foreign observers, that the Spanish had intentionally stirred up the cholera panic. Others were more magnanimous and attributed the governor's procrastination to his fear that a military intervention would spark insurrection. Peter Dobell, an Irish-American serving as the Russian consul in Manila, clearly viewed jealousy as the motivation for the violence. 'After living there a couple of months,' he wrote, 'I perceived that there existed a vast deal of jealousy and envy, against all strangers, and particularly those who resided or intended to form establishments in the country.'[24]

It was only in late October, as the violence abated, that Folgueras intervened and reprimanded the local population for infringing the law under the influence of what he called 'a general frenzy'. He alleged that the populace had been 'led astray and infuriated by certain malicious persons'. Rumours that the foreigners had poisoned the waters were, he asserted, unfounded. Those who had been attacked 'were not only friends and brethren, but the very persons on whom the prosperity of the islands must depend'. Belatedly, he called on the natives to hand over those responsible for the violence, to return any items that had been stolen and to denounce the murderers.[25]

What caused the panic in Manila? Several explanations were offered at the time, chief among them cholera: it was fear of the unknown, or rather, fear at the thought of an agonising death. When the Filipinos let superstition get the better of them, they gave free rein to that fear. There was also a suggestion that the crowd's ignorance had been exploited by those with malevolent intentions. Group anger was dangerous because it could be harnessed by others for heinous political ends. In the same year as the Manila massacre a wave of revolutions shook Europe's established order. Crowds were perceived as threatening, and nowhere more so than in foreign places where cultural differences came to the fore.

Contemporary accounts all seem eager to identify signs that might anticipate the emergence of panic. From their ships at anchor in the bay Europeans scour the shoreline through their spyglasses, interpreting catastrophe in the silhouette of the gathering crowd. Ignorant of Tagalog, the local language, they can only interpret the mood of the people from gestures and expressions. 'I perceived even before I landed,' wrote Captain John Campbell of HMS *Dauntless*, 'that some dreadful catastrophe had marked its progress with desolation and had produced stagnation in the commercial operations on the river, and in the port.'[26] European eyewitness accounts emphasise the role played by rumours and counter-rumours, which were generated by disrupted information flows. During the crisis, communication channels with the Spanish authorities were impeded by historic rivalries. Meetings with Governor Folgueras achieved little, the two sides at odds because of religion and politics. Encounters with the local Filipinos resulted in misunderstandings, which were exacerbated by barriers of language and culture – just as Félix-François Godefroy's natural history collection was mistakenly assumed to be proof of wizardry. To this extent, the Manila panic serves as a case study for how cultures misread each other, with tragic consequences. Panic was both the cause and the outcome of a communication breakdown.

Stereotyping worked both ways. While the Filipinos viewed the foreigners as collective poisoners, the Filipinos were lumped together by the Europeans. Panic for them wasn't all bad. It may have pitted locals against foreigners, but it also brought foreigners together: French, American, British, German, Danish and Russian. Panic distinguished 'them' from 'us', in much the same way as fear of native Americans acted as a unifying force for early American colonisers. Contemporaneous Western accounts of the massacre invariably include a roll call of European victims, implicitly offsetting their names against the unnamed native perpetrators of the violence. It's as if Europe is being called forth to counter an unfathomable world of darkness and fear. However, the European compulsion to make lists may indicate not self-confidence but rather an anxiety about operating in a world that wasn't fully understood. Europeans may have ascribed native panic to 'one of those terrific outbursts of barbarian despair', but there was more than a hint of panic in such denunciations.[27] Like the Filipinos who attributed the epidemic to poison and sorcery, they had little clue where cholera came from and how it spread.

The panicked crowd in Manila is also contrasted with the emptiness of the city when the crowd isn't there. By the nineteenth century this had become a familiar image of epidemic panic. In his account of the plague panic in London, published a century earlier, Daniel Defoe had dwelt on the emptiness of the streets. We're given scenes of jostling pedestrians and wagons and carts hurrying to escape the spread of infection; we're also shown the opposite, the city returned to an unnatural state of nature: 'the great Streets within the City, such as Leaden-hall-Street, Bishopgate-Street, Cornhill, and even the Exchange it self, had Grass growing in them, in several Places'.[28]

Panic is structured around a series of oppositions – crowds and emptiness, frenetic activity and immobility – that by the 1820s defined the template of modern panic.

The historical sources that enabled me to reconstruct the Manila panic are in Spanish, French and English, not in Tagalog, the language of the Filipinos, which would give the other side of the story. While Europeans depict themselves as well-rounded individuals with a capacity to think on their feet, the Filipino mob is portrayed as a blinkered mass. Panic is the characteristic of a violent rabble, driven by emotion rather than reason. Individuals do occasionally stand out in the records – Yang-Po, for example, the generous owner of a tea store who risks his life to help Gironière. Hemmed in by armed Filipinos, the Frenchman is also saved at the last moment by the intervention of a Filipino soldier who distracts the mob so he can slip away. Overwhelmingly, however, the indigenous mob is faceless. Here we have a key assumption about the panicking crowd that would become prevalent as the nineteenth century progressed. Panic reflects a herd instinct, a tendency for individuals to act as one when they're subsumed in a crowd. At the same time, the enervated local mob serves to individuate the composed Western onlooker. In other words, panic may be the flipside of a rational, dispassionate worldview, but one can't exist without the other.

In many accounts, the break-ins by natives symbolise a dangerous disregard for social and political boundaries. When the mob crashes through the door of a European household, it is inverting the social order. Panic isn't just disruptive, it's revolutionary. Underlying this realisation is another perturbing thought that is only hinted at in accounts: what if the rampaging mob was right and foreigners *were* responsible for the epidemic? What if the massacre wasn't the result of blind native panic but the expression of a retributive justice? Supposing the cholera had been ferried to Manila on board the *Merope*? As Western commentators tacitly acknowledged, their sojourn in the Philippines had in part triggered counter-invasions. They may have brought the massacre on themselves.

Panic in 1820 existed at different scales. The epidemic was the outcome of expanding imperial networks and shifting geopolitics, even as it was shaped by highly specific conditions. Years after the massacre, the explorer Gabriel Lafond, a friend of Gironière, agreed with many others when he concluded that the cholera had been the spark that set alight dormant suspicions produced by economic and political stress factors. Panic was triggered not by cholera but by the circumstances that made it possible.[29]

News of the epidemic and massacre soon spread from Manila to Europe, the United States and China. The panic took its place as part of a broader, global diffusion of information, quickly transmuting into a news story that travelled through the same global pathways as cholera itself. A memorial plaque on the wall of the parish church at Kirriemuir in Angus, Scotland, is dedicated to 'Capt. DAVID NICOLL late commander of the ship Merope of Calcutta, who was killed in the massacre at Manila, 9th Oct. 1820, aged 25 years'.[30] While eyewitness accounts stress the immediacy of the violence, the panic now seems to exist in a different, stretched-out temporality: it unfolds as memory, history, hearsay and distant report.

In 1908, after the Americans had defeated the Spanish and annexed the country with a brutal campaign waged against Filipino nationalists, the massacre was once again invoked to explain what was happening in the present. Rumours circulated that the Americans had poisoned the wells and streams to kill off Filipinos, leading to native panic and a spate of attacks on US personnel. As Dean C. Worcester, secretary of the interior for the US colonial government in the Philippines, wrote, 'thus history has repeated itself after so long a time'. Quoting Governor Folgueras's 1820 proclamation, he called the rumour of foreign plots a 'fable' propagated to deceive the suggestible masses.[31]

Lafond asks other questions that are relevant to our story of colonial panic. Was the violence and cruelty of the 1820 massacre a cultural manifestation of latent Filipino fanaticism, or is such violence a universal phenomenon – the consequence of catastrophes, which tend to incite irrational fears? Lafond is certain that violence isn't a demonstration of an inherent native barbarity. Even in America and in Paris – 'the centre of modern civilisation', as he reminds us – the second cholera pandemic in the early 1830s had revealed the precariousness of the social order. The term 'cholera panic' had by then become commonplace, and nowhere was immune.[32]

Panic may exist everywhere, but that doesn't mean it is the same wherever it appears. As European influence extended across the globe in the nineteenth century, racial and cultural views hardened and the idea of a universal panic gave way to a comparative approach: some fears were better than others. The naturalist Félix-François Godefroy, who was killed in the Manila massacre, had been sent to Asia to collect scientific specimens for a cabinet of curiosities. By the mid-nineteenth century science was interested in the study of different human behaviours along with animals and plants. To rule over people, you had to know how they behaved. 'Panic acts on an Oriental population like drink upon a European mob,' the British Indian administrator William Wilson Hunter observed in 1882.[33] The management of native panic, and the racialised science it was based on, were to become key facets of colonial governance.

While the history of Western colonialism and empire is one of violence, it is also in many ways the story of how mutual incomprehension produced mutual fear that served to justify and intensify that violence. Panic was the consequence of an environment where different cultural worlds collided. Colonial governments, ever fearful of native rebellion, were quick to panic. And when they did, they invariably set off a chain reaction of subsidiary panics that could have global effects.

5

Despotism of Liberty

The geopolitical upheaval set in motion by the French Revolution in 1789 provides another context for the violence unleashed in the 1820 Manila panic. In April 1792, anticipating an invasion to quash the Revolution, France declared war on Austria, which was immediately supported by Prussia. Before long Britain, Russia, Spain and Portugal were drawn into the conflict, which extended well beyond the borders of Europe. The Reign of Terror in France was followed by a parliamentary revolt, after which Napoleon Bonaparte seized power. A successful general in the Revolutionary wars, he would become first consul of the French Republic in 1799 and, five years later, crown himself emperor. The Napoleonic Wars, and Napoleon's eventual defeat in 1815, would result in the further expansion of British power.

As these events unfolded, the words 'fear', 'panic', 'horror' and 'terror' acquired new connotations, even as earlier meanings endured. In the seventeenth century, as we've seen, political theorists had lauded terror as an attribute of kingship compatible with virtue and justice. Of all the Bourbon kings, Louis XIV was the one most associated with this terror.[1] However, during and after the Revolution, terror gained new currency. The 'Reign of Terror', or simply 'The Terror', came to describe a period of mass arrests and executions carried out by France's Revolutionary government between September 1793 and July 1794 – a policy of concerted state violence summed up in the radical injunction to 'make terror the order of the day'.[2] 'Terror' now implied both a form of calculated violence and the regime that perpetrated it. And from there it came to designate the breakdown of authority, as well as the negation of those virtuous political principles – liberty, equality, fraternity – that had inspired the Revolution in the first place.[3]

Earlier in the eighteenth century, the word had had very different overtones. In Denis Diderot's *Encyclopédie*, published in numerous volumes from 1751, 'terror' is defined as an emotion that heightens a person's awareness of other people's suffering and in this sense is closely connected to compassion and pity, and to tragic drama.[4] Terror was also associated with the 'sublime', a concept that conveyed disorientation and awe in the face of nature's terrifying vastness.[5] As a form of extreme fear induced by the sight of an external danger, terror jolted viewers into recognition of their limitations and vulnerability in a world that they couldn't control. As the Anglo-Irish politician and political theorist Edmund Burke contended in his 1757 essay *A Philosophical Enquiry into the Origin of Our Ideas of the Sublime and Beautiful*, 'No passion so effectually robs the mind of all its powers of acting and reasoning as fear.' At the same time, Burke insisted, terror was sublime because 'it is impossible to look on any thing as trifling, or contemptible, that may be dangerous'.[6]

There was an ambiguous line between pleasure and pain in this understanding of the sublime. The shock response of terror – Burke calls it 'astonishment', which he defines as 'the effect of the sublime in its highest degree' – triggered by a painting or a book could shatter indifference and expand the mind, not unlike Diderot's understanding in the *Encyclopédie*. But while danger or pain experienced at a remove might be pleasurable, it was an altogether different matter when they pressed too near; at which point, Burke wrote, 'they are incapable of giving any delight, and are simply terrible'.[7]

Terror as an effect of the sublime drew its force from the things we imagine but can't see, which is why, Burke claimed, despotic governments that trade 'on the passions of men, and principally upon the passion of fear' keep their ruler 'as much as may be from the public eye', and why religions throughout history have used 'judicious obscurity' to instil fear in the faithful.[8] However, there was all the difference in the world between sublime terror and the terror associated with Revolutionary tyranny, which gave free rein to self-destructive human propensities – 'rapacity, malice, revenge, and fear'.[9]

Fear was certainly crucial to the events leading up to the French Revolution in 1789 and to the espousal of terror as a political principle in 1793. From the beginning, convoluted political manoeuvrings created uncertainty and confusion, which were amplified by rumour and panic. In April 1789 disgruntled workers rioted in Paris. Later that summer, amid a deepening food crisis in the countryside and as peasants began to prepare to bring in the harvest, reports circulated that marauding brigands were destroying crops as part of a sinister plot, orchestrated by government ministers, to starve the population into submission.[10]

This intensifying unrest was the backdrop to the meeting in Versailles of the Estates-General, the French parliament that was soon reconfigured into a National Assembly. After they pledged to establish a constitution in June 1789, many deputies feared recrimination for opposing the king. These fears, which were heightened by the panicking crowds gathered at Versailles, seemed justified when Louis dismissed the popular finance minister Jacques Necker the following month.[11] By deploying royal troops in and around the capital, the king exacerbated these existing tensions, inciting a Parisian crowd to storm the Bastille, the fortress and prison that had long been an emblem of royal tyranny.

In August 1789 the National Assembly passed a series of decrees that effectively dismantled France's 'feudal' system. Three years later, in September 1792, the newly formed National Convention formally abolished the monarchy and established a republic. And the following year Louis XVI was tried for treason, found guilty and executed. Meanwhile, the

Convention found itself overwhelmed by intensifying factional conflicts, food shortages, riots, war and uprisings in the provinces. As an emergency measure it created a Committee of Public Safety and suspended the new constitution, along with the rights guaranteed in 1789. This marked the beginning of the Reign of Terror, which would only end in July 1794, when the leader of the regime, Maximilien Robespierre, was removed from power. As the country careered from absolutism to quasi-dictatorship via constitutional monarchy and republic, fear and panic shaped responses at every stage.[12]

During the Terror coercion became a tool that was used to enforce order in the name of freedom and equality. New legislation was introduced to streamline the justice system; the 'Law of Suspects' allowed for the arrest and trial of those suspected of betraying the Revolution. Indictment became tantamount to a death sentence, since the Revolutionary Tribunal denied those accused the opportunity to mount a meaningful defence. Fear turned inwards, as Jacobin leaders 'feared one another – the enemy within – even more than they feared their acknowledged enemies'.[13]

Appealing to his erstwhile friend Robespierre, Camille Desmoulins, a deputy of the Convention and member of the Jacobin Club – a group of radical Revolutionaries – wrote, 'remember the lessons of history and philosophy: love is stronger and more durable than fear'.[14] If it didn't offer freedom of expression, he declared, the Republic was no different from the despotic monarchy it had replaced. In an impassioned rebuke to the regime, Desmoulins claimed that democracy had become 'intemperate', with tolerance giving way to 'the cold poison of fear, which freezes thought to the depths of the soul'.[15]

As a strong-arm tactic, terror didn't only involve physical intimidation; it extended to censorship and a general clampdown on nonconformist views, enforced by the threat of violence. Days after writing his denunciation, Desmoulins was arrested, tried on charges of counter-Revolutionary conspiracy and executed.

An atmosphere of fear and suspicion fed rumours of spies and counter-Revolutionary plots. Rumour had long been a feature of life at court, part of the machinations of power at Versailles, where gossip could make or destroy careers. But now it was no longer 'whispered in the corridors or the boudoirs of nobility, but openly proclaimed'.[16] A shadowy enemy alliance was reportedly at work, secretly assembling an army of outlaws to attack the fledgling Republic. Many of these threats were invented or exaggerated by radical leaders, either to reaffirm the urgency of the Revolutionary struggle or as a means of justifying ever more draconian interventions. As terror spread among the political leadership, individuals turned on each other to save their necks.[17] Citizens were arraigned for political crimes, and the Revolutionary Tribunal sent thousands to the guillotine. Many more died in prison awaiting trial, while as many as 200,000 were killed when a royalist uprising in the west of France was crushed.

If despotism's masterstroke was its ability to attach reason to its cause, Robespierre wrote, why couldn't terror be appropriated in the fight for liberty? In a speech before the Convention in February 1794, he justified its use as a form of emergency justice, arguing that it was a means to a democratic end. 'Terror is nothing more than speedy, severe and inflexible justice,' he said. Virtue is terror.[18]

In histories of the Revolution, Robespierre is presented as either the pantomime villain and the prime architect of terror or the incorruptible progressive and firebrand who is brought down by his spineless comrades. In his writings and speeches there's an impressive casuistry, as when he makes an argument for the happy cohabitation of democratic principles with terror. There's also something discomfiting about the way an issue of life and death is treated as a philosophical conundrum.

Picture the scene: fidgety deputies are crammed onto the

benches of the Convention, casting nervous glances at their fellow members as they wonder what's about to happen. It's 31 March 1794, and a few hours earlier Desmoulins and the Revolutionary leader Georges Danton have been dragged from their beds in a dawn raid. The fear in the chamber is palpable; any of the deputies might be hauled off to the tribunal on trumped-up charges. Robespierre enters and realises that these men are frightened, but he doesn't assuage their fears; instead, he hones in on fear itself as a form of betrayal: 'I say that anyone who trembles at this moment is culpable; for innocence never fears public scrutiny.'[19] Those who feel fear in the face of the terror, Robespierre is saying, are *ipso facto* guilty. On one level this is a disingenuous sleight of hand that makes the potential victim guilty of the spurious crimes he fears he'll be charged with. But on another level, it's a reminder, doubtless not lost on Robespierre's audience, that they are implicated in the terror they're afraid of. There can't be a revolution without a revolution.[20]

'What do I care about danger?' Robespierre had declaimed in March 1794. 'My life belongs to my country; my heart is free from fear; and were I to die, I would do so without reproach and without ignominy.'[21] Four months later, he was ousted from power, along with the other Jacobin leaders that dominated the Committee of Public Safety. Holed up in the Hôtel de Ville, he was putting his signature to a proclamation urging patriots to rally to his cause when soldiers sent by the Convention burst into the room. According to one account, a bullet hit Robespierre in the jaw. However, a botched suicide seems more likely – as his colleagues attempted to flee, he was handed a pocket pistol and misfired.[22]

It was to be a miserable end. On the evening of the following day, after a hasty appearance before the tribunal, Robespierre and his associates were taken by cart to the Place de la Révolution, where a guillotine had been assembled. A surgeon dressed Robespierre's wound and patched up his face. But as he was waiting to be strapped down, the executioner ripped off the bandage that held his broken face together, causing him to give an almighty howl – a scream that reverberates well beyond the moment of its utterance.

At the outset, the Revolution had been greeted with enthusiasm by radical politicians and progressives in Britain. There were those, like the Welsh-born Presbyterian minister and reformer Richard Price, who saw it as an example for the British to emulate.[23] In a sermon delivered in November 1789 – and subsequently published as *A Discourse on the Love of* Our *Country* – Price decried anti-French sentiments as a form of blinkered nationalism that promoted vested interests at the expense of universal liberty. It was time, he wrote, 'to correct and purify this passion, and to make it a just and rational principle of action'. To drive home his point, he appended his sermon with a congratulatory address to the French National Assembly, rejoicing in the 'triumph of liberty and justice over arbitrary power'.[24]

For conservative thinkers like Burke this was anathema. The Revolution had created an illegitimate form of government that circumvented sanctioned institutions, such as the monarchy and Parliament, and gave vent to unfettered and destabilising passions. He warned of anarchy and of the real danger that Britain might be 'led through an admiration of successful fraud and violence, to an imitation of the excesses of an irrational, unprincipled, proscribing, confiscating, plundering, ferocious, bloody, and tyrannical democracy'.[25] Revolutionary France was a 'scourge and terror' and in the fourth of his *Letters on a Regicide Peace*, published in 1796, he writes of the 'undisciplined power' of 'those Hell-hounds called Terrorists' – not its first usage in English, but an early one – who are 'the Satellites of Tyranny'.[26]

In September 1792, when hundreds of prisoners were butchered in Paris, even progressives and erstwhile supporters of the Revolution began to wonder how a political movement that had been motivated by an enthusiasm for liberty and fraternity could have descended so quickly into terror. A doctrine of natural rights as formulated in the seventeen articles of the Declaration of the Rights of Man and of the Citizen, which had been approved by the National Assembly in August 1789 and which asserted that all 'men are born and remain free and equal in rights', had been inverted in order to underpin terror. The government's task was no longer to protect and uphold its citizens' inalienable rights but to punish the malefactors who contravened them.[27]

Most commentators agreed that the violence had been driven by fear. In a passionate response to Burke's claims, his former friend Thomas Paine argued that Revolutionary terror was the logical response of a people who'd been brought up in fear. Paine reminded his readers of the barbarous punishments meted out under the old regime, epitomised by the execution of Robert-François Damiens, a domestic servant who was publicly drawn and quartered in 1757 for an attempted assassination of Louis XV. Such 'cruel spectacles' were part of a strategy of 'governing men by terror' and were intended 'to destroy tenderness' in the population. Was it any surprise that citizens who had been brutalised by this 'slavery of fear' inflicted 'in their turn the examples of terror they have been instructed to practice'?[28]

To understand better these debates about Revolutionary terror, fear, panic and their place in political life, we need to look at them in context. During the eighteenth century there was a shift across a range of fields, from political theory and philosophy to art and literature, in how the emotions were understood. For some, emotions weren't antithetical to reason; rather, human language and reasoning faculties had developed out of them. As the Scottish philosopher David Hume put it in 1739, 'Reason is, and ought only to be the slave of the passions, and can never pretend to any other office than to serve and obey them.'[29]

In 1763 the French physician and botanist François Boissier de Sauvages published a new classification of diseases, based on their symptoms. In his discussion of 'perverted desires and aversions', he included the disease 'panophobia', which caused nightmares and groundless terror that could lead to convulsions and epilepsy. Because these fears are symptoms of underlying disorders that have discernible causes, they can be treated and, in some cases, cured. Which is to say that emotional behaviour can be modified with the right clinical intervention.[30]

The year before Boissier de Sauvages's medical textbook appeared, the Swiss-born philosopher Jean-Jacques Rousseau had proposed an altogether different theory of fear in *Émile*, his groundbreaking treatise on education. In contrast to Hobbes and Locke, Rousseau claimed that humans are intrinsically good but become progressively corrupted by society.[31] In our natural state we have no fear of death because we have no consciousness of it; but as we grow up, we are taught to fear it by those who stand to gain from it, losing our freedom and capacity for goodness in the process. 'It is doctors with their prescriptions, philosophers with their precepts, priests with their exhortations,' he wrote, who debase Émile's heart 'and make him unlearn how to die'. Medicine doesn't so much cure us of our maladies as it 'impresses us with terror of them'.[32]

These philosophical and scientific debates about fear coincided with profound transformations taking place in social relations.[33] In *Émile*, Rousseau used the term 'bourgeois' to disparage a new class of person motivated by self-interest and fear rather than the common good: an alienated, contradictory and vacuous individual 'always floating between his inclinations and his duties'. He was arguably the first to use the word in this way, anticipating Karl Marx's later indictment of the exploitative bourgeoisie.[34] In 1790 Burke also recognised that the French Revolution represented 'warfare between the noble ancient landed interest, and the new monied interest', commenting that perhaps 'the most important of all revolutions' taking place in France was 'a revolution in sentiments, manners, and moral opinions'.[35]

*

In the seventeenth and early eighteenth centuries Louis XIV had consolidated power through overt coercion, censorship and the regulation of court behaviour via an elaborate honour code, using fear as a tool. By the end of his reign, however, a booming print culture and an increasingly assertive urban commercial class were challenging this centralised authority. Coffee shops, private *salons*, Masonic lodges, societies and clubs provided less deferential and far more inclusive and rumbustious venues where different social classes could interact, with women playing a crucial role.[36] The German social theorist Jürgen Habermas has claimed that together these spaces constituted a new 'public sphere', where different opinions could be debated and solutions to social problems proposed. In truth, the *salons* remained bastions of a political elite – it was precisely their ambiguous status between the court and an emergent social world that enabled them to survive and flourish.[37]

But all these changes reflected and helped to foster a new optimism in human nature and a growing conviction in the importance of 'sentiment', 'taste' and 'passion' in moral judgements. Novels, poems, plays and operas, which catered to a new public, reinforced this sentimentalism.[38] Portraits in which sitters sat stony-faced were no longer de rigueur, and smiles became fashionable, with improvements in dental hygiene no doubt playing a part.[39]

This new humanism is exemplified by Rousseau's writings, which stress the links between morality and spontaneous feelings. In his *Discourse on the Origin of Inequality*, published in 1755, he had underlined the importance of compassion – an individual's 'natural repugnance against seeing a fellow creature perish or suffer'.[40] It is a theme that he returned to in *Émile*, where pity for the plight of others is viewed as crucial for fostering sociability. 'It is man's weakness which makes him sociable,' Rousseau famously declared. 'Pity is sweet because, in putting ourselves in the place of the one who suffers, we nevertheless feel the pleasure of not suffering as he does.'[41]

The promotion of empathy, which recognised the universality of human suffering, became fundamental to the espousal of human rights. Meanwhile, as social relations became more attenuated, a political order determined by neat subdivisions of the realm into 'estates' – the clergy, nobility and commoners – became less feasible. The family presented another model of community, one in which social divisions could be overcome by familial love.[42] Royal apologists increasingly conceptualised the king's relationship to his subjects as that of an indulgent father to his children, with patriotism identified 'not with a political principle, but with an emotion: the love of the French for their kings'.[43] The father was no longer an austere patriarch who ruled the household with fear but a benignant figure who commanded obedience with affection.[44]

This cult of the family and the promotion of royal authority as a form of paternalistic love created new instabilities, however. On the one hand, the distance between the king and his subjects contracted.[45] But on the other, as citizens gained access to the emotional world of their rulers, the aura of other-worldliness was pierced, and they were viewed as fallible. In fact, the more the world of the court became accessible to public scrutiny, the more suspicion there was of those private spaces that remained hidden.[46]

The question of where the line between the monarch and his subjects should be drawn became contentious. In 1783 the artist Élisabeth Louise Vigée Le Brun painted a portrait of Marie Antoinette, queen consort of Louis XVI, wearing a loose muslin chemise. When it was unveiled at the Salon of the Académie Royale, in her debut appearance there, the portrait caused a scandal, not only because it looked as if the queen had disrobed but because the trappings of power were missing – the depiction was too human and unseemly for a royal portrait. In response to the outcry, Vigée Le Brun was forced to replace it with a more formal painting of the queen in a magnificent silk dress, her hair elaborately coiffed. These two styles of portraiture illustrate the ambiguity of a monarchy that was at once too open and too closed, too public and too private: a monarchy that was neither sufficiently feared nor loved.[47]

In the years before the Revolution, critics of the monarchy had exploited this haziness to disparage the institution. In the Parisian cafés and taverns, the royal household became the butt of lewd *libelles*, small-format pamphlets of burlesque verse or satirical prose. Louis XVI was censured in dramatic symbolism, his portrait accompanied by a caption that identified him as 'false' or 'fake'. The tone of the pamphlets was earthy, even prurient, and the language often foul-mouthed. However, for all their ideological differences, scurrilous pamphlets and modish royal portraits tapped into basic human emotions, whether of disgust, hatred or love. In this sense, the scowl of the radical and the smile of the aristocrat belonged to a single universe of feeling.

The *libelles* also took aim at royal sexual predilections. In the late 1740s anti-royal sentiment had come to the fore during a panic precipitated by rumours that young children were going missing in Paris. Louis XV had a reputation for debauched sexual behaviour, and there were claims that he was implicated in a kidnapping plot. Other rumours alleged that the children had been snatched to satisfy the king's bloodlust, or that their blood had been drained for use in a potion to cure his leprosy.[48]

It was common knowledge that Louis XVI and Marie Antoinette had taken seven years to consummate their marriage. While Louis was depicted in pamphlets as impotent and viewed as a figure of derision, the Austrian-born queen became a hate figure, depicted as a voluptuary with insatiable sexual urges. It was claimed that her neoclassical château in the grounds of Versailles, the Petit Trianon, was the setting for bacchanalian orgies where she engaged in lurid acts of masturbation, sodomy and incest.[49] As the political philosopher Montesquieu had suggested, lust was the hallmark of Eastern despots obsessed with their harems and seraglios.[50] The queen embodied the monarchy, and her illicit behaviour came to symbolise the institution's despotism and illegitimacy. Scabrous satire was a way in which radicals could undermine the quasi-religious mystique of the monarchy while showing the queen for what she was. Her eventual execution in October 1793 in many ways marked the symbolic takedown of the old regime. A sketch of her being ferried to the scaffold, long attributed to the artist Jacques-Louis David, shows Marie Antoinette as a decrepit, saggy-jawed widow in a plain white gown, hands tied behind her back, with her dishevelled hair bunched under a coarse bonnet.[51]

Revolutionaries would seize on the growing ambiguity between private and public lives, which would also present challenges for the Republic. How far should terror go? Where should the law's authority end? And how could the desires of the individual be reconciled with the imperatives of the new polity?[52]

In Britain sympathy for the Revolution turned to repugnance with the news of the Terror. In a 1792 print by the British cartoonist James Gillray an extended family of working-class Revolutionaries sit down to dinner, their home reimagined as a butcher's shop. Diners gorge on a human heart, a severed arm and an eye scooped from a decapitated head; chubby kids shovel handfuls of sloppy entrails into their mouths from a bucket on the floor, their grandma roasts a child on a spit and a wooden rack is piled high with back-up provisions of body parts.

Burke didn't miss an opportunity to excoriate the Revolutionaries for their 'rapacity', murderous 'cruelty' and 'ferocious dissoluteness in manners'.[53] His 1790 bestseller, *Reflections on the Revolution in France,* was intended to shake an English elite out of its complacency, warning of the dangers that lay ahead if dissenters like Richard Price got their way. The result was hysterical melodrama. Take his description of the attack on the Palace of Versailles in October 1789, when a 'band of cruel ruffians and assassins' rushes into the royal bedroom, jabbing the bed with bayonets, while the 'almost naked' queen takes flight.

Then the mob herds the royal family from the palace, which is 'swimming in blood, polluted by massacre, and strewed with scattered limbs and mutilated carcases'.[54]

There are insinuations in this description of acts of torture, rape and cannibalism performed to the depraved score of a hollering horde. Moral and political breakdown is imagined as a form of bodily dissolution. France is a 'shop of horrors' and the members of the National Assembly, Burke writes, are like twisted children who hack their 'aged parent in pieces, and put him into the kettle of magicians, in hopes that by their poisonous weeds, and wild incantations, they may regenerate the paternal constitution, and renovate their father's life'.[55]

Perhaps the artist who captures the terror of the post-Revolutionary period most powerfully, however, is Francisco Goya. Some time between 1819 and 1823 Goya painted a series of murals known as the *Pinturas Negras*, or 'Black Paintings', on the walls of his farmhouse outside Madrid. In a hallucinatory scene that adorned the dining room, a gigantic Saturn, or Kronos – one of the Titans in Greek mythology – grips the headless body of his son as he chomps on morsels of bloody flesh. It's an image that echoes the words of the French lawyer and Revolutionary Pierre Vergniaud, who before his execution in 1793 had declared that the Revolution was devouring its children like Saturn.[56]

The violence precipitated by Napoleon's invasion of Spain in 1808 informed much of Goya's later work. Britain and Portugal had joined with the Spanish in an alliance against the French. The hard-fought campaign was to last six years; and although it concluded with a French defeat, it left Spain divided and economically ruined. When the Spanish king, Ferdinand VII, was restored from captivity in France, he revoked the constitution, clamped down on liberal reformers and reintroduced the Inquisition. It was in response to this post-Revolutionary turmoil that Goya produced a series of eighty-two etchings known as *The Disasters of War*. Like the 'Black Paintings', they are not for the faint-hearted. A garrotted priest clasps a crucifix; women are assaulted and raped; prisoners are shot and stabbed; the mutilated torso and severed limbs of a civilian dangle from a tree.[57]

One of Goya's best-known etchings from the earlier series *Los Caprichos* (1799) is *The Sleep of Reason Produces Monsters*, which shows the artist asleep with his head resting on a desk, while bats, owls, a lynx and a devilish black cat loom out of the darkness. Dreams and nightmares pervade Goya's work, and the series was initially conceived as twenty-eight drawings of dreams, with *The Sleep of Reason Produces Monsters* its original frontispiece.[58] The title is generally taken as an affirmation of Enlightenment rationality; whenever reason goes to sleep, superstition will prevail. However, the Spanish word *sueño* means both 'sleep' and 'dream', suggesting that the title could signify exactly the opposite. 'Underneath all reason,' writes the French philosopher Gilles Deleuze, 'lies delirium, and drift.'[59]

The intensifying violence of the French Revolution after 1792 – and particularly between 1793 and 1794 – suggested to some that, when pushed to its limits, reason could become murderously unreasonable. Such ideas persisted. In the aftermath of the Second World War, the German intellectuals Max Horkheimer and Theodor Adorno came to a similar conclusion when they sought to explain the horrors of the Holocaust. Enlightenment was supposed to have banished fear, but in fact the 'wholly enlightened earth', they said, was 'radiant with triumphant calamity'. The rationalisation of society in the eighteenth century had created a new model of inhumane governance that began with the French Revolution and culminated in twentieth-century fascism. Reason, underpinned by science and technology, had become a dehumanising force that destroyed the freedoms it claimed to preserve.[60]

But many others – Burke among them – saw the Revolution not as the outcome of an alienating rationality but as the perversion of legitimate political processes by 'irregular and capricious feelings'.[61] Through the nineteenth and twentieth centuries the French Revolution became central to such arguments about the place of the emotions in public life.

Reflecting on the history of revolutions in the aftermath of the Second World War, Hannah Arendt was wary of a politics that repudiated the emotions to rely on a steely bureaucratic rationality. Yet she also highlighted the destructive role that the emotions had played in the French Revolution, suggesting that, while histories tend to emphasise late eighteenth-century rationalism, they 'are likely to overlook or to underestimate the strength of these early pleas for passion, for the heart, for the soul'.[62] An emphasis on empathy and pity during the Revolution, she argued, had diverted the focus away from the task of building robust political institutions onto 'the people', who were viewed as a collective object of pity. In contrast, reason was held to be a selfish proclivity that undercut compassion. Here Arendt pointed to the influence of Rousseau, who had accentuated selflessness as a virtue.[63] But it was precisely this loss of the self in the emotive defence of an abstract collective that Arendt viewed as precipitating terror, since it created 'an emotion-laden insensitivity to reality'. Revolutions are invariably conceptualised as a stream or torrent in which individuals are no longer in control of their own destinies, mere spectators of unfolding events. And it is this emotive sublimation of the self that creates the space for terror. 'Since the days of the French Revolution,' Arendt observed, 'it has been the boundlessness of their sentiments that made revolutionaries so curiously insensitive to reality in general and to the reality of persons in particular.'[64]

In the decades after the French Revolution fear of political violence sparked panic across Europe. To many establishment commentators it appeared as if the world was on the brink of collapse. From the outbreak of war with France in November 1793 there were fears that the French would invade England or Ireland. In 1796 Burke wrote that 'out of the tomb of the murdered Monarchy in France has arisen a vast, tremendous, unformed spectre'. 'The revolutionary harpies' that had 'sprung from night and hell,' he warned, 'cuckoo-like, adulterously lay their eggs, and brood over, and hatch them in the nest of every neighbouring State'.[65]

In this atmosphere of anxiety there was a new focus on the threats posed by rumour and panic, which led to an emphasis on the need both to control information and to manage the explosive potential of crowds. Following the Napoleonic Wars, an economic depression in Britain fed into a political crisis. In 1812 the prime minister, Spencer Perceval, was shot in the lobby of the House of Commons. A meeting of radicals at Spa Fields in East London turned ugly in December 1816, and the following month the much-disliked prince regent was attacked in his coach following the state opening of Parliament. Emergency measures, known as the 'Gagging Acts', were introduced to suppress 'seditious meetings', and the Habeas Corpus Act – intended to prevent arbitrary imprisonment – was suspended. In 1819 cavalry charged into a crowd of some 60,000 protesters demanding reform in St Peter's Field, Manchester, killing at least fourteen people and wounding close to 700, an event that came to be known as the 'Peterloo Massacre' in a grim pun on the Battle of Waterloo where Napoleon had been defeated four years before. During the 1830s and 1840s a working-class movement known as Chartism campaigned for a reform of the electoral system. Rioting broke out across the country, triggering fears of revolution.

In many places the threat of revolution led to the stifling of reform and the passing of repressive legislation, along with urgent investment in a police apparatus to enforce it. Counter-revolutionary fears also gave rise to an anti-democracy invective and to a new understanding of freedom based on the protection of private property and citizens' inalienable rights 'to enjoy their lives and possessions in peace and quiet'.[66]

For decades after 1789 European rulers remained fearful of

a 'phantom terror'.[67] In Russia the Romanovs clung to imperial autocratic rule. After a failed coup in December 1825, Nicholas I set about defanging dissent and building a police state. 'This Empire, vast as it is,' wrote one French visitor to Russia in 1839, 'is only a prison to which the Emperor holds the key.'[68]

Writing from Paris in 1842, the German poet Heinrich Heine described the French bourgeoisie's 'instinctive fear of communism' and of an 'invading mob' that might emerge from the debris of a wrecked monarchy. In their fear of a proletarian revolt, he suggested, the middle classes would have no hesitation in ditching constitutional freedoms.[69] When revolutions did sweep across Europe in 1848, they brought back memories of earlier violence. Even after the threat had petered out, the French Revolution remained an example of how easily popular protest could spiral out of control, and of how tyrannical democracy could be. Simmering resentments born of urban poverty heightened fears of social conflict, and the spectre of terror lived on in an industrialising world.

6

The Slave Matrix

Six years before the Reign of Terror began in Revolutionary France, another kind of terror was causing concern in Britain. In 1787 the Anglican clergyman Thomas Clarkson had helped to establish the Society for Effecting the Abolition of the Slave Trade. In 1808 he would write a book, *The History of the Rise, Progress, and Accomplishment of the Abolition of the African Slave-Trade by the British Parliament*, based on fact-finding missions he had undertaken to support the anti-slavery campaign that was being spearheaded by William Wilberforce.

The history of slavery stretches back thousands of years, but from the sixteenth century, as the Portuguese and Spanish expanded their empires in the New World, they began to create a system of trans-oceanic slavery in which enslaved people became chattels of their European owners. They were soon followed by other aspiring imperial powers: the Dutch, British, French and Danish. Over 12.5 million Africans were traded between around 1500 and 1875. Of these, almost 6 million were transported by Portuguese ships, and well over 3 million by British traders. An estimated 1.8 million died en route, and those who survived were sold at auction and put to work as enslaved labour. Meanwhile, slavery became a key facet of the colonial economic system across the Americas, furnishing cheap labour that supported the production of cash crops including sugar, tobacco, cotton, coffee, rice and cocoa.

While slave numbers capture the horrific scale of this trafficking, there's something dehumanising, as the historian

Marcus Rediker suggests, about a history that has to be viewed through 'ledgers, almanacs, balance sheets, graphs and tables'.[1] It's not just that human voices get lost in the statistics; these archives of numbers are themselves the product of an extractive economic system that turned human beings into capital.[2]

Clarkson and other abolitionists drew attention to the systematic use of terror by white traders and slaveholders as a tactic to subjugate Africans; from their initial captivity and the harsh discipline on board the slaving vessels to life on the plantations.[3] 'I am at a loss to describe it,' Clarkson asserted. 'Where shall I find language to paint in appropriate colours the horror of mind brought on by thoughts of their future unknown destination, of which they can augur nothing but misery from all that they have yet seen?'[4] Alexander Falconbridge, a surgeon who had been involved in the trade, wrote in 1788 that the mistreatment of slaves 'must excite in every humane mind, the liveliest sensations of horror'. Deprived of air, the holds where the slaves were kept were sweltering and caked with blood and mucus so that they 'resembled a slaughter house'. 'It is not in the power of the human imagination,' he wrote, 'to picture a situation more dreadful or disgusting.'[5]

After Britain abolished the Atlantic slave trade with the Slave Trade Act of 1807, contraband ships intercepted by the Royal Navy's West Africa Squadron exposed its full horrors.[6] In November 1837 the *Arrogante*, a Portuguese schooner based in Havana, was seized off the coast of Cuba. The slaves on board were found to be in a 'horrible state of disease and emaciation', with the thighs of many slaves no thicker than a wrist. The crew was accused of murder, torture, rape and cannibalism.[7]

A few years later a Spanish coaster, the *Jesus Maria*, was intercepted with 233 surviving Africans on board. The slaves, who were found 'in an extreme state of emaciation and debility', provided harrowing accounts of their abuse. 'I confess to your Excellency,' David Turnbull, the British consul in Havana, wrote to Francis Cockburn, governor of the Bahamas, 'that I have not the courage to enter on this horrid catalogue of crime.' Cockburn sent the evidence of abuse obtained from the slaves to Lord John Russell, secretary of state for the colonies. 'The document,' he wrote in an accompanying note, 'is appalling; for, such unmitigated atrocities thus proved to have occurred in one slave-vessel, there is but too much cause to suppose that similar acts are practised in them all.'[8]

Clarkson had noted how fear in the slave trade skewed relations in surprising ways. While the traders kept their slaves in 'a state of general degradation and misery' through the routine application of violence, the knowledge which they had of 'their own crime in having violated the rights of nature, and of the disposition of the injured to seek all opportunities of revenge', induced a fear that drove them to adopt ever more repressive measures.[9] Terror, in other words, arose from the guilt of terrorising captives – though it was hardly symmetrical.

Violence wasn't only integral to cost-cutting; it also functioned as an instrument of onboard governance. It was in part because they were outnumbered and conscious of their fragile authority that traders kept slaves confined in ships' holds. Intimidation and outright coercion were tools by which they could consolidate their power.[10] The risk of insurrection was ever-present, and crew members were fearful of slave insubordination, acts of sedition and open revolt.[11] 'Seldom a year passes,' wrote the clergyman and abolitionist John Newton, 'but we hear of one or more such catastrophes.'[12] The crew of slave vessels lived in fear that the slaves would poison them using native herbs, or perhaps by employing black magic. In 1751, while serving as captain of the *Duke of Argyle*, a slave ship sailing to Antigua, Newton wrote of the crew's alarm when they learned that the slaves were planning 'to poison the water in the scuttle casks upon deck'.[13] Such threats compounded the crew's insecurities and often led to impulsive retaliation.

Meanwhile, the mariners who worked on the ships were at the mercy of the captain.[14] Sailing to the Gulf of Guinea from

Bristol and then on to the West Indies, the British surgeon James Arnold testified to the abuse of slaves and seamen on three separate voyages. Discipline was brutal, with the crew beaten, often deprived 'of the common necessaries of life' and forced to sleep on deck in all weathers. On one trip, eleven crew members had jumped ship in Africa, four had died on the voyage, while the rest had 'been badly used'.[15] Clarkson had persuaded Arnold to keep a diary during his third trip to the Cameroons, and it was presented as evidence before a parliamentary inquiry into the slave trade in 1789.[16] Arnold attested to the arbitrary violence inflicted on the native Africans, as well as the 'wanton Barbarity' the captain had shown to the crew. 'It is almost impossible for a person to describe in its proper Colours the Treatment which the Crew of the *Ruby* experienced at the Hands of the Captain,' he concluded.[17]

Abolitionists themselves used fear as a means of moral persuasion, repeatedly emphasising the depredations of slavery. John Newton excoriated the 'unmerciful whippings' and 'the torture of the thumb-screws' that gave 'intolerable anguish'. Wilberforce noted how the African trade had 'rendered the whole coast of that vast continent a scene of insecurity, of rapine, and of terror'.[18] Descriptions of predatory sharks trailing slave ships became a metaphor for the monstrosity of a system that chewed up humanity.[19] It was laid bare during a much-publicised incident off the coast of Jamaica in November 1781, when, as a result of navigational errors, the slave ship *Zong* found itself off course and short of water – or so the captain, Luke Collingwood, would later claim. When slaves and crew members began to fall ill and die, the captain ordered the crew to throw 122 shackled slaves overboard.[20] On its return to England, the ship's owners submitted an insurance claim of £30 per head under the terms of the contract that covered the loss of slaves due to 'perils of the sea'. However, the claim was contested by the insurers and the publicity around the ensuing court case helped to promote a growing awareness of the inhumanity of slavery, giving impetus to the abolitionist cause.[21]

When Clarkson's history of the slave trade was reissued in 1836, the artist J. M. W. Turner was among its readers. In 1840 he painted one of his most celebrated works, inspired by the case of the *Zong*. In *Slave Ship (Slavers Throwing Overboard the Dead and Dying – Typhoon Coming)* he wrestled with Clarkson's predicament of how to express the terrors of slavery. The convoluted title of the work suggests the ineffable horror of the episode and, beyond that, of slavery itself. The painting is a hellish vision, the typhoon an expression of divine judgement. In the background, the *Zong* pitches in a rough sea; in the foreground, shackled human forms can be seen in the waves, spectral bodies flailing among predacious fish and squawking gulls that circle as they wait for leftovers.[22]

The dreadful image of the overladen slave ship, imagined as 'a strange and potent combination of war machine, mobile prison, and factory', was conjured by abolitionists to move the public.[23] One of the best-known images was the plan of the slave ship *Brookes*, which launched from Liverpool in 1781 to take slaves from West Africa to Jamaica. Images of the ship were published in December 1788 by the Plymouth Chapter of the Society for Effecting the Abolition of the Slave Trade and were widely circulated by the Quaker publisher, bookseller and activist James Phillips.[24] Clarkson noted that the 'print seemed to make an instantaneous impression of horror upon all who saw it, and was therefore instrumental, in consequence of the wide circulation given it, in serving the cause of the injured Africans'.[25]

Since many Africans died on the voyage, traders would overload their ships to compensate for the loss. With the Slave Trade Act of 1788 limiting the carrying capacity of slave ships, the *Brookes* was legally permitted to carry 454 slaves, but on one journey 740 captives were apparently shipped. Space in the hold was so constricted that it was impossible to move and sometimes hard to breathe; when the weather was bad, a tarpaulin was placed over the ventilation grates. According to one account, slaves were forced 'to lie on their sides, breast to back, "spoon fashion"'.[26] Newton described the slaves packed 'close to each other, like books upon a shelf'.[27]

The diagram in question shows the *Brookes* from longitudinal and cross-sectional viewpoints, tightly packed with rows of captives – a shocking image that conveys the brutality of the slaving system. However, while the image makes claims about a common humanity, it nonetheless places a distance between the white viewer and the Black experience, raising the issue of whether it is even possible to imagine what a slave went through.[28] After all, the very word 'slave' places the enslaved person in a predetermined social role, making the African an abject victim of sociopathic aggression. Even first-person slave narratives conform to a generic template of terror. Such 'spectacular' views of suffering were designed to promote the abolitionist message and play on the sensibilities of a metropolitan readership.[29]

One of the best-known and earliest accounts of the Middle Passage, the route through which African slaves were taken to the West Indies, was written by Olaudah Equiano and published in London in 1789 with funds raised from subscriptions. Abducted with his sister as a child from Igboland, in today's south-eastern Nigeria, Equiano was sold by local slave traders and shipped to Barbados in 1754, and then on to Virginia. Although there is some doubt about the veracity of certain aspects of his narrative, historians in the main agree that the story rings true.[30] Equiano describes 'a scene of horror almost inconceivable', with slaves thrashed and chained in the holds. At first, the Europeans resemble cannibals, but as he becomes more familiar with this white world, Equiano's fears diminish. 'I soon grew a stranger to terror of every kind,' he writes, 'and was, in that respect at least, almost an Englishman.' His early fear, he tells us, dissipates as he begins to learn the language and customs of his captors.[31]

It's hard not to read such texts as abolitionist mouthpieces, since they tend to view slavery from the perspective of a morally outraged onlooker, rather than a participant.[32] John Newton tells us that his opposition to the trade stemmed equally from aversion to the ill-treatment of slaves as it did from unease about 'the effects it has upon our own people'. For Clarkson, the word 'horror' becomes a shorthand to convey the disgust experienced by the white observer, rather than the experience of the captives themselves. The concern often is not so much with the suffering of the enslaved as with the moral consequences for those culpable. As Equiano entreats his readers, 'But by changing your conduct, and treating your slaves as men, every cause of fear would be banished.' Slave narratives like his have a moral message for their white readers: fear isn't just cost-effective; it's redemptive, too.[33]

In his own account, Newton confessed that he had once been 'an active instrument, in a business at which my heart now shudders'. A 'succession of difficulties and hardships' had propelled him to Africa, where he became 'in effect, though without the name, a Captive and a Slave myself; and was depressed to the lowest degree of human wretchedness'.[34] The business of slavery has turned the white man into the Black slave, and it was *his* liberation that the abolitionists were also championing.

This kind of abolitionist tract was part of a growing literature of sensibility that sought to cultivate virtue in readers by eliciting their 'spectatorial sympathy'. As we've seen in our earlier discussion of the French Revolution, the eighteenth century was a period in which pain and suffering were increasingly viewed as abhorrent. And yet, while they were condemned, they were also dwelt upon with an insistence that suggested just how ambiguous the moral line was between disgust and fascination.[35]

There's a problem, then, with the incorporation of the 'slave' into rigid narratives that celebrate progress from slavery to freedom, from fear to non-fear. Wrenched from their homelands, slaves inhabited a far more complex space than the abolitionist storyline suggests. On the one hand, the regime that lumped African people together created a sense of community among captives. In the crowded holds they developed new bonds. As Marcus Rediker has noted, they forged 'a "fictive" but very real kinship to replace what had been destroyed by their abduction and enslavement in Africa'.[36] On the other hand, brutal alienation led, as the cultural critic Paul Gilroy has argued, to a 'double consciousness', summed up in their incarceration on slave ships – 'mobile elements', Gilroy calls them, 'that stood for the shifting spaces in between the fixed places that they connected'.[37] The point is that, in order to survive, captives were forced to navigate different social worlds in ways that defy attempts to box their lives into a summary institutional history of 'slavery' and its abolition.

Terror wasn't confined to the Middle Passage but continued on the plantations in the Americas, where 'a regime of calculated brutality and terrorism' was implemented to cow enslaved Africans into docility.[38] The routine cruelty of the slave owner pervades surviving diaries, such as that of William Byrd II of Westover, the plantation owner and surveyor who'd studied law in London's Middle Temple and is credited with the founding of Richmond, Virginia, where he'd inherited an estate in 1705. Byrd recorded the violence he inflicted on his slaves with disturbing nonchalance. An entry for 10 June 1709, for example, reads: 'In the evening I took a walk about the plantation. Eugene was whipped for running away and had the [bit] put on him. I said my prayers and had good health, good thought and good humour, thanks be to God Almighty.'[39]

Another slave owner who left an incriminating diary is Thomas Thistlewood, from Lincolnshire, who settled in Jamaica in 1750. By the time of his death in 1786 he had accrued an estate valued at more than £2,000 – a tidy sum at this time – and become the owner of thirty-four slaves. Thistlewood didn't demur from describing in meticulous detail the punishments he meted out on those who worked for him. One repugnant practice he developed, called the 'Derby's dose', involved a slave defecating 'into the mouth of another slave whose mouth was then wired shut'. He would cover slaves in molasses and leave them out in the stocks overnight, so they would be feasted on by insects. Like many white slaveholders, Thistlewood was a sexual predator; his diary records a total of 3,852 sex acts with 138 women. Violence was central to the slaveholder's operations.[40]

By 1839, there were some 2.7 million men, women and children in slavery in the United States according to a survey compiled by the abolitionist Theodore Dwight Weld, working with his wife Angelina Grimké and her sister. Newspaper clippings and extracts from letters, periodicals and books were assembled to expose the 'abominations of slavery'. According to an editorial gloss on the testimony of a Southern clergyman, 'Were there nothing else to prove it a system of monstrous cruelty, the fact that FEAR is the only motive which the slave is plied during his whole existence, would be sufficient to brand it with execration as the grand tormentor of man.'[41]

Many later slave narratives dwell on the violence of life on the plantations in the American South, perhaps the best-known being Frederick Douglass's first autobiography, published in 1845.[42] After escaping from slavery in Maryland in September 1838, Douglass went on to become an outspoken abolitionist and social reformer. If slaves feared their violent owners and lived with the prospect of being sold off to 'fleshmongers', Douglass observes, the slaveholders themselves remained distrustful of their slaves, which was why they encouraged them to get drunk during their holidays, as a way of 'keeping down the spirit of insurrection'. Drunken holidays, Douglass writes, functioned as 'conductors, or safety-valves, to carry off the rebellious spirit of enslaved humanity'.[43]

Fear of insurrection dominated slaveholder culture, and it sometimes flared into all-out panic as white owners overreacted to wild speculation.[44] Of course, slave uprisings did occur – among them was the Stono Rebellion in South Carolina in 1739, which saw twenty-three colonists and up to fifty slaves killed. Perhaps a thousand slaves took part in Tacky's Revolt in Jamaica in 1760.[45] The successful Haitian Revolution of 1791, led by Toussaint L'Ouverture, involved liberated slaves challenging French colonial rule in Saint Domingue on the Caribbean island of Hispaniola. In 1831, Nat Turner's Rebellion in Southampton County, Virginia, led to the death of over fifty colonists. Between late 1831 and early 1832 some 60,000 slaves rose up against their owners in the Great Jamaican Revolt under the leadership of a Black Baptist deacon, Samuel Sharpe.

Harriet Jacobs, a runaway slave, describes a slaveholders' campaign of terror, conducted in retaliation for Nat Turner's Rebellion. 'The news threw our town into great commotion,' she observes. Black homes were searched, and drunken white militia bands roamed the land. 'Every where men, women, and children were whipped till the blood stood in puddles at their feet,' Jacobs writes. 'Some received five hundred lashes; others were tied hands and feet, and tortured with a bucking paddle, which blisters the skin terribly.' Women hid in the woods and swamps, while marauders pillaged houses, 'like a troop of demons, terrifying and tormenting the helpless'.[46]

This use of terror had unforeseen effects, and fed the slave owners' paranoia. Rumours of conspiracies reflected different, intersecting fears: the slave owners' worries about slave rebellion, the slaves' dread of punishment and the officials' apprehension that the peace wouldn't hold.[47] Regulations were brought in to deal with runaways, but covert forms of resistance were far harder to manage.[48] As on the slaving ships, owners feared poisoning and witchcraft, as well as the threat of arson. But chiefly it was the menace of violent insurrection that hung over plantation life. Restrictive laws were brought in, along with surveillance and disciplinary measures that allowed slaveholders to terrorise their workers. The aim wasn't just to punish slaves for misdeeds; it was to quell uprisings before they happened. 'The world of white violence and black trauma that scholars have come to recognize was, in truth, a world made and sustained by fear,' writes the historian Jason Sharples.[49]

Far from being inherent, though, fear could be learned, along with prejudice. When Douglass first went to work for his owner's brother's family in Baltimore, his new mistress was a model of compassion, keen to teach him how to read and write. But her attitude quickly changed under the tutelage of her husband, who persistently warned her it was 'unsafe' to teach a slave how to read. Reflecting on this experience, Douglass concluded, 'It was at least necessary for her to have some training in the exercise of irresponsible power, to make her equal to the task of treating me as though I were a brute.'[50] In early abolitionist literature there's often a suggestion that terror dissipates with knowledge, that the more slaves learn about white society, the less they'll come to fear it. Douglass tells us that the opposite is in fact true and he experiences greater anxiety than the slaves who are inured to their suffering because he's glimpsed what it's like to be treated differently.[51]

Although his story conforms to the format of an abolitionist narrative in the way that it moves inexorably towards resolution, concluding with his freedom, Douglass was to become increasingly exasperated by the way abolitionists appropriated his writing. And towards the end of his life he shifted from pacifism to countenancing violent resistance. The optimistic tone of his 1845 autobiography gave way to troubled reflections in *My Bondage and My Freedom* a decade later, and to a more confrontational style in *Life and Times of Frederick Douglass*, published in 1881.[52] As the literary scholar William Andrews has observed, 'the greatest restrictions on Douglass's self-expression in the antislavery movement emerge not from his initial underdeveloped sense of himself *as* an individual but from the abolitionists' inability to allow him to *be* an individual'.[53] 'Give us the facts,' Douglass reports one abolitionist telling him, 'we will take care of the philosophy.'[54] Abolitionists stereotype slaves as passive victims and in so doing claim to speak on their behalf.

There is, perhaps, no more poignant image of this dispossession than Harriet Jacobs's description of the cramped roof cavity where she was forced to hide from her owner for seven years. The 'little cell', or 'dismal hole', as she calls it, both recalls the claustrophobic holds of the Middle Passage and represents the social and intellectual constraints that shackle the slave.[55] As Douglass puts it, slavery keeps the slave 'in mental darkness'.[56]

In a letter to his former owner Thomas Auld, included as an appendix to *My Bondage and My Freedom*, Douglass remarks how 'There are those north as well as south who entertain a much higher respect for rights which are merely conventional, than they do for rights which are personal and essential.' For all the promotion of rights and freedoms, Douglass recognises that prejudice lives on, creating inequalities that stem from imagined, handed-down conceptions about the world that cannot be easily legislated against. 'Few evils are less accessible to the force of reason, or more tenacious of life and power, than a long-standing prejudice,' he writes in his essay 'The Color Line'. There he likens prejudice to 'a moral disorder, which creates the conditions necessary to its own existence, and fortifies itself by refusing all contradiction'. Racists, he tells us, are like people who believe in ghosts and see them wherever they look, no matter what evidence disproves their existence.[57]

It's this mental dimension to fear that undermines democratic processes and imperils freedom. The most powerful way to challenge bigotry, Douglass implies, is to compel his white readers to grasp vicariously what it's like to experience the fear of a slave. As he writes to Auld,

> How, let me ask, would you look upon me, were I, some dark night, in company with a band of hardened villains, to enter the precincts of your elegant dwelling, and seize the person of your own lovely daughter, Amanda, and carry her

> off from your family, friends, and all the loved ones of her youth – make her my slave – compel her to work, and I take her wages – place her name on my ledger as property?[58]

Douglass's first strategy is to appeal to the moral conscience of his white readers by shaming them. Fear operates on the level of making them understand what it would be like if they traded places. Progressively, however, Douglass's position hardened and in his 1854 essay 'Is it Right and Wise to Kill a Kidnapper?' he argues that in certain circumstances armed resistance is justifiable. 'We need not only appeal to the moral sense of these slaveholders,' he writes, 'we have a need and a right to appeal to their fears.'[59]

Douglass was right. Despite the legal abolition of slavery, real and symbolic forms of domination persisted – and continue to exist today. As the historian Thomas Holt has shown in his study of post-emancipation Jamaica, a free-market liberal system created conflict between the demands of the colonial economy and the freedom of former slaves to adopt their own lifestyle. The liberal system assumed the participation of freed slaves, but freed Jamaicans preferred small-scale cultivation and occasional labour to regular employment on large-scale plantations. This reluctance to embrace industrial work reinforced mid-Victorian assumptions about race and provided a justification for withholding political rights from emancipated Black people.[60]

While it's convenient to consign the history of slavery to a tale of exploitation and abolition, this narrative denies the open-endedness of slavery. In many places the abolition of slavery gave way to a different form of servitude, as freed slaves became expendable wage labour in an abusive industrial complex. And while human trafficking still exists, the structural inequalities that slavery has left continue to shape modern societies.

In the 1980s the Brazilian photographer Sebastião Salgado produced a series of twenty-eight photographs of the Serra Pelada gold mine in the northern Brazilian state of Pará.[61] The mine had opened in 1980, after gold was found in a local river, sparking a rush of prospectors. The frontier town of Serra Pelada that grew up around the mine was a rough place, plagued by violence and rampant prostitution that catered to the migrant workers. And the boom didn't last long; by 1986 the mine had been abandoned and the open pit had turned into a turgid lake.

Serra Pelada was a squalid place, and outbreaks of hepatitis, TB and malaria were common. While there were frequent accidents, disputes over mining claims often turned nasty. Other problems bedevilled the place. Effluents discharged into nearby streams and rivers – including mercury used in the gold extraction process – created an ecological disaster.

Salgado's photographs show us individual workers carrying bags of ore, alongside panoramic scenes with thousands labouring like ants on a cliff face. The Portuguese name Serra Pelada means 'Naked Mountain' and it's as if the Earth itself has been peeled back to its geological bones – forests cut down, rivers poisoned and diverted, mountains blasted. Human exploitation merges with the ravages of resource extraction.

Looking at the photographs, you can almost hear the hum of this gruelling, repetitive work, the creaking of limbs, the hammering of rocks. This is Hell, a staggering scene of mass labour that recalls a distant past when legions of toiling slaves built monumental tombs for despotic rulers. As the art critic Parvati Nair has observed of the photographs, 'Innumerable men, rendered alike by a shared abject poverty, become almost indistinguishable from the mud that covers their bodies: humans reduced to mere usage, without value, without name or distinction.'[62]

Slavery was only formally abolished in Brazil in 1888, after three and a half centuries in which the country had received an estimated 4.8 million enslaved Africans – nearly half of all those that were shipped across the Atlantic.[63] The port of Salvador was a hub for this slavery, which was initially geared to the sugar plantation industry before diversifying into other sectors, including mining. Gold was discovered in Minas Gerais, in south-east Brazil, in the late seventeenth century, and by the 1730s diamonds were being extracted.[64] The French botanist Auguste de Saint-Hilaire, who travelled through the region between 1816 and 1822, commented on the harsh life of the slaves, who were obliged

> to stand constantly in water during the diamond panning season; and because they're given bad food, which is invariably cold and undercooked, their intestinal tracts develop problems, rendering them susceptible to incapacitating diseases. Aside from this, they're often at risk from being crushed by loosened rocks, or buried under an avalanche of earth. Their work is gruelling and relentless. Under the ever-watchful eye of the overseers, there's never a moment of rest.[65]

If fear lay at the heart of the slave trade, slavery was also entwined with the rise of global capitalism. Ironically, the civilising mission of European empires to rid the world of barbaric slavery was a key justification for their expansion in the second half of the nineteenth century – even though these imperial powers had established the global system of enslavement in the first place.[66]

In 1867 Karl Marx had linked the Atlantic slave trade and the development of industrial societies, contending that 'the veiled slavery of the wage-labourers in Europe needed the unqualified slavery of the New World as its pedestal'.[67] Much later, during the Second World War, when the writing was on the wall for the British Empire, a similar argument was expounded by the historian Eric Williams, the first prime minister of independent Trinidad and Tobago from 1962. In his pathbreaking book *Capitalism and Slavery*, published in 1944, Williams traced the antecedents of the African slave trade in the use of indentured white labourers who were often forcefully removed to the New World. 'White servitude was the historic base upon which Negro slavery was constructed,' he wrote, adding that slavery 'was not born of racism: rather, racism was the consequence of slavery', a means of rationalising an iniquitous economic system.[68] Williams went on to make two central arguments; first, that the slave trade arose in the seventeenth and eighteenth centuries to solve the problem of how to procure sufficient cheap labour to service the plantations in the Americas; and second, that the wealth from slavery created the capital necessary to catalyse Britain's industrial development in the nineteenth century.[69]

Once this new manufacturing economy had taken off, slavery's importance diminished. Commercial capitalism and monopoly gave way to industrial capitalism and 'free trade'. It was at this point, particularly from the 1780s, when the economic value of the slave trade was already in steep decline, that abolitionists became more vocal. As a schoolboy growing up in Trinidad, Williams had been taught to venerate British humanitarians, like Wilberforce, who had campaigned to end slavery. However, he came to understand that the abolitionists were hardly disinterested witnesses, and neither were they primarily responsible for the trade's abolition. 'Even the great mass movements, and the anti-slavery mass movement was one of the greatest of these,' he reflected, 'show a curious affinity with the rise and development of new interests and the necessity of the destruction of the old.'[70]

Across the British Empire, the anti-slavery cause was viewed as a cornerstone of imperial enlightenment, but despite this anti-slave rhetoric and the ban on indentured labour under Britain's 1833 Slavery Abolition Act, colonial economies were increasingly dependent on cheap workers. The line that divided this technically emancipated workforce from slavery was hazy. A quasi-form of servitude underpinned the trade in 'coolies' – a pejorative term for unskilled contract labourers – that transported hundreds of thousands of Chinese and Tamil workers to service the plantation economies in South-East Asia, across the Indian Ocean in Africa, and in the West Indies. Life for a coolie on the vast Sumatran rubber plantations in the Dutch East Indies or in French Indochina could be a living hell, as it was for many Chinese who worked on the construction of the Central Pacific Railroad in the 1860s. Although technically 'free', they were ensnared in a market system that used strong-arm tactics to ensure their compliance.

The horrors of late nineteenth-century colonial exploitation in equatorial Africa after the formal end of the slave trade were extreme. Under the personal rule of the Belgian king Leopold II as many as 11 million Africans perished in the Congo between 1885 and 1908, forced to work on rubber plantations with a paramilitary army brutally enforcing labour policies.[71] This was the 'land of tears' dramatised by Joseph Conrad in *Heart of Darkness*, which tells the story of a journey up the River Congo into the horrors of Leopold's bloody fiefdom.[72] There a crazed white man rules over the natives like a tyrant and the surrounding jungle reverberates with the 'tremulous and prolonged wail of mournful fear and utter despair'.[73]

Fast-forward a hundred years, and Salgado shows us the terrifying post-colonial aftermath of slavery. The image is a reminder not only of the continuation of human exploitation but also of the problematic relationship between pain, violence, fear and a global economic order. Enslavement has evolved into a form of structural manipulation.

Is it possible to break free from this legacy of industrial slavery? As Salgado's photographs suggest, production processes and supply chains that depend on cheap labour continue to perpetuate shocking inequalities. Perhaps slavery has been so thoroughly embedded in free-market capitalism that it can't be dislodged, at least not without the collapse of the entire system.[74]

Between 2014 and 2016 an Ebola epidemic in West Africa triggered fear across much of the world. News coverage and social media reports of the terrifying disease caused panic in East Asia, Europe and the United States. Particularly affected by the epidemic were the poverty-stricken areas of Liberia's capital, Monrovia, notably West Point, a densely populated township. After the imposition of curfew and quarantine measures to contain the spread of infection in August 2014, there was civil unrest, with security forces firing on angry crowds.[75]

Liberia was established in the early nineteenth century by former African American slaves under the aegis of the American Colonization Society, a coalition of slaveholders and abolitionists. Those who backed this colonisation did so for different and often contradictory reasons, but a key motivation was dealing with the perceived threat posed by emancipated Black people. From the outset there was conflict between the resettled former slaves and the native societies whose land had been extorted from them.[76]

The writer Alan Huffman tells the story of a wealthy cotton planter from Mississippi, Isaac Ross, who, when he died in 1836, decreed in his will that his plantation should be sold, with some of the proceeds used to pay for his slaves' passage to Liberia. After protracted legal wrangling, Ross's former slaves emigrated to West Africa, where they developed extensive plantations in a region they referred to as 'Mississippi in Africa'.[77] Although the descendants of freed slaves were a minority in Liberia, they exploited indigenous labour to amass vast wealth. And they dominated the leadership of the country until 1980, when the president, William Tolbert, was ousted in a coup that brought Samuel Doe, leader of the Armed Forces of Liberia, to power.[78]

Liberia was a deeply unequal society before the coup. The country's resources were siphoned off to benefit an elite, leaving ordinary Liberians disadvantaged and resentful. It was anger at these inequalities that caused President Tolbert to be overthrown. And it wasn't long before the country erupted into full-blown civil war, which degenerated into anarchy as rival factions fought it out. In 1990 Doe was killed by forces of

Charles Taylor, the head of another rebel group known as the National Patriotic Front of Liberia. After six years as president, Taylor was in turn deposed and put on trial by a UN judicial body that in 2012 found him guilty of acts of terrorism, murder, rape, sexual slavery and enslavement.[79]

Unravelling Liberia's twenty-first-century history entails grappling with the complex afterlife of slavery and the terror that permeated it. Africans who had been enslaved by Europeans were freed and repatriated to West Africa by abolitionists, only to remake the abusive system of the enslaved world they'd left behind.[80] Elements of the plantation system recombined to create a new state of servitude, with fear at its heart.

7

Lost in the Crowd

In the nineteenth century full-throttle industrialisation transformed the world, creating new opportunities for wealth but also giving rise to new fears, many of them centred on the threat posed to social order by the urban poor. These fears began to influence architecture and urban planning, as well as the apparatus of governance, from the formulation of new laws to police tactics and modes of surveillance.

If slavery and indentured labour were indispensable to the rise of modern industry, so too were the workers who migrated in large numbers from the countryside to feed the booming mines, mills and factories. The 1851 census in Britain revealed that, for the first time in its history, the majority of the country's population lived in towns and cities.[1] 'The rapid progress of our manufactures and commerce has accumulated great masses of population,' noted one commentator in an article on the plight of the working classes in Manchester.[2] Although industrial development and urbanisation became much-vaunted indices of national progress, mass migration and the pressures it placed on housing and services fuelled concerns about this urban environment, including fears of contagious disease, rising levels of crime and the wanton violence perpetrated by the fulminating, panic-prone hoi polloi.

Modern urban living was creating political, social and psychological instabilities, which in turn fed bourgeois fears of the stereotyped radical mob that had haunted Europe since the French Revolution. As the English journalist and Liberal politician John Morley put it in 1867, as electoral reform was being debated in Parliament, the prospect of 'democracy' brought terror to the minds of many.[3]

Different groups sought to harness these fears. Conservative and industrial interests tended to push for more legislation and the dispensation of harsher penalties to quash antisocial behaviour, while social reformers exploited these same fears as a means of promoting a more radical agenda. Meanwhile, an increasingly bureaucratised state supported an expanding professional class that began to play an important role in managing different facets of these new municipal challenges.

Urban social problems also became the focus of a burgeoning media. New methods of mechanical paper pulp production and steam-powered printing, along with novel communication technologies – notably the telegraph and later the telephone and wireless – were spurs to the development of instant news. If fear sold newspapers, it wasn't long before newspapers themselves were condemned for propagating fear and panic with lurid coverage of garrotters, rioters and the ubiquitous roughs, or 'cornermen', who loitered on city streets. Politicians and professional experts excoriated the toxic effects that these news stories had on a violence-prone riff-raff.[4] Descriptions of grisly homicides and other social evils were damaging to a mass reading public on every level: moral, psychological and physical.

By the mid-nineteenth century fears about the urban 'masses' had come to the fore.[5] They were conjured as an ominous 'slumbering giant' whose 'fearful strength' might at any time be unleashed. It was an appalling prospect, since the hardscrabble masses possessed 'a restless and anarchical energy, which if not counteracted would speedily issue in the destruction of all the cohesive properties of the social constitution'.[6]

'Cities are the abyss of the human species,' Rousseau had concluded in 1763. Overcrowding led to physical infirmities and 'vices of the soul'.[7] As the philosopher and political economist

John Stuart Mill observed, by the 1850s distinctive voices were drowning in the hubbub of the multitude.[8] Previously, the individual had been 'a power in himself', but now he or she was 'lost in the crowd'.[9] Subsumed within the fickle agglomeration of the industrial urban masses, individuals quickly succumbed to the sway of volatile emotions. By the end of the nineteenth century the French sociologist Émile Durkheim was using the term 'anomie' to describe a condition of social estrangement that created morbid anxiety and despair. He attributed the soaring levels of suicide in modern society, at least in part, to moral confusion and to feelings of purposelessness that arose when individuals felt detached from the social transformations taking place around them.[10]

The masses became associated in the imagination of the bourgeoisie with working-class militancy, strikes, riots, violence, alcohol abuse, epidemic disease and crime. They were regarded as ignorant, prejudiced, unpredictable – and dangerous. The word 'mass' derives from the Latin *massa*, meaning 'kneaded dough'. Like dough, the masses could be easily manipulated, but once they were incited, they were difficult to placate.

Even more worrying was the prospect that they might one day accede to power. Back in ancient Greece, both Plato and Aristotle had fretted about the implications of a 'mobocracy', while Thucydides had argued for the importance of a charismatic leader – which is how he viewed the Athenian general and politician Pericles – to moderate the fickleness of the people. Although the English pamphleteer and journalist William Cobbett had denounced 'the oppression of the weak by the powerful', he'd seen in the American Revolution an even graver danger. Democratic government, he wrote in 1805, 'was a despotism of the many over the few', in which 'every act of oppression was committed in the name of the people'.[11] With the French Revolution in mind, Burke likewise noted, 'The tyranny of a multitude is but a multiplied tyranny', suggesting that rule by 'an unthinking and unprincipled multitude' resulted in a level of oppression far worse than that of a tyrannical king.[12]

Despite the fact that they often took opposing views, many nineteenth-century commentators pointed to the contradictory effects of industrial modernity, which was producing different sets of fears. Paradoxically, individuals were becoming increasingly isolated at the same time as they were being de-individualised through their submergence in an anonymous mass. And while society was becoming ever more heterogeneous and unruly, individuals were becoming indistinguishable from one another, victims of a homogenising system that reduced citizens to replicate units and functional equivalents.[13]

Alexis de Tocqueville championed the vitality of American democracy even as he recognised the threat of the masses sleepwalking into servitude. Society seemed to be breaking down and concurrently citizens were becoming more isolated, making them vulnerable to external political pressures. Here Tocqueville used the metaphor of the *massa* to describe how individuals could be 'kneaded' into conformity. A loss of free will, he wrote, would open the door for despotic governments to browbeat the population until it became 'nothing more than a herd of timid and industrious animals of which the government is the shepherd'.[14]

John Stuart Mill, who favoured enlarging the franchise, repeatedly forewarned of the 'tyranny of the majority', pointing out that the imposition of a majority view posed a threat to free thinking and individual liberty. Despite his libertarian views, however, he fretted about the diminishing influence of 'superior minds' over a restive multitude that could no longer be restrained. Power, he noted, was passing 'more and more from individuals, and small knots of individuals, to masses', as a result of which 'the importance of the masses becomes constantly greater, that of individuals less'.[15] Although developments in communication and commerce, along with standardised education, had positive effects, they also promoted 'a general similarity among mankind'; 'individuality' was being destroyed and life reduced to 'one uniform type'.[16]

Everyone was becoming the same because they were reading and listening to the same things and had 'their hopes and fears directed to the same objects'. And this was not the work of some machinating tyrant, but rather a process that Mill considered intrinsic to industrial society; 'when society is itself the tyrant,' he noted, 'its means of tyrannizing are not restricted to the acts which it may do by the hands of its political functionaries. Society can and does execute its own mandates.' It wouldn't be long, Mill claimed, before Britain resembled China, a country that had languished for 'thousands of years' because its people lived within a system that crushed individualism.[17]

Others were far more strident in their denunciation of the masses. 'I believe that the mob, the mass, the herd will always be despicable,' the novelist Gustave Flaubert wrote in 1871, the year that a revolutionary government took control of Paris.[18] In his account of the French Revolution published a few years later, the historian Hippolyte Taine deplored the mercurial nature of crowds which were easily moved to mob violence.[19] Two decades later, Nietzsche didn't mince his words when he decried what he called the 'tyranny of the least and the dumbest' and advocated a 'declaration of war on the masses by higher men'.[20] Even Sigmund Freud would work this denigration of the fractious mob into his account of the psyche. 'Our mind, that precious instrument by whose means we maintain ourselves alive, is no peacefully self-contained unity,' he wrote. 'It is rather to be compared with a modern state in which a mob, eager for enjoyment and destruction, has to be held down forcibly by a prudent superior class.'[21]

The masses were first and foremost the product of the industrial city. In the mid-1840s Friedrich Engels, the political theorist, revolutionary socialist and industrialist, described the 'colossal centralization' that industrialisation had produced. He began his book *The Condition of the Working Class in England* by evoking the turmoil of London's thoroughfares. Despite the crowds, this was a place of loneliness, where pedestrians passed each other without a glance. 'The brutal indifference, the unfeeling isolation of each in his private interest becomes the more repellent and offensive,' Engels observed, 'the more these individuals are crowded together within a limited space.'[22]

'Fear, revulsion, and horror were the emotions which the big-city crowd aroused in those who first observed it,' the critic Walter Benjamin would remark in a commentary on Edgar Allan Poe's short story 'The Man of the Crowd'.[23] Published in 1840 and set in London – the largest city in the world at the time, with a population approaching 2 million – Poe's story is told by a nameless narrator who sits in a coffee shop and watches the restless masses through the smoky windows. While he considers the different social types that make up this 'tumultuous sea of human heads', he also reflects on how isolated individuals are in the city, despite 'the very denseness of the company around'. As night falls, his attention is drawn to an old man in the crowd. Curious, the narrator follows the stranger across the foggy city in the hope of uncovering his identity, but to no avail.[24]

Like Poe, Engels focuses on the social and psychological dimensions of the crowd, on the threatening disarticulations that this urban immiseration produces. As he concludes, 'The dissolution of mankind into monads, of which each one has a separate principle, the world of atoms, is here carried to its utmost extreme.'[25] While the industrial metropolis is imagined as an amorphous multitude, it is simultaneously associated with new forms of segregation and stratification: the ghettos of the poor, homes under siege and self-isolation. These are the alienating conditions that led, as Karl Marx saw it, to the workers' estrangement from their human nature.[26]

According to Engels, the destitute working classes in England's industrial cities lived in a 'whirlpool of moral ruin', in constant fear of hunger, disease and death. Old Manchester was 'Hell upon Earth': 'in such dwellings only a physically degenerate race, robbed of all humanity, degraded, reduced morally and physically to bestiality, could feel comfortable and at home'. Slum tenements were characterised by crumbling brickwork, an absence of windowpanes, mounds of foul-smelling refuse and fumes belching from smokestacks. Material breakdown represented societal disintegration, as Engels wondered how 'the whole crazy fabric' of the city 'still hangs together'.[27] This could be a passage from a reformist tract, the difference being that for Engels the slum conditions are confirmation that capitalism is a spent force. The horrific images he conjured were ultimately a means of transmuting fear, indignation and anger into political action.

Fear is an important dimension of *The Communist Manifesto*, which Engels co-wrote with Karl Marx in Brussels and published in 1848, just as violent anti-establishment protests were erupting across Europe. Summoning the threat of a communist phantasm had its uses, and the *Manifesto* opens with the memorable sentence 'A spectre is haunting Europe – the spectre of Communism,' which immediately casts the book as a sort of ghost story, echoing and subverting Burke's image of the 'unformed spectre' of revolution, in which the power struggle over the fate of industrial Europe is melodramatised as a Gothic horror show.[28]

For municipal authorities and governments, countryside-to-city migration and urban overcrowding, filth and poverty of the sort that Engels described presented different kinds of challenges and opportunities. Slums had to be dealt with because they propagated contagious disease and crime. But what was equally worrying was how readily slum dwellers could be swayed by activists peddling subversive ideologies.

A particular problem posed by this new industrial environment was the proximity of the poor to the wealthy. 'The various orders of society,' wrote one commentator, 'are mutually dependent; their interests are interwoven with a complexity which cannot be unravelled.' Particularly worrying were 'the great masses of habitations, closely peopled by the lowest and least moral of the poor, which, in almost all great cities, threaten ultimately to surround and bury in their bosoms the dwellings of the rich and the refined'.[29]

In 1889 the social reformer Charles Booth produced a survey of London with the capital's socio-economic classes colour-coded on maps, from black for 'lowest class, vicious semi-criminal' to yellow for 'upper-middle and upper classes'. *Life and Labour of the People* didn't just reveal the scale of poverty in the capital; it highlighted the intricate social and economic mosaic of the city. Despite the focus in media accounts and popular literature on the East End as the epicentre of poverty and crime, wealth and destitution in fact existed cheek by jowl.

It was this uncomfortable contiguity that gave rise to crime panics from the mid-nineteenth century, notably the London garrotting panics of 1856 and 1862. The media reporting of street violence – 'garrotting' was a term used to describe violent street robbery, what we'd now call 'mugging' – rattled a middle class that was increasingly concerned with security. In 1856 the bombastic prime minister Lord Palmerston had boasted that, given the reach of British imperial power, it was now safe for 'the humblest British subject' to journey 'to the most distant quarters of the globe'. As *The Times* retorted, however, Londoners cared less about 'security within the Tropics or the Polar Circles' than they did about being able to walk the streets of the capital 'without imminent danger of being throttled, robbed, and if not actually murdered, at least kicked and pommelled within an inch of [their] life'. Muggings were on the rise – and if something wasn't done about it, public fear would spiral into uncontainable panic.[30]

In fact, panic was already being whipped up with lurid reports of street violence. When the Liberal MP James Pilkington was assaulted on Pall Mall while returning home from the House of Commons one evening in July 1862, there were impassioned calls to bring back the transportation of convicts, a practice that had stopped in the 1850s. It was argued that a new and suitably remote penal colony was needed. Why not dump garrotters on the Falkland Islands in the South Atlantic?[31] In the meantime, given the unresponsiveness of the police, urbanites had to fend for themselves. As one editorial put it, '[Now] the long nights are coming we shall have to buy revolvers.'[32] Newspaper sensationalism created a groundswell of hysterical public opinion that was caricatured in the pages of the satirical magazine *Punch*. Cartoons pictured Londoners wearing medieval armour and spiked dog collars, pedestrians chased by their own shadows or spooked by the silhouettes of trees.

Numerous editorials panned the Penal Servitude Act of 1853 for enabling convicts to be released on a ticket-of-leave parole system. As a result of the press-inspired panic, legislation was rushed through Parliament. The Penal Servitude Act of 1864 and the Prisons Act of 1865 created a far harsher regime that sanctioned the use of irons and chains and sentenced those convicted to hard labour. The Security from Violence Act of 1863, known as the 'Garrotters Act', which condoned the whipping of prison inmates, would remain on the books until 1948.[33]

Two decades after this furore, the press coverage of the murder and shocking mutilation of five women in London's East End between 1888 and 1890 sparked another panic in the capital. Rumours about the identity of 'Jack the Ripper' whirled through the city. A few years earlier, the term 'psychopath' had been coined in the pages of the *Pall Mall Gazette* to describe a person who was devoid of morality. 'Beside his own person and his own interests,' the magazine pronounced, 'nothing is sacred to the psychopath.'[34]

Whoever the killer was, this was clearly the work of a 'savage'. London's slums were a perilous urban jungle not dissimilar to 'Darkest Africa' as described by the journalist and explorer Henry Morton Stanley: a place 'where the rays of the sun never penetrate, where in the dark, dank air, filled with the steam of the heated morass, human beings dwarfed into pygmies and brutalised into cannibals lurk and live and die'. Or so General Booth, the Methodist preacher and founder of the Salvation Army, was convinced. 'May we not find a parallel at our own doors,' he wrote, 'and discover within a stone's throw of our cathedrals and palaces similar horrors to those which Stanley has found existing in the great Equatorial forest?'[35]

Panic triggered by the Ripper killings fed into a wider political malaise. The previous year there'd been a violent showdown between police and anti-government protesters in Trafalgar Square. Fearful of 'the rough elements' among the protesters, many of whom were unemployed dockers, the government banned all meetings from being held there. When troops were called in to assist the police, there was a bloody face-off and several hundred protesters were arrested.[36]

Such events reinforced assumptions about the inherent unruliness of crowds that could metastasise at any time into an enraged mob when stirred by a salacious press or by some malicious agency with an axe to grind. The Social Democratic Federation was regarded as one such organisation; as the Metropolitan Police Commissioner, Sir Charles Warren, put it, the group encouraged 'the poorer classes to help themselves from the wealth of the affluent'.[37] According to *The Times*, reporting on the Trafalgar Square clashes in November 1887, 'howling roughs', incited by ringleaders along with segments of the gutter press, had converted 'an English Sunday into a carnival of blood'.[38]

Crowds posed other risks, aside from the danger of mob action. They could foment and facilitate the spread of lethal diseases, particularly cholera, which swept across Europe from the 1830s. It was in an effort to deal with the entwined issues of crime, social unrest and disease that authorities began to invest in large-scale public works. Overcrowded neighbourhoods, with their dark alleyways and dilapidated dwellings, were demolished to create open spaces that allowed for the penetration of light and air, better traffic circulation and easier policing.

This process of modernisation was exemplified by Napoleon III's redevelopment of Paris from the 1850s. Under the supervision of Georges-Eugène Haussmann, the French capital was remodelled with the construction of wide boulevards, parks, squares, railway stations, town halls, a new central market and a modern sewerage system.[39] In his memoirs Haussmann spoke of 'disembowelling' the old city with its 'almost impassable maze' of narrow streets, which made it a magnet for 'riots and barricades'.[40] The urban poor were displaced but not removed. The poet Charles Baudelaire, who witnessed some of these changes, described the roar of traffic along the new boulevards and the faces of the uprooted working classes pressing up against the windows of bustling shops and cafés. Progress had exacerbated inequality, and crowd living produced a new kind of alienation.[41]

One of the best-known late nineteenth-century commentators on the urban crowd was Gustave Le Bon. His book *The Psychology of Crowds*, published in 1895, became an instant bestseller. More than the description of a new mass psychology, it was intended as a manual with 'practical applications' on how to manage crowds for legislators and statesmen.[42] Widely translated from his native French, it was read by the likes of Churchill, Hitler, Lenin, Mussolini, Mustafa Kemal Atatürk and Roosevelt – charismatic leaders who were to put their reading to practical use, with momentous effect.

'Ideas, sentiments, emotions, and beliefs possess in crowds a contagious power as intense as that of microbes,' Le Bon wrote. His definition of the crowd is expansive. Juries in court cases that 'deliver verdicts of which each individual juror would disapprove' demonstrated to him the properties of a crowd, as did parliaments, or any body of persons that has convened to 'make decisions affecting matters of general interest'. The decisions that these assemblies come to, he wrote, 'are not sensibly superior to the decisions that would be adopted by a gathering of imbeciles'.[43]

These various incarnations of crowds are all linked by the idea that individuals lose their sense of self and personal responsibility when they become part of a collective – a process analogous to a chemical reaction, in which different elements 'combine to form a new body possessing properties different from those of the bodies that have served to form it'. Emotions diffuse through a crowd like contagion, or they act upon it like hypnosis so that people unquestioningly adopt dominant ideas, 'to such a degree that an individual readily sacrifices his personal interest to the collective interest'.[44]

There is some kinship between these ideas and the 'traumatic hysteria' that the French neurologist Jean-Martin Charcot diagnosed in his patients, the vast majority of whom were women treated at the Salpêtrière Hospital in Paris. As he put it in 1892, hysteria was 'less a disease in the ordinary sense of the word, than a peculiarly constituted mode of feeling and reaction' of which fear could be an important component, often playing a role 'in the explosion of hysterical symptoms'. While it was triggered by external factors, which he likened to 'agents provocateurs', nervous heredity predisposed individuals to the disorder.[45]

For Le Bon, crowd contagion worked as a similar form of agent provocateur, bringing out predispositions to panic, not just in the individual but on the collective level. While all crowds were 'irritable and impulsive', inherent racial traits exerted an influence on their behaviour. Latin and Anglo-Saxon crowds were strikingly different, he claimed. An excessively emotional French response to the publication of the so-called Ems telegram in 1870, in which the French ambassador to Prussia had been insulted, led to the Franco-Prussian War. In contrast, the British had demonstrated 'only a slight emotion' in the face of the serious setbacks they'd experienced during the Nile Expedition to relieve Major-General Gordon in Khartoum in 1885.[46]

Crowd behaviour is the manifestation of an unconscious process: Le Bon likened it to 'waves, which are the expression on the surface of the ocean of deep-lying disturbances of which we know nothing'. Just as late nineteenth-century bacteriology was intent on identifying the microscopic agents that cause disease, the role of the social scientist was to reveal the subliminal forces working on the mind and body.[47]

Although crowds have existed throughout history, there is something new in the power of the modern crowd. 'The age we are about to enter,' Le Bon intoned, 'will in truth be the ERA OF CROWDS.' 'The substitution of the unconscious action of crowds for the conscious activity of individuals,' he continued, 'is one of the principal characteristics of the present age.'[48] The modern city created an environment for the resurgence of primordial behaviour. Similarly, panic, a characteristic of the modern world, recalls an earlier phase of human development where instinct dominated reason.

According to Le Bon, crowds reflected the turmoil of an age in which the religious, political and social beliefs that anchored civilisation were being fatally undermined. It was in this chaotic interregnum between the old and the new that terror prevailed. Crowds were both symptom and precipitator of a civilisational crisis: 'When the structure of a civilization is rotten, it is always the masses that bring about its downfall.'[49]

Le Bon wasn't alone in his pessimistic thinking. At the turn of the century many others noted the tendency of crowds to panic, observing how, when one individual mimicked another, a contagious knock-on effect could engulf whole populations.[50] The crowd resembled a collection of atoms, and its molecular structure was amenable to scientific analysis.[51] In the early twentieth century the focus shifted onto the nature of the social interactions that shaped collective behaviour. 'When the crowd acts it becomes a mob,' the American sociologists Robert Park and Ernest Burgess wrote in 1921. 'Men in a state of panic,' they declared, 'have like purposes but no common purpose.' In this way, 'panic and the stampede is a society "in dissolution"'.[52]

If 'dissolution' was a keyword at the turn of the century, another was 'degeneration', a socio-biological theory premised on the idea that, if societies could evolve, they could equally regress. After all, didn't organisms that adapted to less demanding environments lose their inherited specialisations? As the British zoologist Sir Edwin Ray Lankester put it in 1880, 'Degeneration may be defined as a gradual change of the structure in which the organism becomes adapted to less varied and less complex conditions of life.'[53]

There appeared to be compelling evidence for degeneration, precipitated by industrialisation. When Britain went to war with the Boer Republics in 1899, the army set about recruiting for the war effort. Before joining, young men had to take a medical test, but the results were disconcerting: it was soon apparent that many men were suffering from a range of disabilities and health issues, leaving them unfit for military service. Major-General Sir John Frederick Maurice ascribed this degeneration to the growth of cities and to new patterns of consumption enabled by 'a vast increase in the facilities of communication and in the organisation of the distribution of commodities', which was causing a prevalence of bad teeth, flat feet and, above all, 'stunted, anaemic specimens of humanity'. With only 'two out of five of the population' fit to bear arms, Britain was faced with 'a national danger which cannot be met by any mere schemes of enlistment'. It was a patriotic duty, he declared, to recognise the security threat posed by the country's enfeebled workforce.[54]

A Committee on Physical Deterioration was duly established, with expert witnesses called to give evidence. A 1904 report recommended, among a raft of measures, regular medical inspections for children, the issuance of leaflets to mothers on how to rear babies, a system for dealing with underfed schoolchildren, and a regular 'anthropometric' survey to record the 'measurements of children and young persons in schools and factories'.[55] It was with a mandate to implement welfare reform that the Liberal Party swept to a landslide election victory in 1906.

Fear of degeneration pervaded the press. The British writer H. G. Wells was to make this a key theme in his writing. If evolution was random, why should human progress and survival be inevitable? In an 1891 article entitled 'Zoological Retrogression' he criticised those who claimed that human development was inexorable.[56] In another essay, 'The Extinction of Man: Some Speculative Thoughts', he asked: if sabre-tooth tigers have become extinct, what makes humans so sure they won't go the same way? 'Even now, for all we can tell,' he wrote, 'the coming terror may be crouching for its spring and the fall of humanity be at hand.'[57]

Urban living seemed to be enfeebling the population, and different kinds of phobias were understood to be manifestations of proliferating disorders. Doctors attributed a rising tide of nervousness to the overstimulation caused by humanity's immersion in increasingly artificial mass environments. In 1869 the American neurologist George Miller Beard proposed the term 'neurasthenia, or nervous exhaustion', to describe patients who exhibited a range of disorders, with symptoms that included dyspepsia, headaches, paralysis, gout and menstrual irregularities.[58]

Ten years later, the British psychiatrist Henry Maudsley described what he called 'melancholic panic' in a revised edition of his book *The Pathology of Mind* – apparently the first use of the term 'panic' in psychiatry.[59] 'Some melancholics,' he concluded, 'are in a state of panic fear without knowing what they fear, and exhibit an excessive susceptibility to every kind of impression.' Melancholics were overwhelmed by a 'discharge of frantic energy'; it was during such paroxysms of melancholic panic, he proposed, that homicides and suicides were committed, 'without premeditation, without reflection, without distinct motive, almost without consciousness at the time'.[60]

Sigmund Freud, who had trained as a neurologist, began by focusing on anxiety's physiological processes, but soon shifted towards a psychological understanding of fear, which he claimed would 'throw a flood of light on our whole mental existence'. In 1895 he developed the concept of 'anxiety neurosis' to differentiate a syndrome – with anxiety as its main symptom – from the miscellany of conditions that Beard had lumped together under the term 'neurasthenia'. This kind of neurotic anxiety, Freud suggested, was the outcome of frustrated sexual urges. 'Anxiety arises from a transformation of the accumulated tension,' he said, and subsequently observed, 'where there is anxiety there must be something one is afraid of'. 'Sexual excitations', or libidinal impulses, became unhealthy when they were blocked – or, to use one of Freud's analogies, the libido soured just as wine turns to vinegar. This idea of blockage would later evolve into a more systematic theory of unconscious repression, and with it a proposal for a psychoanalytic therapy to treat the obsessional neurosis that it caused.[61]

Freud was more concerned with the origins of anxiety in individual psychology, albeit in relation to social norms. Later he did extend his psychoanalytic methods to the study of group behaviour, critiquing Le Bon's idea of a 'collective mind', while recognising that a person's psychology is shaped in relation to other members of a group.[62] By the turn of the century the broader environmental and technological influences acting upon the psyche had become a focus of growing concern. In an essay titled 'The Metropolis and Mental Life', published in 1903, the German sociologist Georg Simmel described how city dwellers were being forced to cope with the 'rapidly changing and closely compressed contrasting stimulations of the nerves' that city living induces.[63] Exposure to constant stimuli was reshaping 'the sensory foundations of psychic life', rendering people less responsive to the world because they erected defensive barriers to shield themselves from this unrelenting bombardment.[64] The material transformation of the expanding city was also creating new pathologies: fears of crowded, enclosed spaces, as well as of open, empty spaces. With some justification, this period has been called 'phobia's *belle époque*'.[65]

In 1889 the Viennese architect Camillo Sitte identified a new ailment called 'agoraphobia', which he linked to the emptiness of 'wide thoroughfares'. From the seventeenth century, cities had been transformed with the construction of broad avenues and boulevards, including the Champs-Élysées in Paris, Berlin's Unter den Linden and the Esplanade in Hamburg. In stark contrast to the constraining twists and turns of old towns, this new urban expansiveness was overwhelming and could create a panic response. 'On our modern gigantic plazas, with their yawning emptiness and oppressive ennui, the inhabitants of snug old towns suffer attacks of this fashionable agoraphobia,' Sitte wrote. 'Overly large plazas have a most pernicious influence on their surrounding structures.'[66]

The Ringstrasse, a centrepiece of Vienna's nineteenth-century transformation, consisted of a 'vast complex of public buildings and private dwellings' on 'a broad belt of land separating the old inner city from its suburbs'.[67] Sitte was critical of its homogeneity and alienating proportions: the grid-like uniformity of the modern city crushed individuality, in contrast to the organic space and human scale of the medieval town centre, with its irregular streets and squares. For Sitte and others, the 'open-plan' city embodied a form of disaffecting modernity that estranged individuals with its 'heartless utilitarian rationalism'.[68]

The term 'agoraphobia' had been coined in 1871 by the German psychiatrist Carl Otto Westphal to describe patients who'd experienced severe anxiety when walking in the streets, crossing squares, taking the omnibus or going to the theatre.[69] A few years later the French psychiatrist Henri Legrand du Saulle detailed what he called 'fear of spaces', which he defined as 'a particular kind of neuropathological state, characterised by anguish, an acute feeling of anxiety, and even genuine terror, occurring suddenly in the presence of a given space'. Among its many symptoms were trembling, palpitations, compulsive sobbing, excessive sweating and occasionally complete paralysis.

Du Saulle preferred the term 'fear of spaces' to 'agoraphobia' because the latter, he thought, suggested a fear restricted to public spaces, whereas clinical observations showed that the onset of the illness could be triggered by exposure to all kinds of spaces. While crossing a road, an individual might suddenly experience extreme dread, as if they were hanging above an inferno, or walking a tightrope over Niagara Falls. One of du Saulle's patients, a forty-three-year-old mother of three, had suffered from a debilitating fear of spaces ever since visiting the Alps. Now she couldn't cross the Champs-Élysées without experiencing vertigo and worrying she might collapse. To counter her fear of open spaces, she'd crammed her apartment with furniture, paintings, statuettes and old carpets.[70]

In 1879, at a presentation given at the annual meeting of the British Medical Association, the Anglo-French physician Benjamin Ball had used the term 'claustrophobia' to describe 'a state of mind in which there is a morbid fear of closed spaces'. This was a word, as Ball acknowledged, originally coined by the Italian psychiatrist and neurologist Andrea Verga. Aside from 'claustrophobia', Verga was responsible for 'acrophobia' (fear of heights) – from which he himself suffered – and 'rupophobia' (fear of dirt).[71] Ball described the clinical case of a young officer in his care who suffered from a 'feeling of irresistible terror whenever he found himself alone in a room with the doors shut'. Claustrophobia, Ball concluded, was a 'depression of melancholy or the furious excitement of mania', and ought to be regarded 'as the result of a distinct and peculiar form of insanity'. The prognosis, he warned, wasn't good.[72]

By the turn of the century agoraphobia was widespread. Among those who supposedly suffered from 'nervous' conditions with agoraphobic symptoms were Marcel Proust and Edvard Munch. A typical case reported in the *Lancet* in 1898 described a thirty-year-old man who was unable to leave his home out of fear that an accident might befall him.[73] The physician John Headley Neale detailed his own experiences of the illness with great frankness. His first attack occurred when he was walking to college as a medical student in Edinburgh, but disorienting feelings of giddiness and faintness could happen anywhere, at any time: while attending a church service with his family or climbing a ladder to enjoy a view from the rooftop of the Leicester Infirmary. Moral determination, concentration, companionship and cheerful conversation could help manage these fears, along with 'avoidance of over-mental strain and of all excesses, a careful diet, aids to digestion and tonics'. To deal with open spaces, he advised, the 'presence of a cart, even a stick or umbrella in the hand, gives a sense of confidence'.[74]

'The psychology of states of feeling,' wrote the French psychologist Théodule-Armand Ribot in the preface to his book *The Psychology of the Emotions*, 'is still in a confused and backward condition.' Despite new scientific research, he observed that 'the part played by the emotions and passions in human life' was still woefully understudied. The field, he argued – in what is one of the most cogent summaries of late nineteenth-century psychology – was polarised between those who ascribed emotions to a mental state and those who viewed them as intrinsic to biological or physiological processes.[75] Ribot was writing in 1896, the same year that Le Bon's study of the crowd was published in English.[76] By then, every fear was being recast as a syndrome.

The vogue for categorising phobias was creating muddled thinking, with description replacing explanation. The list of phobias now filled pages. 'Every morbid manifestation of fear,' Ribot wrote, 'is immediately fitted with a Greek designation, or one so reputed, and we have aïcmophobia, belenophobia, thalassophobia, potamophobia, etc., even siderodromophobia (the fear of railways) and triakaidekaphobia (fear of the number 13!).'[77] The physician Max Nordau was also critical of the discovery of apparently endless 'monomanias'. The list, he argued, 'might be lengthened at pleasure, and enriched by nearly all the roots of the Greek dictionary. It is simply philologico-medical trifling.' More relevant, according to Nordau, was the underlying cause of these 'varied manifestations' of 'phobias' and 'manias', which he attributed to 'the great emotionalism of the degenerate'.[78]

As the twentieth century progressed, the belief that cities were places of proliferating phobias would be eclipsed by a more sanguine outlook. Urban living wasn't just more convenient and entertaining; it made a lot of sense economically and environmentally. But by the late 1960s and 1970s the fear factor had returned, as industrialisation stalled and unemployment rose. Riots in the United States highlighted social and racial divisions and the fragile economic, social and political make-up of cities. A darker view of the city began to prevail, reflecting anxieties about social degeneration that were reminiscent of turn-of-the-century concerns. Cities were now evoked as fearful places plagued by crime, addiction, homelessness, pollution and infectious diseases. More than a century after Engels, many were wondering, as he had, how the 'whole crazy fabric' of the city hung together.

Science was also used to corroborate accounts in the media that cities were dangerous places to live. The urban environment was shown to be a factor that could induce psychotic illness. Evidence now suggested that people raised in cities were more prone to mental disorders than those from rural areas, with the risk for schizophrenia more than twice that in the countryside.[79] Urban living appeared to affect brain biology. A study using functional brain imaging suggested that an urban upbringing influenced the neural processes that managed stress in ways that precipitated psychotic illness.[80]

Cities once again came to be viewed as places that were fundamentally unhealthy and insecure. It was in response to these social, environmental and biological threats that new surveillance technology and forms of defensive urban design were introduced, exemplified by closed-circuit television, the retreat from public spaces and the development of gated communities. An 'obsession with security' fuelled fear and a suspicion of government, particularly in 'fortress America', where gun ownership surged even as crime rates declined.[81]

Meanwhile, the suburbs were also under threat. Neighbourhood vigilantism was one response to a growing fear of crime and disorder in the late twentieth century, along with home security devices. A culture of victimisation arose that didn't just reinforce prevalent fears, perpetuating entrenched social and racial prejudices; it also further empowered privileged communities, magnifying divisions and materialising the very threats that new urban designs had been intended to avert.[82]

8

Diabolus ex Machina

It wasn't just festering industrial cities and the volatile masses that caused panic in the nineteenth century. New fears also coalesced around technology. In May 1851 Queen Victoria had opened the Great Exhibition of the Works of Industry of All Nations in London's Hyde Park, a 'celebration of the triumphs of the useful arts throughout the globe', as *The Times* described it.[1] The venue for this industrial extravaganza was the Crystal Palace, a technological feat of iron and glass designed by the architect Sir Joseph Paxton. It was a fitting venue to showcase miraculous industrial appliances, from Colt pistols and Goodyear hard India rubber goods to hydraulic presses, pumps, steam engines and automated cotton mules. Yet for all this tech boosterism and the shrill paeans to progress, the nineteenth century was also an epoch of tech pessimism, which in many ways mirrors our own. As advances in artificial intelligence (AI), robotics and biotechnology transform our lives, they present both promises and perils.[2] And so it was when steam power, electricity and the mechanisation of production set in motion far-reaching economic, social and political transformations.

As the Industrial Revolution progressed, it became evident that machines, mines, roads, factories and cities were creating a socio-technological system that extended from engineering methods and production processes to new laws, practices and institutions.[3] If the benefits of mechanical innovation were clear, so were its shortcomings, particularly when things went wrong. Government reports and newspaper articles enumerated the gruesome injuries sustained by factory workers. Fingers, hands and arms got chewed up in cumbersome appliances, and it was dangerously easy for women working in cotton mills to be scalped when their hair caught in the rollers of carding machines. One account of life in an English cotton mill, published in 1832, described the 'scene of horror' when the apron of a ten-year-old operative snagged in a shaft and she was sucked into the machine, bones crunching and blood spurting across the shaft frame and floor.[4] Among many other occupational hazards in textile factories were deafness from exposure to the unremitting din of machinery and lung damage from dust inhalation. Boiler explosions could leave workers' bodies disfigured and often impossible to identify.[5]

While the railway was an emblem of modernity, it could also be a death machine.[6] Boilers exploded, axles broke and signals jammed. Fatalities from collisions, derailments and faulty infrastructure were common, with locomotives falling from collapsing bridges, toppling off washed-out embankments or overshooting their buffer stops. Although many accidents were caused by human error, others were discussed as if they were the regrettable by-products of industrial power.[7]

Just like bodies, minds could also break. Trains were linked to a miscellany of conditions described variously as 'railway spine', 'fright neurosis', 'hysterical neurosis' and 'traumatic neurosis'.[8] The physical and psychological aspects of this traumatisation by train travel were catalogued in a number of medical studies on injuries of the spinal cord and nervous system sustained by passengers 'subjected to the violent shock of a railway collision'.[9]

Above all, the train crash exemplified the nightmare that lurked beneath the dream of a tech utopia. Zola's 1890 novel *La Bête humaine* ('The Beast Within') ends with a driverless train, packed with troops, hurtling through the night towards disaster. We're asked to imagine the inevitable train wreck, bodies mangled in metal, comparable to the slaughter that awaits the soldiers on the battlefield. The novel is set during the

Franco-Prussian War of 1870–71, in which the Prussians crushed the French thanks to their use of modern technology. Zola's train, in other words, is part of a broader industrial complex that meshes the military with the civilian.

At the World's Columbian Exposition, held in Chicago in 1893 to celebrate the 400th anniversary of Columbus's 'discovery' of the Americas, the Krupp Pavilion showcased the largest cannon in the world. The fair, a shrine to progress, was abuzz with new inventions, including the first moving walkway or 'travelator', prototypes of the automatic dishwasher, phosphorescent lights, the latest elevators and the zip.[10] Fairgoers could listen to music through telephones and a colossal Ferris wheel – named after the engineer George Washington Gale Ferris, who built it – dominated Jackson Park on the lakefront in the city's South Side, symbolising 'the subjugation of physical forces to human control'.[11] The exposition, which attracted over 27 million visitors, attested to a population that was 'probably at the present moment the most energetic, enterprising, and aspiring set of human beings on the globe'.[12]

There was, however, a dark side to this progress. A short distance west of the fair in Englewood, thirty-three-year-old Herman Webster Mudgett was busy catering to the influx of visitors to Chicago. The top two floors of his three-storey building, billed as the World's Fair Hotel, consisted of a warren of guest rooms rented out to young women; below that were shops, including a pharmacy, which he oversaw. Mudgett, who went by the name Henry Howard Holmes, was a con artist and a bigamist. As it turned out, he was also a serial killer.

When the police raided the premises in July 1895, after his arrest, they discovered a building rigged for murder. The media published what they claimed were floor plans of the building showing a 'death shaft' and 'asphyxiation chamber', along with an elevator for lowering bodies. Sensationalist articles described rooms that were soundproofed and fitted with peepholes;

trapdoors led to a sealed basement; fake walls hid a maze of passageways; and windowless rooms served as makeshift gas chambers. Holmes had studied medicine at the University of Michigan, and in the basement the police apparently discovered a dissection table, acid vats, a gas tank, quicklime and an array of medical tools.[13] Among these, it would later be claimed, was an 'elasticity determinator', a rack with straps that Holmes had invented to test the expandability of the human body.[14] The nondescript façade of the building belied the fact that it 'incorporated the most advanced domestic technologies'. Holmes would later confess to twenty-seven murders, although the exact number of his victims remains unknown. He was hanged in May 1896, apparently showing no signs of fear as he faced the noose; his body, encased in cement, was buried in an unmarked grave in the Holy Cross Cemetery in Yeadon, Pennsylvania.[15]

On 1 May 1893 US president Grover Cleveland had pushed an electric button that ignited the large Corliss engine in Machinery Hall and brought the exposition to life. The same wires that powered the 'scintillating glare of myriads of electric lights' at the fair supplied Holmes's murderous mod cons.[16] The Chicago exposition, which he had visited, presented a triumphant vision of technology harnessed for beneficent progress. But in his 'Murder Castle' technology had been recruited for altogether different purposes. As one New York newspaper wrote, a Chicago building had been turned into 'a veritable murder factory'.[17] A furnace had been installed to dispose of the victims which 'was so arranged', Holmes himself wrote in a confession, 'that in less than a minute after turning on a jet of crude oil atomized with steam, the entire kiln would be filled with a colorless flame, so intensely hot iron would be melted therein'.[18]

Meanwhile, an acrid odour drifted across Englewood from the Union Stockyards in New City, just to the north, where slaughter was being mechanised on a truly mass scale. Some 250 miles of track brought in 10,000 cattle and hogs a day, as well as sheep, all of them herded down chutes in 'a very river of death'. Outside, placards proclaimed the wonder of Imperial Hams and Bacons, Dressed Beef and Excelsior Sausages. Inside, animals swung from chains on a lever system, while the place reverberated with beastly screams.

This is the setting for Upton Sinclair's 1905 novel *The Jungle*, which describes working conditions in Chicago's meatpacking industry. Based on first-hand investigative reporting, these are 'stories to make your flesh creep'. The protagonist sweats at his station on the production line, the 'killing beds' where workers perform with the speed and power of 'wonderful machines'. Nothing is wasted in this system, which, as one character puts it, uses 'everything about the hog except the squeal'. Meat is scraped from the floor where workers tramp and spit, before being thrown into giant mixers to be turned into sausages, along with dead rats inadvertently gathered in the process. At the fertiliser plant, workers occasionally fall into the open vats, all but their bones dissolving into Durham's Pure Leaf Lard.[19] 'It was like some horrible crime committed in a dungeon,' the narrator tells us, 'all unseen and unheeded, buried out of sight and of memory.'[20]

Over the summer of 1904 – the year before Sinclair's book was serialised – packers in the wholesale beef industry had gone on strike, with riots in the stockyards that saw workers shot, attacked and beaten.[21] *The Jungle* refocused attention on the shocking workplace conditions, leading to media coverage, outrage and public panic. The US president, Theodore Roosevelt, was moved to bring in reform with the Meat Inspection Act of 1906, which prohibited the sale of adulterated meat and livestock products for food.[22]

From the late 1860s the Chicago meatpacking industry had developed industrial dis-assembly lines that would later serve as the inspiration for the assembly-line approach that was pioneered at the Ford Motor Company in Detroit. 'The idea came in a general way,' Henry Ford recalled in his autobiography, 'from the overhead trolley that the Chicago packers use in dressing beef.'[23] 'Mass production,' he noted in 1926, 'is the focusing upon a manufacturing project of the principles of power, accuracy, economy, system, continuity and speed.'[24] Fordism, as it came to be known, was predicated on standardisation and efficiency, ideas promoted in the work of the American mechanical engineer Frederick Winslow Taylor. 'It is only through enforced standardization of methods, enforced adoption of the best implements and working conditions, and enforced cooperation that this faster work can be assured,' Taylor declared in his 1911 monograph *The Principles of Scientific Management*.[25]

There were those who feared that, through their increasing interactions with machines, people were becoming less than human. And what if machines were to acquire intelligence and perhaps even sentience, rendering humans obsolete? These fears were offset by – and to some extent took their force from – the exaggerated expectations of a technological future. Tech optimism went hand in hand with a dystopic view of humanity; industrial society was being overpowered by the ingenious technologies on which it had become reliant.

As early as 1829 the historian and philosopher Thomas Carlyle had characterised the nineteenth century as 'the Mechanical Age'. 'For all earthly, and for some unearthly purposes,' he wrote, 'we have machines and mechanical furtherances.' He wondered what the societal impact would be and surmised that this mechanisation would 'change our whole manner of existence' – and not for the better. 'Men are grown mechanical in head and in heart, as well as in hand,' he lamented.[26]

In 1844 Karl Marx argued that in industrial societies workers had become commodities, estranged from the things they made and from one another. 'The *devaluation* of the human world,' he observed, 'grows in direct proportion to the *increase in value* of the world of things.'[27] In the first volume of his magnum opus, *Capital*, published in 1867, he would remind his readers that human disaffection with machines had a long history. In the seventeenth century, he tells us, workers had revolted against the ribbon-loom, a contraption 'for weaving ribbons and lace trimmings'. When the first water-powered wool-shearing machine was introduced in England in 1758, it was set on fire by aggrieved workers who had been made redundant as a result of this mechanisation.[28] As farming and artisanal labour gave way to factory work, these fears proliferated. The more powerful the machine, the less powerful the worker. A conviction that automated machinery was threatening the livelihoods of skilled labour sparked the early nineteenth-century Luddite movement, when textile workers smashed up machinery in the Midlands and the north of England.

Of course, mechanisation had its advocates. The Scottish physician Andrew Ure celebrated the automatic factory system as 'the great minister of civilization'. In his 1835 book *The Philosophy of Manufactures* he championed mechanical manufacturing as a model of social order, a 'vast automaton, composed of various mechanical and intellectual organs, acting in uninterrupted concert for the production of a common object, all of them being subordinated to a self-regulated moving force'.[29] This was an ecstatic vision of mechanical coordination that veered, as Marx pointed out, between contradictory interpretations of the relationship between human and machine. While Ure envisioned a workforce that managed the machines, he also suggested that 'self-acting machines' would be in the driving seat.[30]

And if machines were so marvellous, why not dispense with humans altogether? Marx warned of the relegation of the worker to an incognizant cog in an alienating industrial complex. 'An organized system of machines to which motion is communicated by the transmitting mechanism from an automatic centre is the most developed form of production by machinery,' he declared. 'Here we have, in place of the isolated machine, a mechanical monster whose body fills whole factories.'[31]

This was the *diabolus ex machina* that emerged from an expanding assemblage of spookily biologised machines and turned people into automata. Aside from its demonic power, did this mechanical monster possess a consciousness? To some it certainly looked that way, or at least the line between human and machine seemed to be blurring alarmingly. In Samuel Butler's satirical novel *Erewhon*, published in 1872, a writer contemplates the danger posed to humanity by the rise of intelligent, self-replicating machines. 'Reflect upon the extraordinary advance which the machines have made during the last few hundred years, and observe how slowly the animal and vegetable kingdoms are advancing in comparison,' the narrator remarks. 'But who can say that the vapour engine has not a kind of consciousness? Where does consciousness begin, and where end? Who can draw the line? Who can draw any line?'[32]

While advances in machinery may have raised questions about what it meant to be human, they also foregrounded ethical issues around how this machinery was being used. Electricity, for example, now had deadly purposes. By the 1890s, as Henry Howard Holmes was incinerating his victims in the basement of his Chicago hotel, cremation was becoming more popular as an efficient and hygienic way of dealing with the dead.[33] Meanwhile, execution by electrocution was being hailed for its advantages. In 1890 William Kemmler became the first person to be executed by electric chair in New York's Auburn Prison. Although Thomas Edison had claimed that death by electrocution would be humane, witnesses to Kemmler's death reported that his head was singed and bleeding where the electrodes were fixed, while the execution chamber filled with a ghastly smell. This was hardly 'the instant extinction of life' that the pro-electrocution lobby had promoted.[34] 'They would have done better using an axe,' one witness noted sardonically, a pointed reference to Kemmler's murder of his wife with a hatchet.[35]

When asked about possible words for death by electricity, Edison had come up with 'ampermort', 'dynamort' and 'electromort'.[36] Any of the above would have made an effective subtitle for Munch's *The Scream*, painted in 1893 and today totemic of just about every kind of modern fear imaginable. A phantasmagorical body holds two hands to a horror-struck face: full-moon eyes, mouth agape in an existential howl that appears to emanate from some tenebrous place within. The expressionist whirls of colour are ear-splitting sound waves that dissolve body and landscape into a continuous, overwhelming scream. An electromagnetic surge, the universe tortured with pulsing currents, a case of cosmic shock therapy.

By the 1890s a new age of electrotherapeutics had begun, pioneered by the French 'electrophysiologist' Jacques-Arsène d'Arsonval and the Serbian-American electrical engineer Nikola Tesla. High-frequency alternating currents were applied to the body to treat everything from epilepsy and hysteria to migraines and tinnitus – as well as cancer, constipation, incontinence, insomnia and 'morbid sexual states'.[37] Munch himself received non-convulsive electrotherapy to treat his psychiatric symptoms.[38]

The inspiration for *The Scream* has been traced back to 1889, when Munch left Norway to study in Paris. He was there when the city hosted the world trade fair to celebrate the centenary of the French Revolution with the 'primitive' and the 'exotic' on show beside the hyper-modern, exemplified by dazzling light displays, illuminated fountains and Gustave Eiffel's 300-metre wrought-iron tower. 'Everything shines, glitters, blazes in a perpetual feast for the eyes,' one ecstatic visitor exclaimed.[39]

It may be that Munch visited the Trocadéro, home of the Ethnographic Museum, and saw the mummified remains of a Chachapoyas warrior from Peru.[40] There is certainly a resemblance between the central figure in Munch's famous painting and the mummy's expression. Another inspiration may have been the 'incandescent bulb', a big draw at the exposition, on display alongside Edison's other patented inventions.[41] The similarity between the shape of Edison's lamp and the glowing head of Munch's electrified screamer is certainly striking. Mix these two inspirations together and you get a spectacular resurrection, a body shocked back to life from some dark submergence, gasping for air.

Electricity's power of reanimation had long been touted. In *Frankenstein*, by Mary Shelley, a lifeless monster is infused with 'a spark of being'. 'Perhaps a corpse would be reanimated,' Shelley wrote in the preface to the 1831 edition of the novel; 'galvanism had given token of such things.'[42] She was referring to sensational demonstrations by the Italian physician Luigi Galvani that suggested it was possible to resuscitate the dead. Jolted by electricity, the bodies of animals and recently executed convicts appeared to come back to life, their eyes popping open and faces contorting.[43]

But it was the industrial scale of electricity's application in the late nineteenth century that transformed the nature of these earlier hopes and fears. The bigger the claims made about the transformative power of electricity, the more the fears around it intensified. Writing in 1895, the American electrical engineer Thomas Commerford Martin celebrated Tesla's 'beautiful inventions' which had made the distribution of power possible. All the breakthroughs that electricity had enabled had been extraordinary, but it wasn't until Tesla developed his oscillator that technology could be converted 'into resistless trained forces, sweeping across continents', forces that offered 'unimagined opportunity'.[44]

Electricity was a means of conquering space and subduing superstitions. Innovations in communication technology were transforming the way humans travelled and communicated. In 1893, the year that Munch painted *The Scream*, Tesla declared that powerful machines would soon be able to disturb 'the electrostatic conditions of the earth'. Or, as he put it elsewhere, it would be possible to 'hook our machinery directly to that of Nature'. The energy from Niagara Falls would be harnessed and distributed by electricity as light, heat and power.[45] It was this unchecked acceleration of science and technology, and the impact that it was likely to have on nature, that worried many. Munch, who had briefly studied engineering before dropping out to pursue art, registered his ambivalence to these innovations in his private journals. In one cryptic entry he recorded a fearful presence 'who directed the wires – and held the machinery in his hand'. Christ, he wrote, is 'the spark of the Ur-light', an electrical shock that gives off warmth and produces 'vibrations in the airwaves'.[46]

While newspapers acclaimed the wonders of electricity, they also carried frequent reports about the danger that electric lights and storage batteries posed to city dwellers, with many tales of accidental deaths from electrocution. The tangle of wires from arc lights that were strung across city streets presented a particular threat, not to mention the hazards that existed in a mass culture that was being reshaped by electrical contraptions. Life was speeding up and the working day was being prolonged, thanks to artificial lighting. All of this was putting stress on the body's nervous system, leading to fatigue, premature ageing and – in extreme cases – death. Aside from health and safety concerns, electricity fuelled anxiety about the potential perils of its misapplication, its promotion by private interests with ulterior motives, the unforeseen consequences of its use and fears about its alienating and soul-destroying properties.

Of all his electrical inventions, Edison claimed that none had 'commanded such profound and earnest attention throughout the civilized world' as the phonograph: for the first time in history it became possible to capture elusive sound.[47] Tech cynics immediately worried about eavesdropping and surveillance, not to mention issues of privacy and intellectual property.[48] It was to mitigate these fears that the Berlin Convention of 1908 added photography, film and sound recordings to the literary and artistic works protected under the Berne Convention.

The *New York Times* railed against Edison's contraptions. 'Mr Edison has invented too many things,' the paper declared. Not only was he 'addicted to electricity' but his contrivances, almost without exception, were 'things of the most deleterious character'. If the phonograph was a 'mischievous enterprise', even worse was the so-called 'aerophone', a device for amplifying sound that would ultimately lead to 'the complete disorganization of society'.[49] 'Men and women will flee from civilization,' wrote the *London Figaro*, only slightly tongue in cheek, 'and seek in the silence of the forest relief from the roar of countless aerophones.'[50]

Arguably the most transformative technology of the second half of the nineteenth century, however, was the electric telegraph. In 1844 Samuel Morse – creator of the Morse code, a means of encoding text characters as standardised sequences – sent the first telegraph message from Washington, DC, to Baltimore. This technology laid the groundwork for the development of the telephone and wireless radio, which transformed the nature of fear and panic, since rumour and misinformation could now spread far more easily.

By the 1870s telegraphic cables encircled the globe. For the first time in history messages could be transmitted faster than humans could travel. It was at this point that the word 'communication' acquired its modern meaning: the transmission of information.[51] The disassociation between time and space created opportunities for planning and crisis mitigation; authorities could be apprised of distant threats almost instantaneously, giving them vital time to prepare.

But telegraphy could have adverse effects. Newspapers were now reliant on telegraphic intelligence, which caused 'vast injury'; the speed of the news was simply 'too fast for the truth'.[52] It was even working as an antisocial force. A satirical cartoon in *Punch* from 1906 depicts a man and a woman sitting next to each other in a park as they both stare down at a telegraphy machine. 'These two figures,' the text reads, 'are not communicating with one another. The lady is receiving an amatory message, and the gentleman some racing results.'[53]

There were also fears about the vulnerability of telegraphy to subversion. Networks could be sabotaged, and messages intercepted. During the American Civil War several US states had imposed penalties on those who disclosed the contents of private telegrams. The earliest statute prohibiting wiretapping was introduced in California, after the Pacific Telegraph Company reached the West Coast in 1862; the first person charged under the new law was a stockbroker who had eavesdropped on corporate telegraph lines and sold the information to stock traders.[54]

Across the British Empire similar legislation was introduced, as colonial authorities began to worry about the problems that the telegraph created. In European colonies the technology had seemed to represent a tool that might help manage indigenous, panic-prone populations, but before long it became apparent that this was a naïve proposition; anti-colonial interests began to send telegraphs to plan their activities and spread their propaganda.[55] Aside from this, there was also the issue of information overload. How could important news be filtered from the relentless inflow of data? Giving the public too much information might be just as dangerous as giving it too little.

Many of the issues of distrust involving the electric telegraph anticipated those that later arose in relation to the telephone, which was thought to be unsafe, given the potential for electrocution. It was believed to cause 'nervous' conditions, particularly among female operators, while 'the constant buzz of the system' and frequent interruptions on the line could impair the user's hearing; and there were also real concerns that the technology would produce a population of citizens who were deaf in their left ear.[56] Besides, germs festered in receivers and mouthpieces, with condensation dripping 'from the breath of previous users'.[57] As late as 1933 the writer and cartoonist Clarence Day was lampooning the residual telephonic fears that people had. 'They weren't human, they popped or exploded,' he declared; and people 'were afraid that if they stood near one in a thunderstorm they might get hit by lightning'.[58]

Vision was also being transformed by new optical technologies, including neuroimaging, X-rays and film. It was now possible to photograph a galloping horse, and to see through fluids and soft tissue. Photomicrographic techniques were capturing a dynamic but hitherto invisible world in ever more detail. These breakthroughs suggested that reality could be peeled back, layer upon never-ending layer. And if that was truly the case, would it ever be possible to organise this ever-receding, infinite universe? The greater the complexity that science and technology uncovered, the more moving parts there would be to organise, and the greater the scope for disorder.

An understanding of the role of microorganisms in the spread of disease led to an awareness of the dangers that lurked in the home, giving rise to a 'germ panic', with everyday objects regarded as potential carriers of lethal infection. New germ-busting technologies and routines were developed to deal with this invasive micro-world. The wealthy equipped their homes with plumbing and flushable white ceramic toilets. Windows were secured to keep out insects, and sleek, easy-to-clean electric kitchen appliances were installed, along with refrigerators. Out went heavy Victorian drapes and thick upholstery; long dresses that trailed in the dirt were discouraged, as were beards. Restaurants, hotels, public transport and cinemas were all reorganised around the imperatives of hygiene. Waiters were required to be clean-shaven, and tables were laid with white tablecloths. For manufacturers, the germ panic created an expanding market for anti-germ household products: everything from cellophane, developed in the 1920s by the American company Du Pont, to antiseptic paint, sanitary garbage pails and household cleaners.[59]

Film was another breakthrough technology that caused both excitement and alarm.[60] In the 1890s Louis and Auguste Lumière had devised and patented the *cinématographe*, a prototype motion-picture camera, inspired by Edison's 'kinetoscope'. Their short film *Arrival of the Train*, which was filmed in the coastal town of La Ciotat in 1895, allegedly created panic at its early public screenings as the terrified audience rushed from the auditorium, convinced that the steam locomotive was about to crash into the theatre.[61] While it's possible that the story of the panicked response to the film was no more than a publicity stunt, the Russian writer Maxim Gorky, who saw the film at a fair in Nizhny Novgorod in 1896, wrote that the train 'speeds straight at you – watch out! It seems as though it will plunge into the darkness in which you sit, turning you into a ripped sack full of lacerated flesh and splintered bones, and crushing into dust and into broken fragments this hall and this building.'[62]

But in 1897 film was embroiled in an incident of real-life mass panic, one that claimed numerous lives and put cinematography in the dock. On the afternoon of 4 May the venue for the annual Bazar de la Charité in Paris's prosperous eighth arrondissement was destroyed by fire. This charity fundraising event was held in a large hall, packed with over a thousand well-heeled visitors. A highlight of the evening was the screening of several films by the Lumière brothers, but disaster struck when the projector caught fire, engulfing the heavy drapes and tearing through the hall. Panic broke out as the ceiling caved in and debris fell onto the crowd, with people rushing to the exits. The doors of the premises led to a narrow vestibule, creating a bottleneck. Firemen watched helplessly as people burned alive; the fire claimed 126 lives and left many others with serious injuries.[63]

Following the tragedy, various individuals involved in the event were put on trial for negligence.[64] But the fire also prompted broader debate about the moral dangers of new technology. At a memorial service for the victims held in Notre-Dame Cathedral, a Dominican priest, Father Ollivier, delivered a controversial sermon in which he claimed that the fire was divine retribution – a 'terrible lesson', in his words – for France's abandonment of its Christian inheritance in the vainglorious pursuit of modernity. In an allusion to the fateful film screening he said: 'That which gave the illusion of life has produced the horrible reality of death.'[65]

Father Ollivier wasn't alone in fearing cinema's corrupting effects. At the turn of the century many people felt that film was death masquerading as eternal life, a ghostly realm that Gorky called the 'Kingdom of the Shadow'.[66] A decade after the fire at the Bazar de la Charité, the words *cinéphobie* and *cinémaphobie* were being used to describe those who feared the new technology. Films were dangerous because they could seduce impressionable spectators. Not surprisingly, cinema was viewed as a medium of propaganda. Beyond this, films encouraged antisocial behaviour by blurring the line between truth and fiction, morality and immorality. There was also evidence that they were addictive and unhealthy, inducing over-excitation and causing a new form of vision impairment, which was given the name *cinématophtalmie* in 1909.[67]

As a social space, the cinema was also thought to encourage subversive behaviour. 'Under cover of dimness evil communications readily pass and bad habits are taught,' wrote the American criminologist William Healy in 1915.[68] In this early twentieth-century cinephobia we can see how technological development defined new social relations, and how crucial fear was to the emergence of the modern technological world.

9
Crash

If crowds and modern industrial technologies became objects of fear in the nineteenth century, they were also viewed as conduits of panic.[1] As the century progressed, the bursting of speculative bubbles and financial crashes were increasingly understood as the outcome of panicked reactions to rumour, uncertainty and risk. Panics and the crashes they precipitated reflected that mass psychology identified by Gustave Le Bon and others, which worked through crowd contagion. They were manifestations too of an ambivalent new global interconnectedness that created immense wealth but also produced new uncertainty. Minor perturbations in the financial system, originating in distant places, could now escalate into what the American writer Thomas Lawson called a 'panic cyclone' that highlighted the limits of state authority and the growing influence of international capital.[2] As the political geographer Sir Halford Mackinder declared in 1900, the world had become interdependent: 'We are now a closed circuit – a machine complete and balanced in all its parts. Touch one and you influence all.'[3]

In his 1841 book *Memoirs of Extraordinary Popular Delusions* the Scottish journalist, editor and poet Charles Mackay catalogued the 'moral epidemics' that had given rise to 'national delusions', in which individuals had acted irrationally and en masse. 'We find that whole communities suddenly fix their minds upon one object,' Mackay wrote, 'and go mad in its pursuit.' 'Money,' he declared, 'has often been a cause of the delusion of multitudes. Sober nations have all at once become desperate gamblers, and risked almost their existence upon the turn of a piece of paper.'[4] Here, we have the elaboration of a theory that identifies in market behaviour a paradigm for collective 'hysteria', 'mania' and 'madness'.

Four years later, a speculative mania in England led to a boom in the value of railway shares, which doubled but then dramatically collapsed when their inflated price became apparent and the Bank of England stepped in to raise interest rates, which had been at historic lows.[5] A market frenzy had been fuelled by politicians with vested interests in the railways who petitioned Parliament to authorise the formation and promotion of hundreds of new railway companies. Shrewd marketing, including newspaper advertisements that trumpeted the handsome profits to be made from the railways, had targeted inexperienced investors.[6] When the bubble burst, thousands of individuals who had subscribed to shares lost their investments. Perhaps unsurprisingly, fears of financial instability, bankruptcy and unscrupulous speculators feature prominently in Victorian fiction. Fortunes are lost when markets crash and businesses go under, and characters commit suicide when their fraud is exposed – a prime example being the reprobate Mr Merdle in Charles Dickens's *Little Dorrit*, who slashes his throat with a penknife when his Ponzi-like banking scheme fails.[7]

Although speculation intensified with the expansion of credit and the growth of stock markets, producing heightened volatility of prices, panics were nothing new. An early example of a public mania that Mackay alludes to is the one that gripped Dutch society in the 1630s. An obsession with the exotic tulip among the newly wealthy middle classes led to frenzied speculation and to an extraordinary spike in the price of tulip bulbs, which then collapsed when panicking investors pulled out of the overheated market. Analysts would later explain the panic as the convergence of multiple factors: developments in the

Dutch market system, social transformations, psychology and global interconnectedness. While many details of this Dutch tulip bubble have been embroidered for effect – there isn't much evidence of bankrupt burghers throwing themselves into canals, as is sometimes claimed – 'tulipmania' continues to be cited as 'a tale of stupidity, greed, and madness', an early example of the dangers of feverish speculation and the lure of 'fictitious capital'.[8]

Holland was at the forefront of financial innovations in the seventeenth century, and panic was understood to be an inherent feature of the market system. In 1602 the Dutch East India Company became the first company in history to issue transferable shares to the general public.[9] Joseph Penso de la Vega, a Sephardic Jew who traded diamonds on the new Amsterdam stock exchange, published an account of modern trading instruments in 1688, including a discussion of buying and selling options and price manipulation. His book *Confusion of Confusions* is written in the form of a dialogue between philosopher, merchant and stockbroker which is interspersed with philosophical digressions. Though it makes for a rather stilted read, the book identifies common practices and pitfalls for the aspiring trader. As the title suggests, disorder and panic are features of the trading world he describes, and we're given insights into how contagious fear can arise in the marketplace. As Penso de la Vega remarks when commenting on a sudden market collapse: 'Such a panic, such an inexplicable shock was produced that the whole world seemed to crumble, the earth to be submerged and the heavens to fall.'[10] Markets may have been catalysts for a new kind of sociability, but they were also inherently destabilising, encouraging ruthless competition and fierce national rivalry.[11]

Another early instance of market madness was the bursting of the South Sea Bubble in 1720. By the eighteenth century London had grown in importance as a financial and insurance hub, servicing the needs of a global maritime trade. Joint-stock companies, which acquired their capital from investors who bought shares in them, enabled the rapid growth of businesses. In 1694 the Bank of England was founded by royal charter to raise funds from private investors to support the government's war against France. Meanwhile, equity and commodity markets had developed around the Royal Exchange, and coffee houses served as meeting places where merchants traded stocks, with stock and commodity prices listed in *The Course of the Exchange*, a twice-weekly broadsheet.

The South Sea Company had been established in 1711 as a joint-stock company and held exclusive rights on British trade with Spain's American colonies, including the slave trade. This monopoly had been granted as part of a debt-for-security swap initiated by the British government to help service the crippling national debt. A promotional campaign had encouraged investors to buy stock in the company with the prospect of significant profits and the assurance that their investments were backed by the state. The price of South Sea shares rose dramatically between January and July 1720, before plummeting as the slave trade proved far less lucrative than anticipated. As fear of defaults grew among investors, they scrambled to recoup their investments – one contemporary noted the 'wild confusion in the crowd' in Exchange Alley, where traders congregated – and the state was threatened with bankruptcy.[12] The market crash in Britain converged with another crisis in France, triggered by the simultaneous collapse of the Mississippi Company – which held a monopoly on trade in France's West Indian and North American colonies – creating an international financial crisis that led to panic and scapegoating, with anti-Jewish riots in Amsterdam.[13]

It was at this time that the word 'panic' began to be used more routinely to describe reactions to financial events that necessitated emergency interventions. Adam Anderson, a Scottish economist who worked for the South Sea Company, spoke of the panic that spread among fearful investors.[14] In 1734 Daniel

Defoe wrote: 'Men are not now blamed on that Account: South Sea was a general Possession.' Earlier he had denounced mercenary 'stock jobbers' who bought up stock to resell quickly for profit, jeopardising 'the Credit of the Nation'. The country, he suggested, had been 'bewitched' during the South Sea Bubble and was almost ruined by a 'terrible infatuation' that had 'overspread the whole Body of the People'.[15] As one director of the company remarked before the 1720 debacle, credit was 'liable to be overturn'd by the least puff of Wind or panick Fear amongst us'.[16]

From the mid-eighteenth century journalists, merchants, bankers, economists and government officials began to focus more concertedly on elucidating the nature of these panics and the fears that drove them, in the hope of discovering ways of preventing them. In the 1750s Joseph Harris, a government adviser to the Royal Mint, noted that economic stability depended on the faith that citizens had in the integrity of a currency. If this was eroded, it could produce 'infinite disorders, distrusts and panics'. Similarly, when governments used monetary policy as a way of writing off debt, this could result in a 'universal panic', destroying public confidence in the state's finances, and ultimately in its authority. And once these genies were out of the bottle, it was almost impossible to put them back.[17] Following a spate of market upheavals in Britain, Europe and the Americas from the late 1790s, the term 'panic' became closely associated with 'crisis', originally a medical term used to signify a critical phase in the progress of a disease. The meaning of 'panic', 'crisis' and 'crash' began to overlap, with the words often used interchangeably.

By this time mercantilism – an economic policy that prioritised exports with subsidies but discouraged imports with heavy tariffs – had fallen out of favour. Market theorists such as David Ricardo and Adam Smith were outspoken proponents of laissez-faire market capitalism, even though the market 'freedom' with which they became associated was in fact dependent on a range of interventionist measures, including the expropriation or 'enclosure' of common land that forced agrarian communities to migrate to towns and cities for wage labour.[18]

Ricardo, the British political economist who made a fortune by speculating on the outcome of the Battle of Waterloo in 1815, was a particularly shrewd analyst of market behaviour.[19] One of the panics he wrote about occurred in 1796, when fears of a French invasion coincided with a downturn in the credit markets in Britain and America, resulting in a panic that caused a financial crash. Bank of England investors had begun to convert banknotes into gold, draining the bank of its reserves. Fearing insolvency, the directors suspended payment under the Bank Restriction Act, which was rushed through Parliament in February 1797.

In his analysis of what went wrong, Ricardo argued that banks have no security against such panics, since their loans inevitably exceed their reserves. No bank in the world would ever have enough coin or bullion to repay investors once panic had set in. Although the Bank of England had certainly overstretched itself by extending large amounts of credit to the government for its war effort, this wasn't the reason for the crash. As Ricardo puts it, '[a] panic situation of this kind was the cause of the crisis'. In other words, panic was a psychological and behavioural response to risk. 'Neither the Bank nor Government were at that time to blame; it was the contagion of the unfounded fears of the timid part of the community, which occasioned the run on the Bank,' he claimed.[20] And while panics obviously had the potential to cause problems, they also offered opportunities to the cool-headed speculator. Ricardo himself was to make his fortune, after all, as a share manipulator taking advantage of market panic.

The Scottish moral philosopher and economist Adam Smith, Ricardo's near-contemporary, called the political use of fear 'in almost all cases a wretched instrument of government'.

At the same time he noted the myriad ways in which fear shaped society and government policy. Farmers, he argued, had 'nothing to fear from the free importation' of corn, and he criticised the 'popular fear' of new commercial practices – 'forestalling', buying corn when prices are low to resell later at a profit, and 'engrossing', buying in one locale to sell elsewhere at a higher price – suggesting that fear of these activities resembled 'the popular terrors and suspicions of witchcraft'.[21] Smith also maintained that it was fear of losing their jobs that kept workers in line. And while 'fear of misfortune' was rarely sufficient to curb rash speculation, it could nonetheless be the basis for mutual interests, as when merchants and kings found common cause in their fear of the nobility who threatened their wealth and power.[22]

As for panic, Smith believed that the element of surprise was crucial. We fear what we don't know, while foreseeable outcomes rarely prompt sudden and extreme behaviour.[23] Financial turbulence underlined the unpredictable nature of the markets. It also highlighted the role of rumour in panic, since the slightest whiff of negative news could trigger volatility and unleash panic selling. Central to this definition was the notion of trust: panic was what happened when trust in financial instruments and institutions was fatally undermined.

In tandem with this theoretical literature, the nineteenth century saw the publication of increasing numbers of popular books aimed at teaching novice investors how to negotiate the markets. The assumption underlying these self-help manuals was that the more understanding there was about how the markets worked, the better equipped people would be to manage future downturns, and the less panic would result. As the pioneering British statistician William Farr expressed it, 'knowledge will banish panic'.[24]

In her nine-volume *Illustrations of Political Economy*, published after a major panic in 1825, the British writer Harriet Martineau set out to show her readers how the free market worked. Confusion and collapse are part of the nature of markets, she insisted, and as long as investors steel themselves for inevitable vicissitudes, the ending can be happy. Martineau's approach to market panic was extrapolated from a more general method for dealing with personal fears and panics. As she wrote in her autobiography, she was herself prone to panic attacks, which she had learned to cope with by training her fear: 'panic struck at the head of the stairs, and I was sure I could not get down; and I could never cross the yard to the garden without flying and panting, and fearing to look behind, because a wild beast was after me.'[25]

Martineau's homespun market theory had many admirers, from Queen Victoria to the poet Samuel Taylor Coleridge, from the Conservative statesman Sir Robert Peel to the radical Liberal MP Richard Cobden. But if she seemed to offer a way of navigating market turbulence, her insistence on the need to pre-empt and manage crises implied the pervasive nature of the threat that investors were up against.[26]

Published forty years after Martineau, the banker Arthur Crump's guide to the pitfalls of the markets was similarly aimed at first-time speculators. Crump begins *The Theory of Stock Exchange Speculation* by stating that his aim is 'to show to persons who may contemplate trying their hand at Stock Exchange Speculation, the improbability of their hopes being realized'.[27] For the majority, speculation will spell disappointment, loss and ruin. As the *New York Times* observed in a review of the book, Crump had produced 'a very plain and searching account of the practices which prevail on the Exchange, and of the facts which make it a dead certainty that in the long run the outside speculator will lose'.[28] Unless, that is, the novice avails himself of a guide to pilot him 'through the Stock markets, and bring him out to a certainty with profit'. Market behaviour, according to Crump, is influenced by a plethora of interlinked variables, including the 'temper of the public' and 'meteorological influences'. The time of year and fluctuations in weather play such a crucial role in the psychology of speculation that Crump advises his readers to hang a barometer in their home and pay attention to weather forecasts.[29]

Crump invites us to think of speculation as a test of strength, like the navigation of a morass, beneath which lie 'hidden the remains of unwary travellers'. In a disconcertingly mixed metaphor, he claims that only those who display the cool-headedness of a surgeon and the ruthless determination of a tiger will survive. The stock markets are haunted by the flabby-minded, who are as easily frightened 'as a stray rabbit'. These feeble men

> are always fidgetting in and out, first as little bulls, and then as little bears, disappearing after a sharp panic like flies from a joint of meat that is rudely disturbed by the shop-boy, with the important difference that whereas the flies always get something, the speculators invariably drop their money.[30]

Different interpretations of how to manage panic reflected different views of how the global financial markets worked. Were they social inventions that could be reconfigured at will? Or were they natural phenomena that obeyed intrinsic laws, making human intervention at best futile and at worst dangerous? Was market turbulence structural or cyclical?

From one perspective, market vagaries were stages in a natural process. The collapse of a market was the inevitable result of a recurrent cycle of boom and bust.[31] Some analysts diagnosed market panic as a form of illness, the symptom of an ailing economy. A satirical playing card produced in 1721 to commemorate the South Sea Bubble depicts three doctors consulting on how 'To Cure the South Sea Plague, that Spoils the Nation'. The speculative bubble is imagined here as a sickness that requires therapy.[32] Mackay similarly regarded bubbles as examples of 'manias' and 'madness' where the 'normal', healthy state of the market was compromised. Writing in the aftermath of a panic triggered by the collapse of the London bank Overend, Gurney and Company in 1866, Walter Bagehot, editor of *The Economist*, argued that panic was the convulsive symptom of an underlying pathology, 'a species of neuralgia, and according to the science you must not starve it'. 'The best remedy for the worst malady,' Bagehot advised, was the intervention of a central bank – in this case, the Bank of England – as a lender of last resort.[33]

By the 1870s analogising financial crisis with infectious disease had become commonplace, as had the notion that speculation was an 'intermittent fever'.[34] During another financial panic, this time in 1907, the former governor of Ohio, Myron T. Herrick, declared that the financial system 'is in a susceptible condition, and it may easily become infected by panic germs'.[35]

These ideas persist in modern theories of financial contagion. In the late twentieth century fears about globally emerging infectious diseases – notably HIV/AIDS, Ebola and avian influenza – informed attitudes to financial crashes and were used to explain the spread of market panic. Economists drew on epidemiological models to track 'contagion'; fear spreads like a disease, they claimed, creating shockwaves that are hard to predict. In the aftermath of the 2008 global financial crisis, triggered when a housing bubble burst in the United States, the economist Nouriel Roubini and the historian Stephen Mihm wrote: 'History confirms that crises are much like pandemics: they begin with the outbreak of a disease that then spreads, radiating outwards.'[36]

Panics raised issues of trust and responsible governance, and they exposed tensions between private and public interests. The 1837 crash in the United States led Henry Charles Carey, the American economist and adviser to Abraham Lincoln, to rethink his views on global trade.[37] It was a crisis caused by multiple factors, from lax monetary policy and unregulated lending to fluctuating cotton prices and land speculation, that triggered a major depression.[38] This was the context for Carey's criticism of free-trade capitalism, which he felt produced financial panics through centralisation on the one hand and unequal exchanges on the other.[39] He was forthright in criticising the view that crises and panics were natural occurrences, 'like epidemic visitations', about which little could be done.[40] The answer, he held, was for the government to protect domestic markets with tariffs.

By the late nineteenth century the 'panic fear' produced by financial crises had become a central concern for governments. Meanwhile, arguments about state regulation versus the 'free market' came to be equated with the political left and right. Responses to panics exposed divergent political positions, as illustrated by cartoons published in response to the American bank crash of 1873.

In an illustration by the caricaturist Thomas Nast, which appeared in *Harper's Weekly*, the crash is depicted as a violent collision of industries. Steam engines, trucks and cattle are flung into the air in a giant explosion, while dark clouds envelop Wall Street; the iconic Trinity Church looms in the background like a stranded lighthouse, a moral beacon from an old world. The speculators who have caused this market detonation aren't that different from the anarchists who dreamed of blowing up the Stock Exchange – both groups were looking to profit from chaos, regardless of the collateral damage.

In another cartoon by the artist and illustrator Frank Bellew, published on the cover of New York's *Daily Graphic*, panic is caricatured as a giant health officer – a monstrous and hairy King Kong-type figure – sweeping the garbage from Wall Street, with one foot at the door of the newly completed Drexel Building.[41] Two telegraph poles and a tangle of wires are visible in the background, as agitated speculators swarm onto the street. Implicit in this cartoon is the notion that financial disasters and the panics that precipitate them can be cleansing. Panics, far from always being unmitigated disasters, can function as a natural rebooting mechanism that irons out glitches and recalibrates the system when it gets overheated, or they can be harnessed to streamline market processes for efficiency.

For Karl Marx, himself a dabbler on the stock market, financial crises were signs of the coming revolution. In 1856 he was certain that a major crash was on its way – the big one that would bring down Europe's industry and destroy the propertied classes. In an article for the *New-York Daily Tribune* he drew attention to the speculative activities of the Crédit Mobilier, a bank that had lent substantive sums to the French government. 'What distinguishes the present period of speculation in Europe is the universality of the rage,' he wrote. 'The ruling principle of the Crédit Mobilier, the representative of the present mania, is not to speculate in a given line, but to speculate in speculation, and to universalize swindling.'[42]

Market turbulence has long been exploited for profit. If, to borrow the catchphrase of Gordon Gekko, the fictional villain of Oliver Stone's film *Wall Street*, 'greed is good', so too is panic. For some investors, bear markets – sustained falls in market prices – create opportunities for 'panic profits' as stocks can be snapped up cheaply.[43] Market crashes may also provide opportunities for corporations to monopolise business, and for the state to extend its authority and gain consent for controversial post-crisis policies, an essential element of what the Canadian writer and activist Naomi Klein calls 'disaster capitalism'.[44]

The idea that panic can be manipulated for personal gain recurs in late nineteenth- and early twentieth-century fiction. As the literary historian David Zimmerman has argued, it was partly in response to the 1890s recession and the subsequent economic boom that many American novelists began to explore the theme of market crashes and financial panics. To explain the psychological dimensions of market events, writers drew on new theories of 'mob psychology, psychic investigations, new conceptions of sympathy, and new forms of conspiracy discourse'.[45]

Thomas Lawson's novel *Friday, the Thirteenth*, published in

1907, features a young broker who loses his fortune – acquired in the first place through the exploitation of a panic – when the price of sugar collapses, a fall orchestrated to allow the powers-that-be to line their own pockets. In retaliation he creates a counter-panic, choosing Friday the thirteenth as the day to implement his scheme. While he almost destroys Wall Street and brings misery to many in the process, he makes all his money back – with a sizeable profit to boot.[46]

Upton Sinclair's 1908 novel *The Moneychangers* is another tale of deliberately induced panic, where powerful capitalists plot to sabotage the market in order to ruin their rivals. Panic, as one of the plotters whispers to a fellow conspirator, is a useful curb. 'Don't they realise what they'll do?' another character asks. 'There'll be a panic such as New York has never seen before! It will bring down every bank in the city!' 'The panic was stopped,' the narrator tells us later, 'but the business of the country lay in ruins.'[47]

As much as this literature focuses on the panic that can result from financial collapse, it struggles to provide a convincing description of how markets work. In his 1903 novel *The Pit: A Story of Chicago*, Frank Norris imagines the market as a force for chaos. It is depicted, by turns, as an implacable natural phenomenon, like a cyclone, or as a malevolent creature devouring those who block its path. The novel's protagonist, Curtis Jadwin, buys and sells stocks of wheat on the trading floor of the Chicago Board of Trade Building, becoming increasingly greedy and power-crazed. Eventually, as a result of his reckless speculation, the market crashes, bringing misery to investors.

The pit in Norris's book is the eye of the storm, a primordial morass and a monster's lair. 'Within there, a great whirlpool, a pit of roaring waters spun and thundered,' the narrator tells us, 'sucking in the life tides of the city, sucking them in as into the mouth of some tremendous cloaca, the maw of some colossal sewer; then vomiting them forth again, spewing them up and out, only to catch them in the return eddy and suck them in afresh.'[48] In this description of the market, a drum-roll of suspense reaches a climax when the object of fear and the trigger for panic are finally disclosed – only for it to be anti-climactic. Norris's pit can only be described in terms that are familiarly hyperbolic. It's a monster, a maelstrom, a whirlpool and a machine. Speculation and panic are elusive; they lack a core, which is what makes them fundamentally ungraspable and dangerous. In the end, we're left with a void.

At the time Norris was writing, criticism of the markets had become more strident, spurred by the rise of socialism and the consolidation of trade unions. During the Progressive Era in the United States – the period from the 1890s to 1920s when activists took up the cause of labour rights, women's suffrage and economic reform – the American economist Thorstein Veblen attacked the notion of production for profit and the 'conspicuous consumption' of the 'leisure class'.[49]

Financial crises also created public resentment towards financiers and speculators, with attacks on those with a stake in the financial system coming from many quarters. Sponging elites, thought to be in cahoots with power-hungry politicians, were denounced for exacerbating poverty and sacrificing national interests to those of global capital. Some anti-capitalists were even prepared to take up arms to topple the system. Acts of violence perpetrated by anarchists against business leaders, politicians and heads of state became more frequent from the 1880s. Alfred Nobel's invention of dynamite in the 1860s didn't only have military and industrial applications; it was also an impetus to terrorism. Among many assassinations were those of Tsar Alexander II, blown up in St Petersburg in 1881; President Sadi Carnot of France, stabbed in Lyon in 1894; the empress Elisabeth of Austria, also stabbed, in Geneva in 1898; and US president William McKinley, shot in Buffalo, New York, in 1901. Stock exchanges were also targeted for attack. In 1886 the young Breton anarchist Charles Gallo threw a bottle of prussic acid from the visitors' gallery of the

Paris Bourse, before discharging a revolver and shouting, '*Vive l'anarchie!*'[50]

In the history of financial crashes, the collapse of the New York stock market in October 1929 stands out as a defining moment. Despite the global fallout from the 2008 financial crisis, 1929 remains the crash that has shaped what financial panics are supposed to look like: markets spiking and crashing like irregular heartbeats on an ECG monitor; mayhem on the trading floor; the frenzied selling of investments; and, at its worse, devastated speculators throwing themselves from top-floor windows.

Panic in its post-1929 manifestation is alternatively a collective and a singular experience. It involves violent stampedes and sullen crowds in the canyons of Lower Manhattan, or a solitary trader, head in his hands, tie askew and splayed against a brick wall. Panic unfolds across the vertiginous modern city, as if the more vertical a city becomes, the greater the potential there is for suicidal falls.

The actor Will Rogers, writing from New York on 'Black Thursday', 24 October 1929, commented: 'When Wall Street took that tail spin, you had to stand in line to get a window to jump out of, and speculators were selling space for bodies in the East River.'[51] When James J. Riordan, the forty-eight-year-old president of the County Trust Company, was found shot dead in his bedroom a few weeks later, his associates decided not to announce his suicide until after the markets had closed for the day, afraid that the news would start a run on the bank.[52]

The film *King Kong*, directed by Merian C. Cooper and Ernest B. Schoedsack – surely the greatest fantasy adventure film of all time – came out in 1933, at the lowest point of the post-1929 Great Depression. Its heroine, Ann Darrow, is an out-of-work actress, played by Fay Wray, who only agrees to shoot a movie because times are hard and she's 'in a fix'. In Manhattan we're shown a bread line outside the Women's Home Mission, and Carl Denham, the filmmaker protagonist (played by Robert Armstrong), runs into the starving Darrow after she's been accused of stealing an apple from a street stall. Later, on a remote island in the south Pacific, the film crew discovers a land that time forgot inhabited by a giant gorilla and a fearful tribe who sacrifice humans to propitiate the beast. Captured and taken back to New York as a theatre spectacle, the gorilla manages to break loose – and the rest is history. The climax of the film sees the building-smashing ape swinging from the recently completed Empire State Building, his fist wrapped around Fay Wray, while crowds panic on the streets below. King Kong is doing what the markets have already done: smashing the place up. It doesn't take much of a leap to see this big ape as a monstrous echo of the crash itself.

The Wall Street Crash is often taken to mark the end of the 1920s boom, epitomised by the glitzy parties thrown by the enigmatic Jay Gatsby, the eponymous anti-hero of F. Scott Fitzgerald's 1925 novel *The Great Gatsby*. 'In his blue gardens men and girls came and went like moths among the whisperings and the champagne and the stars,' Nick Carraway, the book's narrator tells us. It's a wistful evocation of fleeting life – flitting moths, shooting stars, bursting bubbles – that hints at an incipient collapse. And this anticipation of tragedy, it turns out, is rooted in past panics. When asked by Carraway whether he inherited his money, Gatsby lies and claims that he had, 'but I lost most of it in the big panic – the panic of the war'.[53] It was a panic that H. G. Wells had predicted in 1908, when he wrote that war would cause the 'flimsy fabric of credit' to dissolve, dragging down millions who now lived 'in an economic interdependence that no man clearly understood'.[54]

Billions of dollars were wiped off investments when the market plunged almost 13 per cent on 28 October 1929, 'Black Monday', followed by another fall of nearly 12 per cent the next day. By July 1932 the US stock market had lost over 89 per cent of its value. The *Times* of London called the market sell-off a 'Niagara of liquidation'. 'Never before, even at the outbreak of the Great War,' the paper declared, 'was there such a volume of transactions.' To reassure panicking investors, Morgan Lamont, a partner at J. P. Morgan, claimed in the press that there had been 'a little distress selling' on the Stock Exchange and the problem was 'technical rather than fundamental'.[55]

Addressing the District of Columbia Banking Association days before the crash, Irving Fisher, professor of economics at Yale, typified this faulty optimism when he downplayed 'the public's speculative mania'.[56] He had earlier dismissed the risks posed by the 'shaking out of the lunatic fringe that attempts to speculate on margin', while reiterating his prediction that stock prices 'have reached what looks like a permanently high plateau'.[57] 'There may be a recession in stock prices,' he declared, 'but not anything in the nature of a crash.'[58]

In reality, of course, the collapse of the market led to a rout that forced the closure of the Stock Exchange. 'Thus ends, for the time being,' reported *The Economist*, 'the most dramatic week in Wall Street's history since the crisis of 1907.' While the boom had lasted, New York had been 'a magnet for the world's floating resources', but now, after the crash, the newspaper predicted 'that few branches of American life will escape the repercussions of the break'.[59]

A US government investigation of the crash and the speculative craze that had triggered it failed to shed much light on the crisis, although by the early 1930s it was generally agreed that 'the Wall Street panic undoubtedly contributed largely to the world-wide reaction which followed'.[60] What had gone wrong? In the words of the 'American financial titan' McGafferty, the protagonist of Archibald MacLeish's *Panic*, a play in verse which premiered in March 1935 at the Imperial Theatre in Manhattan: 'And why? What's done it? Who's behind it?' At the height of a banking crisis, McGafferty, who is modelled on the banker J. P. Morgan, struggles to keep afloat and prevent the country from being knocked 'clean through the crack of panic' while all around him businesses foreclose, factories shut and banks default. As the play's blurb puts it, the scene shifts 'back and forth between a group of distraught and bewildered capitalists desperately attempting to shore up the old order, and the people outside whose voices rise from the street like the chorus of a Greek tragedy'. 'All afraid – and of what?' the bankers in the play ask in unison.

The roots of the crisis, MacLeish intimates, lie not just in greed or in panic whipped up by a sensationalist media – much of the action takes place 'in a street before an electric news bulletin of the Times Square type' – but in a destructive fatalism that envelopes the crowds and the bankers alike, and which in the end brings about McGafferty's downfall when his peers lose confidence in him. The crisis, MacLeish suggests, reflects a failure on all sides to envision a plausible alternative to the defunct economic system that's on the brink of imploding. As he observed in a letter to Henry Luce, the owner of *Fortune* magazine, after the 1929 crash America's business leaders were 'fearful, vacillating, bewildered and void. Their one hope has been to hang on. Their greatest fear has been the fear of falling off.'[61]

In 1933 the Glass–Steagall Banking Act attempted to separate retail banking from investment banking to ensure that depositors' funds weren't used in risky investments. Commentators were now stressing the role of psychology in market behaviour. In November 1929, with the extent of the crisis apparent, Irving Fisher attempted to justify his flawed prediction by arguing that the crash had been the result of 'the psychology of panic'. 'It was mob psychology,' he asserted. 'The fall of the market was very largely due to the psychology by which it went down because it went down.' In other words, the panic produced a self-fulfilling momentum that defied rational assessment of key market predictors.[62]

The 1929 crash helped to shape an iconography of market panic that remains familiar to this day, from pundit soundbites to news coverage of the consequent sell-off. It also perpetuated and reinforced an idea of panic psychology that still endures. In December 1930 the *Evening World* bemoaned the fact that so many people were 'giving a too eager ear to wild rumors and spiteful gossip', which were sapping confidence and creating 'an atmosphere of general distrust'. 'The victims of vague fear, on the street and in the market place, are a menace to the community,' the newspaper declared. 'They are the feeders of that mob psychology which creates the spirit of panic.'[63] In the twenty-first century, different 'fear indexes' are used to track the volatility of option prices and to measure stock market sentiment based on the assumption that fear drives prices down, while greed drives them up. Meanwhile, panic continues to be viewed, at least by some analysts, as the expression of a 'mob psychology' or 'herd behaviour' similar to that which caused the 1929 crash and the depression that followed – but with the difference that in a world of digital connectivity, its scope and potential for damage have been drastically extended.

10

Horror in the Trenches

Imagine every turn-of-the-century fear combined: the growing power of the masses, dehumanising machines, mechanical slaughter and volatile markets. This was the First World War, a 'smash up of empires and diplomacy' that led to industrialised killing.[1] It was a new kind of war, but one that had been anticipated. Six years before its outbreak, H. G. Wells had foreseen a future in which 'Europeanised civilisation was, as it were, blown up'.[2]

Previous conflicts had demonstrated the strategic importance of industrial weaponry, trains, steamships and telegraphy. Photography was another new technology that became central to modern warfare. Aside from its deployment for tactical observation and reconnaissance, it had important propaganda value and could be used to shape public awareness. *Valley of the Shadow of Death*, a famous shot taken in 1855 during the Crimean War by the British photographer Roger Fenton, captures the new landscape of modern warfare. This is a powerful vision of futility, where war is less a presence than an overwhelming absence. An empty road crosses a rugged hill strewn with cannonballs. As Fenton wrote in a letter to his wife, 'in coming to a ravine called the valley of death, the sight passed all imagination: round shot and shell lay like a stream at the bottom of the hollow all the way down, you could not walk without treading upon them'.[3]

It may well be that the scene was staged, as some have suggested, but the details are still evocative. Instead of a gory view of the injured or the dead, we get a landscape littered with instruments of mass destruction that are barely distinguishable from rocks. It's as if war has pulverised humanity, leaving nothing but silence and rubble, scattered shot and shell. What we're shown, in other words, is the no-man's-land that modern war creates. As the nineteen-year-old protagonist of Gabriel Chevallier's thinly veiled autobiographical novel *Fear* declares after he's been wounded in northern France in 1915, the war has killed God and left 'nothing in the sky but shells and all the other murderous devices made by man'.[4]

The First World War was waged in Europe, Asia and Africa. A slugfest fought with plane, tank, automatic weaponry, poisonous gas and submarine, it redefined fear on many levels: as an experience, a military tactic, a logistical challenge and a medical condition. It also posed an aesthetic predicament. How could the experience of war be credibly represented when it existed on such vastly different scales, from the staggering magnitude of 20 million military casualties and over 10 million deaths to the terror of a single combatant at the front or the gassed soldier choking on his own blood?[5] Even as the meaning of fear expanded, it moved inwards: the war would be the spur for the development of new medical practices that were geared to treat suppressed fears, namely psychiatry.

In early 1915, with mounting carnage in Europe, the *Scientific American* ran a special series on 'the lesson that history teaches', bemoaning the United States' total unpreparedness for a modern war that was fought 'like a thunderbolt from heaven'. Seven months after the conflict had begun, Americans had every reason to be fearful.[6] The industrial scale of the First World War marked it out from previous conflicts. On the first day of the Battle of the Somme in July 1916, close to 20,000 British soldiers were killed, with over 30,000 wounded. By 18 November, when the battle ended, approximately 1.3 million men were left dead or wounded.

Was it possible to grasp this level of mass violence? Many

thought not. As Fenton's photograph suggested, the horrors of modern warfare had to be conjured obliquely. The writer John Berger, born eight years after the war, described how his father, who spent four years as an infantryman, never spoke about his experiences. Instead, 'he would sometimes finger and look at his mementos: a field compass, a revolver, some trench maps, a few letters and lists, some machine-gun rounds, the ring of a hand grenade'.[7] Recollections of the war unfolded through objects, with experiences revealed via buttons, medals, discharge papers and brief notes scrawled on the back of postcards.

In First World War fiction stories are often told through letters and diaries retrieved from chests. It's only after the event that the intensity of repressed fears can be acknowledged, and even then only indirectly, through bric-a-brac. As Paul Bäumer, the twenty-year-old narrator in Erich Maria Remarque's novel *All Quiet on the Western Front*, observes: 'The terror of the front sinks deep down when we turn our back upon it.'[8] *Life in the Tomb*, by the Greek novelist Stratis Myrivilis, who fought on the Macedonian front in 1917, takes the form of a journal retrieved from an old army field chest amid 'a pile of mementoes'.[9] What happened must be pieced together from fragments because the sheer magnitude of the event makes it hard to comprehend.

The war artist Paul Nash expressed this idea in a letter to his wife, observing that the scene at the front was 'utterly indescribable'.[10] In the same year, 1917, the American film director D. W. Griffith was given unrestricted access by British high command to the Western Front at Ypres in Belgium. The British government had earlier approached him to make a film that would sway the American public's view of the war and jolt the country out of its neutrality. When he got to the front, however, the sight amazed him. As Griffith would later confide to a journalist, 'It is too colossal to be dramatic. No one can describe it. You might as well try to describe the ocean or the Milky Way. The war correspondents of today are staggered almost into silence.' 'Everyone is hidden away in ditches,' he continued. 'As you look out across No

Man's Land, there is literally nothing that meets the eye but an aching desolation of nothingness – of torn trees, ruined barbed wire fence, and shell holes.'[11] In the event, the silent film *Hearts of the World*, which appeared in 1918, was shot on Salisbury Plain in England and at the Lasky Ranch studio in Hollywood.

Fenton's famous photograph gives us a view looking up a hill towards the vacant sky, but in the First World War aeroplanes provided a unique vantage on this territory. Aerial photographs of the battlefields show networks of trenches spreading out across the land, interspersed with dugouts and concrete bunkers. Hedged between them is a pitted waste ground, and in the hinterland behind are miles of abandoned farms, villages and towns, with some, such as Ypres, razed to the ground.

To airmen, who were shocked at what they saw and found themselves scrambling for metaphors, the trashed landscape of northern France and Belgium resembled 'the humid skin of a monstrous toad'.[12] The poet Wilfred Owen saw the battlefield as the putrefying face of a dead soldier, pockmarked and cleft by the slimy tracks of slug-like caterpillars – the tread marks of tanks that 'roll without feeling into the craters', Remarque's narrator tells us, 'invulnerable steel beasts squashing the dead and the wounded'.[13] The American nurse Mary Borden imagined a great wave had washed over the land, a biblical flood that had left 'the muddy bottom of the earth uncovered'.[14] From above, it appeared as an earth-shattering, quasi-geological event. As the Anglo-Irish writer Elizabeth Bowen once observed, 'I see war (or should I say feel war?) more as a territory than as a page of history.'[15]

The French novelist Henri Barbusse begins *Under Fire*, his account of the war on the Western Front, with a description of the trenches glimpsed through murky clouds that cloak the earth 'like evil spirits'. An immense plain comes into view, churned to mud by heavy artillery and with minuscule human forms clinging to the surface, 'blinded and borne down with filth, like the dreadful castaways of shipwreck'. Mud in this place is a monster that ensnares humanity, pulling men into a squelching, mephitic morass, concealing them 'like a monstrous hand' and transforming their macerated, mud-caked bodies into 'inanimate objects'.[16] Ideals were lost 'in the mud and the flood and the blood'. 'It was mud, mud, everywhere,' British gunner John Palmer said about Passchendaele in 1917. 'Every shell hole was a sea of filthy oozing mud.'[17]

Aeroplanes, of course, were also implicated in this devastation. At the start of the war, bomber crews relied on the naked eye to hit their targets, but soon rudimentary bombsights were in use. German Zeppelin airships conducted raids on European cities, and the British armed forces leveraged the popular fear of enemy air attacks in a recruitment drive; in one poster a Zeppelin shines a white beam over a blacked-out London, with the tagline 'It's far better to face the bullets than to be killed at home by a bomb.'

Borden described an enemy plane appearing out of nowhere, an ominous speck in the sky, before the bombardment commenced. 'The unconscious map lay spread out beneath it,' she wrote: 'the wide plain, the long white beach and the sea, lay there exposed to its speeding eye.'[18] Remarque, in *All Quiet on the Western Front*, captured the fear that gripped the men in the German trenches when they heard the menacing drone of reconnaissance planes overhead, presaging a full-on assault with the thunder of artillery batteries and the whine of shells.[19]

Fear was disruptive because it could paralyse soldiers and trigger panic, which might then spread among the troops before travelling behind the lines to sap the morale of a nervy civilian population. Arthur Gristwood, who was wounded at the Somme, wrote of 'fear ever lying in wait to grow to panic'.[20] When a battalion became dispersed, noted the psychiatrist Charles Stanford Read,

> the individual soldier, losing the sense of protection of the herd, will find his fear probably return, and the love of

> self-preservation may bring about flight reactions. The signs of fear are very contagious, and if they spread in the vital moments of attack a panic resulting in a disorderly retreat may occur.[21]

Military authorities used a range of tactics to prevent this contagious fear. Censorship, which extended from the press to personal communications, cables, pamphlets and books, was used to weed out bad news, avert defeatism and instil confidence. Another stratagem was the threat of court martial. Punishment, even execution, awaited those who feigned illness or injury to shirk their duty, with malingerers branded cowards. As one report put it bluntly, 'Cowardice is a military crime for which the death penalty may be exacted.'[22]

Troops were also trained to manage fear. The aim was to free the soldier 'from the danger of succumbing to the collapse of terror or the blind flight of panic' and to inculcate in him 'such a state that even the utmost horrors and rigours of warfare are hardly noticed, so inured is he to their presence'.[23] Practice and routine were promoted as countermeasures that would repel any latent propensity for terror and panic, a message that was reinforced in operational manuals that emphasised the role of the drill in the preparation of troops for battle. The influential Russian military theorist Mikhail Dragomirov stressed the difference between self-preservation and self-sacrifice: military training was tasked with eliminating the former and cultivating the latter through exercises that stimulated fear.[24] While the drill sought to eliminate fear among the ranks, it was also a means of developing 'shock' tactics that would induce panic in the enemy. When training failed to pay off, extreme measures might be adopted. As one commentator asserted in 1914, in the event of panic on the front line it was permissible for officers to shoot their own men.[25]

The wartime press, muzzled by state censorship, reinforced this cultivation of fearlessness. Newspapers and magazines celebrated thrilling new technologies and advances in medical science, with pictures of mobile operating units and ambulance trains intended to suggest efficiency and an unflagging commitment to the future. The purpose of this propaganda was to boost public morale and foreground emotions that would counteract fear, such as pride and hope.[26]

In 1916 the British medical officer Robert W. Mackenna concluded from his many interviews with veterans of the South African War and those experiencing combat in the ongoing conflict in Europe that 'in the heat of battle the fear of death is absolutely obliterated'. It was only in the moments leading up to battle and after 'the din of battle had ebbed into a great and vague silence' that soldiers felt apprehension. The publisher John Murray, who wrote the foreword to Mackenna's book *The Adventure of Death*, agreed. Faced with 'sudden peril', he noted how he'd often had 'no consciousness of fear'; the shock of the ordeal kicked in afterwards when he experienced 'a recurrent sense of shuddering'. Was this, he wondered, 'a form of retrospective fear'? When, in 1918, C. S. Lewis was hit by shrapnel, which killed the man beside him, he felt no fear. Thinking back on the experience, it was as if the war had 'happened to someone else'.[27]

When soldiers began to present for treatment for shock with no visible signs of physical trauma, it was initially thought that they must be suffering from concussion caused by proximity to exploding shells. In February 1915 Charles Myers, consultant psychologist to the British armed forces in France, published a paper in the *Lancet* in which he described three cases of 'shell shock', a condition associated with the loss of memory, vision, smell and taste. One of the cases involved a twenty-year-old private whose battalion had been targeted by German artillery in November 1914. As Myers noted, 'up to that time he had not been feeling afraid; he had "rather been enjoying it", and was in the best of spirits until the shells burst about him'.[28] As the soldier crept under the barbed-wire entanglements, in the midst of enemy fire, he panicked and struggled to free himself from the wire. An exploding shell blasted the haversack off his back, leaving him scorched and bruised. It felt, he said, 'like a punch on the head, without any pain after it'. His vision became blurry, objects seemed to dissolve and he started to sob, thinking he was going blind. Still, he somehow managed to throw himself into a trench, and when he finally rejoined his battalion, an ambulance took him to a dressing station, where he was given brandy and conveyed onwards to a hospital behind the lines. Myers concluded about such cases, 'They appear to constitute a definite class among others arising from the effects of shell shock.'[29]

It soon became apparent that soldiers who hadn't been exposed to shelling were nevertheless showing the same debilitating symptoms, ranging from trembling to memory loss. At this point military and medical authorities concluded that they were probably dealing with a form of mental collapse brought on by fear – what we would now call post-traumatic stress disorder. After the Battle of the Somme in 1916 there was a surge in cases of mental breakdown leading to panic. The British authorities were forced to contend with the logistical consequences of this; a report on medical services during the war, published in 1923, noted that 'the severe wastage of manpower which the psycho-neuroses were causing in France made the problem of dealing with them urgent'.[30]

In its extreme form shell shock manifested with uncontrollable shaking, twitching and contorting. In 1917 the British physicians Arthur Hurst and J. L. M. Symns filmed the tics and 'hysterical' gaits of shell-shocked patients. Their resulting documentary, *War Neuroses*, aimed to provide evidence of how 'Increased experience in the treatment of the hysterical symptoms which form one of the largest classes of war neuroses has led to gradual simplification of methods and increasing certainty and rapidity of cure.'[31]

The 27-minute silent film includes captions that give the name, rank and medical condition of each patient, along with a description of their symptoms and the duration of their treatment. 'Clinical features shown include a variety of ataxic and hysterical gaits,' a summarising caption states dispassionately, enumerating a catalogue of life-shattering infirmities: 'hysterical paralyses, contractures and anaesthesias; facial tics and spasms; loss of knee and ankle-jerk reflexes; paraplegia; "war hyperthyroidism"; amnesia; word-blindness and word-deafness'.[32]

'Nowhere do the sheer horror and savagery of modern warfare appeal so vividly to the mind and senses as in a tour of these wards,' declared an article in the *Daily Mail* in 1916, describing the soldiers who'd had their faces blown off.[33] The nose and jaw were particularly exposed in trench warfare and vulnerable to flying debris from bombs and shells. The appalling facial injuries suffered by men at the front were traumatising to witness, even for seasoned surgeons. 'Hideous is the only word for these smashed faces,' wrote Ward Muir, a corporal in the Royal Army Medical Corps (RAMC).

> [The] socket with some twisted, moist slit, with a lash or two adhering feebly, which is all that is traceable of the forfeited eye; the skewed mouth which sometimes – in spite of brilliant dentistry contrivances – results from the loss of a segment of jaw; and worse, far the worst, the incredibly brutalising effects which are the consequence of wounds in the nose, and which reach a climax of mournful grotesquerie when the nose is missing altogether.[34]

A 'chamber of horror' is how the doctor and artist Henry Tonks described a hospital ward of the wounded.[35] Trained as a surgeon, he had switched careers to take up art, teaching at the Slade School of Fine Art in London. When war broke out, he was dispatched to the front as a medic, but was soon recruited by the New Zealand surgeon Harold Gillies to draw diagrams of surgical procedures for his patients' records. Influenced by the operations he'd seen performed in France, Gillies pioneered new methods of reconstructive surgery, including skin grafting, that helped lay the basis for modern plastic surgery.

The loss of a face wasn't only a question of disfigurement; it gave rise to serious psychological trauma. Working in a war hospital, Muir discovered how hard it was to look a disfigured patient in the eye without 'betraying, by his expression, how awful is their appearance'. When 'the patient was going about with his wrecked face uncovered', Muir felt embarrassed and fearful. 'I feared, when talking to him, to meet his eye,' he writes. Despite the notional ban on mirrors in these hospitals, the soldier with his mangled mess of a face – 'a broken gargoyle' – invariably knew what he looked like. As Muir put it, 'he is aware that you are aware, and that some unguarded glance of yours may cause him hurt. This, then, is the patient at whom you are afraid to gaze unflinchingly: not afraid for yourself, but afraid for *him*.'[36] The scarred faces depicted in Tonks's sketches of patients before and after surgery take us into the drama of shattered selfhood that Muir describes so astutely.

Pathological images of the war-wounded would later give rise to an aesthetic that was popularised in horror movies featuring the living dead and other monsters of the night. But in Tonks's drawings the patients become objects of empathy rather than fear. However crude Gillies's plastic surgery may now appear, it speaks of hope and the possibility of reconstructed life. This isn't the case in the film by Hurst and Symns, where the staggering shell-shocked victims are obliged to parade before us in an exhibition of their rehabilitation, 'a sort of aquarium for the psychopath to study'.[37] The public showcasing of managed trauma feels like a form of secondary violence; first comes the war, and then the treatment.

Although Hurst and Symns had begun by using hypnotism, this was ditched in favour of other treatments, principally 'persuasion and re-education continued with manipulation'.

Electric shock therapy was used in cases of 'flaccid paralysis' – a neurological condition that caused muscle weakness – but in the main the emphasis was on what Hurst and Symns called 'the creation of a proper atmosphere'. This involved convincing the patient that he would be cured as a matter of course, even if that often entailed telling a white lie.[38]

Very different approaches were adopted to treat shell shock. The Canadian-born psychiatrist Lewis Yealland was among those who advocated a hard-line intervention. 'Hysteria' was associated with women, and by implication 'hysterical' shell-shocked patients were those who had been deprived of masculine virtues. Fear and panic, it was believed, had turned these he-men into she-men, and patients had a moral duty to toughen up. Based at the National Hospital for the Paralysed and Epileptic in London's Queen Square, Yealland was renowned for his use of electrotherapy, a method that he'd pioneered with the electrophysiologist Edgar Adrian, and which he applied on soldiers who displayed symptoms of shock.[39]

Pain was an essential element of this shock treatment. 'The current can be made extremely painful if it is necessary to supply the disciplinary element which must be invoked if the patient is one of those who prefer not to recover,' Adrian and Yealland wrote in a 1917 paper describing their method, 'and it can be made strong enough to break down the unconscious barriers to sensation in the most profound functional anaesthesia.'[40] In his manual *Hysterical Disorders of Warfare*, published the following year, Yealland elaborated on his various techniques, including shaming and the threat of punishment, designed to mend the minds of those corrupted by 'the hideous enemy of negativism'. Reading the book now is a reminder of how different medicine was in the early twentieth century: a boot-camp approach that lingered well into the 1960s. 'Remember you must behave as becomes the hero I expect you to be,' Yealland reports telling one of his patients as he applies an electric current to the man's body, a process called 'faradization'. 'A man who has gone through so many battles,' he chides the soldier, 'should have better control of himself.'[41]

Yealland wasn't alone, of course. In Germany faradization was widely used to treat soldiers suffering from male hysteria, a disorder that had first been identified in workers on the railways and in factories.[42] At the same time, the use of electrotherapy reflected a prevalent view that shell-shocked patients were using their illness as an excuse to dodge their duty on the battlefield.[43] In France electric currents were similarly applied to treat soldiers with 'intractable' neuroses, a process known to the soldiers as *torpillage*, or 'torpedoing', because of the intense pain that it caused.[44]

Other physicians took a more humane approach. William Rivers, who had qualified as a doctor and developed a medical focus on neurology and experimental psychology – alongside an interest in anthropology, to which he made important contributions – was a lecturer at Cambridge when war broke out. Physicians were in high demand to meet the surge in shell-shock cases and among the hospitals requisitioned as treatment centres was the Moss Side Military Hospital in Maghull, Merseyside, which became a specialist institution for the treatment of 'abnormal psychology'.[45] In July 1915 Rivers took up an appointment there on the recommendation of Grafton Elliot Smith, who a few years later was to co-author the book *Shell Shock and Its Lessons*, in an effort to dispel the prejudice that still clung to 'even the mildest forms of mental abnormality'. 'Of all varieties of fear,' Elliot Smith wrote, 'the fear of the unknown is one of the greatest.' Tackling 'this public wound' required overcoming the 'apathy, superstition, helpless ignorance and fear' that continued to surround mental illness.[46] At Moss Side, war neuroses were treated with experimental psychopathological approaches, including hypnosis, psychoanalysis and dream interpretation.[47]

Rivers was soon appointed a captain in the RAMC and transferred to Craiglockhart War Hospital outside Edinburgh. Originally built as a clinic where the wealthy would go to take water cures, the gloomy Italianate building had been repurposed as a hospital to treat officers diagnosed with shock. Rivers was convinced that war neuroses developed from an impulse to repress memories of traumatic experiences or 'unacceptable emotions', fear being one of them. It was evident from his research that, while some violent event, such as an explosion, could act as a trigger for mental illness, the stress of warfare produced new susceptibilities to this kind of 'morbid process'. Often, he noted, fear could be 'wholly displaced by the affect of horror associated with some peculiarly painful incident of war'. He describes one case in which a young officer had been flung by the force of an explosion into 'the swollen corpse' of a dead German soldier. The dead man's putrefying entrails had filled his mouth and afterwards he was haunted by memories of the 'horrid sensations of taste and smell'.[48] By encouraging patients to describe their traumatic experiences, Rivers hoped to reverse their suppression; it was a method he called 'autognosis', from the Greek for 'self-knowledge'. Freud was clearly an influence on Rivers's talking cure, and in a paper on Freud, published in 1917, he pointed out the 'wonderful turn of fate' that Freud's theory of the unconscious was being hotly debated at a time when the war was producing 'on an enormous scale just those conditions of paralysis and contracture, phobia and obsession, which the theory was especially designed to explain'.[49]

The atmosphere at Craiglockhart may have been different from the hospital in Queen Square, but it was nonetheless a gloomy place. The poet Siegfried Sassoon, who was treated there in 1917, noted in his autobiographical novel *Sherston's Progress* that while the hospital was outwardly cheerful, once the lights were switched off the place reverberated with the cries of traumatised patients. 'By night,' he wrote, 'each man was back in his doomed sector of a horror-stricken front line where the panic and stampede of some ghastly experience was re-enacted among the livid faces of the dead.'[50] Rivers was a light in this disconsolate world, and the method he developed for treating war neuroses made him a true innovator.

Other physicians were also applying forward-thinking approaches to treat shock, among them the Scottish psychiatrist Hugh Crichton-Miller, who had made a plea for 'rational psychotherapy' in 1912.[51] Drawing on his wartime experience, he would go on to establish the Tavistock Clinic in 1920, where the 'new psychology' was used to treat mental disorders in the civilian population, particularly children.[52]

Different approaches to shell shock reflected uncertainty about its cause. As the Welsh psychiatrist Sir Robert Armstrong-Jones conceded in 1917, 'although an indescribable, unknown fear is a preliminary condition, it is impossible to dogmatise when the symptoms are so variable'.[53] Was it a real condition, or a scam to get out of service? Was it neurological, or was it psychological, the consequence of industrial warfare? Others wondered whether some individuals were predisposed to shell shock, and whether it was inherited. Views shifted and were often inconsistent. Many physicians shared Armstrong-Jones's inference that the condition was set off by an external shock that caused 'neurotic changes', triggering a strong emotional reaction and instinctive behaviour. Most cases of shell shock were the result of 'sudden, unconscious fears and awe' and could be 'quite restored if treated early'.[54]

The American physiologist Walter Cannon emphasised physiological processes and the physical triggers of fear. The initial focus of his research was on the association of traumatic shock with acidosis – an excessive buildup of acid in the blood – and on treating this chemical imbalance with an infusion of sodium bicarbonate. Cannon, the originator of the term 'fight or flight response', which he had used to describe animal response to threats, stressed the role of biochemical processes in mental illness: 'the emotion of fear', he concluded in a study on the subject, 'is associated with the instinct for flight, and the emotion of anger or rage with the instinct for fighting or attack'.[55]

Meanwhile, the neuropathologist Frederick Mott distinguished different kinds of shock, identifying various environmental, social and neurological causes. A soldier's exposure to high explosives and trench warfare were clearly key factors. Men were traumatised by the privations and violence they had experienced at the front, which was expressed as 'a dread of impending death or of being blown up by a mine and buried alive'.[56] Aside from extrinsic physical triggers, Mott argued that there were other factors, including the pre-existing state of a soldier's nervous system and his inherited neuropathy, that might predispose him to shock. Dealing with fear was central to any treatment. 'Fear, in its depressive effects upon the mind and body, plays a very important part in the production of a hysteric or neurasthenic condition,' Mott wrote. At the Maudsley Hospital in London, which he was instrumental in founding, he experimented with a range of treatments to deal with these different causal factors. The 'mental hygiene' rubric included giving patients warm baths 'with a drink of warm milk at bedtime', and ensuring they had 'quiet and unstimulating diversions of the mind' – although in 'severe cases, the noise of gramophones, pianos, the click of billiard balls, and even musical instruments, excite and aggravate symptoms'.[57] In this 'atmosphere of cure', patients could overcome their illness by resting and pursuing leisurely activities, including gardening.[58]

While clinicians may have held different views on what shock was and how it ought to be treated, the stakes for military physicians were high. In addition to the issue of manpower wastage, there were financial implications. If shell shock could be attributed to combat, the state would have to compensate veterans; if not, it was off the hook. On top of this, there was the moral quandary. Medical personnel were responsible for deciding whether wounded soldiers were well enough to remain at the front, whether they ought to be admitted to a hospital or whether they should be invalided out of the army. Inevitably, unmasking imposters was also part of their job.

'Malingering as shell shock is quite common at the front,' Mott conceded, noting that detection was difficult because the symptoms of the condition could easily 'be mistaken for malingering'.[59] Rivers clearly wrestled with the predicament of being both a physician and an officer; his job wasn't just to treat the wounded but also to make sure the men under his care could resume active service as soon as possible. He was also conscious of the internal struggle in his patients between duty and fear. In his book *Conflict and Dream* he describes the case of a suicidal Canadian officer torn between recognition that the war must go on and 'deeper feelings' of the horrors that awaited him there.[60] As a 1922 War Office report into shell shock noted, the challenge for the military was in determining whether a soldier 'has or has not crossed that indefinite line which divides normal emotional reaction from neurosis with impairment of volitional control'.[61]

The report advocated dispensing with the term 'shell shock', since it was too vague to be useful. Among its recommendations, it stressed the imperative of training to promote a military 'morale, esprit de corps and a high standard of discipline', which would act as a corrective to cowardice in those who were unable to exercise self-control. It also emphasised the importance of weeding out through a screening process those with 'abnormalities from which mental or nervous instability may be inferred', as well as recruits who were using sickness as an excuse to shirk duty. The report was categorical that 'no soldier should be allowed to think that loss of nervous or mental control provides an honourable avenue of escape from the battlefield'.[62]

Shell shock added to the logistical problems faced by the medical services, who were swamped by wounded soldiers, but it also gave impetus to the development of a bureaucratic system to manage medical staff and patients efficiently.[63] Progressively, shell shock was understood in relation to the alienating and dehumanising effects of industrial warfare and became the focus of a vocal anti-war literature. When Jean Dartemont, the protagonist of Chevallier's novel *Fear*, is admitted to hospital after being peppered by shrapnel from a grenade, he finds himself in a bed next to a soldier with a suppurating gash criss-crossed by so many drainage tubes that he resembles a piece of machinery. Dartemont begins to see the war as a perverse system of production that devours the humanity it claims to serve; 'suddenly there before us lay the front line, roaring with all its mouths of fire, blazing like some infernal factory where monstrous crucibles melted human flesh into a bloody lava'.[64]

It hadn't always been so. Social transformation wrought by nineteenth-century industrialisation may have given rise to anxiety about living in a dehumanising technocracy, but before the war there were many who championed industrial development. Futurist artists in Italy exalted the energy, power and speed of the 'Machine Age', which were enhancing human capacities to the extent that it was possible to speak of a 'renovated consciousness', as the painter and sculptor Umberto Boccioni put it.[65] In 1909 the poet Filippo Tommaso Marinetti provocatively claimed in his 'Futurist Manifesto' that the motor car was 'more beautiful than the Winged Victory of Samothrace', a famous statue of Nike, the Greek goddess of victory, in the Louvre. Artists such as Carlo Carrà, Gino Severini and Giacomo Balla signed up to the cause, producing work that depicted humans merging with machines in a celebration of what Marinetti called a 'nonhuman, mechanical species of extended man'.[66] Tanks, aeroplanes and battleships were acclaimed as manifestations of a new industrial power, fearless heralds of a 'Machine Kingdom' that would shatter the status quo and allow for the regeneration of a stronger, energised nation.[67]

Many of the Futurists enthusiastically signed up to fight as soon as war broke out. Marinetti, who fought in the campaign against Austria-Hungary on the Isonzo front, wrote of 'the shame of being fearful' and continued to celebrate war as an expression of the new industrial spirit, although as the art critic Lucia Re has noted, this may have been an attempt 'to suppress the opposite, all-too-real experience of war'.[68] 'Disorder panic,'

Marinetti records in his diary. 'Injured and sick hastily cleared out. Stretchers. Injured. Cries of Terror. Wagons. Ambulances. Buzzing airplanes.'[69]

After the mass destruction of the war, the euphoric man-as-machine credo was no longer possible. Instead, we get visions of human monster machines by the German artists George Grosz and Otto Dix, with patched eyes and truncated limbs strapped to crude prostheses – a ghastly antithesis to the Futurists' celebration of machines. The French cultural historian and theorist Paul Virilio has even suggested a link between the carnage of the Great War and the violence that's implicit in 'pitiless' twentieth-century avant-garde art, where human forms are progressively disassembled before disappearing into abstraction.[70]

Dix, who had served in a machine-gun unit, was haunted by his wartime experience. In the print *Stormtroopers Advancing under a Gas Attack*, part of a series of engravings published in 1924, a group of soldiers in gas masks looms out of the mist. While technology has enlarged the scope of violence, it has diminished the role of human beings. In this wasteland of barbed wire, soldiers are simultaneously victims and faceless monster-automata.

Revulsion at the bloodbath of the war led to an efflorescence of horror movies in the 1920s and 1930s. Many of the pioneers of German expressionist cinema had first-hand experience of combat, and many horror motifs that have now become clichés – vengeful revenants, monsters, animated dolls and the like – can trace their roots back to the First World War. Often war reports and descriptions of the front in letters, diaries and memoirs sound like stories from a horror repertoire. Take the rumour that circulated in September 1914, after the Battle of the Marne, that dead men had been discovered 'standing in the trenches, apparently in possession of their faculties'.[71] Or C. S. Lewis's account of 'sitting or standing corpses' and 'horribly smashed men still moving like half-crushed beetles'. 'In every horror movie we see, every horror story we read, every horror-based video game we play,' writes the film historian W. Scott Poole, 'the phantoms of the Great War skittle and scratch just beyond the door of our consciousness.'[72]

The writer Hans Janowitz, who co-wrote the script of the trailblazing 1920 silent horror film *The Cabinet of Dr Caligari*, had fought in the war, an experience that made him a pacifist. Told as a series of flashbacks, the narrative centres on an evil hypnotist who manipulates a somnambulist to commit brutal murders. It's hard not to read the plot as an allegory of Europe sleepwalking to slaughter in 1914.

F. W. Murnau's 1922 masterpiece *Nosferatu: A Symphony of Horror* is another film where characters are gripped by fear, but this time the plot is a clear retelling of Bram Stoker's *Dracula*. Horror in the film bears a striking resemblance to the crepuscular world of the trenches. The swarming rats that bring the plague to Germany recall the pests that invade and infest the trenches – those repulsive 'corpse-rats', as they're called in *All Quiet on the Western Front*, with their 'shocking, evil, naked faces'. Another motif is that of the fog that rolls in off the ocean, evoking the mist and poison gas that shroud the front. The ominous image of a deathly mist is a classic index of horror to come: 'Only the mist is cold, this mysterious mist that trails the dead before us and sucks from them their last, creeping life.'[73]

11

Death Camps and Dictators

In October 2018 the House of History, a museum in Bonn, staged an exhibition entitled *Fear: A German State of Mind?* Its immediate inspiration had been the fear sparked by the influx of nearly a million refugees into Germany in 2015 and the panic triggered by reports of attacks on German women by young 'Arab' and 'North African' men in Cologne and other cities. Aside from immigration, the exhibition dealt with collective German fears of nuclear war, the destruction of forests and the threat posed by encroaching surveillance.

While the show spanned some six decades, the curators suggested a more expansive historical context to this *angst*, raising the question: is any discussion of contemporary fear possible without addressing Nazi terror and the horrors of the Holocaust?[1] The sexual assault of German women allegedly by Moroccan and Algerian men on New Year's Eve in 2015, for example, was presented in some media as an instance of German *Wehrlosigkeit*, or 'defencelessness', with online commentary attributing German docility to a disavowal of a Nazi past associated with 'violence, aggression, genocide, and biological racism'.[2]

One striking exhibit was a large photographic installation by the photographer Gerhard Vormwald that depicted a group of naked men and women with barcodes etched across their shaven heads. The work was originally produced in 1983 in protest at a proposed census in West Germany that gave rise to fears of Big Brother-style surveillance, but it also called forth a darker history – a message reinforced by the title, *Wider die Totalerfassung*, 'Against Total Control'.

Worries about the ethics of data privacy in Germany stem from the grim uses of compulsory registration during the Third Reich. Information recorded on Nazi censuses ensured that Jews and other 'undesirables' could be easily tracked, incarcerated and ultimately exterminated.[3] International corporations were complicit in this coercion. The Hollerith punch-card machines that were manufactured by IBM, for example, were used in the administration of the Holocaust. After the war, the Allies overlooked this collusion since the machines' data-processing capacity was convenient in their post-war occupation of Germany.[4]

While Nazi surveillance helped to cultivate fear among German citizens, *angst* soon took on a life of its own. The playwright and poet Bertolt Brecht, who fled Germany in February 1933, was an insightful analyst of this fear. In his 1937 poem 'The Fears of the Regime' a traveller returns from a trip to Germany and is asked who's in charge there, to which he replies with one word: 'Fear'. It infects the whole of society, from academics and teachers to doctors, parents and even the dying, who 'lower their failing voices' because they're scared.[5]

Brecht's anti-Fascist play *Fear and Misery of the Third Reich*, which premiered in Paris in 1938, consists of twenty-four scenes of life under the Nazis that explore different facets of this fear. Rather than focus on the top-brass purveyors of terror, Brecht shows us fear as it manifests itself in everyday situations: inside a courtroom, a hospital ward, a town square, a factory, a farmyard and in private residences – although we're also given glimpses of life inside concentration camps. While individuals get caught up in bureaucratic processes, it's the mundane choices they make that ultimately determine their fate.

We're not talking here about the chilling, edge-of-your-seat scare that a horror film might produce; this is an altogether more prosaic and pettier emotional world where doubt, mistrust and betrayal lead to conflict between husbands and wives, parents and children, neighbours and colleagues. Seemingly trifling and misplaced fears get magnified until they overwhelm relationships and produce misunderstandings that accumulate into a bigger, more consequential fear. It's precisely because terror emerges from this jostling, everyday space of mutually reinforcing *angst* that it's so difficult to manage.

Fear of persecution by the German state's security agencies was only one aspect of the story, then, though an important one. Founded by Hitler in 1925, the SS, or 'Protection Squad', developed into a powerful police and military institution, vested with the authority to root out the state's enemies. Under the leadership of Heinrich Himmler, it oversaw the concentration camps and coordinated the systematic murder of Jews from 1941, a genocide referred to euphemistically by the Nazis as 'The Final Solution of the Jewish Question'. The SD, the 'Security Service', and the Gestapo, the 'Secret State Police', were other vehicles of terror that were officially merged in a new central security office after the invasion of Poland in 1939. These agencies worked through a network of uniformed and undercover agents and informants; citizens could be arrested and detained at any moment.[6]

In Brecht's docudrama, however, fear isn't confined to the persecuted; it also grips the persecutors. The same is true in his poem 'The Fears of the Regime', where the Nazis themselves, despite their use of brute force and access to the paraphernalia of power, are still

> Driven by fear
> They break into homes and search through the bathrooms
> And it is fear
> That drives them to burn whole libraries. So
> Fear holds sway not only over those who are ruled, but also
> Over those who rule.[7]

Similarly, in the opening scene of *Fear and Misery of the Third Reich*, set on 30 January 1933, the day that Hitler became chancellor, two dazed SS officers are anything but celebratory. They're jumpy and suspicious as they patrol the city, as if their ascension has set them up for a fall. When they wander into an unfamiliar neighbourhood, the soldiers' fear intensifies until one of them begins to fire indiscriminately for no apparent reason, hitting an innocent bystander. The suggestion is that power breeds paranoia and for all their arrogant swagger, the Nazis are deeply insecure.[8]

It's this veiled but explosive fear, nestled within the outward appearance of strength, that Winston Churchill identified when he observed of the Nazis,

> On all sides they are guarded by masses of armed men, cannons, aeroplanes, fortifications, and the like – they boast and vaunt themselves before the world, yet in their hearts there is unspoken fear. They are afraid of words and thoughts; words spoken abroad, thoughts stirring at home – all the more powerful because forbidden – terrify them.[9]

In Brecht's play, unfounded fears become self-fulfilling prophecies. In a scene entitled 'A Case of Betrayal' a man denounces his neighbour simply because he hears foreign broadcasts coming from the man's apartment. In 'The Spy' a boy's parents are mistakenly convinced that he's betrayed them when he goes out to buy some chocolate; it's fear rather than treachery that destroys the family. In 'Release' a prisoner is discharged from a concentration camp but returns home to find that his friends and neighbours no longer trust him, suspecting that he may be working as an informer. Fear corrodes community, exploiting uncertainty and sowing discord. Its intractable power lies in the way that it acquires a life of its own, insinuating itself into everyday social interactions and conjuring imaginary threats. As the Russian-American poet Joseph Brodsky once remarked,

'Tragedy, as you know, is always a fait accompli, whereas terror always has to do with anticipation.'[10] It was through the anticipation of terror that totalitarian fear gained its force.

Where did these German fears come from? Hitler and his henchmen traded on public disillusion in the aftermath of the First World War; craving security at a time of political and economic uncertainty, people turned to extremist parties. According to the legal theorist and political philosopher Carl Schmitt – a Nazi sympathiser – Germany in the 1920s was experiencing a 'parliamentary crisis' that resulted from 'the inescapable contradiction of liberal individualism and democratic homogeneity'. Individualism was in the end incompatible with equality, which in any case was a deception – it was clear that party politics was based on horse-trading and backroom handshakes. Politics hinged on the fundamental distinction between 'us and them', despite liberal cosmopolitan claims to the contrary. What was needed, according to Schmitt, was a strong leader to cut through the quagmire of red tape, pacify 'internal antagonisms' and give voice to the people's fears.[11]

A febrile fear, verging on paranoia, is apparent in the post-war work of German artists such as Dix, Grosz and Max Beckmann. In Beckmann's 1919 print series *Hell* we're presented with scenes of chaos and wanton violence. In Dix's *Prague Street* two amputees are shown begging on one of Dresden's main shopping streets. A gloved hand drops a paltry 5-pfennig stamp into one of the beggars' outstretched hands as pedestrians shuffle past, unmoved by these wretched scroungers. A beggar with no legs, precariously perched on a makeshift trolley, clings to a pamphlet with the headline 'JEWS OUT!'

These art works show a society starkly divided between the haves and the have-nots, a society so brutalised that human relations have all but broken down. The ex-soldiers, relics of the horrors of the trenches and now cast aside like rubbish, are emblems of a society that has lost its moral bearings. Fear seems to provide the only way out.

The *angst* of social breakdown is one explanation for Hitler's rise to power. Fear was entwined with a sense of victimhood that was born from Germany's defeat in the First World War and the punitive terms imposed at the Treaty of Versailles – relinquishing territory, paying hefty reparations and demilitarising – followed immediately by political and economic turmoil. Like Dix's veterans, Germany had been dismembered – politically, economically and territorially.

The Nazis used this story of national humiliation to justify their tub-thumping revanchist policies and to stoke popular fears about Germany's pending annihilation. As the historian Peter Fritzsche writes, the rise of the Third Reich was 'premised on both supreme confidence and terrifying vulnerability; both states of mind co-existed and continuously radicalized Nazi policies'.[12] Their violence was, in a sense, pre-emptive; like Brodsky's anticipatory fear, it summoned its objects as a precondition for their obliteration.

Claims of a Jewish world conspiracy were used to fuel paranoia and panic. This form of terror wasn't just used to silence political adversaries; it also functioned as a way of bringing the masses to heel. The scapegoating of public enemies coexisted with an 'ecological panic' set off by fear of a global food shortage, which the Nazis exploited to justify German expansion.[13] The concentration camps existed as components of a larger political system in which fear and discriminatory panic played key roles. And this all worked within the fears that drove, and were produced by, war. Although the people might not want war, they could 'always be brought to the bidding of the leaders,' the Nazi Luftwaffe commander Hermann Göring told the American psychologist Gustave Gilbert at his Nuremberg trial in 1946. 'All you have to do is tell them they are being attacked and denounce the pacifists for lack of patriotism and exposing the country to danger. It works the same way in any country.'[14]

*

It wasn't only in Germany that fear was unleashed in the 1920s and 1930s. Two revolutions in Russia in 1917 were followed by the abolition of the monarchy, a civil war and the establishment of the USSR in December 1922. Within a year Lenin had died after suffering a series of strokes, precipitating a struggle among the Bolshevik Party leadership that brought Joseph Stalin to power.

Political manipulation and terror were crucial to Stalin's ascent, and to the consolidation of his authority through the elimination of rivals. In his memoirs Nikita Khrushchev, Stalin's successor, wrote that anyone who fell out with Stalin was considered an 'enemy of the people'. 'Everyone lived in fear in those days,' he wrote. 'Everyone expected that at any moment there would be a knock on the door in the middle of the night and that knock on the door would prove fatal.'[15] Fear permeated Soviet society to a far greater degree than it did in Germany under Hitler – unless, that is, you were a designated public enemy such as a Jew, communist, gay person, gypsy, Pole or member of some other offending community.[16] Looking back at these years, the Russian poet Yevgeny Yevtushenko remembered how 'fears slithered everywhere, like shadows'.[17]

Despite Khrushchev's claims, Stalin wasn't solely responsible for the 'Great Terror' that purged the Party of dissenters in the 1930s. It may have been a ruthless strategy to consolidate his grip on power, but this terror had a prehistory.[18] Documents released after the collapse of the USSR in 1991 reveal the extent to which Stalin was reliant on others among his leadership clique for the formulation and implementation of policy. This isn't in any way to diminish his central role, which was reinforced by an unrelenting propaganda machine that promoted him as the charismatic leader, the father of the nation adulated in paintings, posters, statues and eulogistic poems.[19] Buoyed by this cult of personality, he lived up to the name he'd adopted as a young revolutionary – the word *stal* being Russian for 'steel'.[20] Gruff and pockmarked, with 'thick fingers, fat like worms', as the poet Osip Mandelstam wrote in 1933 in a satirical poem that would cost him his life, Stalin was 'Genghis Khan with a telephone', in the words of the Bolshevik revolutionary Nikolai Bukharin. He was a leader who found his role models in the tyrants of the past, including the first tsar of Russia, Ivan the Terrible.[21] We still have the lists of individuals marked for execution with Stalin's initials scribbled in red pencil, together with his annotations, crossings out and underlinings, as if violence was no more than a bureaucratic chore: the epitome of what Hannah Arendt would controversially call 'the fearsome, word-and-thought-defying banality of evil'.[22]

After Stalin's death, attributing atrocities to his psychopathy became a convenient way for the Soviet elite to distance itself from the violence in which it was implicated. When Khrushchev was appointed general secretary of the USSR in 1956 and denounced Stalin's regime of terror, he did so as a means of self-exoneration.[23] In his magnum opus *The Gulag Archipelago*, written between 1958 and 1968, the dissident writer Aleksandr Solzhenitsyn maintained that the vast prison system that developed under Stalin known as the 'Gulag' – an acronym far more evocative than the nondescript designation 'Main Camp Administration' – was Lenin's legacy, rather than Stalin's invention.[24] After all, a 1918 decree had called for the incarceration of 'class enemies' in concentration camps, and Solovetsky, the first corrective labour camp, had been established in 1923. Fear and violence were the twinned instruments of revolution from the outset, with earlier antecedents in the forced labour brigades of tsarist Russia.[25]

Still, fear was central to Stalin's rule and stemmed from an awareness that the achievements of the Bolshevik Revolution could at any moment be reversed or cancelled by counter-Revolutionary reactions. A sensitivity to threats led to distrust, suspicion and often hysterical overreaction. Even the threats that *were* real were inflated, and this paranoia expressed itself in Stalin's phobias: his aversion to flying, for example, and his fear of being poisoned. Meanwhile, fears of domestic sabotage intersected with worries about external threats posed to the USSR by the rise of the National Socialists in Germany and an expansionist Japanese Empire that menaced Soviet territory in the Far East.

From 1929 Stalin initiated a process of enforced collectivisation to transform agriculture and increase productivity by replacing traditional farms with large state-owned enterprises. This was part of an ambitious five-year plan that included a drive to modernise and expand industry. Impossibly ambitious production targets were set, and all of this played out against a background of near-hysteria in the face of the fear of invasion and disruption by reactionary elements within the country. 'Is it not clear that as long as capitalist encirclement lasts,' Stalin remarked, 'there will continue to exist among us wreckers, spies, saboteurs, and murderers, sent into our hinterland by the agents of foreign states?'[26] While propaganda posters acclaimed the strengths and heroism of the Soviet people, they also conjured up a shadow world of bogeymen waiting to sabotage the nation's glorious future: rapacious capitalists, conniving monarchists, disgruntled Mensheviks, along with a host of other degenerates.

The prosperous landowning peasants, or *kulaks*, were viewed as 'class enemies' who might be susceptible to manipulation by these foreign-backed interests. As such, in the grim parlance of mass-managed violence, the USSR was *dekulakized*.[27] A shortage of labour, along with the social and economic upheaval brought about by collectivisation and industrialisation, inevitably put pressure on food supplies. A devastating famine between 1932 and 1933 killed at least 5 million people, with grain-producing regions such as Ukraine the hardest hit. Some historians have suggested that the Soviet state viewed the disaster as an opportunity to destroy the Ukrainian peasantry. During the *Holodomor* – Ukrainian for 'death by hunger' – Communist Party activists confiscated all available food and the republic's borders were closed; peasants were forced to forage off the land, eating boiled grass and tree bark, frogs, rats, cats and dogs, and in some cases resorting to cannibalism. An estimated 4 million people died in Ukraine alone.[28]

Following the famine, the regime increased its efforts to eliminate opposition. Between 1936 and 1938 a million citizens were killed and many more who were regarded as traitors – labelled 'scum', 'filth' and 'vermin' – were dispatched to the Gulag. Using the assassination of a Leningrad Party official as a pretext, the ranks of the Communist Party and the Red Army were purged in a campaign spearheaded by the dreaded secret police, the infamous NKVD, or People's Commissariat for Internal Affairs, overseen by Genrikh Yagoda and later by Lavrentiy Beria, Stalin's faithful lieutenant.

The hunt began for a fifth column of spies and wreckers who, as Stalin saw it, were waiting for the moment to strike.[29] A series of show trials were held, in which prominent Revolutionaries were found guilty of reactionary plots and summarily executed in a 'bacchanalia of repression'.[30] Leon Trotsky, who had fled the Soviet Union in 1929, was tried and found guilty in absentia; a decade later he was tracked down and murdered in Mexico. But it wasn't just the political elite who were targeted. In July 1937 the Politburo signed off an order that instigated a crackdown on 'anti-Soviet elements who undermine the foundations of the Soviet state'. By the end of the operation in 1938 some 767,000 people had been arrested, with 386,798 of them executed.[31]

The Gulag, a vast system of prisons that stretched across the Soviet Union, was designed with several purposes, the first being to sustain fear. In 1939 the Belarus-born Jewish writer Julius Margolin was arrested by the NKVD and sentenced to five years' forced labour. In 1940 he was sent to a camp on the northern shore of Lake Onega, where prisoners provided the labour for the construction of the White Sea–Baltic Canal. On his release in 1945 he published an account of his experiences. 'My attitude toward the Soviet regime now is completely defined: fear,' he wrote. 'Until I arrived in this country, I did not really fear people. Soviet Russia taught me to fear man.'[32]

The Polish writer Gustaw Herling, arrested in Soviet-occupied Poland in 1940 and sentenced to two years' hard labour, describes the pervasive fear among the prisoners in the camp and how fear of death, which could strike at any time, was 'transformed into the fear of night'. 'Like a phantom ship pursued by death,' he writes, 'our barrack floated out into the moonless sea of darkness, carrying in its hold the sleeping crew of galley slaves.'[33]

Solzhenitsyn, having been sentenced to eight years in the camps for 'anti-Soviet agitation and propaganda', spent three years in northern Kazakhstan, working first as a bricklayer and then in a machine shop. These were experiences that he drew on in his novel *One Day in the Life of Ivan Denisovich*, which tells the story of a man falsely accused of being a German spy and condemned to ten years' hard labour. In *The Gulag Archipelago*, Solzhenitsyn described the USSR as a country meshed by terror networks. Prisons and transit centres were the conspicuous parts of a system that operated through the covert activities of informers, spies, secret police and interrogators. In the Gulag, prisoners were recruited to be guards, becoming jailmasters in the institutions that repressed them. The publication of the book may have shone a light on Soviet oppression, but under Leonid Brezhnev, who took over from Khrushchev in 1964, Solzhenitsyn was persecuted and eventually exiled. Soviet authorities, the writer once remarked, showed an 'animal fear of exposure'.[34]

From 1929 the original Gulag system was extended, with the NKVD eventually taking charge when it merged with the OGPU, or Joint State Political Directorate, in 1934. While many knew of the Gulag's existence, the state kept a lid on its scale. Half-knowledge created a climate of uncertainty, meaning that citizens lived with an ever-present worry of being denounced and arrested. Fear was perpetuated by stories about the harshness

Graffiti on a bridge outside the Hong Kong Polytechnic University, 23 November 2019

Pieter Bruegel the Elder, *The Triumph of Death* (1562–3)

Francisco José de Goya y Lucientes, *Saturn Devouring His Son* (from *The Black Paintings*) (1820–3)

Sebastião Salgado, *The Gold Mine, Brazil* from the *Serra Pelada* series (1986)

Edvard Munch, *The Scream* (1893)

Train crash at the Gare Montparnasse, Paris, October 1895

Otto Dix, *Shock Troopers Advance Under Gas*, etching and aquatint from *The War* (*Der Krieg*), published in Berlin in 1924 by Karl Nierendorf

The Enemies of the Five Year Plan, 1929

Shoes of victims of Auschwitz

George Tooker, *Subway* (1950)

Cover art of *Atomic War!* #1 (November 1952)

of camp life that seeped out via correspondence from inmates, or those lucky enough to make it home.

This dynamic of hearsay and half-truths created a society of informers, just as it did in China during the Cultural Revolution. Denouncing your neighbour as a saboteur was encouraged and might be enough to save your skin or at least buy you time. Some citizens used accusations 'to settle scores, get rid of annoying neighbors sharing the same communal apartment, or eliminate those competing for the same job'.[35] The writer Anatoli Rybakov captures this atmosphere of paranoia in his novel *Fear*, which begins in 1934 as Stalin's purges are commencing and tells the story of a young engineer, Sasha Pankratov, who like Rybakov himself has been exiled to Siberia on trumped-up charges of counter-Revolutionary activity. Stalin appears as a protagonist in the book and in one scene he reflects on the nature of terror. Taking issue with Engels's claim that terror is a policy of 'useless cruelties' espoused by those who are afraid, Stalin cites with approval the words of the Marxist Revolutionary Georgi Plekhanov, who, inspired by the French Revolution, had declared that terror 'is a system of actions, the goal of which is to frighten a political enemy, to spread horror in his ranks'.[36] But terror, at least as it figures in Rybakov's novel, isn't only state policy, it's also a psychological state – albeit one perpetuated by state institutions.[37]

Hannah Arendt, who escaped from an internment camp in south-east France in 1940, argued that totalitarianism was distinguished from other forms of autocracy by its emphasis on 'dominating and terrorizing human beings from within'. The aim was no longer to neutralise political opponents but to monopolise every aspect of the individual's intellectual and emotional life. Alienation, which Arendt calls 'loneliness', provided fertile ground for totalitarian leaders to exploit. Nurturing suspicion and self-doubt created a dependency on the ideology of the state.[38]

In his novel *Life and Fate*, set during the siege of Stalingrad in 1941, the Russian-Jewish writer Vasily Grossman noted that fear could be overcome. For example, 'children pluck up their courage and enter a dark room, soldiers go into battle, a young man can leap into an abyss with only a parachute to save him'. 'But what about this other fear,' he asks, 'this fear that millions of people find insuperable, this fear written up in crimson letters over the leaden sky of Moscow, this terrible fear of the State?' Grossman's novel is in many ways an exploration of these conflicting, overlapping and converging fears. One character lives in fear 'that he might be dragged back into the world of the camps, the world of hunger', while another feels a fear 'always lurking in his heart – fear of the State's anger, fear of being a victim of this anger that could crush a man and grind him to dust'. As the narrator puts it, this is a story about the 'fear of living in fear'.[39]

Far from being a well-conceived, centrally directed policy, fear in the Soviet Union was often produced by arbitrary, haphazard processes. It infused the elite as well as the rank-and-file, and it spread out into Soviet society as citizens began to anticipate and internalise the repressive apparatuses of the system they were part of. 'Party terror,' writes the historian Igal Halfin, 'was the result of a never-ending interrogation of the self.'[40] The poet Anna Akhmatova, whose husband and son were sent to the Gulag, began writing her 1935 poem 'Requiem' as an elegy to those who had been imprisoned. Fearful that the authorities would discover the poem, she asked her friends to help her memorise the lines, as if the world had returned to a 'pre-Gutenberg' age.[41] Grossman wondered why, having so thoroughly crushed freedom, Stalin continued to be afraid of it.[42]

Aside from its function as an instrument of fear, the Gulag was justified on the grounds that it performed a vital economic role, providing labour for state enterprises, often in remote regions where free labour was impossible to find. Convicts, or *zeks*, built railroads and factories, and worked in manufacturing, lumber operations and mining, with strict production targets determined by the state.[43] Of course, this was also true in other camp systems, including the internment camps managed by the Japanese imperial army from the 1930s and during the Second World War, where military and civilian prisoners were set to work on construction projects, in mines, fields and factories, including those run by some of the biggest Japanese corporations. Similarly, the *laogai* system established in China after 1949 involved the use of prison labour on state farms and in a network of industrial operations across the country, including coal mines and textile factories.[44] In Germany there were both concentration camps and death camps. Auschwitz shifted from one function to the other, but it was also conceived by Himmler as a centre for agriculture and manufacturing to support the war effort, with the slogan *Arbeit Macht Frei* ('Work Brings Freedom') illuminated above the camp's entrance.[45]

The Soviet carceral system, however, was on a whole other scale of 'terror by quota' and was central to Stalin's economic model of state-operated industry.[46] The Kolyma region in Siberia came to symbolise the Gulag system, with remote towns built around camps where prisoners dug for coal, tin, uranium and gold. The Russian journalist and blogger Yuri Dud's 2019 documentary *Kolyma: Birthplace of Our Fear* explores the legacy of the Gulag in this remote part of Russia, where the temperature can drop below −50 °C. At the Butugychag Corrective Labour Camp in 'Death Valley' convicts were forced to mine uranium ore without protective gear, and inmates were allegedly experimented on in a secret medical research facility. And yet, according to a 2018 survey, almost half of young people in Russia aged between eighteen and twenty-four had no idea about Stalin's repressions.

Today the term 'Gulag' stands for more than the name of a Soviet institution; it represents a system of rule by terror of the kind that Orwell described in his satirical 1945 novella *Animal Farm*, where an idealistic animal revolution unravels into tyranny. Although Orwell himself intended the work as a critique of the 'Soviet myth' and after his death the film rights were bought by the CIA to promote anti-Soviet propaganda, the book spoke to the danger of totalitarianism wherever it might be.[47]

In contrast, 'concentration camp' has become a shorthand for the terror of the Nazi regime, even though it was also used to describe the Spanish detention centres built in Cuba in the 1890s and the camps constructed by the British for Boer prisoners of war in South Africa in 1900. In June 2019 US congresswoman Alexandria Ocasio-Cortez announced on her Instagram page that Donald Trump's administration was 'running concentration camps on our southern border'. In summoning the ghost of the Holocaust, she provoked a strong reaction from those who questioned the equivalence between US detention centres for undocumented immigrants and a comprehensive system of state terror that killed 6 million Jews. Ocasio-Cortez later tweeted the link to an article suggesting that federal detainment facilities, being institutions for the 'mass detention of civilians without trial', met the basic definition of 'concentration camp'.[48] Conversely, the Holocaust survivor Ruth Klüger has cautioned against generalising about the camps and the terror they produced. Of the death camps, she writes, it is 'easier to comprehend if we put them all into the basket of one vast generalization, which the term *death camps* implies, but in the process, we mythologize or trivialize them. Even terror and deprivation are different from case to case.'[49]

The issue of how a 'camp' ought to be defined had come to the fore in the late 1940s. For some, Nazi concentration camps were an historical aberrance, but for others the camp was an integral component of totalitarianism. In France the horrors of the 'Gulag' were denounced by the writer David Rousset. The Soviet camp system, he argued, was on a par with Nazi concentration camps. Rather than distinguishing one from the other, he emphasised the common plight of the victims, arguing that the Nazi camps ought to be viewed as part of a broader dehumanising economic and bureaucratic system that worked through terror. 'Normal people,' he wrote, 'aren't aware that anything is possible.'[50]

Rousset's focus was on concentration camps and prison labour rather than on death camps, and he was drawing on his own experience. Photographs in the archives of the US Holocaust Memorial Museum show him wearing a striped prisoner's uniform and helping to evacuate emaciated inmates from a newly liberated camp, or standing beside American soldiers in a brick outhouse as he shows them naked corpses on the floor. A committed Trotskyist, he'd been active in the French resistance until his capture by the Gestapo in 1943, before being deported to Buchenwald and then to Wöbbelin.[51] After the war he wrote about his experiences in a book, *L'univers concentrationnaire* (translated as *The Concentration Camp Universe*), and in 1949 he pleaded for former inmates to join him in bearing witness to the equivalence between the terror of the concentration camps and the Soviet Gulag system.[52]

When Rousset suggested that the Gulag was the logical consequence of totalitarianism, many pro-Soviet intellectuals demurred. After all, Stalin had helped to defeat Hitler. The journalist Pierre Daix, a fellow camp survivor, accused Rousset of falsifying history, and alleged he was a stooge of the West working to spread anti-Soviet propaganda. Rousset took Daix and his editor to court for defamation in 1951, calling on witnesses who had experienced the Gulag – including Julius Margolin – to testify and denouncing what he called Soviet 'crimes against humanity'. 'The people who justify Soviet camps,' Margolin later wrote, 'are preparing a second edition of Hitler in the world.'[53] Rousset went on to win the case.

In the same year the American Federation of Labor produced a map of the USSR that showed the locations of nearly 200 labour camps that comprised the Gulag system. The '"Gulag" – Slavery, Inc.' map was soon being used as a weapon in the Cold War, reportedly becoming 'one of the most widely circulated pieces of anti-communist literature'.[54]

Whatever position one takes in the argument about the equivalence of the Gulag and German concentration camps, the former tend to be met with relative indifference. It's a discrepancy that struck the historian Anne Applebaum when she noticed crowds of hawkers selling Soviet-era military paraphernalia on the Charles Bridge in Prague. Why, she wondered, were Western tourists who would be appalled at the idea of buying Nazi merchandise happy to snap up Soviet propaganda? Why was it, she asked, that 'while the symbol of one mass murder fills us with horror, the symbol of another mass murder makes us laugh'?[55]

Looking back three-quarters of a century after the event, it's hard to comprehend the terror experienced by the victims of Nazi violence. In December 1943 the twenty-four-year-old Primo Levi was captured by fascist militia in northern Italy and imprisoned in Fossoli di Carpi, a prisoner-of-war camp in Emilia-Romagna. A few weeks later German SS officers ordered that the prisoners be moved to Auschwitz. 'The different emotions that were roused in us,' Levi writes, 'of conscious resignation, of futile rebellion, of religious abandon, of fear, of despair, now, after a sleepless night, converged in a collective, uncontrolled panic.' On their arrival at the camp, the passengers were divided into two groups: those who could be put to work and those who were regarded as superfluous. They were then stripped, shaved and tattooed. Few were to survive. 'Among the forty-five people in my car,' writes Levi, 'only four saw their homes again; and ours was by far the most fortunate.'[56]

Viktor Frankl, who later became a psychiatrist, describes the moment of being on the train and realising they were arriving at Auschwitz, the name itself standing 'for all that was horrible: gas chambers, crematoriums, massacres'. 'My imagination led me to see gallows with people dangling on them,' he writes. 'I was horrified, but this was just as well, because step by step we had to become accustomed to a terrible and immense horror.'[57] For children, Ruth Klüger writes, the terror of the camp was crushing in a way that it wasn't for grown men. After she'd been hauled off the train, gasping for air, she'd wanted to cry but her tears had 'dried up in the palpable creepiness of the place'. Although terror filled her throat like vomit, it had 'a kind of logic to it' – after all, she'd already been stripped of her rights 'piece by piece'.[58]

Many of those who survived the camps later spoke of the panic and loss of rational thinking they had experienced. Frankl observed that while many prisoners initially suffered from a 'delusion of reprieve', they often reacted to the horrors of the camp with compulsive laughter or attempted suicide by running headlong into the electric fences.[59] In a study of 200 victims conducted after the war it was found that, whatever their background, those who had been interned exhibited symptoms of chronic anxiety, the result of constant exposure to fear. Managing their response was crucial to survival. As one former internee put it, 'Fear gave me strength.'[60]

But note the confusion of terms here: fear, terror, horror. Confronted by the scale of this mass killing, words themselves are inadequate. Margolin noticed that in the Gulag the meaning of words seemed to change; 'they say the words: man, culture, home, work, radio, dinner, cutlet, but not one of these words means what it normally signifies in freedom.'[61] When he wrote about his experiences in his book *If This Is a Man*, published in 1947, Levi commented on the failure of language to grasp what he experienced. 'We say "hunger", we say "tiredness", "fear", "pain", we say "winter" and they are different things,' he observed. 'They are free words, created and used by free men who lived in comfort and suffering in their homes. If the Lagers [camps] had lasted longer a new, harsh language would have been born.'[62] Elsewhere, he reflected on how the moral content of words such as 'good' and 'evil', 'just' and 'unjust', die inside a world of barbed wire.

In 1975 Levi published a collection of twenty-one autobiographical short stories – each named after a chemical element

– that dealt, in part, with his time in the camp. *The Periodic Table* was a way of bringing order to his experience of a system that not only crushed people but also destroyed the semantic and expressive capacities of language.

At the end of his account of life in Auschwitz, Frankl remarks that there comes a time in the life of the liberated prisoner 'when all his camp experiences seem to him nothing but a nightmare'. 'The crowning experience of all, for the homecoming man,' he writes, 'is the wonderful feeling that, after all he has suffered, there is nothing he need fear any more – except his God.'[63] But Levi's fear never went away. In a short story contained in *The Periodic Table* entitled 'Vanadium', he describes an experience he had working as a chemist in Italy in the 1960s. One day the factory received a shipment of resin that was used in varnishes, but it wouldn't dry. When Levi contacted the German company about the faulty product, he discovered that his counterpart, a Dr L. Müller, had the same name as one of the German supervisors of the lab where he'd worked in Auschwitz. Could it be the same person? When he wrote to ask, a reply came back from Müller acknowledging that he was indeed the same individual. A brief correspondence ensued in which Müller attempted to justify his life and implored Levi to meet him. 'About the "hoped-for meeting" I said nothing,' Levi writes, 'because I was afraid of it. No point in having recourse to euphemisms, to talk about shyness, disgust, reticence. Fear was the word.' This was fear of what might be said, of the memories it would bring back, and of meeting somebody who had been, after all, his 'captor'. But Müller caught him unawares with a phone call and, flustered, Levi agreed to a rendezvous on the Italian Riviera. Eight days later, however, he received a message from Dr Müller's wife, informing him of her husband's unexpected death at the age of sixty.[64]

If there's a moral to this tale, it is that fear doesn't easily harden into indifference; like the defective resin that triggers the exchange and reawakens memories of the camp, fear sticks to the lives of those it affects. We read this story with the knowledge that in April 1987 Levi fell to his death from his third-storey apartment in Turin at the age of sixty-seven, an episode that the coroner ruled as suicide. Whether or not that was the case, the Holocaust survivor and activist Elie Wiesel was surely right when he wrote at the time, 'Primo Levi died at Auschwitz forty years later.'[65]

Given the extent of the violence and the numbers murdered, the terror of the Holocaust can all too easily slip into abstraction. Arendt suggested that it marked a point 'in the final stages of totalitarianism' where 'an absolute evil appears (absolute because it can no longer be deduced from humanly comprehensible motives)'.[66] 'From the Rhine to the Oder I took no pictures,' the photographer Robert Capa confided in his 1947 memoir of the Second World War. 'The concentration camps were swarming with photographers, and every new picture of horror served only to diminish the total effect.'[67] Capa here raises the question of how we represent this scale of horror, let alone comprehend it. As Adorno was to put it in 1951, 'To write poetry after Auschwitz is barbaric.'[68]

In *If This Is a Man*, Levi ditches the question of meaning to focus on the details of camp life. Surrounded by mass executions and faced with the prospect of his own extinction, the only thing to do is fix on the mundane – it is through the small, apparently incidental objects and events in this bare existence that restorative meaning might ultimately be found, like the shoes which prisoners are forced to remove carefully in case they are stolen. 'Someone comes with a broom and sweeps away all the shoes,' Levi writes, 'sweeps them out the door in a heap. He's crazy, he's throwing them all together, ninety-six pairs, they'll be unmatched.' Later he observes, 'And do not think that shoes constitute a factor of secondary importance in the life of the Lager. Death begins with the shoes; for most of us, they prove to be instruments of torture, which after a few hours of marching cause painful sores that become fatally infected.'[69]

Among the displays at the Auschwitz Museum is a mound of prisoners' shoes. Forty cubic metres of anonymous footwear remind us of the lives subsumed within the horror. The shoes bring us closer to those who perished in this place than the photos of the dead massed in pits. They belong to an inventory of objects either taken from prisoners or used against them, such as empty cans of lethal Zyklon B poison gas pellets. Aside from the shoes, the museum houses clothes, prayer shawls, prosthetic limbs, pots and pans, suitcases and human hair shaved from the heads of those sent to the gas chambers. This isn't just Nazi loot or the display of twisted power – many of these personal effects were used in a barter economy.[70] As the Polish writer Tadeusz Borowski shows us in his Auschwitz stories, for those who weren't immediately killed in the crematoria – after the money, gold and diamonds had been extracted from them – life in the camp centred on survival and trade-offs for bread, marmalade, sugar, shirts and sturdy shoes.[71] But now, nearly eighty years on, these things are a means of remembrance. And something else happens as we look at the display of shoes in the museum. They seem to be lifted into the realm of fairy tale, where for a brief moment terror is overshadowed by the hope that freedom might still materialise before the stroke of midnight.

12

A Contest of Nightmares

Reflecting on the menace of the atomic bomb in 1945, George Orwell warned of an indefinite 'peace that is no peace'. East and West were now at loggerheads, the world locked in competing geopolitical power blocs. Fear of nuclear annihilation might have 'put an end to large-scale wars', but this would probably lead to a new kind of 'cold war': a struggle for power between 'monstrous super-states' waged through propaganda, covert operations and the promotion of political and economic interests in global spheres of influence.[1]

In 1947 the American journalist and political commentator Walter Lippmann popularised the term 'Cold War' in a book of the same name, where he argued against a US policy of containment against the USSR on the grounds that it would involve backing dubious satellite states and puppet governments in return for their support.[2] The same year the financier and statesman Bernard Baruch expanded the definition of 'Cold War' when he suggested that industrial labour disputes in the United States were serving foreign interests. 'Let us not be deceived, we are today in the midst of a cold war,' he proclaimed. 'Our enemies are to be found abroad and at home. Let us never forget this: Our unrest is the heart of their success.'[3] It was to assuage this fear of agitation that the Taft–Hartley Act came into law in June 1947, restricting the activities of labour unions who were barred from organising wildcat strikes, boycotts and picketing. Union officers were also obliged to sign non-Communist Party affidavits. As the US economy took off in a post-war boom, anticipation of unrest perpetrated by home-grown agitators, vulnerable to manipulation by foreign agents, created new fears and a growing conviction that novel forms of 'psychological warfare' were required to defeat the enemy within.

Cold War fears were to feature prominently in US president Dwight Eisenhower's speeches in the 1950s. In his inaugural address in January 1953 he warned of the 'forces of good and evil' that were 'massed and armed and opposed as rarely before in history'. The atomic bomb presented a new threat – the power to obliterate life on Earth. Dreams of post-war peace were now in jeopardy; as he put it, 'the shadow of fear again has darkly lengthened across the world'.[4]

Eisenhower's fear stemmed from the threat posed by foreign aggression, but he also recognised that new tools were required to meet the propaganda challenge at home. Cold war meant stealth, the ability to influence without being seen – and this was the rationale for the creation of the US Psychological Strategy Board in 1951, four years after the establishment of the CIA. 'Our aim in "cold war" is not the conquest of territory or subjugation by force,' Eisenhower announced. 'The means we shall employ to spread this truth are often called "psychological".'[5]

The American artist George Tooker captured this age of psychological warfare in his 1950 painting *The Subway*. By then, wartime fear had thawed into a murky post-war atmosphere of suspicion and insidious threat. Tooker's claustrophobic urban setting resembles a prison, with its labyrinthine passageways, metal bars and turnstile. Androgynous figures in suits appear trapped in an underground world saturated with violent intent. A man loiters with his hands in his pockets and his back to a white tiled wall, while other characters look over their shoulders – 'harassed', as one reviewer described them in 1955, and 'filled with fear, anxiety or despair'.[6] The estrangement depicted brings to mind the convoluted plot lines of a Hollywood film noir. We're about to witness a crime, or perhaps one is in progress. This is neither the underworld nor an entirely familiar world; it's a place in between, washed with a cold, inquisitorial fluorescence – the territory of the Cold War.

Writing after the Second World War, the writer and philosopher Albert Camus characterised the twentieth century as 'the century of fear' in which people seemed to have lost all faith in the future.[7] Meanwhile, the poet W. H. Auden was working on his long poem *The Age of Anxiety: A Baroque Eclogue*, published in 1947. And in the same year as Tooker painted *The Subway*, Hannah Arendt sought to capture the contradictions of a world that felt torn between 'desperate hope' and 'desperate fear', 'unavoidable doom' and 'reckless optimism'. While European empires were collapsing and former colonies were asserting their independence, democratic regimes were pitted against emergent totalitarian powers. After two world wars, wasn't a third one just a matter of time? There was no prospect now of returning to an old-world order that had been comprehensively shattered. Looking ahead, it was evident to her that 'Progress and Doom are two sides of the same medal'. A sense of humankind's mastery over the world was offset by a sense of disintegration and powerlessness to manage the destructive political forces that had been unleashed. The terror of twentieth-century dictatorships called for a reappraisal of the past. 'The subterranean stream of Western history,' Arendt wrote, 'has finally come to the surface and usurped the dignity of our tradition. This is the reality in which we live.'[8] It is this 'subterranean stream' that Tooker's painting encapsulates so well.

Subways, of course, had played an important role in London during the Blitz between 1940 and 1941, when for eight months Britain was the target of concerted attacks by the German Luftwaffe. Over a million London buildings were damaged or destroyed by bombs, and over 20,000 civilians perished in the capital, with roughly the same number killed in 'blitztowns' across the country. Thousands sheltered in the capital's underground train system, creating a community bound by shared fear, as documented by the photojournalist Bill Brandt in his poignant images of Londoners huddled on platforms, tunnels and stairways. Elizabeth Bowen, who served as an air raid warden in central London and whose home was bombed in 1941 and 1944, observed that 'many people had strange, deep intense dreams' during the Blitz, in which 'the overcharged subconsciousness of everybody overflowed and merged'.[9]

While the subway provides a powerful image of the subconscious, it is also a striking metaphor for the political underground: a cloak-and-dagger world that lurks beneath the façade of the everyday. The historian Eric Hobsbawm once called this world 'a contest of nightmares', an apt description of the Cold War.[10]

In the summer of 1945 the Potsdam Conference divided continental Europe into two camps: East and West, cleft by an 'Iron Curtain', as Churchill famously put it in 1946. The United States, he declared, 'stands at this time at the pinnacle of world power'. And yet there was cause for anxiety, and not only because of the threat to the West posed by the Soviet Union in an era when 'war can find any nation'. 'If you look around you,' Churchill told an audience in Fulton, Missouri, 'you must feel not only the sense of duty done but also you must feel anxiety lest you fall below the level of achievement.'[11]

Bankrupt and bombed-out Europe – London, Berlin and Vienna – was another setting for this Cold War. Among the ruins of these old-world cities, sinister forces prowled in the shadows, waiting to unsettle the fragile post-war peace and insinuate themselves into the inner life of democratic societies. An atmosphere of suspense and foreboding pervades Graham Greene's screenplay for the 1949 film *The Third Man*, the plot of which centres on a shadowy gangland network that carries out its business under cover of post-war confusion in bomb-ravaged Vienna, a city divided into an Allied sector and a Soviet zone.

Berlin was likewise split into different American, British,

French and Soviet sectors, with the free city encircled by the communist German Democratic Republic, created by the Soviets in October 1949. As Khrushchev put it with characteristic bluntness, it was a city 'stuck like a bone in the Soviet throat'.[12] Amid growing tension between the West and the Soviet Union in the late 1950s, the East German government constructed a wall in just two weeks, a blitzkrieg effort to stem the flow of defectors to the West. Begun in August 1961 – originally in brick and concrete slabs and subsequently in concrete and reinforced steel – the Berlin Wall was twelve feet high and more than a hundred miles long by the 1980s, as it snaked through the city and around the Western sectors.

The wall didn't only give material form to Churchill's 'Iron Curtain'; it was also a reflection of broader conflicts and fears. Checkpoints, watchtowers, barbed wire, German shepherds straining at the leash and anti-tank barriers made it the archetype of the Cold War border: the place of handovers, switchovers and double-crosses; an obstacle to be overcome with escape by air balloon and tunnel, by swimming across the River Spree or, in the years before they were demolished, by leaping to freedom in the West from buildings on Bernauer Strasse. The divided city was the locus of the spy thriller par excellence, beginning with Richard Burton as the British agent Alec Leamas in the screen adaptation of John le Carré's 1963 novel *The Spy Who Came in from the Cold* and Michael Caine as the inimitable Harry Palmer in the film version of Len Deighton's *Funeral in Berlin* (1966).

But the most poignant cinematic reflection on Cold War Berlin is surely Wim Wenders's *Wings of Desire*. The film captures the city at the end of the Cold War, in 1987, two years before the wall came down. Angels walk among humans, unable to intervene, their omniscience an echo of some ever-watchful state. Berlin is a haunted city that's divided between the angels and their fearful human counterparts, and between East and West. The graffitied wall is the marker of a violent severance, a 'death strip' that casts a shadow over every life. And yet, while the film suggests a place mired in divisive history, it also hints at the prospect of unification.

From the late 1940s fears of internal subversion were evident across the world, from the United States to the People's Republic of China. In 1949 the Chinese Communist Party, led by Mao Zedong, seized power. And from June 1950 the country was at war with the United States and Britain in North Korea. The strategic use of fear, as we've seen, has always been a vital instrument of autocratic and totalitarian government. But Mao, not unlike Stalin, whose policies he emulated, had a special gift for the political use of fear.[13] He was highly effective in leveraging it to break his enemies and impose discipline within the ranks.

In 1952, during the Korean War, Mao exploited anti-Western sentiment at a moment of crisis, using collective fear to advance his transformative social agenda. The previous year, North Korea and the Soviet Union had accused the US military of using germ warfare in Korea. American planes, they claimed, were dropping pests to spread lethal disease: plague, cholera, encephalitis and anthrax. The allegations were repeated in Chinese newspapers, and Mao ramped up the tension, putting the country on a biological war footing and calling on patriotic citizens to hunt down and exterminate the invading pests, whether they be flies, fleas, mosquitoes, rats or dogs.[14] The accusations, and the fear they produced, provided the communist leadership with a convenient front for promoting a radical programme of collectivisation.

Fear remained a catalyst for revolution in Mao's campaigns against landlords and the suppression of 'counter-revolutionaries'; it was also cultivated to ensure the cooperation of the masses in the Great Leap Forward from 1958 – a campaign designed to transform the country's agrarian economy into a communist society, which would kill tens of millions of Chinese citizens in the process. But as collectivisation in China took off, fear gave way to more systematic violence. 'Violence became a routine tool of control,' writes historian Frank Dikötter. 'It was not used occasionally on a few to instil fear in the many, rather it was directed systematically and habitually against anybody seen to dawdle, obstruct or protest let alone pilfer or steal – a majority of villagers.'

Meanwhile, in the 'shadow world of rumours', stories of food shortages, war and impending invasion spread fear that not only challenged officialdom but 'promoted a sense of cohesion'.[15] In her autobiographical novel *Wild Swans*, Jung Chang describes how she joined the Red Guards as an idealistic teenager during the Cultural Revolution in the 1960s, as Mao attempted to wipe out residual reactionary elements within Chinese society. Soon Chang's parents were arrested and tortured, while Chang herself was exiled to the countryside for re-education. As she would later observe, 'the Chinese must be the most traumatized people in the world. Fear is embedded in the national psyche.'[16]

When Bernard Baruch had spoken about the 'enemies at home' in 1947, he'd given voice to growing fears that communism was taking seed in America. Foreign spies were working to undermine the country's security, and Americans were being inveigled to their cause. The most important task was ferreting out these rogue citizens – easier said than done, because turncoats and spies blended in. 'Commies' were shapeshifters, indistinguishable from everyone else, just like the comic superheroes who fought against evil from the late 1930s, most notably Superman with his off-the-shelf suits and Clark Kent spectacles. Until, that is, he ripped off his disguise and revealed his muscular, logo-emblazoned alter ego.

The scene was set for the 'Red Scare', which was triggered not just by the prospect of communist infiltration but also by the limitations of detection. 'Commies' may have been everywhere, but they were difficult to spot, which is one reason Hollywood films in the 1940s and 1950s were obsessed with watching and being watched, with the power of dissimulation and the uncertainty of what has been seen or can't quite be seen – Alfred Hitchcock's *Rear Window* (1954) being a good example.

During the Second World War there had been widespread fear in the United States that a network of Nazi spies and saboteurs was undermining the war effort.[17] But after Germany's defeat in 1945, the USSR and the international communist movement more generally were viewed as the principal threat. In 1949 the historian Arthur Schlesinger warned that the Soviets were busy recruiting local American Party members to their cause, creating a fifth column that represented 'a fearful warhead to the traditional energies of Russian expansionism'.[18] It was a threat of an altogether different magnitude to earlier German attempts at sabotage, which had been 'crude and ineffective'.[19]

Senator Joseph McCarthy and his House Un-American Activities Committee, set up in 1938, helped to fuel the 'Great Fear'.[20] Americans suspected of pro-communist ties were investigated and those who didn't cooperate were blacklisted. McCarthy claimed to be uncovering 'a conspiracy so immense and an infamy so black as to dwarf any previous such venture in the history of man'.[21] Although Harry Truman may have opposed the Internal Security Act of 1950, which gave the president emergency powers to arrest and detain anyone believed to be involved in espionage or sabotage, the communist containment doctrine he formulated in an address to Congress three years earlier had been calculated 'to scare the hell out of the country', as one US senator put it.[22] Worried about a communist insurgency in Greece and growing Soviet influence in Turkey, Truman asked Congress to sanction $400 million in military and economic aid to 'support free peoples who are resisting attempted subjugation by armed minorities or by outside pressures'. The United States, he said, was 'distinguished by free institutions, representative government, free elections, guarantees of individual liberty, freedom of speech and religion, and freedom from political oppression'. In contrast, communism relied on 'terror and oppression, a controlled press and radio; fixed elections, and the suppression of personal freedoms'.[23] Four months later the 1947 National Security Act was brought in, creating the CIA. At his second inauguration, in January 1949, Truman restated the dangers posed by communism and the challenges of a world torn between 'great hopes and great fears'. 'We are aided by all who wish to live in freedom from fear,' he said, 'even by those who live today in fear under their own governments.'[24]

Although the communist witch-hunt was driven by fear, it claimed to be banishing it in the name of freedom. Anti-communist scares weren't anything new either. There had been widespread fear of communist infiltration in the United States after the 1917 Bolshevik Revolution.[25] During the First World War this fear converged with other anxieties, chief among them the threat posed by foreign interlopers to the dominance of 'Anglo-Saxon' culture.[26] But loathing of the Germans soon shifted to the Bolsheviks and their godless propaganda, bringing 'a sense of unease, a fear that something malignant and foreign was contaminating the nation'.[27]

The intensity of this disquiet reached new levels during and after the Second World War. Anything containing the name 'red' was now regarded as dodgy and susceptible to scrutiny. Even the baseball team the Cincinnati Reds was renamed the 'Cincinnati Redlegs' in 1953 to avoid being tarnished with communist associations.[28] In 1954 the Communist Control Act terminated the 'rights, privileges, and immunities' which the Communist Party of America had been granted – effectively banning it – on the grounds that it wasn't a genuine political party but 'in fact an instrumentality of a conspiracy to overthrow the Government of the United States'. Membership of the Party and of any '"Communist-action" organization' became a criminal offence punishable under the terms of the 1950 Internal Security Act.[29]

Fears of a communist takeover were everywhere between

1946 and 1954. The front cover of the 1947 comic book *Is This Tomorrow: America under Communism!*, several million copies of which were produced by the Catechetical Guild Educational Society of St Paul, Minnesota, depicted flames engulfing the American flag as military personnel and civilians fought off a communist advance. The book cautioned readers 'to be alert to the menace of Communism: The average American is prone to say, "It can't happen here." Millions of people in other countries used to say the same thing. Today they are dead – or living in Communist slavery. IT MUST NOT HAPPEN HERE!'

Feverish stories of communist plots pervaded the American mass media, often carrying the same message: subversive elements were scheming to overthrow the government and had to be stopped before it was too late. In 1948 *Life* magazine reminded its readers that the communists had seized power in the Soviet Union through a combination of infiltration and bare-knuckled violence. They'd taken advantage of economic turbulence and social discontent to stir up the people 'with a relentless drumfire of propaganda slogans'.[30] In the same year the anti-communist cartoon *Make Mine Freedom* was distributed by MGM. Produced by the Extension Department of Harding College in Arkansas, the film claimed to promote 'a deeper understanding of what has made America the finest place in the world to live'. In the film an unctuous salesman wearing a purple suit and yellow bow tie tries to persuade a group of Americans to sign away their freedom in return for a restorative tonic called 'Dr Utopia's ISM'. When they taste the potion, however, they get a glimpse of what their lives would be like under Dr Utopia's regime: every one of them is in servitude to an oppressive, iron-fisted state. Aware now of the danger the salesman poses, the crowd runs him out of town.

Something had to be done to get Hollywood on board with the fearmongering message. A young Richard Nixon, then a Republican congressman, urged the film studios to help produce anti-communist movies in a counter-agitprop offensive. 'People react to fear, not love,' Nixon was later reported to have claimed. 'They don't teach that in Sunday school, but it's true.'[31] The late 1940s and 1950s saw a spate of agit-movies – all unsuccessful at the box office, and no surprise, given their leaden plot lines – including *The Iron Curtain* (1948), *The Red Menace* (1949), *I Married a Communist* (1949) and *Invasion, USA* (1952).[32]

All these films – and many others like them – used fear to train viewers how to look at the world, and presumably how to behave. They are cheesy B-movies scripted around a single obsession to a degree that, watching them now, one wonders how viewers ever took them seriously. Perhaps the highly strung audience, primed by an anti-communist media, found some relief by slotting their prejudicial fears into Hollywood screen ciphers.

Attempts to re-politicise popular culture, which went hand in hand with a crackdown on suspicious content, reflected a realisation of just how important the media were in shaping public attitudes. Although they could be used as a tool for countering the Red threat, films and books could also be a destabilising force when they glorified 'aggressions which are impossible under civilized restraints – with fists, guns, torture, killing, and blood'.[33] Americans were falling victim to the pernicious influence of all the junk they were reading and watching. The fifth column was being aided and abetted by the producers of films, books and magazines who put commercial interests above morals and stoked the kind of fear that sold copies, encouraged copycat behaviour and nurtured consuming addictions.

This was the context for the culture wars of the late 1940s and 1950s, in which fear played an important part. There was a new front in the psychological war. If popular culture couldn't be reappropriated, it had to be banned, or at least censured. The controversies surrounding comic books are a case in point. Comic strips had been around since the late nineteenth century, but they took off in the 1930s, a decade that saw the creation of Superman and Batman. During the Second World

War patriotic superheroes like Captain America and Superwoman were added to the roster and tapped into a growing youth market.

Even by 1945, however, there was mounting scepticism about the values embodied in these superhero vigilantes. Walter Ong, a Jesuit priest and professor of English literature, argued that the comic hero 'stands as the raw, elemental prototype, constructed on a monumentally primitive pattern'. He traced the history of Superman back to Nietzsche's *Übermensch*, the term the German philosopher had used in 1883 to describe the perfect human of the future, but which later became associated with Nazi racial ideology. Ong stressed the covert nature of this malign influence and suggested that oppressive forces were working surreptitiously to overwhelm the democratic world. As he put it, 'fishing about in the murky depths of mass reactions, one is sure to encounter strong movements of those often unconscious impulses which have powered the various new orders'.[34] To some, like Ong, superheroes reflected a dangerous anti-democratic and atavistic current within mass culture.

Meanwhile, cheap pulp magazines began to publish other genres of comic, with grittier plot lines that featured crime, horror and gore. The seditious content of these comic strips soon began to cause concern, especially as their popularity grew. Some commentators drew connections between the gruesome scenarios depicted in them and the rise of juvenile delinquency. Cold War anxieties about nuclear war and communist takeover converged with a gamut of social anxieties that revolved around youth crime and antisocial behaviour.[35]

Comics sparked a moral panic that was fuelled by a much-publicised congressional investigation. But even before that, things came to a head on 26 October 1948, in Spencer, West Virginia, where children – supervised by parents, teachers and priests – incinerated a mound of objectionable comics. Other towns across the country soon followed suit. In Binghamton,

New York, Catholic students collected '2,000 comic books and pictorial magazines' in a 'house-to-house canvass', which they then set alight in the school courtyard 'to dramatize their movement to boycott publications which they say stress crime and sex'. In an open letter encouraging the faithful to join the 'Legion of Decency', Bishop Edmund Gibbons of the Albany Catholic Diocese asserted, 'Another evil of our times is found in the pictorial magazine and comic book which portray indecent pictures and sensational details of crime.'[36] Meanwhile, boy scouts in Rumson, New Jersey, chickened out of book-burning and instead handed their comics to the Salvation Army to be used as scrap paper.[37]

In 1954, with the McCarthy witch-hunt reaching a climax, the German-born American psychiatrist Fredric Wertham published his book *Seduction of the Innocent*, condemning comics on the grounds that they were corrupting America's youth. 'A common clinical syndrome in comic-book readers,' he argued, 'is rough and blustering conduct during the day, associated with fear dreams at night.' Scenes of extreme and gratuitous violence, including hanging, flagellation, rape and the torture of women, gave rise to 'sex fears of all kinds'. Comic heroes, Wertham maintained, were 'psychopathic deviates'. Wonder Woman – the red-booted, short-skirted, leather wrist-banded, ass-kicking DC Comics heroine who had first appeared in 1941 – was unquestionably gay. 'For boys, Wonder Woman is a frightening image,' Wertham wrote. 'For girls, she is a morbid ideal. Where Batman is anti-feminine, the attractive Wonder Woman and her counterparts are definitely anti-masculine.' Among his other aspersions were that the insignia on Superman's chest reproduced the Nazi SS symbol and that the only reason children could possibly be interested in a pair of binoculars was to spy on their neighbours.[38]

By 1949 comic books had become an urgent political issue. A New York Joint Legislative Committee to Study the Publication of Comics was set up in response to allegations that they were 'inherently objectionable' and tended 'to provoke acts of juvenile delinquency and crime'. Wertham pushed for a new law that would 'forbid the sale and display of all crime comic books to children under the age of 15 years'. At a closed session of the committee in 1950, he cited the case of a thirteen-year-old who had shot a youth, knifed another boy and flung a cat from a roof. It wasn't a coincidence, the psychiatrist insisted, that the perpetrator's comic book collection consisted of numerous murders by, among other methods, shooting, choking, stabbing, beating, hanging and submersion in a bathtub of acid.[39]

Estes Kefauver, an ambitious Democrat senator from Tennessee, who had earlier chaired the Senate's Special Committee to Investigate Organized Crime, became a key figure in a new body established to tackle the problem of juvenile delinquency. The focus soon turned to comics, given the pervasive news reports that linked comics with juvenile crime, as well as the denunciation of comics by leading political figures, including J. Edgar Hoover, director of the FBI, who claimed that comics could 'serve as the springboard for the unstable child to commit criminal acts'.[40] An upshot of this was the establishment in 1954 of the Comics Magazine Association of America, which created the Comics Code, an independent authority charged with self-regulating the industry.

Freedom didn't mean the ability to say whatever you wanted; it meant supporting culture that opposed the propaganda being pumped out of the Soviet Union while adhering to the tenets of the *right* propaganda. This was the message of the CIA-backed Congress for Cultural Freedom campaign that launched in 1950. Whatever the Soviets didn't like, Western agencies would champion. It was an unexpected and unlikely fillip for atonal music and abstract expressionism, the antithesis to the Soviet-sanctioned doctrine of social realism.[41]

But undoubtedly the biggest Cold War fear focused on the threat of nuclear war. The use of atomic bombs by the United

States on Hiroshima and Nagasaki in 1945 along with the development of nuclear technology in the 1950s had an important psychological impact. The black-and-white photographs taken of the mushroom cloud over Hiroshima by George 'Bob' Caron, tail gunner of the B-29 *Enola Gay*, created a new iconography of fear. The Soviet Union's first test of nuclear weapons in Kazakhstan in 1949 fed into growing concerns about the possibility of all-out nuclear war, as did the US hydrogen bomb test, codenamed 'Bravo Castle', on Bikini Atoll in the central Pacific in 1954, and the 'Tsar Bomba' H-bomb test by the Soviets in the Arctic seven years later. As John F. Kennedy declared in an address to the UN General Assembly in September 1961, 'Every man, woman and child lives under a nuclear sword of Damocles, hanging by the slenderest of threads, capable of being cut at any moment by accident or miscalculation or by madness.'[42]

In the United States fears about the atomic bomb merged with the Red Scare. In the propagandistic movie *The Atomic City* (1952), Frank Addison is a physicist at Los Alamos, the New Mexico nuclear facility that built the world's first nuclear weapons – whose young son is kidnapped and held to ransom by a group of communists eager to get their hands on the H-bomb formula.

The short-lived comic series *Atomic War!* launched in 1952 with *The Sneak Attack*, which contains multiple scenes of nuclear destruction. The cover depicts Manhattan being destroyed by a nuclear blast, with the Empire State and Chrysler buildings toppled and flames consuming the streets. This was to become a familiar spectacle of terror. In 1950 a cover illustration in *Collier's* magazine showed a mushroom cloud enveloping Manhattan, accompanied by the words 'HIROSHIMA, USA: Can Anything Be Done About It?' It was a vision of annihilation conjured up a few years later in the same magazine by the politician and diplomat Val Peterson, head of the Federal Civil Defense Administration (FCDA), a new government agency tasked with creating training programmes to prepare the public. In an article that ran alongside fictional headlines announcing nuclear strikes on Buffalo and New York, Peterson imagines the panic caused by a direct hit on the city. 'Those who did succeed in fleeing the island,' he writes, 'would pour into adjacent areas to become a hungry pillaging mob – disrupting disaster relief, overwhelming local police and spreading panic in a widening arc.'[43]

As early as 1946 nuclear scientists were warning that panic caused by a nuclear attack might be as destructive as the bomb itself. It was to meet this threat that Truman had established the FCDA. Between 1951 and 1958 the organisation produced films and pamphlets to teach Americans how to respond to an attack, with anti-panic measures high on the agenda.

Civil defence education materials didn't only deal with practical advice; they were also concerned with how to keep calm in a crisis, even though there was some evidence, as the American sociologist Enrico Quarantelli noted in 1954, that the 'frequency of panic has been exaggerated'. 'Compared with other reactions,' he observed, 'panic is a relatively uncommon phenomenon.'[44] But the aim of 'emotional management' wasn't to expel fear altogether, since a degree of fear in the face of an attack was unavoidable and could be channelled as a motivational force to sustain survival efforts. The short film *Our Cities Must Fight* (1951), for example, aimed to re-educate what it called the 'take-to-the-hills fraternity', those individuals who might stampede in the face of danger and trigger mayhem. *Survival under Atomic Attack*, produced in the same year, gave advice on what to do as soon as the sirens warned of an imminent attack, as well as how to prepare in advance to ensure a nuclear shelter was equipped with a first aid kit, bottled water, canned food and back-up batteries for radios and torches.[45] *Duck and Cover*, produced in 1952, was aimed at teaching children how to 'duck and cover' whenever they saw 'the flash'.[46]

In tandem with the distribution of such material – films, broadcasts and booklets – other programmes were rolled out.

Home economics courses were introduced in schools to train students in practical skills ranging from food preparation to first aid and the construction of shelters. The Alert America roadshow, created in 1951, involved a convoy of trucks criss-crossing the country to display survival products and information about nuclear war at temporary expos, with tips on how to prepare for an attack, along with screenings of federally supported films.[47] 'Operation Alert', launched in 1954, was a national civil defence exercise that drilled the public for a nuclear attack.

Such initiatives were informed by two basic assumptions: first, that people panicked; and second, that panic was manageable with the right education. These were the findings of a series of reports issued by a research group – codenamed 'Project East River' – convened in 1951 to look into civil defence and disaster relief in the event of a nuclear strike on a US city.[48] At the same time simulations of such attacks were carried out to train emergency workers. One citywide exercise in New York, in April 1952, involved 50,000 workers responding to an imagined attack in which two nuclear bombs had been dropped. As soon as unfriendly planes were detected approaching the city, an alert went out to key services across the boroughs – police precincts, fire departments, schools and hospitals – followed by an air siren, although 'as a precaution against panic or confusion, radio and television stations broke in on their programs to emphasize that a drill was in progress'.[49]

In his 1953 article 'Panic: The Ultimate Weapon?', Val Peterson noted that panic could 'produce a chain reaction more deeply destructive than any explosive known'. 'Mass panic – not the A-bomb,' he added, 'may well be the easiest way to win a battle, the cheapest way to win a war.' To meet this challenge, fear had to be leveraged as a generative force. As he elaborated, 'Fear itself is not panic; it's merely the raw material of panic.' Peterson thought it was perfectly possible for Americans to become 'panic-proof', or at least 'reasonably panic-resistant', and he included a 'Test Yourself' panic quiz for readers. 'MAKE

FEAR WORK FOR YOU' was one of his mottos. 'Don't be ashamed of being scared. If an attack comes, you will be scared and so will everyone else. It is what you do when you are afraid that counts. Fear can be healthy if you know how to use it.'[50]

Meanwhile, the risks of nuclear war were increasing as technology developed. By 1959, intercontinental ballistic missiles had made a nuclear strike as straightforward as punching in a code. From JFK onwards, US presidents began to travel with a briefcase – the so-called 'nuclear football' – with which they could launch an immediate nuclear strike. The time frame for destruction had also shrunk; if bombers needed hours to get to their destination, it was now only a matter of minutes; plus, once the button was pushed, the decision was irreversible. 'The terrifying spectacle of atomic warfare has put Hamlet's words, "To be or not to be," on millions of trembling lips,' Martin Luther King declared. 'Our problem is not to get rid of fear altogether, but to harness it, master it.'[51]

In 1962 the world appeared to be on the brink of nuclear war when American U-2 spy planes identified Soviet bases under construction in Cuba, just 90 miles from Florida – sites from which ballistic missiles could easily strike US cities, including Washington, DC. On the evening of Monday, 22 October 1962, President John F. Kennedy gave a twenty-minute televised address to the nation. 'Within the past week, unmistakable evidence has established the fact that a series of offensive missile sites is now in preparation on that imprisoned island,' he said. 'The purpose of these bases can be none other than to provide a nuclear strike capability against the Western Hemisphere.' The Soviets had prevaricated about the build-up, he went on, before stating that a missile launched from Cuba would be met with 'a full retaliatory response'. 'We will not prematurely or unnecessarily risk the costs of worldwide nuclear war in which even the fruits of victory would be ashes in our mouth,' he said, but 'neither will we shrink from that risk at any time it must be faced'.[52]

Even now, Kennedy's address makes for chilling listening.

This was perhaps the first time the world grasped the irrevocability of the nuclear button option, and Kennedy himself clearly understood the momentousness of the occasion. After all, as he had declared at his inauguration address in January 1961, 'the world is very different now; for man holds in his mortal hands the power to abolish all forms of human poverty and all forms of human life'. In a line allegedly written for him by the economist J. K. Galbraith, he'd also declared, 'We shall never negotiate out of fear. But we shall never fear to negotiate.'[53]

In that same year, tensions between the United States and the Soviet Union had intensified. Khrushchev had demanded that the United States and its allies give up their control of West Berlin, which they refused to do. Talks to resolve the Berlin crisis broke down, with tensions mounting further when a US spy plane was shot down over the USSR. In August 1961 the East German government began to build the wall cutting off the East from the West.

It was against this backdrop that Kennedy warned Congress that the US government had limited means at its disposal to protect its citizens from a nuclear attack. In another address in July 1961 he told the nation that 'in the event of an attack, the lives of those families which are not hit in a nuclear blast and fire can still be saved if they can be warned to take shelter and if that shelter is available'.[54] So began a push to construct nuclear shelters, with Congress allocating federal funds to the effort and the media taking up the cause. On the cover of its 15 September 1961 issue *Life* magazine showed a man in a 'civilian fallout suit' with the words 'How You Can Survive Fallout'.

The Cuban Missile Crisis came to a head on 27 October 1962, the final day of diplomatic negotiations that became known as 'Black Saturday'. As he'd left the Oval Office, US Defense Secretary Robert McNamara later confided, 'I thought I might never see another Saturday night.'[55] While people reportedly stockpiled food and prepared fallout shelters in anticipation of an attack, there is less evidence of widespread panic than is sometimes suggested. On the contrary, fear encouraged caution, at least on the political front.[56] Recent research in the Soviet archives, including access to declassified KGB files, has revealed the extent to which fear permeated the decision-making process on both sides. As the Soviet historian Serhii Plokhy has noted, 'both sides had one thing in common that proved decisive – fear of nuclear war'.[57] After a tense thirteen-day showdown, during which the world held its breath, Khrushchev pulled back. He would later respond to accusations of cowardice by emphasising the political virtues of fear in the nuclear age. 'If being frightened meant that I helped avert such insanity,' he said, 'then I'm glad I was frightened. One of the problems in the world today is that not enough people are sufficiently frightened by danger of nuclear war.'[58]

The stand-off over Cuba was to reanimate nuclear fears in ways that shaped the views of the public and officials alike through the 1970s and 1980s. An arms race triggered by the deployment of US Pershing II ballistic missiles to Europe in 1983 threatened the Soviet Union, while the death of the Soviet leader Leonid Brezhnev in 1982 gave rise to political instability. In the face of this political tension, the mid-1980s saw a spate of terrifying films about nuclear war. *The Day After*, a US TV drama, was transmitted in 1983; in Britain, Mick Jackson's post-nuclear TV movie *Threads* was screened in 1984, and a year later *The War Game*, a controversial pseudo-documentary about a Soviet attack on the UK, was broadcast. This last film had been made in 1965 but was pulled by the BBC – under pressure from the Ministry of Defence and the Home Office – because it was judged 'too horrifying for the medium of broadcasting'.[59] It wasn't until the collapse of the Berlin Wall in 1989 and the dissolution of the Soviet Union in 1991 that the nuclear fear of the Cold War receded; however, it didn't vanish – as Vladimir Putin reminded the world in February 2022 when, during his invasion of Ukraine, he ordered his generals to put Russia's nuclear forces on 'special alert'.

In the United States, meanwhile, the Cuban Missile Crisis was a reminder of the political value of fear. During the presidential campaign that followed Kennedy's assassination in November 1963, Lyndon Johnson seemed to trade on the fear created by the crisis. His so-called 'Daisy Girl' TV commercial began with a three-year-old in a meadow, counting as she picks the petals from a daisy; when she reaches the number nine, a man's voice interjects with 'ten' – the start of a missile launch countdown. At the end, the screen blacked out and then filled with a nuclear flash before cutting to a mushroom cloud, as a voiceover by Johnson reminded viewers, 'The stakes are too high for you to stay home.' The film suggested, in no uncertain terms, that Johnson stood for security; the implication being that a vote for the Republican nominee Barry Goldwater was a vote for possible annihilation.[60]

The H-bomb exemplified the unforeseen dangers that science and technology were posing to human survival, but there were other tech threats to reckon with too. To win the propaganda war, mass communication had become a crucial dimension of government. While technology played an important role in the government's ability to gather and store increasingly large amounts of data, its use also raised issues about freedom of expression and the right to privacy. This was a concern that George Orwell had raised more than a decade earlier in his novel *Nineteen Eighty-Four*, which is set in a totalitarian state where cameras watch public spaces and screens monitor behaviour in the home. This is a society, we're told, 'whose prevailing moods are fear, hatred, adulation, and orgiastic triumph'. So extensive is the surveillance culture that citizens censor themselves in a disturbing mimicry of the machines.[61]

By the 1960s the burgeoning field of data science was also being used for political advantage – and not just by corporate giants like IBM. In 1961 the writer Thomas Morgan published a story in *Harper's* claiming that Kennedy's narrow victory over

Nixon in the presidential election had been facilitated by a computer dubbed the 'People Machine', which had provided simulations of the election based on the analysis of past voting behaviour. The machine in question was the creation of the Simulmatics Corporation, for which Morgan would later serve as director of publicity. The company had been founded in New York in 1959 with a mission to create profitable data-informed messaging campaigns; its name conflated 'simulation' with 'automatic'.[62] Morgan's piece highlighted many of the public concerns around automation. 'If, in a free society, information is power,' he asked, 'how do we prevent tampering with the data provided by the machine? As we approach a consensus of opinion, what happens to freedom and spontaneity? As we seek more and more data for the machines, can we maintain our traditions of privacy?'[63]

There were risks to being so reliant on technology. Beyond the ethics of data storage were questions of independence, freedom and the limits of the state's authority. Many feared that, in the wrong hands, the 'People Machine' would undermine the democratic process. In the words of one commentator, it would make 'the tyrannies of Hitler, Stalin and their forebears look like the inept fumbling of a village bully'.[64] As the historian Jill Lepore has suggested, the story of Simulmatics, albeit ultimately a failure, encapsulates 'the data-mad and near-totalitarian twenty-first century' with its dreams and nightmares of information extraction and voter or consumer prediction.[65]

Fear of runaway technology may have prefigured the Cold War, but in the 1950s and 1960s new technologies and communication theories created new challenges: from automation and cybernetics to artificial intelligence and genetics. In 1956, the Logic Theorist computer programme – 'the first artificial intelligence program' – was presented at a conference that brought together AI researchers at Dartmouth College in New Hampshire organised by the mathematicians John McCarthy and Marvin Minsky.[66] It was in their proposal for this event, which aimed to study 'how to make machines use language, form abstractions and concepts, solve kinds of problems now reserved for humans, and improve themselves', that the term AI was coined.[67] While these developments and their practical applications were celebrated by some, they also gave rise to fears about the loss of independent thought and freedom.

In 1960 the scientists Manfred Clynes and Nathan Kline coined the word 'cyborg'. Space travel, they argued, had created an environment that challenged human physiological functions, but technology could play an important role in ensuring man's survival. As they wrote, 'it is becoming apparent that we will in the not-too-distant future have sufficient knowledge to design instrumental control systems which will make it possible for our bodies' to survive in space.[68]

In the same year the MIT mathematician Norbert Wiener, a pioneer in cybernetics – the 'study of control and communication in machines and living beings', as he defined it – argued that human reliance on machines was eroding human autonomy.[69] 'It is my thesis,' he asserted, 'that machines can and do transcend some of the limitations of their designers, and that in doing so they may be both effective and dangerous.'[70] What would happen, Wiener wondered, if wars were fully automated? Imagine a war 'playing-machine' programmed for victory; it would pursue its 'goal at any cost, even that of the extermination of your own side', Wiener concluded, 'unless this condition of survival is explicitly contained in the definition of victory according to which you program the machine'.[71]

From the battlefield to the office, machines threatened to overpower humans, and those who celebrated the benefits of automation were countered by an increasingly vocal 'automatophobia'.[72] Writing in the mid-1950s, as 'the danger of a destructive war' hung over humanity, Erich Fromm argued that humans had created a standardised world of mass consumption, in which the ideal citizen was now 'the automaton, the alienated man' who was 'free and independent' but 'willing to be commanded, to do what is expected of them, to fit into the social machine without friction'.[73] Automation spelt apocalypse. Mass media and advertising were turning people into passive consumers and imposing a new form of social control by stealth. In his provocative book *One-Dimensional Man*, the philosopher and political scientist Herbert Marcuse asserted that the so-called free democratic states of the West weren't in the end much different from the totalitarian regimes of the East.[74] These fears pervaded pop culture from the 1960s, in films such as *2001: A Space Odyssey* (1968), which features a sentient supercomputer called HAL, or *Dr Strangelove* (1964), where human folly leads to nuclear annihilation.

One definition of panic might be a 'pervasive set of anxieties about the way technologies, social organizations, and communication systems may have reduced human autonomy and uniqueness'.[75] This sounds a lot like a summary of Philip K. Dick's 1968 novel *Do Androids Dream of Electric Sheep?*, the inspiration for Ridley Scott's film *Blade Runner* (1982). Set in a post-apocalyptic near future – the year is 2021 and radioactive fallout has devastated the planet – most humans have migrated to Mars and robots are banished from Earth. Rick Deckard, the eponymous 'blade runner', works for the police department as a bounty hunter assigned to track down and 'retire' six renegade droids – a tall order, since they're hard to distinguish from humans. Applying the Voigt-Kampff Empathy Test is one way of doing it, along with assessing a subject's reflex responses to external stimuli. However, it turns out that bioengineered humanoids may be able to feel emotions after all, while human feelings can be induced by a machine. By 2021 humans appear to have lost their humanity, a plight emblematised by the lone, horror-struck figure in Munch's painting *The Scream*, which Deckard sees at an art exhibition.[76]

The mid-twentieth century is crowded with fearful images, from the mushroom clouds of Hiroshima and Nagasaki to Nick Ut's photograph of the nine-year-old Vietnamese girl Kim

Phúc running down a road naked near Trảng Bàng in 1972. 'It was a time for an Agonizing Reappraisal of the whole scene,' Hunter S. Thompson's alter ego Raoul Duke tells us in *Fear and Loathing in Las Vegas*. The backdrop to this gonzo novel's drug-addled 'journey to the heart of the American dream' is the Vietnam War, the death of the 1960s counterculture and the media's sell-out to political interests. 'When the going gets weird,' Thompson wrote, 'the weird turn pro.'[77]

But it wasn't all fear and loathing; the other side of the Cold War story, which can sometimes be hard to see amid the dire headlines, was hope. In the 1960s, with the Cold War at its height, the architect Douglas Murphy reminds us of the alternative lifestyles that were imagined in the communes of California and the cooperatives of Vienna, and by a new generation of avant-garde thinkers.[78] Fear and hope were interwoven; hippiedom, rock 'n' roll, civil rights, feminism and the Pill were also part of the story. While governments, politicians and business interests may have harnessed fear to further their aims, hope found a new voice in this new age of protest. 'We are not afraid,' the twenty-two-year-old folk singer Joan Baez sang in 1963 to a defiant crowd gathered on the National Mall in Washington, DC. 'We shall overcome some day.'

13

Break-Up, Breakdown

In the 1980s geopolitical realignments and deepening global interdependence brought new pressures to bear on existing institutions: from the nation-state that struggled to secure its borders – against viral disease, drugs, terrorists and foreign threats – to social institutions that were vulnerable to corrosive influences from without. At least, that was the fear. Ironically, as we'll see, the staunchest defenders of these threatened borders were those who pressed for deregulation and clamoured to bring down the barriers that hamstrung the 'free' market.

By the end of March 1973 the United States had removed the last of its forces from South Vietnam, where it had been embroiled in a protracted proxy war against the Soviet Union and China, which had backed communist North Vietnam. Two years later communist forces seized South Vietnam, creating a new socialist republic. Alarmed by the Soviet invasion of Afghanistan in 1979 and the deployment of SS-20 ballistic missiles in Soviet bloc countries, Ronald Reagan, who became US president in 1981, ditched containment and adopted a more belligerent foreign policy, arguing that enhanced military capabilities were essential to protect US interests.

The so-called 'Reagan Doctrine' sought to roll back communist influence, which meant intervening abroad to support anti-communist forces, from the Contra rebel groups fighting to overthrow Nicaragua's Sandinistas to the insurgent Mujahideen in their war against the Soviets in Afghanistan.[1] To meet this obligation, defence spending rose almost 40 per cent during

Reagan's first term in office – 'arguably, the largest peacetime expansion of military spending in American history'.[2] As part of a NATO upgrade, intermediate-range Pershing II and cruise missiles were deployed in Britain and West Germany. In 1980 Britain announced that it would replace the Polaris missile system used by its nuclear submarine fleet, which had been in operation since 1968, with new American Trident missiles.

In Germany, as elsewhere, this military escalation combined with concerns about nuclear weapons to produce what the historian Frank Biess has described as 'an intense, almost apocalyptic fear' that played an important role in the politicisation of young people. The language with which this fear was described – for example, in the notion of a 'nuclear holocaust' – brought back memories of the Second World War, linking 'a catastrophic past with an apocalyptic future'.[3]

The Chernobyl nuclear disaster in Ukraine on 26 April 1986 was taken by some Western commentators as a harbinger of the USSR's disintegration, while others saw it as hastening the Soviet state's collapse.[4] One of the core reactors in the power station had erupted during a safety test, spewing radioactive contamination into the atmosphere. According to the International Atomic Energy Agency, the explosion released 400 times more radioactivity than the atomic bomb at Hiroshima.[5] Mikhail Gorbachev, General Secretary of the Soviet Communist Party, had been in office for just over a year, and *glasnost*, his commitment to more open government, was little more than a catchphrase. The Soviet response to the catastrophe was far from open; the 'immediate instinct of most Soviet officials was to pretend that nothing serious had happened', and the Politburo imposed a news blackout to prevent panic. 'Panic is even worse than radiation,' Boris Shcherbina, the engineer later tasked with heading the first government commission on the disaster, was reported as saying.[6]

Three years later, in 1989, a wave of revolutions swept across Central and Eastern Europe, beginning in Poland and

Hungary, and culminating with the fall of the Berlin Wall and the Velvet Revolution in Czechoslovakia. Yugoslavia, a communist federation created after 1945, began to disintegrate, setting the stage for war between its constituent republics. In the summer of 1992 images of skeletal Muslim Bosniak prisoners shocked the world. In July 1995 news emerged that thousands of half-starved Bosniaks had been massacred in a UN 'safe area' in Srebrenica as part of a Bosnian Serb 'ethnic cleansing' campaign. Eyewitness accounts in the subsequent trial of the Serbian war criminal Radislav Krstić showed – as the judgement concluded – that fear 'was part of the purpose of a joint criminal enterprise'.[7]

It was against this backdrop that the American political scientist Francis Fukuyama suggested that Western liberal democracy had effectively won the Cold War or, as he put it in an essay published in 1989, humanity had reached 'the end of history as such; that is, the end point of mankind's ideological evolution and the universalization of Western liberal democracy as the final form of human government'. There no longer seemed to be any viable alternative to liberal democracy – every other political system had run out of steam.[8] But this grand claim would soon be challenged, not least by the reinvention of the USSR as the Russian Federation after 1991, China's newfound status as a superpower and the rise of militant Islam.

As Fukuyama was writing, governments around the world were adopting neoliberal policies as a response to the new global environment. President Reagan and the British prime minister Margaret Thatcher exemplified this shift to limited government, laissez-faire economics and privatisation. As Reagan had declared in 1981, 'government is not the solution to our problem; government is the problem'.[9] The word 'globalisation' has come to embody the opportunities and challenges of this post-Cold War period, although it remains a deeply ambiguous and divisive term. To some it implies a healthy meshing of the world through reciprocal flows of investments, information and people; to others it denotes a world driven by finance, unregulated multinational corporations and money lobbying in a process dubbed 'casino capitalism'.[10]

Many of the worries associated with globalisation had their origins in the 1970s.[11] When members of the recently formed Organization of Arab Petroleum Exporting Countries (OAPEC) embargoed oil exports to several countries, including the United States and Britain, in retaliation for their support of Israel during the Yom Kippur War, soaring oil prices marked the end of a post-war economic boom. The demise of this 'Golden Age', and the economic turmoil that was unleashed, triggered a shift to the political right, 'shaped by fears of failing and concerns that one's children might have it worse, not better'.[12] Governments struggled to cope with the tailspin created by the combined effects of an energy crisis and a financial downturn, together with soaring unemployment.[13]

In Britain inflation soared to over 25 per cent and in 1976 prime minister Jim Callaghan's Labour government was forced to borrow from the International Monetary Fund. The 1978–9 'Winter of Discontent' saw widespread industrial action and fierce trade union opposition to the government's measures introduced to curb inflation. There were periodic power cuts and sometimes extended blackouts. Gravediggers and refuse collectors went on strike, and some hospitals, blockaded by picket lines, could only provide basic services. All of this, along with high taxation, caused middle-class jitters that found expression in hyperbolic books such as *The Decline and Fall of the Middle Class and How It Can Fight Back*, published in 1976. 'That this is a time of crisis for the nation is a commonplace,' wrote the journalist Patrick Hutber, 'but it is equally a time of crisis for the middle classes, who are subjected to unprecedented pressures, and, at the same time to considerable denigration.'[14] The cover of Hutber's book summed up the crisis. While the tax-evading wealthy had decamped abroad – the Rolling Stones relocated to France – the middle classes were under siege. A suburban house is shown surrounded by protective sandbags, with armed occupants under a fluttering Union Jack.

The Australian writer and historian Robert Moss put this panic in a broader context in *The Collapse of Democracy*, published in 1975. There he examined states where democracy had become defunct, from Portugal and Czechoslovakia to Chile, and pondered the dangers posed to free societies by 'egalitarian socialism' and 'totalitarian democracy'. Subversive minority groups, he suggested, were threatening liberal democracies, necessitating the promotion of what he called 'civilised intolerance'.[15] The economic and social fears he articulated were responses to global shifts, from immigration to labour conditions that were increasingly shaped by global market competition. These economic transformations weren't only putting pressure on the cash-strapped state; they were raising the spectre of social and political breakdown.

These were the circumstances in which the British sociologist Stanley Cohen coined the term 'moral panic'. The media scapegoating of minority groups as criminals or deviants – Cohen used 'mods' and 'rockers' as his examples – stoked panic that deflected scrutiny away from underlying issues, while also serving political ends.[16] Hysterical media stories in Britain about white people being mugged by young Black men similarly led to panic and reflected deeper anxieties that stemmed from political and economic uncertainties. As Stuart Hall and colleagues argued in 1978, 'crime in general, and "mugging" in particular', were viewed 'as an index of the disintegration of the social order, as a sign that the "British way of life" is coming apart at the seams'. The crime-ridden 'inner city' was the dark locus of these threats, a British version of the American 'ghetto', and spurred a white flight to the suburbs.[17]

Perhaps nowhere exemplified the 1970s panic triggered by urban decline better than New York. By 1975 the city was all but broke, and to many people it felt on the brink of collapse.

Visitors arriving at the city's airports were handed a 'Welcome to Fear City' leaflet with a skull drawn on the front. 'Until things change,' it cautioned, 'stay away from New York City if you possibly can.' Pitched as 'a survival guide for visitors' and produced by a council of firefighters and law officers, the leaflet painted a grim vision of the city as a crime-riddled hellhole. Crime was 'shockingly high' and 'getting worse every day'. Data was quoted as evidence: between January and April 1975 robberies had shot up by 21 per cent, aggravated assault by 15 per cent, larceny by 22 per cent and burglary by 19 per cent. Visitors were advised 'to stay off the streets after 6 p.m.', to remain in midtown areas of Manhattan and to avoid riding the subway 'for any reason whatsoever'.[18]

While this picture of the run-down city may have been overblown, it reflected a widespread feeling that New York was in crisis. The Bronx was now regularly evoked in the media as a badland. Bryant Park, a public park in Manhattan, was an open-air drug market. Grand Central Station, saved from dereliction by a last-minute appeal from Jackie Onassis in 1978, was a homeless encampment. There were frequent muggings and break-ins, and vandalism was rampant. The mild-mannered President Ford all but washed his hands of the city in 1975, when he called its mismanagement 'unique among municipalities throughout the United States'. As New York 'tottered on the brink of financial default', its 'day of reckoning' had come, he declared, but he refused a federal bailout all the same.[19] Reporting on the story, the *New York Daily News* carried the memorable headline 'Ford to City: Drop Dead'.[20]

The Big Apple seemed caught in a loop of perpetual violence: a purgatory of fiscal crisis, ferocious austerity and street crime. A place of shoot-ups and shoot-outs, graffiti-daubed buildings, grungy streets, burned-out cars, gang fights and vagrants keeping warm over steaming manhole covers. Jerry Schatzberg's 1971 film *The Panic in Needle Park* is set in a dingy neighbourhood on the Upper West Side where, as the trailer puts it, 'drug addicts live and steal and hustle and somehow manage to exist from one day to the next'. Fear was a constant in this feral, garbage-strewn landscape of urban degeneration. The 'panic' of the title had a specific meaning among drug users. When the heroin supplies run out on the street, addicts forced to go cold turkey panic and turn on each other. Panic meant break-up and breakdown, in every sense: of body and mind, social and economic relations, city and order.

New York in the 1970s was, as the historian Kim Phillips-Fein has called it, 'Fear City', where political and economic uncertainty, coupled with an infrastructural near-collapse, produced new social fault lines. Fear cast a wide net of prejudice that included a host of fear figures, from drug addicts to down-and-outs. It was a city that seemed designed for dystopian films such as the 1974 action thriller *Death Wish*, featuring Charles Bronson as an architect who becomes a vigilante when his wife is killed in a burglary, Martin Scorsese's 1976 *Taxi Driver*, where Robert De Niro plays an unhinged taxi driver-cum-vigilante, or *Escape from New York*, released in 1981, set in a near future where Manhattan has been turned into a giant maximum-security facility.

For some, fear of societal breakdown had its uses. As Phillips-Fein shows, politicians, bankers and speculators took advantage of the city's dire straits to make their fortunes. They conjured visions of a broken New York, not only as proof that social liberalism was defunct but also to peddle cost-cutting policies that stripped back services and froze pay. Among those who exploited this politics of austerity and gamed the system was a young real estate developer from Queens. His name was Donald Trump, and Fear City was his making.[21]

In the early 1980s New York was to become the epicentre of another kind of panic, one that would be closely associated with the drug users of Needle Park. The social and economic troubles of the 1970s – drug subcultures, crime, the fiscal crisis, the rise of the New Right, as well as the racial tensions that followed Martin Luther King's assassination and the riots of

1968 – converged to create 'undercurrents of opportunity' and the perfect panic storm for HIV/AIDS.[22] The biologist Stephen Jay Gould would sum up the views of many when in 1987 he declared that this new disease was 'an issue that may rank with nuclear weaponry as the greatest danger of our era'.[23]

In the late 1960s there had been considerable optimism about infectious diseases. Improved diagnostics, along with drug therapies and vaccines, meant that many killer diseases of the past were finally overcome. Headway was made against smallpox, which was declared eradicated by the WHO in 1980 – to justified fanfare. But optimism soon faded in the face of new emerging and re-emerging diseases. In 1976 a deadly haemorrhagic infection broke out in Zaire, which was subsequently recognised as a new disease and named Ebola after a tributary of the River Congo. A few years later rumours began to circulate in New York, San Francisco and Los Angeles of an infection that caused impairment to the immune system and appeared to target gay people.

As the gay activist, historian and sociologist Jeffrey Weeks has argued, the story of HIV/AIDS is too easily treated as 'a monolithic whole', while in reality there were distinct phases to the epidemic.[24] For Weeks, AIDS had 'all the characteristic signs of a classic panic'.[25] Rather than a momentary crisis, though, this panic didn't go away, leading some to question whether 'panic' is the right term for such a long-term, collective fear-driven response.[26] It seems clear now that the experience of AIDS in the 1980s and 1990s has influenced how we think about crises and panics. The notion of a 'crisis' as a sudden break from normalcy has given way to a far more elastic definition – perhaps even to a permanent, endemic situation. Similarly, the temporal scope of 'panic' has widened so that panics are viewed as 'the product of historical processes', rather than just spontaneous, non-rational responses to a perceived threat.[27]

The first cases of the disease in the United States were

officially reported by the Centers for Disease Control and Prevention (CDC) on 5 June 1981. Five gay men had been admitted to hospitals in Los Angeles suffering from a rare form of pneumonia, along with a range of other infections that pointed to compromised immunity.[28] Days later, a cluster of gay men in New York were diagnosed with Kaposi sarcoma, a rare and aggressive form of cancer, one symptom of which is the appearance of distinctive skin lesions – more evidence of a weakened immune system. In this early phase fear of the disease was confined to those in the communities most at risk: gay men, members of the Haitian community and haemophiliacs.

In his bestselling book *And the Band Played On*, the San Francisco journalist Randy Shilts traces the emergence of HIV/AIDS against the backdrop of Reagan's election as president and the ascendancy of Moral Majority, the conservative organisation founded by the televangelist Jerry Falwell in 1979.[29] The title of Shilts's book captures the indifferent 'business as usual' approach that distinguished initial responses to AIDS.[30] Walter Dowdle, deputy director of the CDC, later observed that the press had at first shown little interest in covering the story. 'Then, when the press finally did pick up on it, it was a sort of blood, sex and politics approach.'[31] As cases rose and news of the disease spread, fear and stigmatisation began to play a major role in the epidemic, with members of the gay community who had fought hard for increased rights pushing back against the media's portrayal of the disease as a 'gay plague'.[32]

In 1982 the name of the new infection was changed from GRID, 'gay-related immune deficiency', to AIDS, 'acquired immune deficiency syndrome', reflecting a growing concern that it posed a threat to society at large. This was the point at which a more widespread panic began to take hold, particularly in the face of government unresponsiveness. Susceptible groups were viewed as a moral threat, and the disease became increasingly associated with promiscuity, permissive lifestyles and crime.

Reagan had been elected on a mandate to cut public expenditure and pare back federal welfare. Budgets for Medicaid, food stamps, federal education programmes and the Environmental Protection Agency were slashed. As we've already seen, by the late 1970s an austerity politics was being promoted as an antidote to pernicious social liberalism, which critics alleged was bankrupting the country. New York and San Francisco were taken as paradigms of this wrong-headed governance that was fuelling crime, addiction and antisocial behaviour.

A report about the disease appeared on the front page of the *New York Times* on 24 May 1983 with an announcement from Edward Brandt, assistant secretary of Health and Human Services, that the government was making a concerted 'effort to identify the cause and find a cure for the mysterious illness, known as AIDS, which leads to a breakdown of the body's immune system against disease'.[33] The actor Rock Hudson's death in 1985 prompted Reagan to make his first public mention of AIDS, in response to a reporter's question. Meeting its challenge, he declared grudgingly, was a 'top priority'. But it wasn't until 1987 – six years after the first report of the disease – that he gave his first speech on the epidemic, at a benefit dinner sponsored by the American Foundation for AIDS Research, in which he called for a programme of state and federal testing. 'AIDS is surreptitiously spreading throughout our population,' he said, 'and yet we have no accurate measure of its scope.' By then, the *New York Times* was reporting that US public health authorities had recorded over 35,000 cases and nearly 21,000 deaths from AIDS.[34]

The previous year Reagan had entrusted Charles Everett Koop, the US surgeon general, to prepare a report on the disease. 'The impact of AIDS on our society is and will continue to be devastating,' Koop wrote. From the outset, the epidemic had 'evoked highly emotional and often irrational responses', a panic that Koop ascribed 'to fear of the many unknowns surrounding a new and very deadly disease'. 'Rumors and misinformation spread rampantly,' he observed, further frustrating attempts to contain the spread of infection. It was therefore crucial to launch a nationwide sex education programme to dispel the prevalent myths – that AIDS could be caught by sharing a glass with a sufferer, sipping from a communion cup, being sneezed on or sitting on a lavatory seat. This was a measure intended to combat both the disease and the panic it was causing.[35]

AIDS continued to be cast as a 'plague' in the media, however – a loaded word that carried suggestions of divine judgement. 'HIV may be a new virus,' wrote the sociologist Janet Holland and colleagues in 1990, 'but the fears it invokes about death, sex and deviance are already embedded in our culture and social structures.'[36] Reporting from the city of Arcadia in Florida, where three haemophiliac boys who had tested positive for HIV had been ostracised from a Methodist church, the journalist Charles Krauthammer suggested that 'AIDS hysteria' was caused by too much media coverage, not too little. As he put it, 'irrationality in the face of improbability is not the product of ignorance, but of a media-fed national panic. AIDS is one case where the truth is not making people free. It is so packaged in hype and hysteria that it is simply making people afraid.'[37]

Polls conducted in 1986 and 1987 found that just under 44 per cent of Americans ascribed AIDS to 'God's punishment for immoral behavior', while 21 per cent of those surveyed agreed that 'people with AIDS should be isolated from the rest of society'.[38] Meanwhile, those who tested positive for HIV faced discrimination and HIV-positive children were excluded from schools. The writer and commentator William F. Buckley reflected the homophobic hysteria when he infamously suggested that 'everyone detected with AIDS should be tattooed'.[39]

It's easy to forget that the fear of AIDS wasn't just political; it was personal. Those who developed the disease in the early and mid-1980s were handed a death sentence. Fear was visceral and painful. Watching his former partner Fred Nogales die of AIDS, the young poet Joel Zizik – who was to commit suicide a few years later, aged just thirty – wrote of 'the fever rising until you were liquid / inside your skin, like a small, young planet'.[40] The gay British poet Thom Gunn, then living in San Francisco and a witness to the death from AIDS of many friends, described a similar process of bodily disintegration. 'Dying,' he observed, 'is a difficult enterprise.'[41] The pain and fear of AIDS are recurring themes in the poet Mark Doty's memoir *Heaven's Coast*, which chronicles the last years of his partner Wally Roberts's life. 'Illness is anticipation,' Doty tells us. 'Illness surrounds us with the vertiginous, the branching paths of what *could* happen.' Hope and anger battle through this 'psychic distress, terror of uncertainty, the fear of what opened up before him'. However, physical pain, the kind that 'horse-pill-sized ibuprofen' and codeine find hard to fix, always brings the illness back to a primal 'panic and fear'.[42]

In Britain, by the mid-1980s, it felt as though the AIDS epidemic was about to explode. In a special report on the disease, the journalist Christine Doyle wrote that 'the number of AIDS victims in Britain is doubling every eight months'; unless radical measures were taken, it seemed inevitable that 'we will inexorably follow America, where public health officers describe "rivulets of heterosexual infection" snaking out beyond the risk groups'.[43] Infection was framed as an insidious snake, an emblem of temptation and sin, a 'powerful Satan Bug'.[44] These 'rivulets of infection' seemed to recall the fears expressed in 1968 by the Conservative politician Enoch Powell in his infamous 'Rivers of Blood' speech. Like hordes of unwanted immigrants breaking through Britain's porous borders, HIV was seeping from the leaky bodies of the sick, 'carried in any body fluid – blood, semen, secretions in the vagina, saliva and tears'.[45]

Annihilation was the central thrust of the 'Grim Reaper' advertisement produced in 1987 by Australia's National Advisory Committee on AIDS, an extreme example of the shock approach that featured a personification of death in the form of a giant, scythe-bearing reaper. In a melodramatic gamification of the disease, death is shown in a bowling alley, knocking over skittles that represent AIDS victims.

'Slowly, slowly, the government is waking up – or at least says it is – to the extent of the threat of AIDS,' wrote *The Economist* in late 1986, when the British government announced it was commissioning the advertising agency TBWA to create a hard-hitting information campaign with the catchphrase 'AIDS: Don't Die of Ignorance'.[46] 'The British public is in a state of "AIDS phobia" or generalised fear, based on lack of knowledge about the disease,' declared the *Daily Telegraph*, citing a survey by an American psychologist.[47] So panic would have to be countered by government-directed fear. The role of the media, government and NGOs was crucial: fear and panic would be neutralised with an informed counter-fear, although the dangers of going too far were recognised. 'The balance is a desperately difficult one to strike,' the journalist Richard Evans observed about the campaign, 'between creating panic and encouraging complacency, between the general good and individual liberty and between spreading knowledge and attracting prejudice.'[48] Earlier proposals for a campaign in Britain had apparently been toned down at Margaret Thatcher's insistence; she feared offending Tory voters and encouraging promiscuity.

As Malcolm Gaskin, the designer of the 'Don't Die of Ignorance' campaign, later remarked, 'scaring people was deliberate'; the aim, he said, was to create a 'doom and gloom sci-fi aesthetic'.[49] Leaflets were sent out to homes across the country in January 1987, and the accompanying films were shown on TV. One of the most memorable, by the British director Nicolas Roeg, begins with a terrifying explosion before switching to workers drilling at a rock face. 'There is now a danger that has become a threat to us all,' the actor John Hurt intones. 'It is a deadly disease and there is no known cure.' The final shot reveals a monolithic tombstone inscribed with the word 'AIDS'.

Hollywood soon began to pick up on the message of doom, with science used to justify fear of viruses and give credence to panic plot lines. Wolfgang Petersen's 1995 pandemic thriller *Outbreak* begins with a quotation from the Nobel Prize-winning microbiologist Joshua Lederberg: 'The single biggest threat to man's continued dominance on the planet is the virus.' A host of eminent scientists, clinicians and epidemiologists would later serve as consultants to Steven Soderbergh's 2011 movie *Contagion*.

Scare strategies in public health messaging weren't new in the 1980s, of course. They had been the staple of campaigns warning of sexually transmitted infections during the Second World War, when posters alerting servicemen to the dangers of venereal disease featured pictures of vamped 'pick-ups' and 'good-time girls' along with images that evoked violence and death: a loaded pistol, women with skull faces, booby traps and ominous syringes. Although the instrumentalised use of fear continued to be central to government messaging during the Cold War, there was also growing doubt about the efficacy of fear-based appeals and recognition of the harm that panic could do. In the 1980s fear came to be viewed, at least by many AIDS activists, as counterproductive. While it created paranoia, the moralistic messages that characterised many fear-driven health campaigns perpetuated homophobic and racist stereotypes.[50]

AIDS didn't only tap into old fears, though; it gave rise to new ones. Janet Holland and her colleagues were right when they wrote in 1990: 'What is new about AIDS in Britain and the USA, is the way in which the realisation that we are in the middle of an epidemic has brought together particularly potent fears of death, with confusion and uncertainty over sexual identity.'[51] Fear about HIV/AIDS brought to the fore the contested nature of sex and gender categories, ultimately making more space for the articulation of queer, non-binary and transgender identities.

But fear was still the dominant response to the disease. The confusion between the HIV virus and the AIDS-related diseases that manifest when a person's immune system is compromised added to this fear.[52] As did the casual statistical blurring in the media between those infected with HIV and those who had died from AIDS. At the same time, while it could take 'years to erupt', AIDS was viewed as a 'disease time bomb' with the virus exerting 'a remote-control effect'.[53] HIV could apparently 'lurk undetected in the blood stream from nine months to seven years before it strikes'.[54] This state of maleficent suspension, and the lack of visible symptoms, made it even more frightening. The virus was imagined as a loiterer, a brainwashed death agent sent by the corrupt leaders of the 'Evil Empire', as Ronald Reagan had dubbed the Soviet Union in 1983.[55]

In the booming, market-oriented 1980s, the commercialisation of fear was also an important feature of the HIV/AIDS epidemic. The catchy acronym AIDS, easy to pronounce and remember, had the draw of a commercial brand; as the American singer-songwriter Prince put it in his 1987 hit 'Sign o' the Times', it was 'a big disease with a little name'. AIDS turned a word for help, encouragement and support into a killer syndrome – it was a disease masquerading as a cure.

Put bluntly, the fear created by AIDS sold – and not just newspapers and magazines but condoms, medicines and the accoutrements of a healthy lifestyle. As Susan Sontag pointed out in 1989, it wasn't only that public information campaigns were caught up in consumerism; it was the fact that commercial interests had contributed to the spread of HIV/AIDS by promoting recreational sexuality in the name of freedom.[56] AIDS was more than a health concern; it was an economic issue. Research and public health campaigns required money, while the race was on 'to find the money spinner' drug.[57] 'Hysteria about AIDS seems to have swept even more quickly through the fund management community than among those most at risk from the disease,' the *Financial Times* noted in 1986.[58] AZT, an antiretroviral drug designed for cancer therapy, gained Food and Drug Administration (FDA) approval for use in treating AIDS in the United States in 1987, with other drugs following in the early 1990s.

The ambiguous line between public health and consumerism lay at the heart of the controversy over the AIDS awareness posters produced by the Italian clothing company Benetton as part of its 'Shock of Reality' campaign in the early 1990s. One series was based on a black-and-white picture taken by the American photographer Therese Frare, then a student at Ohio University, which shows the gay AIDS activist David Kirby on his deathbed, surrounded by grieving family. Even though Kirby's family had consented to its use, the colourised picture caused a furore in 1992. Magazines, including *Elle* and *Vogue*, declined to use it, and groups called for a boycott of Benetton's clothes. The Terrence Higgins Trust – a well-known British AIDS charity – denounced it as 'unethical' and in 'bad taste'. Writing in the *Sunday Times*, the novelist Helen Fielding declared, 'For the offended consumer, the only way to stop this self-perpetuating madness is to vote with our cash.'[59]

Many commentators were repelled by what they regarded as Benetton's exploitation of the image for self-promotion, its logo appearing prominently at the bottom of the picture. 'They're exploiting AIDS to make a buck,' David Eng, of the New York-based non-profit Gay Men's Health Crisis, observed. The activist organisation ACT UP responded by re-appropriating the image and inserting the tagline 'There's only one pullover this photograph should be used to sell', alongside a picture of a condom and their logo 'Silence = Death'. As the cultural theorist McKenzie Wark observed at the time, fear could sell activism as well as clothes.[60]

The associations between AIDS and the marketplace were also evident in China, which from the late 1970s had been undergoing progressive market liberalisation. This was the context for the first HIV/AIDS epidemics there. Aside from intravenous drug users, the disease was linked to a semi-official blood market that had developed alongside the deregulation and piecemeal privatisation of health services. The profits to be had from the sale of plasma for commercial use sparked a rush to set up blood collection centres. As the anthropologist Ann Anagnost writes, 'Provincial authorities found in biotechnology the illusory promise of big profits that could revitalize a devastated landscape left in the wake of the rural economic reforms.'[61] However, those who sold their blood weren't screened for disease; as a result, many people became infected with either HIV/AIDS or hepatitis, although authorities tried to hush it up. The Chinese writer Yan Lianke's novel *Dream of Ding Village*, published in 2006 but now banned in China, gives a disturbing account of how this blood economy led to social implosion as AIDS took its toll, with fear and panic creating violent divisions that tore families and communities apart. 'The most contagious virus was fear' is the tagline of the American-Hong Kong filmmaker Ruby Yang's award-winning documentary exposé *The Blood of Yingzhou District* (2006).

One striking feature of the Western HIV/AIDS panic in the 1980s and 1990s was the extent to which experiences of the disease in other places were marginalised, particularly in Africa, where millions of people were dying. When it was mentioned, Africa was invariably viewed as the ground zero of the disease – just as it is in the movie *Outbreak*, which begins with the bombing of a US army camp in Zaire to contain a mysterious and highly infectious viral disease.

Randy Shilts, who was to die of an AIDS-related illness in 1994, also began his story of the AIDS epidemic in Zaire, at the sickbed of a forty-six-year-old Danish doctor in 1976. The disease Grethe Rask was suffering from would later be identified as AIDS. 'The battle between humans and disease was nowhere more bitterly fought,' Shilts wrote, 'than here in the fetid equatorial climate, where heat and humidity fuel the generation of new life forms.' In a portentous metaphor that conflates disease control with population control, Shilts noted that Central Africa 'seemed to sire new diseases with nightmarish regularity'.[62]

While viruses posed real threats, they were also a convenient metaphor for a dangerous new interdependence, which was being fuelled by globalisation. The Institute of Medicine's 1992 report *Emerging Infections: Microbial Threats to Health in the United States* had underlined the new global dimension of the security challenges posed by disease. 'In the context of infectious diseases,' the report noted, 'there is nowhere in the world from which we are remote and no one from whom we are disconnected.'[63] The pathways that sustained the global economy were the same ones that now served as conduits for the circulation of dangerous diseases.[64] The fear and panic of the late 1980s and early 1990s arose from the challenge of containing pathogenic threats without shutting down the whole system.

AIDS in Africa affected different populations from the high-risk groups in North America and Europe. While the vast majority of AIDS victims in the United States were 'male homosexuals and intravenous drug addicts', in African countries such as Uganda and Zaire – which became the Democratic Republic of Congo in 1997 – the disease affected 'men and women alike'. Local conditions, including the use of unsterilised needles and the prevalence of other sexually transmitted diseases, were key factors that were driving AIDS in the heterosexual African population.[65] By 1999 *The Economist* was writing of 'a global disaster', noting that 47 million people had been infected, the majority of them in Africa. The advent of antiretroviral drugs meant that, at least in wealthy countries, the 'sense of crisis is past' and AIDS was no longer considered a death sentence.[66] This was in stark contrast to sub-Saharan Africa, though, where by 1999 it was estimated that 24.5 million adults and children were HIV-positive.[67]

Even when retroviral drugs were available in the early 2000s, many Africans were fearful of taking them. To understand why, the South African journalist Jonny Steinberg spent time in the district of Lusikisiki in the Eastern Cape Province, a Black rural slum where in 2008 nearly one out of every three pregnant women was reportedly HIV-positive. Ironically, the district had an excellent AIDS treatment programme, with well-stocked clinics that were run as a partnership between local health authorities and the French NGO *Médecins Sans Frontières*.

Steinberg discovered that fear was the main reason for people's failure to seek treatment. First, there was fear of what others in the community might think if you turned out to be HIV-positive. Second, there was fear that this knowledge might be used to undermine your livelihood. And finally, there was fear that the illness might originate from the very medicines and personnel who claimed to be saving you. What if HIV/AIDS was a form of bewitchment? The disease's association with sex added to these conspiracy fears.[68]

Such fears weren't confined to Africa. Rumours circulated in the United States that HIV/AIDS was a plot by the CIA to exterminate African Americans, gay people and other 'undesirables'. The Tuskegee Study of Untreated Syphilis, conducted by the US Public Health Service from 1932 to 1972, played into these rumours. Nearly 400 impoverished African Americans with syphilis had been left untreated so that researchers could observe the natural history of the disease, even though the volunteers had been promised free medical care as an incentive for their participation.[69] There were also claims that HIV was linked to the programme to eradicate smallpox, while other rumours connected it to a US government hepatitis B vaccine study launched in San Francisco in 1978 that enlisted several thousand gay and bisexual men.[70]

In Africa AIDS denialism came from the very top. Thabo Mbeki, president of South Africa between 1999 and 2008, rejected evidence that HIV causes AIDS, instead signing up to the discredited theories of the Berkeley-based molecular biologist Peter Duesberg, who from the late 1980s had suggested that drug abuse was responsible for spreading the disease. A self-proclaimed dissident of the 'HIV-AIDS hypothesis', he insisted that the immunocomprised conditions associated with the disease were, in fact, the symptoms of other illnesses caused by environmental and lifestyle factors.[71]

Meanwhile, Mbeki's health minister, Manto Tshabalala-Msimang, caused an outcry in the South African press when it was reported in 2000 that she had given copies of *Behold a Pale Horse*, by Milton William Cooper, to colleagues. Among madcap theories involving extraterrestrial life, the Club of Rome, freemasons, communists and the Illuminati, Cooper – a former US Navy officer – claimed that the WHO had spread smallpox and that AIDS was a manufactured plague targeting 'the black, Hispanic, and homosexual populations'.[72] It wasn't only Mbeki and Tshabalala-Msimang who espoused such theories. Many other well-known figures supported claims of an AIDS plot, including the Kenyan ecologist Wangari Maathai, who won the 2004 Nobel Peace Prize for her contribution to sustainable development, human rights and democracy.

What is striking about the Tshabalala-Msimang controversy is the large number of people who gave credence to such conspiracy theories, whether they were middle class or lived in the deprived townships. It was these fears that delayed the distribution of antiretroviral drugs, at a time when an estimated 20 per cent of the adult population of South Africa was HIV-positive, with life expectancy predicted to fall dramatically.[73]

In 'normal times', writes the physician and anthropologist Didier Fassin, we tend to view the world through 'similar lenses', but at crisis moments 'a disquieting counter-narrative emerges with peculiar plots and maleficent agents' offering a different worldview. 'Conspiracy theories,' he suggests, 'express social imaginaries and political anxieties that remain unspeakable or unheard.'[74] Colonial memories of oppression have been crucial to the persistence of such theories.

Although panic is often viewed as disruptive, it actually draws its force from continuity: those who are embroiled in a crisis often seek to make sense of it by drawing parallels with the past. As the historian Luise White has shown, during the colonial period Africans in Central and West Africa told each other terrifying vampire stories about white colonists apprehending unwary locals before slitting their throats.[75] While these may have been unfounded, there are plenty of examples of coercive colonial biomedical interventions. Under the Contagious Diseases Prevention Act of 1885, Black South Africans suffering from syphilis were forcefully detained out of fear that the disease might spread to the white population. Racist public health measures were extended in subsequent decades. When epidemics of bubonic plague threatened urban centres such as Cape Town and Port Elizabeth between 1900 and 1904, the amended Public Health Act of 1897 was cited as a justification for moving 'coloured' South Africans into makeshift camps, which were to become the model for the townships during apartheid.[76]

Given this historical context, not to mention the framing of Africans as biological threats by the West – think of the xenophobic backlash that the Ebola outbreak in West Africa sparked in the United States in 2014, when Africans with no exposure to the disease were shunned – it isn't surprising that suspicion surrounds Western biomedical interventions. At the same time, accidental side effects of health interventions have reinforced this mistrust. Hepatitis C was transmitted via syringes in Central and West Africa during public health campaigns, and the Canadian microbiologist Jacques Pépin has argued that this could explain how HIV/AIDS became pandemic.[77] At some point, probably in the 1920s, he argues, human contact with chimpanzees resulted in the spillover of the simian immunodeficiency virus into human populations. According to Pépin, when unsterilised needles were used in large-scale public health campaigns in French Equatorial Africa and the Belgian Congo to tackle tropical diseases such as malaria and sleeping sickness during the 1930s and 1940s, it started to spread more widely.[78]

Urbanisation, road and railway construction and a pronounced gender imbalance were other factors in the spread of HIV. While colonial authorities encouraged male workers to relocate to cities like Léopoldville in the Congo, they discouraged women from moving.[79] As a result, prostitution thrived in urban areas, and it was in the clinics treating men and sex workers for STDs, where needles were reused, that HIV spread between the cities of Central and West Africa – and ultimately far beyond.[80] The AIDS epidemic, and the rumours spread about its origins and means of transmission, rekindled memories of these discriminatory and badly managed public health policies.[81]

The reaction to the US-led polio eradication campaign in Nigeria, Afghanistan and Pakistan highlights the degree to which misgivings about Western medicine persist among local populations. Some people worry that it may be a US ploy to sterilise Muslim children or an elaborate cover for Western government spies. These suspicions have been further fuelled by Western conspiracists: in 1999, for example, the journalist Edward Hooper claimed that HIV/AIDS had originated in the 1950s from an experimental polio vaccine using chimpanzee cells.[82] They're also given weight by US military interventions, such as the killing of Osama bin Laden by US Navy SEALs in May 2011. The CIA had recruited a Pakistani physician, Shakil Afridi, purportedly with the cooperation of Save the Children, to front a spurious hepatitis B immunisation campaign as a way of gaining intelligence on the residents of the compound where bin Laden was living. Not surprisingly, the use of a fake public health campaign as a pretext for a US military operation only strengthened conspiracy theories around polio vaccination; the result was that despite the vast amounts of money and effort that have been spent on immunisation, the disease has yet to be eradicated.[83]

Beneath Reagan's bullish promotion of US power in the 1980s 'lay fear – fear of national decline, of enemies abroad, of dangerous classes at home'.[84] Looming over these was the communist menace and the terror of nuclear war. Meanwhile, globalisation brought with it new risks and fears too.

There was a dark side to the burgeoning global economy in the increasing divide between industrialised nations and debt-ridden countries in Africa and Latin America, for whom the 1980s is often viewed as a 'lost decade'. In the United States, structural changes to the economy led to the offshoring of jobs and the deindustrialisation of American cities, particularly in the Midwestern and north-eastern 'Rust Belt'. The trafficking of illegal drugs, notably cocaine, from South America prompted a scaling up of the 'war on drugs'. An epidemic of crack cocaine was viewed as the root cause of social breakdown; lurid media reports, which reinforced racial stereotypes of Black gang violence and 'crack babies', gave rise to a moral panic. The death of the American college basketball player Len Bias from a cocaine overdose in 1986 served as a further catalyst; the Anti-Drug Abuse Act brought in minimum sentencing for drug offences, but it was seen as racially biased since it disproportionately targeted African American crack users, ultimately leading to the explosion of the Black prison population.[85] Poverty, crime and addiction created a toxic urban nexus, a concatenation of fears that drove the HIV/AIDS epidemic, which by 1990 had claimed over 100,000 American lives.[86]

In his farewell address to the American people, delivered in January 1989, Reagan urged his successors to be vigilant when negotiating with foreign powers like the USSR. 'And don't be afraid to see what you see,' he famously said.[87] A few weeks earlier, on 21 December 1988, Pan Am Flight 103 from Frankfurt to Detroit via London and New York had exploded over the town of Lockerbie in Scotland, when a bomb hidden in a cassette player detonated, killing all passengers and crew on board. As the Soviet threat diminished, another kind of terror was coming into view, and it would redefine the world.

14

War on Terror

Many of the economic and geopolitical developments discussed in the previous chapter were crucial in shaping the fears that formed around new terrorist threats from the 1990s. The rise of China and India, along with the collapse of the USSR, shifted the balance of global power, as did the growing influence of the European Union. And the Middle East became a flashpoint for conflict. Support of Israel led to Arab and Muslim distrust of the United States and its allies, while US diplomatic relations with Iran were severed after the 1979 Iranian Revolution, which toppled the pro-American Shah and established a theocratic Islamic republic under Ayatollah Khomeini. In response to the Iraqi dictator Saddam Hussein's invasion of Kuwait in August 1990, the US headed a military coalition to the Gulf to protect Saudi Arabia – a major oil-producing country, like Kuwait – and to expel Iraqi forces from the region.

There was also growing alienation among the large Muslim communities in Europe and North America, which in turn fed white resentment that fuelled populist anti-immigrant parties. And yet, in 1990, despite the Lockerbie bombing and the terrorist violence perpetrated by the Palestine Liberation Organization, there was little inkling of the new terror that was to come. Writing that year, one American terrorist expert predicted that 'the 1990s will see a moderate increase in left-wing terrorist activity' along with violence from a more unified and tech-savvy far right.[1]

There were good reasons for these prognostications. The

9/11 attacks on New York and Washington have tended to overshadow this earlier terror, as well as the numerous attacks by domestic terror groups in the 1960s and 1970s on landmark buildings, corporate institutions and government offices across America. The FBI's response to these 'revolutionary' threats, which took place against the backdrop of anti-Vietnam War protests, included the creation of Squad 47, an intelligence unit based in New York that was tasked with shutting down radical organisations.[2]

In 1969 the Weathermen, a breakaway faction of the Students for a Democratic Society who took their name from the Bob Dylan song 'Subterranean Homesick Blues' – 'You don't need a weatherman to know which way the wind blows' – organised a series of violent actions in Chicago, known as the 'Days of Rage'. Rebranded as the Weather Underground, the militant group was responsible for a slew of 1970s bomb attacks on, among other targets, the headquarters of the State Department, the Capitol, Pentagon, California Attorney General's office and a police station in New York.[3] In the words of their 1974 manifesto, the group's mission was to promote 'anti-imperialism and revolution inside the imperial US'. To do this required them to mobilise people's 'fears and discontents and hopes'. They cited as their inspiration the 'fearless determination' of the Palestinians and pointed to the ways in which a discriminatory education system taught young people nothing but 'lessons of competition, self-hatred, fear and loneliness'. America was a land saturated with fear, which could only be overcome with violent disruption:

> For people in the US the basic fact of life is fear. People are afraid of society. No one knows what is going to happen. Fear of illness, fear of getting laid off. Afraid to go outdoors. Afraid of Black people moving into the neighborhood, afraid of loss of status, afraid of not looking right, afraid of being taken advantage of, afraid to speak up, afraid of growing old.[4]

One of the most notorious episodes of home-grown American terror was the kidnapping in 1974 of the nineteen-year-old publishing heiress Patty Hearst from her Berkeley apartment by the Symbionese Liberation Army (SLA) – a story that took a surreal twist when the hostage joined her kidnappers and took part in a bank robbery. The SLA had been founded by radicals in the San Francisco Bay area and operated in 'the twilight zone of hit-and-run terrorism', spreading its radical message with kidnappings, executions and bank robberies.[5] Its slogan was 'Death to the Fascist insects who prey upon the lives of the people' and its symbol was a seven-headed cobra.[6] 'In the true-life world of the 1970s, where fantasy often has difficulty approximating actuality,' wrote Leroy Aarons, a staff writer for the *Washington Post*, 'the Symbionese Liberation Army is frighteningly or mysteriously real.'[7] After a shootout with police, Patty Hearst went on the run with other SLA members but was eventually apprehended and sentenced to thirty-five years in prison, which was subsequently commuted to twenty-two months by President Jimmy Carter.

Religious terrorist campaigns were also perpetrated by the likes of the right-wing Jewish Defense League, while ethnic and nationalist groups carried out attacks, among them the Black Panther Party, formed in Oakland, California, in 1966 and described by J. Edgar Hoover as 'the greatest threat to the internal security of this country'. Between 1968 and 1972 there were well over a hundred domestic US plane hijackings.[8]

These were 'days of rage' in Britain, as well. Terrorism there was a fact of life, an anxiety kept simmering by reminders over loudspeakers not to leave unattended bags on public transport and posters urging vigilance. The operations of the Provisional Irish Republican Army (IRA) – the evolution of a paramilitary organisation formed in 1919 during Ireland's struggle for independence – escalated from the late 1960s and particularly after 30 January 1972, when British Army paratroopers killed fourteen demonstrators on a march in Londonderry, which led to a retaliatory bombing in Belfast. The 'Troubles' would last until the signing of the Good Friday Agreement in 1998.

While shootings and bombings were a regular occurrence in Northern Ireland, IRA violence also spilled over onto the streets of mainland Britain. Two pubs were bombed in Birmingham in November 1974, and an assassination attempt was made on the British prime minister Margaret Thatcher and members of her government at the Conservative Party conference in Brighton in October 1984. This escalation of violence was triggered in part by the death in 1981 of seven IRA and three Irish National Liberation Army prisoners on hunger strike at the Maze prison outside Belfast. Viewed in retrospect, the images of Bobby Sands on his deathbed anticipate those of AIDS patients like David Kirby. Images of the emaciated male body invoked fear but also political determination. 'Their arguments increased and multiplied as furiously as their bodies decomposed,' wrote the critic Maud Ellmann of the IRA strikers, 'as if their flesh were being eaten by their words.'[9]

Nor was Continental Europe an exception to terror. In Germany the far-left Baader–Meinhof group was responsible for assassinations, kidnappings and armed bank robberies through the 1970s. Their actions culminated in the so-called 'German Autumn' of 1977, a series of terrorist attacks that caused widespread panic across the country. They kidnapped Hanns Martin Schleyer, a prominent businessman and former Nazi, holding him hostage in an attempt to secure the release of several of their members from prison, and later shooting him when their demands were rejected. When the kidnapping and the hijacking of Lufthansa Flight 181 in Mogadishu by the Popular Front for the Liberation of Palestine failed, imprisoned Baader–Meinhof leaders committed suicide in Stammheim.[10] In *Germany in Autumn*, a 1978 film about the crisis that conveys the mood in Germany at the time, the well-known director Rainer Werner Fassbinder expressed concern that the German government was exploiting public fear as a pretext for curbing democratic freedoms.

One of the most dramatic episodes of terror in the 1970s was the abduction of the former Italian prime minister Aldo Moro by the Red Brigades, a militant left-wing group that was involved in numerous terrorist acts during the 1970s and early 1980s. In 1978 members of the group dressed as Alitalia employees ambushed Moro, killing five of his bodyguards. After holding him hostage for fifty-four days and realising that the government wasn't about to capitulate to their demands by releasing imprisoned members of the group, they shot Moro and left his body in the trunk of a Renault 4 parked on Via Caetani in Rome. Pictures of his dead body appeared on the front page of most newspapers the following day.

In 1994 the German writer Hans Magnus Enzensberger pointed out that Western commentators still tended to discuss violence as if it was something that happened overseas. Writing against the backdrop of the LA riots, the Gulf War, the break-up of the USSR and genocide in Bosnia, he suggested that it had become increasingly difficult to overlook the brutal continuum that linked foreign hostilities with backyard battles.[11]

Terror may have flourished in the late twentieth century, but it took on new proportions on 11 September 2001. The scale and audacity of the al-Qaeda-inspired attacks on New York and Washington revealed the dark side of globalisation with shocking clarity: from brazen, cross-border terrorist activity to mobile technology that enabled the global flow of information and funds that allowed the mastermind of the bombing, Osama bin Laden, to operate his terror network from a remote hide-out in the Tora Bora cave complex in the Spīn Ghar mountains of eastern Afghanistan. Nineteen hijackers taking over four planes – two Boeing 757s and two Boeing 767s – en route to Los Angeles and San Francisco from Boston, Washington and New York was a logistical operation on a different scale.

The shock of the terror attacks on US soil 'at the center of a great city on a peaceful morning', in President George W. Bush's words, created an atmosphere of fear that was amplified by the media – and has persisted. 'After all that has just passed,' Bush told the nation days after the attacks, 'all the lives taken and all the possibilities and hopes that died with them, it is natural to wonder if America's future is one of fear.'[12] 'Instead of the next big thing being some new technological innovation,' wrote the policy analyst David Rieff at the time, 'the next big thing is likely to be fear.' According to an ABC News and *Washington Post* poll, 76 per cent of Americans remained fearful of a 'major' terrorist attack in the United States in 2015. Following '9/11', the historian Peter Stearns has suggested, Americans 'have come, as a nation, to fear excessively'. Stearns has compared the public's responses to 9/11 with those to Pearl Harbor, arguing that Americans 'were over three times as likely to be afraid [post-9/11], and the level of their fear, when expressed, ran much deeper as well'.[13]

The World Trade Center was chosen for spectacular effect, just as it had been in 1993, when a terrorist truck bomb exploded in a garage under the North Tower, killing six people and wounding many others.[14] Rieff called the destruction of the buildings 'the revenge of those for whom modernity has, rightly or wrongly, seemed like a curse'. The towers were landmarks in a skyline that not only defined American financial might but also served as cultural identifiers for the country, along with the Statue of Liberty and the Empire State Building. Many New Yorkers who had initially written off the towers as an eyesore had changed their tune by the mid-1990s.[15]

Formally opened in April 1973, in the midst of a recession, the World Trade Center stood as the symbol of a progressive future, technology-led and driven by commerce; what Nelson Rockefeller, the New York governor who attended the building's dedication, called a 'great marriage of utility and beauty'.[16] The buildings weren't easy to fill in a difficult economic climate, but they received a boost when the French high-wire artist Philippe Petit rigged a cable between the towers in 1974 and spent forty-five minutes walking between them with a thirty-foot balancing pole, a quarter of a mile off the ground. 'Sometimes the sky grows dark around the wire, the wind rises, the cable gets cold, the audience becomes worried,' Petit wrote. 'At those moments I hear fear screaming at me.'[17]

You can date a film by the presence of the towers in the backdrop. When they appear in pre-9/11 movies, we read their presence as a foreboding of the future. After 9/11, the symbolic meaning of the towers was reversed: they were now a memorial to fear. Watching events unfold on TV, it was hard not to think of all the films the towers had featured in, or of disaster movies like *Towering Inferno*, *Die Hard* and *Godzilla*. Spectators compulsively looked on as if events belonged to a Hollywood storyline. At the time of the attack, a trailer promoting the new *Spiderman* movie showed the getaway helicopter from a downtown heist suspended in a giant spider's web between the towers. In *Independence Day*, the Empire State Building and the Twin Towers get hit in an alien invasion.

If this was a 'clash of civilisations', as many were now billing it, the terrorists were on the same page when it came to the aesthetics of disaster.[18] 'The movies set the pattern, and these people have copied the movies,' the veteran director Robert Altman told the *Hollywood Reporter* a few weeks after the attack. 'Nobody would have thought to commit an atrocity like that unless they'd seen it in a movie. How dare we continue to show this kind of mass destruction in movies? I just believe we created this atmosphere and taught them how to do it.'[19] Michael McCaul, Chair of the US House of Representatives' Homeland Security Committee, later blamed 9/11 on a collective 'failure of imagination'. Political leaders and members of the intelligence agencies, he asserted, couldn't think laterally enough to anticipate the unorthodox threats to the United States's security.[20] The irony here is that the bombing of the World Trade Center had already been imagined. It didn't require any out-of-the-box thinking: it was there, primed to go off, in a Hollywood film.

*

Terror, and the global networks that facilitated it, was often analogised with an infectious disease. Like a novel and fast-mutating viral life form, terror required new tools for its identification, management and eradication. As Richard N. Haass, director of policy planning in the US State Department, told the Council of Foreign Relations in October 2001, international terrorism was 'analogous to a terrible, lethal virus', which was 'sometimes dormant, sometimes virulent'. 'Like a virus, international terrorism respects no boundaries,' Haass said. 'We therefore need to take appropriate prophylactic measures at home and abroad to prevent terrorism from multiplying and check it from infecting our societies or damaging our lives.'[21]

In his 2002 State of the Union Address, President Bush spoke of waging a war against the 'terrorist parasites' that lived in 'remote jungles and deserts', and lay in wait in 'the center of large cities'.[22] It was a plot line echoed by the British prime minister Tony Blair when he addressed Congress in 2003 following the invasion of Iraq by a US-led coalition, which took place at the same time as the SARS epidemic began to spread from China. According to Blair, 'a new and deadly virus has emerged. The virus is terrorism, whose intent to inflict destruction is unconstrained by human feeling.'[23]

Viral terror gave rise to nationwide panic days after 9/11, when letters laced with deadly anthrax spores were anonymously sent to media outlets and politicians, leading to twenty-two infections and five deaths.[24] When the first letter arrived on 18 September, it was initially thought that the anthrax episode – codenamed 'Amerithrax' by the FBI – was linked to the World Trade Center attacks, fuelling worries of a new phase of biological terror.[25] As it turned out, the letters had been sent by a disgruntled army biodefence expert, but in the aftermath of the attacks the media 'blurred distinctions between viruses, bacteria and radiation, creating a generalized environment of fear which facilitated and legitimized controversial government initiatives'.[26]

Bush's use of the term 'war on terror' in a speech to Congress in September 2001 was misleading, since the word 'war' suggested that terrorists were conventional military adversaries who could be outmuscled using tried-and-tested methods. In fact, after the 9/11 attacks, governments began to mimic the terrorists' tradecraft by building counterterrorist networks and new surveillance capacities modelled on those of their opponents. In this 'everywhere war', satellites, GPS and drones assumed increasingly important roles. 'Predator' and 'Reaper' Unmanned Aerial Vehicles were flown on bombing expeditions to Iraq, Afghanistan and Pakistan from trailers in the desert of Nevada 'using joysticks and computer screens'.[27] The post-9/11 formulation of a 'war on terror' demonstrated how the word 'terror' now meant an 'asymmetrical willingness and capacity to destroy the other without the formalities of war'.[28] As Vice President Dick Cheney had warned in the wake of 9/11, the United States would have to enter 'the dark side' to defeat the threat of global terror, playing dirty 'in the shadows'.[29]

Conventional, boots-on-the-ground strategies weren't ditched, however. In October 2001 Bush launched a war in Afghanistan to overthrow the Taliban, who were giving shelter to al-Qaeda. And in March 2003 he invaded Iraq with a military coalition to topple Saddam Hussein. The US report 'A Decade of Deception and Defiance', published in September 2002, alleged that Saddam had acquired weapons of mass destruction and possessed biological and chemical capabilities, as well as ambitions for nuclear arms. In a speech to the UN General Assembly, Bush warned that the Iraqi regime was 'a grave and gathering danger'. Fear and hope were central to his remarks. 'The United Nations,' he declared, 'was born in the hope that survived a world war – the hope of a world moving toward justice, escaping old patterns of conflict and fear.' Today, he continued, 'our greatest fear is that terrorists will find a shortcut to their mad ambitions when an outlaw regime supplies them with the technologies to kill on a massive scale'. If the UN did nothing, Bush asserted, its members would be 'condemning the Middle East to years of bloodshed and fear'. 'We must choose between a world of fear and a world of progress,' he urged.[30]

Fear was used as a means of justifying and gaining public support for an invasion, even as it was condemned as a refutation of hope and a capitulation to terror. As Bush kept reminding Americans, 'Freedom and fear are at war. The advance of human freedom, the great achievement of our time and the great hope of every time, now depends on us.'[31] In other words, fear was simultaneously the poison and the remedy. When US Secretary of State General Colin Powell made the case for an invasion before the UN Security Council in February 2003, he drew on the evidence of intercepted telephone calls and satellite images to point to 'an accumulation of facts and disturbing patterns of behavior'. Among these facts was Iraq's possession of chemical weapons, suggested by aerial views of a munitions facility.[32] No such facility was ever discovered, inspiring the Spanish-born American artist Iñigo Manglano-Ovalle to produce a poignant installation art piece, entitled *Phantom Truck* (2007), that used Powell's fragmentary evidence along with post-invasion photographs of American and Kurdish military trailers to reproduce an alleged mobile biological weapons lab. Manglano-Ovalle's point was that Powell had conjured a phantom object of fear to justify military intervention.[33]

In Britain the so-called 'Iraq Dossier' made similar claims. Allegations that Saddam had extended the range of his ballistic missile programme – and in particular the claim that he could 'deploy chemical or biological weapons within 45 minutes of an order to do so' – caused widespread fear as rumours quickly circulated that Britain could be bombed in forty-five minutes. This suggestion was later debunked and turned out to have originated in all probability when a taxi driver on the Iraq–Jordan border recalled a conversation he'd overheard two years earlier. Anything could pass for hard fact in this volatile climate of fear.[34]

The end of the Cold War, as we've already seen, had unsettled the global status quo. Since 1945 the West had shaped its institutions and ideals in opposition to those of the Soviet bloc – and when the USSR collapsed in 1991, it was faced with what the international relations expert Barry Buzan has called a 'threat deficit'. The terror attacks provided Washington with a convenient solution.[35]

While Islamic Jihadism – a controversial term used by Western commentators, particularly after 9/11, to describe a militant form of Islamic extremism – had sought to instil panic in the United States, the Bush administration deployed this fear to promote a political agenda, extend a policy of military intervention and introduce new security legislation. In 2003 former vice-president Al Gore condemned the government for exploiting terror as an excuse 'to use fear as a political tool to consolidate its power and to escape any accountability for its use'.[36] As Zbigniew Brzezinski, a former national security adviser, noted some years later, the 'war on terror' had been designed to produce fear that 'obscures reason, intensifies emotions and makes it easier for demagogic politicians to mobilise the public on behalf of the policies they want to pursue'.[37]

A few days after 9/11, Congress passed a law granting the president unlimited power 'to use all necessary and appropriate force against those nations, organizations, or persons he determines planned, authorized, committed, or aided the terrorist attacks that occurred on September 11, 2001, or harbored such organizations or persons'.[38] The 2001 Patriot Act radically extended the surveillance remit of federal law enforcement agencies, permitting them to tap domestic and international phones and mobilise all available resources in counterterrorism efforts. The definition of 'terrorism' was expanded and the penalties for those charged with terrorist crimes increased. A military order passed two months after the attacks vested the president with the authority to apprehend suspected terrorists anywhere in the world and detain them indefinitely.

This was the climate in which Bush established the Guantánamo Bay detention camp in 2002, conveniently located in Cuba and therefore outside US legal jurisdiction. Combatants suspected of being terrorists were held there without trial and questioned using 'enhanced interrogation techniques', a CIA euphemism for torture; 'waterboarding' involved covering a prisoner's face with a wet cloth to simulate the experience of drowning. US Secretary of Defense Donald Rumsfeld described the camp as a detention centre for 'the worst of the worst', while the attorney general, John Ashcroft, declared, 'Terrorists have no constitutional rights.'[39]

Allegations that prisoners were being held in secret detention centres and transferred across national borders led to several investigations. A June 2006 report estimated that at least a hundred individuals had been abducted from Europe by the CIA with the connivance of European Union member states. Another report, produced by the European parliament, claimed that the CIA had conducted over a thousand flights to countries where prisoners might face torture, in violation of Article 3 of the UN Convention against Torture.[40]

As Corey Robin has observed, 'one day, the war on terrorism will come to an end. All wars do. And when it does, we will find ourselves still living in fear: not of terrorism or radical Islam, but of the domestic rulers that fear has left behind.'[41] In the wake of 9/11, journalists were less inclined to criticise the government and unwittingly turned a blind eye to the abuse of civil liberties, while the stereotyping of Muslims and Arabs led to a surge in hate crimes.[42] What is certain is that the attacks resulted in significant investment in homeland security and led to the rise of a 'terrorism industry' that overstates the threat posed. In the United States there is about as much chance of drowning in a bathtub as of being killed in a terrorist attack, notes John Mueller, an expert in defence policy and counterterrorism.[43] The 9/11 attacks have 'extended and sustained the permanent war economy', an industrial–military complex that hinges on fear and is comprised of government agencies and mega-corporations like Lockheed Martin and Northrop Grumman, along with numerous 'subcontractors and supportive nonmilitary firms and organizations', which all stand to gain from a perpetual war on terror.[44]

The effect of fearmongering soundbites – such as Bush's 'war on terror' – had struck me long before 9/11. When I travelled through northern Pakistan and Afghanistan in 1988, Soviet troops were still very much in evidence. The day before my arrival in Peshawar, the offices of the *Frontier Post* had been bombed, a reminder that there were many in the North-West Frontier Province who opposed a free press, and security was tight. It would be no exaggeration to say that in 1988 Peshawar was Fear City. While the president of Pakistan, Zia ul-Haq, worked with the United States to coordinate the Afghan Mujahideen against the Soviet occupation, millions of refugees poured over the border into his country, flooding the city with arms and giving rise to vast shantytowns. It was here from the late 1980s until around 1991 that al-Qaeda had its headquarters.

The Reagan Doctrine would backfire, of course; the Mujahideen that the US had helped to train and arm became America's nemesis in the 1990s. Beyond that, high-level political fearmongering caused unstoppable chain reactions in places like Peshawar. A geopolitical fear enacted in American foreign policy had fearful ramifications in this border city, just as it also had an impact on national and regional politics. And by the same token the fears that fanned through the refugee camps on the outskirts of Peshawar could boomerang back to the United States. In August 1988 Zia was killed in an unexplained plane crash near Bahawalpur in the Punjab, along with several of his top military brass and two US diplomats.

We need to think about how this web of fear operates: terrorists bombed New York to create fear, which was then harnessed and redirected into a war on terror, which precipitated other fears. Fears emerged from fear like viruses budding from a cell – all the way to the Federally Administered Tribal Areas on the Afghan–Pakistan border. And in a way, to my own paranoiac fear as I crossed a street jammed with hooting buses, bikes, cars and rickshaws by Chowk Yadgar, a square in Peshawar's old walled city. As I passed the domed memorial to Bacha Khan's followers who had been killed in a clash with British troops in 1930, I felt people stare at me with such intensity that I worried for my safety.[45]

Terrorism seeks to achieve its ends through terror. While 9/11 did just that, the fear it produced was also mobilised by governments and other interests for their own purposes. Naomi Klein has compared this 'disaster capitalism', as she calls it, to the shock therapy treatments developed from the late 1950s by the psychiatrist Donald Ewen Cameron, in collaboration with the CIA. When a society has been sufficiently pummelled by disaster, it is often too dazed to put up resistance. Fear makes societies compliant and exploitable. Given that homeland security is big business, it's not surprising that some stocks rise at the news of terrorist attacks. In a 2007 interview Klein emphasised the links between security and the media, noting that General Electric owns NBC and the Californian company InVision Technologies, which manufactures security screening devices for airports. 'A company like that gains from the atmosphere of crisis and fear that is spread through media outlets,' she said. 'It's war against evil everywhere with no end. That's a war that can't be won, and you couldn't ask for a more profitable business plan. The only thing that threatens it is peace.'[46]

And so the terror goes on. In March 2004 a coordinated terror attack on Madrid's commuter train network killed 193 and left some 2,000 injured; the following July a suicide attack on the London underground killed 52 and wounded over 770. In November 2015 Islamic State militants targeted venues across Paris, including the Bataclan concert hall, killing 130 people and leaving many others injured in what President François Hollande described as an 'act of war'. Five years later, a French schoolteacher, Samuel Paty, was decapitated by a Chechen-born teenager outside his school in the Parisian suburb of Conflans-Sainte-Honorine. The same month, three people were stabbed to death in Nice, this time by a young Tunisian immigrant. These killings followed the 2015 attacks on the offices of the satirical French magazine *Charlie Hebdo*, which had published cartoons of the Prophet Muhammad, in which twelve people died, and the death in 2016 of 86 people when a truck ploughed into crowds celebrating Bastille Day.

In response to Paty's beheading the French president, Emmanuel Macron, vowed to 'make fear change sides', but that isn't easy. This is why, in tandem with Bush's retaliatory measures, the two decades after 9/11 saw massive investments in surveillance, enabled by the internet and the rise of social media.[47] Their extent became apparent in 2013, when Edward Snowden, who worked as a contractor for the US National Security Agency (NSA), leaked classified intelligence on its global surveillance programmes that hinted at the involvement of European governments and tech companies including Google, Microsoft and Yahoo.[48] Snowden's leaks suggested that governments, in cahoots with big tech, were hacking personal email accounts and social networking platforms to intercept emails, texts and direct messages – not to mention trawling through contact lists – without the consent of users. A mushrooming apparatus of state surveillance, which had been designed to protect citizens from attack, had itself become a source of fear.

While US authorities condemned Snowden as a threat to the state, his disclosures stoked public fears about privacy and freedom. In September 2020 the US government's mass surveillance programme was ruled illegal and possibly unconstitutional by a federal court.[49] The consequences of this eavesdropping are far-reaching. Online shadowing will doubtless give rise to fears that everything people say or write may be held against them. The invasion of privacy on this scale by government agencies and powerful corporate institutions erodes confidence in the democratic process. And beyond that, it raises the spectre of the deep state, driving conspiracy theories of powerful networks operating under cover in pursuit of ugly agendas of their own.

15

Eco-Panic

Panic and climate change may at first glance seem unrelated; while panic happens quickly, climate change takes so long to manifest that it is hard to conceptualise. The philosopher Timothy Morton suggests that we can't help but think of the climate as a 'hyperobject', a phenomenon too vast to pin down.[1] This is a crisis of the imagination that, as the novelist Amitav Ghosh tells us, is resistant to representation in art and literature; we just can't get our heads around it.[2]

The term 'Anthropocene', proposed in 2000 by the Dutch chemist Paul Crutzen and his colleague Eugene Stoermer, an ecologist, captures the scale of the problem. The human impact on the environment caused by our exploitation of the Earth's natural resources, population growth, urbanisation, the use of fossil fuels, fertilisers, chemicals and carbon emissions has been so profound that a new geological epoch has replaced the Holocene, the post-glacial period that began when human societies first began to settle around 12,000 years ago.[3]

In a pre-modern world, the threats posed to humans came predominantly from natural disasters and epidemics. Then came industrialisation, the result of which has been that modern societies have had to contend with proliferating insecurities of their own making. If you think about it, this is the ultimate feedback loop. Humans have created societies that transform the environment, producing new risks that those societies have to manage by imposing ever more regulation on themselves. The shift from 'external' to 'manufactured' risks has also changed the nature of fear. It's one thing to fear an earthquake or tsunami, quite another to face a hazard that you're in some way accountable for.[4]

But differentiating human-made risks from natural disasters ignores the extent to which they are entangled. Uncertainty about the multiple causes of the environmental challenges we face is driving many of the eco-panics that we're witnessing today. As we've seen, when fear can't be hitched to a specific object, it turns into anxiety. And in the case of climate change, anxiety coexists with the fear produced by tangible phenomena such as shrinking sea ice, thawing permafrost, melting glaciers, droughts and so on. Because it is such a drawn-out and diffused process, we view climate change through its many symptoms, which are presented to us in full catastrophic colour in footage of wildfires, floods, storms, damaged shorelines, ice floes, stranded polar bears and refugees, as well as in graphs, charts and satellite images.

There's an emphasis on the fast and the slow in modern environmentalism, on the blistering pace of technological development and required action versus the need to understand environmental change as the outcome of a process that takes place over millennia.[5] It's this conflation of the immediate with the incremental that has created the ground for a new kind of eco-panic. The environmentalist Bill McKibben sums it up thus: 'The climate fight is the first timed test humanity has faced. If we don't win quickly, we won't win at all. It's the definition of urgent.'[6] Or, in the words of the Swedish climate activist Greta Thunberg, 'the climate crisis is a ticking clock that is rapidly approaching the countdown's end'.[7] Urgency, emergency, crisis: this is the language that frames climate change – one that in recent years has been promoted by activist movements such as Fridays for Future, founded by Thunberg, Extinction Rebellion, a protest group that pushes for direct action and civil resistance to raise awareness of environmental breakdown, and Just Stop Oil, a UK organisation campaigning for an end to fossil fuels.

But eco-panic isn't just triggered by what's already happening; it's also a response to fears about what *might* happen. Some years ago the novelist Jonathan Franzen, a keen bird watcher, had a public spat with the National Audubon Society, a US bird conservation group. Franzen took issue with the way conservationists were prioritising climate change over more pressing problems such as loss of bird habitat.[8] It was easier to fundraise for an intractable future threat, he suggested, than to raise money to solve more immediate problems. Meanwhile, as McKibben has observed, climate change is a 'test' that needs to be 'won'.

The cultivation of panic as a stratagem for environmental awareness is nothing new. In *Silent Spring*, published in 1962, the conservationist Rachel Carson had condemned the indiscriminate use of pesticides and the toxic effects of the first modern synthetic insecticide DDT, which she argued was killing wildlife and jeopardising human health. The controversy that her book sparked, and the eventual banning of DDT in the United States ten years later, set a precedent for the intermeshing of politics and panic in environmental campaigns. As we'll see, this approach caused a backlash that has defined subsequent environmental debates.

In the late 1960s catastrophic events often appeared linked in ways that pointed to a world out of kilter. In June 1969 the Cuyahoga river in Ohio caught fire when sparks from a train ignited industrial material dumped in the water. Startling images of billowing smoke and a fire tug battling flames followed coverage of an oil spill off the coast of Santa Barbara. Meanwhile, it was claimed that peregrine falcons were on the brink of extinction in America, and bald eagle populations were being decimated by DDT, while whales were being hunted to oblivion. Taken together, these reports triggered fears of an imminent environmental collapse. It was in response to this that Gaylord Nelson, a Democrat senator from Wisconsin, launched Earth Day on 22 April 1970, in order to promote environmental awareness. Demonstrations were held in cities across the United States, marking 'the dawn of a new era of "ecological politics"'.[9] The National Oceanic and Atmospheric Administration and the US Environmental Protection Agency were both established later that year, and Congress passed the Clean Air Act, a federal law regulating air emissions.[10]

All of this took place against increasingly gloomy predictions about the future of the planet. It was high time, scientists suggested, for panic. In a speech at the University of Rhode Island in November 1970 the Harvard biochemist and Nobel laureate George Wald suggested that 'civilization will end within fifteen to thirty years unless immediate action is taken against problems facing mankind'.[11] One prominent doomster was the Stanford biologist Paul Ehrlich, who published his controversial book *The Population Bomb* in 1968. 'The battle to feed all of humanity is over,' he declared. 'In the 1970s hundreds of millions of people will starve to death in spite of any crash programs embarked upon now.'[12] Ehrlich's book followed other publications that predicted imminent food shortages: in one of these, *Famine, 1975!* by William and Paul Paddock, the exclamatory title was an indication of what had by then become a prevalent panic.

In a 1969 essay entitled 'Eco-Catastrophe!' Ehrlich forecast the impending extinction of ocean life, claiming that 'a combination of ecosystem destabilization, sunlight reduction, and a rapid escalation in chlorinated hydrocarbons', would precipitate 'the ultimate catastrophe'. Food shortages and toxic smog would lead to political chaos, and the world would be in free fall. 'Most of the people who are going to die in the greatest cataclysm in the history of man,' he wrote, 'have already been born.'[13] Later that year, during a visit to London, Ehrlich anticipated 'worldwide plague, thermonuclear war, overwhelming pollution [and] ecological catastrophe'. 'If I were a gambler,' he opined, 'I would take even money that England will not exist in the year 2000.'[14] In his contribution to a collection of essays entitled *The Crisis of Survival*, published to celebrate Earth Day 1970, he imagined a post-apocalyptic world viewed from the year 2000. Famine has killed 65 million Americans and almost 4 billion people have perished globally in the 'Great Die-Off'.[15] As a 1970 sci-fi anthology for which Ehrlich wrote the introduction proclaimed, this was the 'Nightmare Age'.[16]

In December 1972 a crew member on board the Apollo 17 space mission took a photograph of the Earth. The so-called 'Blue Marble' image shows a luminescent planet mottled with white cloud. Suspended in darkness, the Earth appears as an autonomous life-sustaining system, with the camera's gaze extending from Africa to the Mediterranean and Antarctica – a perspective that intimates vulnerability and 'planetary interdependence'.[17] The image was reproduced on the cover of James Lovelock's 1979 book *Gaia*, which argued that all living organisms interact with their environments to create a complex, self-regulating system, a planet in balance.[18] As the UN report *Our Common Future* put it in 1987:

> From space, we see a small and fragile ball dominated not by human activity and edifice but by a pattern of clouds, oceans, greenery, and soils. Humanity's inability to fit its activities into that pattern is changing planetary systems, fundamentally. Many such changes are accompanied by life-threatening hazards. This new reality, from which there is no escape, must be recognized – and managed.[19]

In the same year as the photograph was taken, a report entitled *The Limits to Growth* presented another planetary vision of interconnectedness. Commissioned by the Club of Rome, an international think tank, it was the work of the system dynamics group at MIT's Sloan School of Management, who used a computer model to study the consequences of global growth. 'If the present growth trends in world population, industrialisation, pollution, food production, and resource depletion continue unchanged,' the authors concluded, 'the limits to growth on this planet will be reached sometime within the next one hundred years.' They also warned of a 'sudden and uncontrollable decline in both population and industrial capacity'.[20] The report sold millions of copies worldwide, making it one of the bestselling environmental books of all time.

Although Ehrlich and the Club of Rome are often lumped together and viewed as fellow drum beaters of the apocalypse, their aims were very different.[21] Ehrlich attributed the depletion of the world's resources to overpopulation and warned of a demographic time bomb. Reading *The Population Bomb* today is a disquieting experience, not least because of the way it invokes the planet's roiling masses as an infestation. A passage in the prologue describes Ehrlich's experience in Delhi as a forewarning of the planet's congested future: 'People eating, people washing, people sleeping. People visiting, arguing, and screaming. People thrusting their hands through the taxi window, begging. People defecating and urinating. People clinging to buses. People herding animals. People, people, people, people.'[22] The people in this racist harangue are statistical ciphers, stripped of humanity and reduced to basic physiological functions, indistinguishable from the animals they herd.

In contrast, although branded neo-Malthusian by some, the Club of Rome was more concerned with the multifaceted dimensions of growth, and above all with the political and economic systems that sustained global inequalities. Population was one element of a broader critique aimed at the global hegemony of a Western model of progress which, although unsustainable, was so deeply entrenched that it had become unchallengeable.[23]

But at that time it was the cooling of the Earth that was causing alarm. In January 1970 the *Washington Post* declared that colder winters heralded a new ice age. A *Newsweek* article in 1975 with the headline 'The Cooling World' warned of 'ominous signs that the Earth's weather patterns have begun to change dramatically' and pointed to 'a drop of half a degree in average ground temperatures in the Northern Hemisphere between 1945 and 1968'.[24] 'This cooling has already killed hundreds of thousands of people,' the science journalist Lowell Ponte asserted in his book *The Cooling* in 1976. 'If it continues and no strong action is taken, it will cause world famine, world chaos, and world war, and this could all come before the year 2000.'[25] It was a prediction that also appeared in popular books such as *The Weather Conspiracy*. In 1973 and 1976 *Time* magazine produced special issues on 'The Big Freeze' and 'The Cooling of America', along with a 1979 cover story on 'How to Survive the Coming Ice Age'. In a 1978 documentary titled *The Coming Ice Age*, scenes from a severe winter in Buffalo, New York, included reports of people freezing to death in marooned cars. This brutal Buffalo winter, we are told, will soon become the norm across the world, as climatologists predict a coming ice age in which 'Arctic cold and perpetual snow could turn most of the habitable portions of our planet into a polar desert'.

Climate change debates in the 1970s occurred in the context of the global oil crisis, which had significant political effects. As the historian Meg Jacobs has shown, it wasn't just the empty gas tanks in America that indicated a nation in decline – there was also the absence of Christmas tree lights, the imposition of daylight saving time, lowered thermostats and a 55 m.p.h. speed limit to conserve gas consumption. The oil embargo, which lasted for six months in 1973, led to a recession and underlined the dangers of America's energy dependency; five years later, the oil shortage caused by the Iranian Revolution was another reminder.[26]

If environmentalism began as a panic, it's a response that has persisted. As *Time* declared in a 2006 headline to introduce a report on global warming, 'Be Worried. Be VERY Worried.' Contemporary environmental documentaries, such as Al Gore's *An Inconvenient Truth*, which appeared in the same year, were also designed to instil fear at the prospect of imminent environmental catastrophe.[27]

Writing in the *Washington Post* in 2011, the environmental activist Mike Tidwell described how his approach to climate change had shifted. A decade earlier he had installed solar panels on his roof, switched to eating locally grown produce and 'bought an energy-efficient refrigerator that uses the power equivalent of a single light bulb'. But now he was making other changes, including fixing deadbolt locks on his doors and installing a portable power generator in his garage for back-up electricity. 'I'm not normally the paranoid type,' Tidwell wrote, 'but when extreme weather alternately baked and flooded wheat fields in Australia and Russia, helping to jack up grain prices more than 40 per cent worldwide and leading hungry people to protest from Mexico to Mozambique to Serbia, I took notice.' When food production falters in the United States, Tidwell anticipates social unrest: food riots, violence and panic.[28]

As part of a campaign from the World Wide Fund for Nature to 'Stop climate change before it changes you', launched in 2008, an advert depicted a mutant human with a fish head, suggesting that climate change was triggering a terrifying devolutionary process. In the short film *Please Help the World*, which was screened at COP15, the UN Climate Change Conference held in Copenhagen the following year, a young girl wakes from a nightmare that feels like a mishmash of clichés from Hollywood horror films. A giant fissure opens in the earth to suck in her teddy bear, while empty swings creak outside. Then a cyclone is followed by a rising ocean that barrels across the bare land, all capped by the obligatory scream. Climate change is a bad dream – but one that is about to become real.

Ten years on, the message is still pretty much the same. Seeing is believing, or is it the other way round? It's only when we have faith in the science that we are able to see what's at stake. In an animated video produced by Extinction Rebellion with the title *Climate Crisis, and Why We Should Panic*, the actor Keira Knightley informs us over a plangent soundtrack that 'governments must enter crisis mode before it's too late'.

Panic is the desired effect of books such as *The Uninhabitable Earth*, the bestseller in which David Wallace-Wells charts the devastating impact of global warming, from extreme heat events and extinctions to geopolitical conflict. 'It is, I promise, worse than you think,' he wrote in a 2019 article for *New York Magazine*. 'If your anxiety about global warming is dominated by fears of sea-level rise, you are barely scratching the surface of what terrors are possible, even within the lifetime of a teenager today.'[29] Or as he put it in an op-ed with the headline 'Time to Panic': 'The planet is getting warmer in catastrophic ways. And fear may be the only thing that saves us.'[30]

A theme that runs through much of this writing is our imperviousness to panic in the face of justifiable terror. Simply put, we ought to be fearful because we're not frightened – and fear may save us. This is the message of the 2021 sci-fi satire *Don't Look Up*, in which Jennifer Lawrence and Leonardo DiCaprio star as astronomers who try to elicit the help of the media to warn of a planet-threatening comet hurtling towards Earth. The film shows a world divided between those who are trying to smash inertia with fear and those who can't see what all the brouhaha is about. And needless to say, it doesn't end happily. The anti-panickers are the villains because, while they can see, they just don't believe.

As a strategy, eco-panic has been driven largely by charismatic activists, private foundations, NGOs and international organisations. A 2018 report produced by the UN Intergovernmental Panel on Climate Change called for 'urgent and unprecedented changes' from governments and the public.[31] At the 2019 World Economic Forum in Davos, Greta Thunberg declared, 'I want you to panic. I want you to feel the fear I feel every day.' The Earth, she said, was like a house on fire – and we had to escape before it was too late.[32] Panic in such situations isn't a choice; it's a matter of survival.

How do you make the threat of climate change feel real when it's part of a geological scenario that's unfolding too slowly to see? One answer, as we've already seen, is to use fear to get people thinking about specific disasters that might be heading their way. But it's easy for this fear to turn into fatalism and despondence. After all, the word 'disaster' comes from the Latin word *astra*, meaning 'stars', reflecting an historical belief that earthly calamities are beyond human control.[33] It's this sense of climate change as unstoppable cosmic event that the former US Special Envoy for Climate Change, Todd Stern, evoked when he described the climate challenge as 'another meteorite heading our way'.[34]

From the beginning, eco-panic fuelled vitriolic counter-arguments by those who dismissed environmentalists as zealots and frauds. In their book *The Disaster Lobby*, Melvin Grayson and Thomas Shepard Jr criticised environmentalists' assault on US business and technological progress. Gullible Americans had been duped by Rachel Carson's argument in *Silent Spring*, they claimed, 'as avidly as the buxom hausfraus of Bavaria had bought the garbage of Adolf Hitler'. *Silent Spring* was castigated as 'The Book That Killed' and the resurgence of malaria in poorer countries was attributed to the banning of DDT.[35] The electrical engineer Petr Beckmann, a champion of nuclear power, reserved special venom for the Club of Rome's 'doomsday machine' in his 1973 book *Eco-Hysterics and the Technophobes*, describing *The Limits to Growth* as tantamount to a takeover by 'econuts' and their 'ecocults'. Science, he said, was under attack by a band of 'benighted fanatics' who preached 'vicious nonsense'.[36] The shrill tone of books like this undermines their claims to be impartial. Written in capitalised, exclamation-marked panic, they adopt the hyperbolical language their authors purport to condemn. 'Don't panic!' is, after all, what people scream when they're panicking.

These accusations have coalesced in a powerful lobby of eco-doubters and climate change deniers. Among these was the novelist Michael Crichton, an avowed climate change sceptic who tackled the issue of environmental militancy in his 2004 thriller *State of Fear*.[37] Although a work of fiction, the book is presented as the outcome of extensive research and incorporates graphs, footnotes, appendices and a substantial bibliography. The plot centres on an attempt to thwart the activities of an eco-terrorist guerrilla organisation called the Environmental Liberation Front – a thinly veiled allusion to the Earth Liberation Front, a radical British environmental group. In the novel the ELF is prepared to kill whoever gets in its way. To draw attention to global warming, the group plans a series of terrorist attacks that will look like natural disasters, including engineering a mega-tsunami to destroy the West Coast of the United States.

In this eco-war the stakes are high – and fear is a game changer. Perhaps the most sinister aspect of the book is its suggestion that eco-terrorists are working in cahoots with big business, the media and what might be termed the 'deep state'. Crichton regards climate change as part of what he calls the 'state of fear', a consortium of institutions that use fear as a form of social control. In the post-Cold War era, environmental fears have taken the place of the Red Scare.

There were certainly connections between the Cold War and the rise of environmentalism in the 1960s and 1970s, and not just in the lexicon of threat that persisted in terms such as the 'population bomb'. More specifically, worries about a nuclear winter informed the science of climate change, while studies on the atmospheric impact of nuclear weapons testing influenced Paul Crutzen's work on ozone depletion, for which he received the Nobel Prize in Chemistry in 1995. But if environmentalists were censured by doom-denying critics for manufacturing fear, it was environmental scientists and their supporters who often found themselves aggressively targeted.

In the 2020 memoir of Greta Thunberg's family, *Our House Is on Fire*, the fear of climate change is linked to the family's struggle to deal with a range of psychological issues. In 2014 Greta suffered a breakdown, which manifested in constant crying and panic attacks. She also stopped eating, and in 2015 she was put on antidepressants. 'I should not have written a book about how I felt,' Greta's mother, Malena Ernman – a well-known Swedish opera singer – concedes, '[but] I had to. We had to. Because we felt like shit. I felt like shit. Svante [Greta's father] felt like shit. The children felt like shit. The planet felt like shit. Even the dog felt like shit.' Like everyone else, they were 'burned-out people on a burned-out planet'.[38] As one reviewer pointed out, Greta's family came to the decision that 'freaking out was the only rational response, not only to climate change but to modern life'. All that shitty, existential dread could be transformed into a movement.[39]

But while 'freaking out' is here conceived as an antidote to a familial and planetary health predicament, climate change has increasingly been identified as a cause of mental illness. Over the last few years psychologists have identified 'eco-anxiety' as a new condition brought on by fear at the prospect of the world's imminent collapse. The Oxford English Dictionary noted a 4,290 per cent increase in the use of the term 'eco-anxiety' in 2019 alone.[40]

Eco-anxiety has been defined as a 'psychological disorder afflicting an increasing number of individuals who worry about the environmental crisis'.[41] Visions of collapse are everywhere in the media, from news reports and documentaries to Hollywood films. The 'die-ins' staged at transport hubs and shopping centres by Extinction Rebellion activists reinforce the idea of societal collapse as a result of climate change. In his 2005 book *Collapse*, Jared Diamond had argued for the likelihood of a catastrophic near future as societies fail to get to grips with the threats posed by environmental degradation, the effects of climate change, conflict and trade wars. More recently, it's been argued that our collective failure to tackle the climate crisis has fatally undermined our ability to deal with its root causes; instead, we're entering a doom loop, 'a spiral of accelerating environmental shocks and counterproductive, defensive reactions'.[42]

A 2017 report by the American Psychological Association studied the effects of climate change on mental health and identified 'eco-anxiety' as 'a chronic fear of environmental doom'. As the report states, 'watching the slow and seemingly irrevocable impacts of climate change unfold, and worrying about the future for oneself, children, and later generations', induces a sense of helplessness and frustration.[43] Symptoms of eco-anxiety include depression, rage and panic attacks. In 2019 a group of psychiatrists formed the non-profit organisation Climate Psychiatry Alliance 'to educate the profession and the public about the urgent risks of the climate crisis, including its profound impacts on mental health and well-being'. In the United States, the Good Grief Network has developed a 10-step programme that 'brings people together to metabolize collective grief, eco-distress, and other heavy emotions that arise in response to daunting planetary crises'.[44]

This eco-anxiety is related to 'ecophobia', a term apparently coined in the late 1980s and used by the American environmental educator David Sobel to describe 'a fear of ecological problems and the natural world. Fear of oil spills, rainforest destruction, whale hunting, acid rain, the ozone hole, and Lyme disease.'[45] The cultural critic Wai Chee Dimock has argued that fears of natural catastrophes and terrorism are converging. The 2001 bombing of the World Trade Center and the devastation caused in 2005 by Hurricane Katrina both served to destroy 'the illusion that the United States is sovereign in any absolute sense'. As she puts it, 'The nation seems to have come literally "unbundled" before our eyes, its fabric of life torn apart by extremist groups, and by physical forces of even greater scope, wrought by climate change.'[46]

Terror and eco-panic have become embedded in mainstream environmental thinking. In *Learning to Die in the Anthropocene*, the army veteran Roy Scranton draws lessons from his experiences in war-torn Iraq. The bombed-out country he lived in as a private in the US Army for fourteen months – wrecked by foreign invasion, internecine conflict and ethnic and religious strife – seems to foreshadow the violence that's soon coming our way. The Earth's doomed future, Scranton insists, will resemble Baghdad after 'shock and awe', the term coined in 1996 to describe the strategic use of spectacular military power to overwhelm an enemy. He saw in Iraq 'what happens when the texture of the everyday is ripped apart'. 'Disaster will strike,' he tells his American readers, 'you can be sure of that, so we must begin preparing today for the next shock to the social order, and the next, and the next.'[47] The assumption here is that framing climate change as a crisis akin to war will work as a motivating strategy. When it comes to spurring action, fear is more effective than hope.[48]

There are those who criticise this panic-mongering modus operandi on political and economic grounds. The environmental commentator Michael Shellenberger has apologised for his role in the 'climate scare'. 'Climate change is happening,' he concedes, before adding, 'It's just not the end of the world.'[49] According to Shellenberger, the environmental movement has locked itself into an invidious narrative of sin and doom, which in the end is counterproductive. He doesn't deny climate change, but he abjures what he calls 'climate alarmism' that distorts scientific data, suggests that fear negates hope and constrains any possibility of smart solutions.[50] In a similar vein, the Danish political scientist Bjørn Lomborg is critical of the 'false alarm' approach to global warming. Throwing billions of dollars at the problem, he protests, will have little effect and is likely to hurt the poor and reinforce social inequality. 'If you have a gun to your head,' he has said, 'you don't make smart decisions.'[51]

At the other end of the spectrum, the British environmental activist Paul Kingsnorth is among those who are dubious of how climate change mitigation is promoted by the corporate world as a form of 'greenwashing'. 'Doomers' and 'crazy collapsitarians' like Kingsnorth reject the idea that the planet can be saved by biotechnology, synthetic biology, nuclear power and geoengineering. In fact, the emphasis on tech salvation, they argue, perpetuates the myth of progress that is responsible for climate change in the first place.[52]

Meanwhile, futurists who are concerned with sustainability such as Alex Steffen, founder of the non-profit organisation Worldchanging in 2003, argue against viewing climate change in binary terms; rather than reversing it or accepting that the end of the world is inevitable, we ought to recognise discontinuity and build resilience against an apocalyptic future. 'The fight can't be won but we shouldn't despair,' Steffen writes. 'We are heroic only to the extent we mold ourselves into people who can succeed with purpose on a planet in permanent crisis.' As the 'fabric of the biosphere' unravels and we're left 'tugging on the loose threads', we need a new, shockproof model of development.[53]

However, arguments such as these about the need for pragmatic adaptation are in danger of being overwhelmed by well-funded anti-climate interest groups. In 2022 the Climate Action Against Disinformation (CAAD) alliance – a global coalition of climate and anti-disinformation organisations – established a taskforce to track anti-climate attacks around the COP27 summit in Sharm el-Sheikh, Egypt. The alliance's report published in January 2023 highlighted the extent of climate denialism, which it suggested was reminiscent of the 1970s. It noted that the hashtag #ClimateScam had spiked on Twitter during the summit and that 'climate scam' was the top recommendation when the word 'climate' was plugged into a search.

According to CAAD, the climate agenda has 'been co-opted by "anti-woke" and conspiracist movements, underscoring climate as a central pillar in the "Culture Wars"'. At the same time, 'wokewashing' was identified as a growing issue. This is when those who oppose climate action adopt a 'progressive rhetoric', alleging, for example, that electric vehicles are worse for the environment than those using fossil fuels, or suggesting

– as Russian and Chinese networks do – that climate change is a form of Western imperialism.

The report also called attention to advertisements for fossil fuel-linked entities on Facebook and Instagram, stressing the influence wielded by PR and lobby groups acting for the petroleum industry, as well as the growing problem of 'greenwashing' and 'nature-rising', when companies that are heavily biased towards oil and fossil gas seek to clean up their image by promoting their green-friendly credentials. Fear is an important part of this lobbying that plays on the dangers to livelihoods and national security posed by climate-change mitigation policies.[54]

The often rancorous debates around climate change, and the battle to dispel misinformation and prevent disinformation, raise profound cultural and political issues. What happens if one community's panic isn't shared by another? Can you compel people to panic if they don't want to? And how can hope be salvaged amid this polarised politics of fear?

Greta Thunberg's comparison of the overheated planet to a house on fire suggests the need for an urgent suspension of the status quo. When caught in a burning building, the emphasis is on getting out, not on careful planning. The writer and activist Rebecca Solnit, on the other hand, continues to make a powerful case for hope. The climate initiative Not Too Late, with which she is involved, aims to promote viewpoints on the crisis that counter incapacitating despair. To this end, the project's website displays a quote from Václav Havel – poet, playwright and dissident who became the first democratically elected leader of Czechoslovakia and after its dissolution in 1992, president of the Czech Republic for ten years – 'Hope is not the conviction that something will turn out well, but the certainty that something is worth doing no matter how it turns out.'[55]

Issues over equality and climate change have also come to the fore as celebrities have become involved in climate change science, policymaking and awareness campaigns. In 2019

Google founders Larry Page and Sergey Brin invited A-listers to brainstorm climate change at the Google Camp, an annual gathering at a luxury Sicilian resort. Palermo Airport prepared for the arrival of 114 private jets. Among the VIP participants who reportedly attended were the internet entrepreneur and Facebook founder Mark Zuckerberg, Prince Harry, Hollywood actor Tom Cruise and pop singer Katy Perry. There was public criticism of the way in which these flashy eco-warriors and Doomsday preppers were summoning visions of the darkening apocalypse to advocate a post-industrial economy of organic food, carbon offsetting and eco-housing. Climate change might affect everyone, but not everyone is in the same boat – indeed, fashion designer Diane von Furstenberg, former Google CEO Eric Schmidt and DreamWorks co-founder David Geffen allegedly turned up on private yachts. In this world of superstar climate change advocacy, the global picture sits uncomfortably next to the world of the elite.

The global picture also works as a means of reinforcing national interests. China is often vilified in the West for its track record on pollution; it doesn't just pose a military threat but is also a menace to the global environment. The Canadian photographer Edward Burtynsky's photographs of China's industrial rise since the 1980s capture the terrifying scale and pace of the country's industrialisation – and its environmental toll. Burtynsky shows us: the Three Gorges Dam, the world's largest engineering project; Bao Steel, China's mammoth steel producer; villages that have sprung up to recycle electronic waste, plastics and metals; mega-factories the size of cities, such as EUPA, where thousands of workers are involved in the manufacture of irons, electric cookers and coffee makers; Yu Yuan, a sports shoe manufacturer; and Deda, China's biggest chicken processor. These industrial zones have driven the expansion of high-density supercities like Shanghai. Mass consumerism, Burtynsky writes, 'and the resulting degradation of our environment intrinsic to the process of making things to keep us happy and fulfilled frightens me. I no longer see my world as delineated by countries, with borders, or language, but as 7 billion humans living off a single, finite planet.'[56]

Chinese growth has been fuelled by Western economic interests, with foreign companies taking advantage of China's low labour costs to satisfy the West's rampant consumerism. In other words, coverage of the environmental fallout from China's industrialisation is an expedient way of touting a narrow, nationalistic approach to a global predicament.[57]

In an interview in 2022, Al Gore declared, 'every night on the TV news is like a nature hike through the Book of Revelation, that builds demands for meaningful action'.[58] And in the following year, UN Secretary-General António Guterres told the UN Security Council that a rise in sea level threatened 'a mass exodus on a biblical scale'.[59]

If we began this book with a discussion of a pandemic that challenged the Catholic Church's monopoly on fear in the Middle Ages, we end with a return to another credo: ecologism, a movement that seeks to capture fear in order to combat climate change. The French philosopher Pascal Bruckner has argued that ecologism reproduces an 'apocalyptic scenography' that borrows 'from medieval forms of messianism'. As he puts it, the adherents of ecologism 'beat the drums of panic and call upon us to expiate our sins before it is too late'.[60] An all-too-real threat is reimagined through a language of regret and guilt that harks back to an earlier age of sacral fear. The problem with this brand of apocalyptic environmentalism is that it plays into the hands of those who claim that climate activism is akin to a messianic religion requiring absolute submission from its adherents.

'Today, one of the most powerful religions in the Western World is environmentalism,' Michael Crichton declared in 2003. 'Why do I say it's a religion? Well, just look at the beliefs. If you look carefully, you see that environmentalism is in fact a perfect 21st century remapping of traditional Judeo-Christian beliefs and myths.'[61] In the 2020 documentary *Religion of Green*, produced by the conservative non-profit PragerU, an organisation that has consistently debunked climate change, we are told that the environmental movement is one of 'Doomsday cultists' that are using fear to push their agenda. As one interviewee declares, 'There is no possibility of a climate catastrophe.'[62] Under the guise of an upbeat message that aims to discredit an extreme, end-of-the-world scenario, another fear is introduced: what if the eco-nuts take over?

Epilogue

Pandemic and the Rule of Fear

When Alexis de Tocqueville wrote *Democracy in America* in the 1830s, he was aware that the society he was describing hadn't yet 'fixed its form'. 'The world that is arising,' he observed, 'is still half entangled in the debris of the world that is falling.'[1]

While the same could be said today, it is possible to identify salient features of the twenty-first century; and in many aspects they are disconcertingly similar to the world Tocqueville imagined, where democracy is in danger of spawning a new form of 'tutelary power' to manage citizens' lives via 'a network of small, complicated, painstaking, uniform rules'.[2] Fear of anarchy produces an imperative for security that gives rise to a form of despotism, which in turn promotes a new set of fears. This double bind resonates uncannily with those who argue that a culture of fear is feeding public distrust, paranoia and a predisposition to panic – all of which provide further justification for new layers of security.[3] The irony is that the more secure we get, the more fearful we become. Perhaps because the more we focus on the business of keeping safe, the more we come to realise that there is no 'absolute security', as the writer Salman Rushdie observed wryly when death threats forced him into hiding after the publication of *The Satanic Verses* in 1988, 'only varying degrees of insecurity'.[4]

But as we've seen, after 9/11 security became institutionalised in new ways. The US Department of Homeland Security was formed with a sweeping remit to instil 'a culture of relentless resilience' with a focus on anti-terrorism, border security, disaster prevention and cybersecurity. It's this last threat that has come to the fore, in relation not just to terrorism and national security but also to fears of hacking and stalking that call for ever more robust safeguards.

The advent of Bitcoin and other cryptocurrencies, which are anonymous and hard to trace, has made it easier for hackers to extort payment and avoid detection. In 2017 hackers unleashed the WannaCry malware that targeted Microsoft Windows operating systems in Ukraine, the United States and many other countries around the word, demanding payment of a ransom to a Bitcoin address. In 2021 the Colonial Pipeline, which carries refined oil from Texas to New Jersey, was forced to shut down after ransomware infected its computer systems. The company allegedly paid the hackers nearly $5 million in cryptocurrency for decryption tools to restore its operations.[5]

As early as 2003, in the midst of the SARS panic which saw the boycotting of Chinese businesses in the United States, the Nobel Prize-winning virologist and president of Caltech, David Baltimore, was warning of the danger of 'media viruses [which] are immune to rational inoculation'. 'The chief means of avoiding an HIV-style scenario are strong and open public health measures,' he wrote. 'Openness, however, breeds fear and overreaction.'[6]

The sheer volume of media traffic was giving rise to 'infodemics', a term coined in the same year by the political scientist David Rothkopf in a *Washington Post* opinion piece, where he argued that an information epidemic, or 'infodemic', had transformed SARS 'from a bungled Chinese regional health crisis into a global economic and social debacle'. As he put it, 'a few facts, mixed with fear, speculation and rumor, amplified and relayed swiftly worldwide by modern information technologies, have affected national and international economies, politics and even security in ways that are utterly disproportionate with the root realities'.[7]

Two decades on, and the struggle to distinguish these 'root

realities' from fiction has become even harder as news stories and rumours proliferate online in chatrooms, blogs, Tweets, on Facebook and TikTok. Today AI technology anticipates our behaviour and short-cuts our decision-making. Social media connect us with the like-minded; algorithmic search engines confirm our biases; and targeted marketing feeds our fears and the hopes we have of overcoming them. We're captives of the burgeoning clickbait industry, consumers in a metaverse that rejigs our psyches and modifies our behaviours. Fear always comes back to haunt us online, so it's no wonder that fear of the internet is a major theme in the cinema. In Japanese director Kiyoshi Kurosawa's 2001 film *Pulse* the internet is a two-way demonic portal: a gateway for ghosts to terrorise the world and a black hole that sucks victims in.

Kurosawa's ghosts belong with many of the fears we've discussed in this book, all of which are triggered by phenomena that are fundamental to our lives and yet hard to predict: God, death, markets, technology, terrorism, war, climate change and novel viruses. The abstruse nature of these disparate phenomena and the often incalculable risks they present make them both a challenge and a boon for governments. As we've seen, the fear and panic they induce may be channelled to further a cause, but they may just as easily undermine it.

During the Covid-19 pandemic, fear was a constant refrain. At different stages, panic manifested in different ways: with the evasion of state-directed social distancing and lockdown measures and the rush to stockpile food; with the stigmatisation of individuals and communities as disease carriers; and with jittery markets that brought back worrisome memories of the 2008 financial crash.

Governments weren't immune to overreaction, either, as they scrambled to stop the virus. In May 2020 Norway's prime minister, Erna Solberg, conceded that she may have panicked when she closed schools during the lockdown, adding that she'd been influenced by the images of mass deaths in Italy and 'probably took many of the decisions out of fear'.[8] In some instances, draconian citywide and nationwide lockdowns reflected top-down panic. That said, given the stringent public health procedures backed by force – in the case of the Philippines, President Rodrigo Duterte implemented a shoot-to-kill policy for those flouting quarantine – what was remarkable was the *lack* of widespread panic.

Donald Trump's promotion of fear as a political tool made it far harder for him to assuage public fear of Covid-19. The adult film actress Stormy Daniels, who claims she had an affair with him in 2006, has described Trump's terror of sharks and how she walked into his private bungalow in the Beverly Hills Hotel to find him watching *Shark Week* on the Discovery Channel with fascinated horror. 'And what is this fear in him?' asks the journalist Michael Lewis. 'In public, Trump preys on the fears of others while acknowledging no fear of his own. But alone in his hotel room he wants nothing more than to experience fear on an endless loop.'[9]

Personal phobias aside, fear was certainly central to Trump's presidency. Interviewed as a presidential candidate in 2016, he asserted, 'Real power is – I don't even want to use the word – fear.' A pronouncement lifted from Machiavelli's playbook, as the French historian Patrick Boucheron has observed.[10] True to his word, Trump traded on fear when he assumed office, with alarmist talk of drug dealers, criminals and rapists rushing across the Mexican border.

And then came the pandemic. At the outset the Trump administration chose to make light of it, insisting that there was no cause for alarm. Speaking to Bob Woodward, a doyen of investigative reporting, the president minimised the coronavirus. 'I still like playing it down,' he said, 'because I don't want to create a panic.'[11] In subsequent White House briefings Trump re-emphasised his determination to avert panic and in June 2020 Vice President Mike Pence impugned the media for 'sounding the alarm bells over a "second wave"', insisting that the 'panic is overblown'.[12]

By contrast, Joe Biden, the Democrat nominee in the 2020 election and eventual victor, used fear to fight the pandemic, while repeatedly claiming that 'Trump is the one who panicked'.[13] In the split-screen town hall debate that followed the president's Covid-19 diagnosis in October 2020, Biden declared of Trump, 'He said he didn't tell anybody because he was afraid Americans would panic. Americans don't panic. He panicked.'[14] Hope was the cornerstone of Biden's inaugural address in January 2021, when he concluded, 'And together, we shall write an American story of hope, not fear.'[15]

Whatever one's view of the causes or extent of the coronaphobia, it's clear that fear was a recurrent theme during the pandemic. As of April 2023 the WHO had reported over 761 million confirmed cases worldwide, with some 6.9 million deaths. The symptoms experienced by sufferers drove home the seriousness of the disease: high fevers, coughing, breathing difficulties and the loss of smell. Images of patients struggling on respirators and mass burials around the world highlighted the stakes: row upon row of coffins and mass graves at the Parque Tarumã cemetery in the northern city of Manaus, Brazil; a night-time military convoy rumbling through the streets of Bergamo, Italy; a temporary morgue in Brooklyn. Displayed as a mural or a sepia photograph, these could be depictions from another century: the Black Death, bubonic plague in the 1890s or the Influenza Pandemic of 1918–19.[16]

One of the reasons the WHO initially refrained from calling the outbreak a 'pandemic' was concern about the effect the word might have. 'Instead of spending time on fear and panic, we should say this is the time to prepare,' WHO director-general Tedros Adhanom Ghebreyesus said in February 2020. 'Pandemic is not a word to use lightly or carelessly,' he later declared. 'It is a word that, if misused, can cause unreasonable fear, or unjustified acceptance that the fight is over, leading to unnecessary suffering and death.'[17]

Early on in the outbreak, when widespread panic threatened to take hold, some commentators suggested that it posed a bigger threat than the disease. Under pressure to impose a lockdown in New York in March 2020, Governor Andrew Cuomo told journalists: 'The fear, the panic, is a bigger problem than the virus.'[18] Fear and constant exposure to dire media reports, government warnings and public health directives, it's been claimed, affected people's mental health and skewed their psychological responses by compromising their 'behavioral immune system'.[19] Research has suggested that we're hardwired to close ranks when threatened by an epidemic. Fear makes us less tolerant of difference and more judgemental of others.[20] According to the psychiatrist Mark McDonald, Covid-19 induced a collective 'delusional psychosis' and in some people created an 'addiction to fear' that has continued even after President Biden declared the pandemic over in September 2022. 'For this latter group,' McDonald says, 'fear appears to be (oddly) a source of security.'[21]

During the pandemic, technology and the media were viewed as engines of disruptive fear, with misinformation that spread online sparking panic. In many countries, the closing of schools and colleges alongside work-from-home policies led to a reliance on online communication. As people spent their days in front of home computers, their exposure to misinformation inevitably increased.

'We're not just fighting an epidemic; we're fighting an infodemic,' Tedros declared. Social media, he claimed, had produced 'an over-abundance of information' to the extent that it was becoming impossible for people to tell truth from fiction.[22] The suggestion here is that panic arises from an information glut and proliferates in the blurry realm between having too much information and not enough knowledge. As Rothkopf had noted in 2003, 'If information is the disease, knowledge is also a cure.'[23] 'This is a time for facts, not fear,' Tedros pronounced. 'This is a time for rationality, not rumours. This is a time for solidarity, not stigma.'[24]

As science grappled to understand Covid-19 in 2020, conspiracy theories snowballed. The problem of online misinformation had been recognised for some time. In 2013 the World Economic Forum warned of the 'digital wildfires' that misinformation could spark in a hyper-connected world, citing the panic that resulted when Americans confused a radio adaptation of *The War of the Worlds* with a real news bulletin in 1938. Convinced that Martians were invading the United States, listeners allegedly panicked and called the police.[25] A report published in March 2021 by the Center for Countering Digital Hate, a London-based NGO, concluded, 'Digital spaces have been colonised and their unique dynamics exploited by fringe movements that instrumentalise hate and misinformation.'[26]

The weaponisation of disinformation is increasingly viewed as one among many existential risks posed to human security by disruptive AI systems with human-like intelligence, another being the development of autonomous weapons systems, or 'slaughterbots'.[27] AI can now replicate human voices and create 'deepfake' images and videos, while ChatGPT, a chatbot developed by the US research company OpenAI and supported by the GPT-4 language model, can perform a range of 'creative and technical writing tasks, such as composing songs, writing screenplays or learning a user's writing style'.[28] In an open letter published in March 2023 in response to the launch of GPT-4 and issued by the Future of Life Institute, a non-profit organisation headed by the MIT physicist Max Tegmark, several thousand leading AI experts from academia and industry – among them Elon Musk and Steve Wozniak, co-founder of Apple – called for a six-month moratorium on the development of powerful AI systems in order to formulate 'a set of shared safety protocols'. 'Contemporary AI systems are now becoming human-competitive at general tasks,' the signatories declared, 'and we must ask ourselves: Should we let machines flood our information channels with propaganda and untruth?'[29]

Although online conspiracy theories may reflect and amplify

uncertainty and mistrust, they also provide a way of making sense of inexplicable events, with fear plugging an information vacuum. As Big Pharma rushed to produce Covid-19 vaccines, anti-vax conspiracies abounded. In November 2020 a rumour that the Pfizer vaccine 'tampers with your DNA' trended on Twitter, while another claimed the pandemic was a covert operation engineered by Bill Gates to implant microchips in people. A YouGov poll suggested that 28 per cent of Americans believed the Gates accusation.[30]

A more enduring conspiracy theory has been that of the 'Great Reset', which alleges that a clique of powerful capitalists and world leaders engineered the Covid-19 pandemic to take control of the global economy and impose a new world order. The origins of this conspiracy lie in an economic recovery and sustainability initiative launched in June 2020 by the then Prince of Wales and Klaus Schwab, head of the World Economic Forum, who called for 'action at revolutionary levels and pace' to meet the crisis. Covid-19 had 'dramatically torn up the existing script of how to govern countries, live with others and take part in the global economy', Schwab argued. A video of Canadian prime minister Justin Trudeau claiming that the pandemic was an opportunity for a 'reset' then went viral. 'I think we're in a time of anxiety, where people are looking for reasons for things that are happening to them,' Trudeau later said, adding 'we're seeing a lot of people fall prey to disinformation'.[31]

Opposition to vaccination dates back to the nineteenth century, but 'the panic virus' has spread exponentially with the rise of the internet and social media.[32] In 2020 it was feared that anti-vaxxers would undermine the roll-out of a Covid-19 vaccine in some countries. So-called 'vaccine hesitancy' has become a pressing issue, given that some 70 per cent of a population needs to be immune, whether through vaccination or exposure, before herd immunity can be achieved.[33] So too has the role of well-funded anti-vax organisations. The 26-minute 'documentary' *Plandemic: The Hidden Agenda Behind Covid-19,* produced by the filmmaker Mikki Willis and released in May 2020, claimed to be exposing 'the scientific and political elite who run the scam that is our global health system'. The video went viral with 8 million views in a week, despite YouTube, Vimeo and Facebook removing links to it on the grounds that it made unverified claims and violated policies on Covid-19 misinformation. In a longer sequel, *Plandemic: Indoctornation,* Covid-19 was again presented as part of a global conspiracy by a nefarious cabal who were using fear to control the world.[34]

To push back against such misinformation, the WHO created channels for the public to report false or misleading online content – but policing the boundary between truth and falsehood isn't easy. The diverse and sometimes contradictory views on the coronavirus held by experts – scientists, clinicians, public health professionals and epidemiological modellers – have underlined the scale of the problem. In March 2021 many European governments panicked over the alleged side effects of the Covid-19 vaccine produced by AstraZeneca, leading to its suspension despite rising infection rates, and even though the WHO and the EU regulator dismissed safety fears as unfounded.

But Covid has also raised fears about the attrition of freedom and the extension of state power exemplified by the draconian measures adopted in China and Australia as part of their 'zero-Covid' policies, which sought the total suppression of the virus. Rows of prefabricated dwellings in a giant quarantine camp on the outskirts of Shijiazhuang, the provincial capital of Hebei Province, or photographs of the Covid facility at Howard Springs outside Darwin in the Northern Territory, represent a new bio-medical tyranny. The mandating of vaccination, the issuance of digital 'vaccine passports' and the implementation of measures that restrict basic freedoms have all been criticised as forms of oppressive control. In February 2022 a 'Freedom Convoy' of truckers protesting against the Canadian government's mask mandate, lockdowns and vaccination policy brought Ottawa to a standstill and shut down the country's cross-border traffic with the United States. The government's use of emergency powers to target demonstrators was slammed by civil rights organisations, as was Justin Trudeau's labelling of the protesters as 'anti-vaxxer mobs'.[35]

For some, vaccination is a proxy for a new system of authoritarianism. Let's not forget that lockdown was first used as an emergency response strategy in China, where it became a means of cracking down on civil rights. In braiding capitalism with communism, China has produced new ways of channelling fear that are extending the frontiers of its power. According to the writer Paul Kingsnorth, we're witnessing the 'systematic censoring of dissent' in the West and the 'deliberate creation by the state and the press of a climate of fear and suspicion', which is based on the Chinese model and serves 'to justify the creation of a global police state'. The question, he reflects, is whether these control systems will 'fade away as the viral threat does, or whether – more likely – they are permanently cemented in place, with radical consequences for the future shape of society'.[36]

Although the terms 'misinformation' and 'disinformation' are widely used to describe the spread of unsubstantiated or wilfully distorted information, they also raise the vexing question of who gets to decide what the truth is. As a matter of course, President Trump slammed any criticism levelled at him as 'fake news'. As his former chief strategist and the former executive chairman of Breitbart News, Steve Bannon, observed in 2018, 'The real opposition is the media. And the way to deal with them is to flood the zone with shit.'[37] While it may not be a new concept – the expression 'fake news' was used in the late nineteenth century – today it's been digitally enabled. Following the Russian invasion of Ukraine in February 2022, the Putin regime clamped down on dissent, with those spreading 'false' information liable for a hefty fine and prison sentence. At the same time, Western governments closed down outlets and websites that were working with Russian intelligence to promote 'false and misleading' reports of the invasion. More recently, tech companies have taken on the task of arbitrating public conversations. Twitter suspended millions of accounts on the basis that they violated its terms of service, a move to stop the flow of disinformation that provoked heated debate about the limits of free speech.[38]

Definitions of what constitutes 'misinformation' or 'disinformation' also depend on where you live. In totalitarian regimes, they are terms used to silence recalcitrant voices the authorities don't want to hear. Any information that isn't sanctioned by the all-powerful state is presented as wrong and, more seriously, illegal. Russia and China, twisting a Western media template where news is sold as entertainment, have been at the forefront of a digital offensive against the factual. The sowing of confusion, rather than outright fibbing, has become a crucial tool of power in the era of 'post-truth'. Spin enough fakery and people become distrustful and begin to lose their grounding in a shared reality. Suspicion spawns fear, which starts to erode the consensus that undergirds pluralist democracies.[39] This is why the enthusiastic endorsement of China, a one-party gerontocracy, by the WHO during the early weeks of the Covid-19 pandemic was problematic. China was at the time involved both in the concerted spread of misinformation and in the suppression of vital information about the virus – twinned policies of strategic discombobulation that fanned conspiracy theories in the United States.

As with SARS in 2002 and 2003, officials concealed the nature and extent of the problem in the pandemic's early stages. It wasn't until 31 December 2019 that China formally alerted the WHO to cases of unusual pneumonia in Hubei. The following day, the Huanan Seafood Wholesale Market in the city of Wuhan was closed, and on 8 January 2020 the disease was formally linked to a novel coronavirus. China reported its first death from the virus on 11 January, but doctors had been warning of human-to-human transmission long before this. Whistleblowers, such as Li Wenliang, an ophthalmologist who had tried to share information about the virus and subsequently died of it, were hounded by the police. Finally, on 20 January 2020 – by which time the coronavirus had spread internationally – Chinese authorities reluctantly acknowledged that the coronavirus was transmissible between humans.

The Chinese artist and activist Ai Weiwei claims that Chinese officials exploited fears over Covid-19 to extend the apparatus of state surveillance. This is the underlying theme of *Coronation*, his documentary that focuses on Wuhan, where the first outbreak occurred. On 23 January 2020 authorities sealed off the city for seventy-six days, making it the first city in the world to go into lockdown. Soon this was extended to the whole of Hubei, encompassing some 56 million people. Air and rail links were cut. Bus, metro and ferry services were scrapped. Residents were forced to remain in self-quarantine, with threats of imprisonment if they didn't comply.

In the opening sequence of the film a drone view of Wuhan's vast railway station – one of China's key transport hubs – conveys not only the magnitude of the challenge but also the scale of the response. In the people's war against the virus, over 42,000 workers from elsewhere in China were sent to help and provisions were shipped in from neighbouring provinces. We watch as a prefab hospital is bolted together with lightning speed and citizens are taught how to wash their hands, miming the action to a pop track. Later, a cadre of healthcare workers are inducted into the Communist Party as 'probationary members' in token of their loyal service. These upbeat messages are juxtaposed with scenes and events that underscore people's isolation, disorientation and distrust of the system. A couple drive through a snowy, deserted city at night in search of a petrol station; a worker, marooned in the locked-down city, lives out of his car in an underground garage; a doctor walks down an interminable corridor plastered with state propaganda; a man and woman burn paper money on an empty street as an offering to the dead.

Beating Covid comes at enormous cost. As people collect

the ashes of their dead relatives, shadowy state officials dressed in personal protective equipment hover on the edges, making sure grief doesn't turn to rage. Ai's message here is clear: China's leveraging of technology and institutional process to contain and neutralise fear, grief and anger may be crucial to its infection control methods, but it is also a dehumanising operation that undercuts democratic aspirations. Even the doctors who monitor patients in the hospitals are watched by prying cameras. What's more, the system is prone to glitches from human error and bungled policy, as well as shoddy tech, with digital thermometers that malfunction, ICU machines on the blink and frozen petrol pumps. In one scene a crematorium worker pummels a bag of human ash so it will fit inside an urn – humdrum labour that encapsulates the violence of the state's enforced conformity.

Everyone is caught between a rock and a hard place: between fear of the virus and fear of the state. And while the film's title puns on the coronavirus, it also hints at an authoritarian form of political power that emanates from Xi Jinping, General Secretary of the Chinese Communist Party and Chairman of the Central Military Commission. Despite China's outward projection of hyper-modernity, its disciplinary system is a throwback to an imperial mode of governance that was supposed to have been swept away in 1949, with the Communist Party victory in the War of Liberation.

In the documentary Wuhan is a city on edge in spite of, or perhaps because of, state efforts to clamp down on the virus. This is a view echoed by the Chinese writer 'Fang Fang', who used social media platforms and messaging services to share her experiences of daily life in the locked-down city under a pen name. By one estimate, her postings on Weibo – a Chinese microblogging platform – garnered 380 million views and generated close to 100,000 discussions.

In the first week of the lockdown most people 'were in a state of utter panic', Fang Fang noted. Anyone with the slightest fever rushed to hospital, which helped to spread infection and added to the pressure on medical staff. Physicians and officials interviewed on TV tried to reassure viewers, but every announcement designed to mollify fear had the opposite effect. After forty days of lockdown, many people reached a 'psychological breaking point' and vented their frustrations online. But as Fang Fang observed, 'if you cry and make all your complaints public, they will claim that you are creating a panic, you are sabotaging the war against the coronavirus, and you've become part of the "negative energy"'. Predictably, given her call to end internet censorship in China, it wasn't long before Fang Fang became the target of online trolls who claimed that she was making up stories to spread fear.[40]

Perhaps the most blatant political use of pandemic-related fear was in Hong Kong, where Covid-19 provided the Chinese government with an excuse to crack down on the protests that had brought the city to a virtual standstill in 2019. Although they had begun as demonstrations against the government's plan to introduce legislation which would have allowed for the extradition of criminal suspects to mainland China, they soon morphed into a mass pro-democracy movement. In June 2019 hundreds of thousands of Hongkongers took to the streets in defiance of the government. At the end of August there were public screenings of *Winter on Fire*, a documentary film about the Maidan protests in Ukraine that had toppled the pro-Russian government of Viktor Yanukovych in 2014.

But with the world distracted by the pandemic, on 30 June 2020 a national security law came into place that circumvented the legislature and eroded the city's autonomy, which had been guaranteed under the constitutional principle of 'one country, two systems'. The law had been quickly rubber-stamped the previous month by the National People's Congress in Beijing, giving Xi Jinping's government broad powers to suppress dissent, with life imprisonment for those found guilty of 'grave' offences.

'At this pivotal moment for Hong Kong,' Amnesty International declared, 'it is imperative that the national security law is not used to trample human rights and undermine the freedoms that distinguish the city from Mainland China.'[41] Sixteen months later Amnesty would shut its Hong Kong offices, declaring that the law 'has made it effectively impossible for human rights organisations in Hong Kong to work freely and without fear of serious reprisals from the government'.[42] 'The message is clear,' *The Economist* pronounced, 'rule by fear is about to begin.'[43] In the words of a *Financial Times* op-ed, 'Beijing's Hong Kong takeover is a masterclass in creating fear.'[44]

Ironically, fear was used by the government as justification for the new law. Carrie Lam, Hong Kong's chief executive, claimed that in this polarised atmosphere residents were frightened to go about their daily business. This was a national security threat, she said, and 'residents are living in fear. Some ask whether Hong Kong is still a city with the rule of law, or whether it is rule of fear.'[45] We were edging closer to the double-talk world of Chinese censorship. Intimidating billboards went up around the city announcing the new law. An extrajudicial agency of the Chinese state now had an apparently limitless scope to ensure 'security'.

Across the campus of the University of Hong Kong, where I worked, fear was palpable. Universities had long been criticised by government officials and pro-Beijing factions as liberal incubators of social protest, a view they claim was confirmed by violence at the Chinese University and the two-week siege of the Polytechnic University. The security law made it clear that these institutions were firmly in the authorities' cross-hairs; in the era of 'patriotic education', dissent would no longer be brooked.[46] Following the implementation of the new law, the Education Bureau offered to review school textbooks and expunge any offending material. While government officials continued to emphasise the importance of academic freedom, they made it clear that any criticism of China would no longer be tolerated. Carrie Lam warned that, if universities didn't reform, 'law enforcement of course will have to go in and resolve it'.[47]

Although the government claimed that the law would only apply to 'a small minority who endanger national security', it was soon being used to go after pro-democracy politicians, activists, academics and anyone else considered a threat.[48] In the absence of any word from the university's senior management, rumours swirled that those who advocated 'political' views would be fired or denied tenure or extensions to their fixed-term contracts. Many colleagues questioned whether they could stay in Hong Kong and worried that this might be the end of their careers.

Professors began to rewrite lectures, omitting content that might be deemed 'sensitive'. Those who studied modern China were especially worried about inadvertently infringing the law, given the scope of its provisions and vague wording. What did 'conspiring' to provoke 'hatred' of the Chinese government actually mean? Even Teresa Cheng, Hong Kong's justice secretary, didn't appear to know when asked by journalists.[49] Some colleagues abandoned their research and focused on less contentious areas, but it wasn't only faculty members who were afraid. Students requested securer platforms for submitting their assignments and worried about the safety of Zoom as a forum for expressing their views. Some of them advised us that informers had infiltrated our classes and were reporting back to the authorities in China.

Meanwhile, thousands of residents stopped sending messages on WhatsApp, out of fear that they could be hacked, and switched to apps with end-to-end encryption. TikTok announced it would quit Hong Kong, and Google, Facebook and Twitter suspended handing over user data to Hong Kong law enforcement agencies. The Hong Kong police were starting to monitor people's online behaviour, and in November 2020 a hotline was launched for residents to send in anonymous tip-offs; in effect, this was a state-sponsored informer network that smacked of the Cultural Revolution.[50]

All of this took place against a background of unrelenting recriminations in mainland China. In November 2020 Zhang Zhan, a former lawyer and citizen journalist, was sentenced to four years in jail for 'picking quarrels and provoking trouble'. Her on-the-ground reporting of the coronavirus epidemic in Wuhan had challenged the official version of events. Before her sentencing she went on hunger strike and was force-fed. Zhang's lawyer reported that when he met her in custody her hands were tied, and a nasogastric tube had been inserted against her will. Concerns about her treatment were raised by Amnesty and the UN Human Rights Office, which called for her immediate release and criticised her detention as an 'excessive clampdown on freedom of expression linked to Covid-19'.[51]

Back in Hong Kong, security guards now monitored the entrances and exits of the university's public campus. As an article in the *New York Times* put it, the city's universities had 'become potent symbols of the shrinking space for dissent or even discussion'.[52] In August 2021 the University of Hong Kong's students' union disbanded and in December the 'Pillar of Shame' statue memorialising those killed in the 1989 Tiananmen Square massacre was removed from the campus on the grounds of 'potential safety issues'.[53]

What happens when people are fearful of speaking out? How does fear of totalitarian shutdown relate to the fears extending their hold over Western societies? It's been suggested that in the late 1980s and 1990s overwrought Western media reports of violent crime, child abuse and satanic cults created a new set of pervasive fears that often tipped into panic and came to fill the vacuum left by Cold War paranoia.[54] In fact, worries about the varied and intensifying threats to children began to dominate the media from the mid-1970s. 'Whether we are looking at drugs, sexuality, or cult activities,' writes the US historian Philip

Jenkins of this period, 'much of the cultural shift in domestic affairs involved a new view of threats (plausible or not) against children.'[55] Although the Millennials and members of Generation Z, born between the late 1980s and 2000s, grew up in an era of exceptional safety, they 'internalized society's push for safety at all costs'. A perception of escalating threat produced a sense of vulnerability that called for more security.[56] Meanwhile, an 'epidemic of self-censorship' reflects the contradictions of a society that 'demands consensus while being wilfully blind to its own tyranny'.[57]

But are all fears equal? Should we equate the rising tide of anxieties in the West with the fear experienced by Ukrainians sheltering from Russian bombs, young Hong Kong protesters tear-gassed by riot police, Uyghurs locked up in Xinjiang's re-education camps, Yazidi women enslaved and raped by Islamic State fighters in Mosul or those detained and beaten by the morality police in Iran? And what about the fears of sexual and racial abuse voiced by movements for social justice and civil rights? Should these mega-fears count for more than fear of a microaggression?

Whatever one's view on this, the fact is that in many parts of the world – China comes to mind – autocratic regimes are leveraging fear to shut down freedoms in the name of security. Meanwhile, in progressive democracies another kind of fear is at work, but with a similar end result: freedom of thought and expression are curtailed. Freedom in one place is being eclipsed by tyranny, but in the other, freedom of expression is being undermined by an insistence that all fears are equivalent. How can we say what we think if anything we say may provoke fear in others?

The case of Edward Snowden, the NSA whistleblower, highlights the complexities of a world in which fear, freedom and control are entangled. Having exposed the infringements on privacy taking place in the democratic West, Snowden sought refuge in two states that retain overt control on information,

China (albeit Hong Kong) and Russia, where in 2022 he took up citizenship. And Snowden isn't alone in his willingness to stomach an authoritarian system for the freedom to expose Western collusion. After all, Julian Assange, the founder of WikiLeaks, who faces criminal charges in the United States for publishing leaked US military intelligence and diplomatic cables, once hosted the *World Tomorrow* show on the state-controlled TV news network Russia Today (RT), widely considered a vehicle of Kremlin misinformation. This isn't to condone the US government's dogged pursuit of Assange, particularly given his disclosure of information that may point to war crimes, as well as the concerns his trial and extradition raise about censorship and freedom of expression – it's simply to illustrate the awkward accommodations required to champion freedom in a mediatised world skewed by competing interests.[58]

Is Tocqueville's premonition finally coming true? Is liberalism being swamped by illiberal forces of its own creation? Is the internet, long touted as an instrument of democratisation, in fact ensnaring its users in the profit-rich demesnes of their digital overlords?[59] What's clear is that the incompatibility of freedom and equality is drawing out latent contradictions within democratic institutions to the point where they seem unworkable. We've entered a world of illiberal democracy and authoritarian populism. A world in which the right and the left alike are at war with what used to be called the middle ground. The right believes that liberalism is yoked to a progressive politics that is eroding 'traditional' values. For the left, neoliberalism is pushing a free-for-all market economy that has exacerbated inequalities, while right-wing pundits are accused of cooking up a moral panic around illusory fears of the unforgiving 'woke mob'.

So where does this leave fear? In the 1830s, as he witnessed the quickening pace of industrialisation and the emergence of a new system of democratic governance, Tocqueville made a plea for a 'salutary fear' that would keep citizens watchful and engaged, rather than 'a soft and idle terror' that could pave the way for authoritarianism. Perhaps we should be making a similar appeal today: for a benevolent fear that prepares us for the challenges of the future without overlooking the possibilities for change in the present – a fear that sees grounds for hope, not despair, in uncertainty.

One of this book's aims has been to highlight the political nature of fear; political in the sense that fear has always infused and shaped our systems of government, from the principles that subtend them to the institutional mechanisms that make them possible. As political systems evolve, the fears within them are reworked too. Fear of God transmutes to fear of the state; the terror of the absolute monarch is reconstructed as revolutionary terror, which then transforms into fear of mob rule and mechanical takeover of the kind that haunted industrialising democracies, and so on.

My other aim has been to show how fear connects us, as individuals and societies, in ways that we often don't see. On the face of it, fear divides by creating an oppositional view of the world; we fear the menacing other or some endangering object, whether it's the Devil, a military adversary, a novel technology or a raging fire. We can fear ourselves too, but we deal with our self-fears by externalising them, whether that means apportioning blame elsewhere or locating fear's origins in a past trauma or even in an inherited propensity. Fear is always outside us, even when it's within.

Although we may be unaware of it, our fears exist in a complex interdependency with others. Take as an example Western condemnation of China's environmental record, which we touched on in the previous chapter. According to the World Bank, China is responsible for over a quarter of global carbon dioxide and a third of the world's annual greenhouse gas emissions.[60] While media coverage of air pollution from Chinese industrialisation feeds Western fears of a planetary meltdown, this industrialisation has been driven by Western demand for cheap Chinese products and by Western companies manufacturing their goods there. Fear becomes a means of redirecting attention away from a complicity in the global processes that are driving the environmental crisis.

Here's another example. Over the last few decades avocados have become identified with healthy living in the Western world, causing a global boom that has created new pressures for producers. In the state of Michoacán, the heartland of Mexico's avocado production, small-scale growers now use armed vigilantes to guard against extortionists. As an Associated Press report put it, 'the scent of money has drawn gangs and hyperviolent cartels that have hung bodies from bridges and cowed police forces'. Avocado growers, the report continues, live 'in fear of assault and shakedowns'.[61] The wonderfruit, celebrated for its nutrients and monounsaturated fats, turns out to be part of a political economy that depends on checkpoints and AR-15s.

The nexus between fear, violence and the reach of global labour and capital has been central to the stories I've told about the rise of the centralised state in early modern Europe, colonisation, the slave trade, industrialisation and neoliberal globalisation since the 1980s. Panic may be triggered by cross-border threats – from immigration, contaminated foods, pollution and financial shocks – but we've also seen how fears are borderless, spreading in ways that are often difficult to discern, let alone manage.

At the same time, pinning fear to a singular crisis, say a war or a pandemic, can deflect attention away from everything else, obscuring the underlying continuities that link seemingly disparate events. As we've seen, an approach to crisis that underplays complexity to focus on some discrete fear factor – a military foe, a threatening social group or a virus – can be advantageous for political leaders and their parties, corporations and other vested interests that weaponise and profit from fear.

In February 2022 German chancellor Olaf Scholz called

Putin's invasion of Ukraine a *Zeitenwende* – 'an epochal tectonic shift' or 'watershed moment'.[62] Although it was met with praise by Germany's allies as a sign of the country's commitment to a more engaged and robust foreign policy, what Scholz's snappy formulation omits is the complex history of terror that's bundled into the 2022 Russian assault, one that stretches back to the dissolution of the USSR in 1991, Cold War geopolitics, Nazi occupation, Stalin's engineered famine in the 1930s, Russian imperialism from the late eighteenth century and more. Similarly, the Covid-19 pandemic isn't an event with a neat beginning and ending. Its effects will continue, even as political orbits shift and the crisis is formally declared over.

While history may seem irrelevant, perhaps even obstructive, in the face of these urgent challenges, the fears we experience in the present are also rooted in the past. Our responses to any crisis are inevitably shaped by earlier crises, just as they are influenced by events unfolding in places far removed from those we assume to be the critical hot spots. In this sense, fear is always intersectional, an unnerving confluence of past, present and future, a convergence of the here and there.

Acknowledgements

In the decades since my trip to Jalalabad many friends and colleagues have helped me to think about the meaning of fear and panic. First, though, thanks to my travelling companions in the *Frontier Post* van from Peshawar, and to Sayeed Khan, Aziz Siddiqui, Farhatullah Babar and Timothy Hyman.

Some years later, as the Soviet Union fell apart and the archives opened there, I was given the opportunity to review books on Russian literature, history and current affairs for the *Independent* and *New Statesman* – among them Lev Razgon's account of his life in the Gulag, *True Stories*, and Anatoli Rybakov's novel *Fear*. Although it was a short interlude, it was an experience that gave me a deeper understanding of totalitarian fear at a moment when the 'end of history' was being euphorically proclaimed. I remain grateful to Robert Winder and Boyd Tonkin for commissioning this modest journalism, as I do to my extraordinary Russian teacher and friend Kyril Zinovieff, who long after those lessons in Chiswick – the highlight of the week – remains an important presence in my life and a connection to the momentous past. Kyril remembered catching a glimpse of Rasputin guffawing on a street in St Petersburg and as a seven-year-old watched the 1917 Revolution unfold from his nursery window.

Two workshops in 2012 – one at the Lichtenberg-Kolleg Institute for Advanced Study at the Georg-August-University of Göttingen and the other at the University of Hong Kong (HKU) – provided creative venues for testing ideas. The first, hosted by Harald Fischer-Tiné, resulted in the book *Anxieties, Fear and Panic in Colonial Settings: Empires on the Verge of a Nervous Breakdown* (2016); the second, which I convened with the support of the Louis Cha Fund (HKU), led to the edited collection *Empires of Panic: Epidemics and Colonial Anxieties* (2015), later published in Chinese by Zhejiang University Press (2021). I should like to thank all of those involved: in particular, David Arnold, Alison Bashford, Amy Fairchild, Harald Fischer-Tiné, Nicholas King, Alan Lester and Chris Munn.

A version of Chapter 4 on colonising panic was given in 2017 as a lecture entitled 'Fatal Entanglements: Manila in the Time of Cholera' in the Faculty of History at the University of Cambridge. My thanks to Tim Harper for the kind invitation.

Aside from the many colleagues acknowledged in the notes, I am indebted to the following individuals for generously commenting on drafts of the book, or relevant portions of it: Paul Cartledge, Mark Clifford, Malcolm Gaskill, Ed Lake, Catherine Peckham, Maria Sin – and the inspirational Joe LeDoux, whose band, The Amygdaloids ('neuroscience meets rock and roll'), provided the original soundtrack to *Fear*. Conversations with Chris Bayly, David Clarke, Frank Dikötter, Didier Fassin, Heidi Larson and Mark Seltzer on imperial networks, fear and art, China, global health panics, vaccine hesitancy and crime have, at different times, all been crucial to my thinking. My grandfather Alexander King – co-founder of the Club of Rome with his friend Aurelio Peccei in 1968 – remains a huge influence and I couldn't have written on eco-panic without him. His apartment on rue de Grenelle in Paris, with its throughflow of impassioned visitors, was the most exciting place to be.

Although the bulk of *Fear* was written in Hong Kong, it was conceived and completed in New York and I am grateful to Katherine Fleming for finding me a perch at NYU's Remarque Institute, where I spent a productive sabbatical year in an office on Fifth Avenue filled with books by the institute's founding director, Tony Judt – what more could one ask? In 2007, the year before he'd discovered he was ill – and a year before the global financial crisis led to bank bailouts, recession, indebtedness and dangerous disillusionment – Tony had written with characteristic prescience: 'Fear is reemerging as an active ingredient of political life in Western democracies.' I like to think that something rubbed off in the course of that year working amid his writing, perhaps a keener appreciation of just how entangled the history of fear is with hope.

Thanks to Peter Hoffmann at the Stiftung Haus der Geschichte in Bonn for providing information on the exhibition *Fear: A German State of Mind?* and to the librarians at HKU who, in difficult book-banning times, were always accommodating.

My brilliant and indefatigable agent, Chris Wellbelove, has encouraged and supported this project from the outset; Helen Conford championed the book before it was a book; and Nick Humphrey, my editor at Profile, has been an assiduous reader, guiding me through the process with astonishing efficiency – thank you.

For almost two years, during the Covid-19 pandemic, I was cut off in Hong Kong, unable to rejoin my wife, Rebecca, and children, Lily Mei and James, in New York. Many friends stepped in to help and I shall always be grateful to this extended family, and above all to Brian and Ellen Rose and to Sami and Babel Suhail.

And then, of course, there's the elephant in the room: the onslaught against democratic protest in Hong Kong. My students and friends there – you know who you are – will forever be a source of inspiration; their probity, enthusiasm and courage in the face of the crackdown on freedom and civil rights will never be forgotten.

Finally, this book is dedicated to my brother, Alexander, who made a damn fine cider. Although he'll never get to read it, in more ways than he could have imagined, he helped to write it.

Notes

Dates given in square brackets are those of the original edition.

Preface

1 There was optimism, but also growing apprehension about Hong Kong's future. An occupation protest, known as 'Occupy Central', took place between 2011 and 2012, and in 2014 there were mass pro-democracy sit-in street protests, dubbed the 'Umbrella Revolution'.

2 Stephen Vincent Benét, 'Freedom from fear', *Saturday Evening Post* (13 March 1943), p. 12.

3 The picture was later reproduced in a poster campaign launched by the US Office of War Information during the Second World War and, along with the other three of the 'four essential human freedoms', was taken on a tour of major US cities by the Treasury Department, reportedly raising nearly $133 million worth of war bonds; see Norman Rockwell, *My Adventures as an Illustrator*, ed. Abigail Rockwell; fwd Steven Heller (New York: Abbeville Press, 2019), p. 384.

4 These are definitions based on the Oxford English Dictionary. The journalist and writer Moisés Naím has defined power 'as the ability to direct or prevent the current or future actions of other groups and individuals': *The End of Power: From Boardrooms to Battlefields and Churches to States, Why Being in Charge Isn't What It Used to Be* (New York: Basic Books, 2013), pp. 15–16; see also *The Revenge of Power: How Autocrats Are Reinventing Politics for the 21st Century* (New York: St. Martin's Press, 2022), where he develops the concept of 'power tools', which are 'specific psychological, communicational, technological, legal, electoral, financial, and organizational techniques' that autocrats wield 'to assert their power' (p. 61).

5 On the 'liquid fear' that characterises postmodernity, see Zygmunt Bauman, *Liquid Fear* (Cambridge and Malden, MA: Polity, 2006).

6 Glück is here commenting on the 'panic' that characterises the work of the poet Richard Siken; see her review, '*Crush* by Richard Siken', in *American Originality: Essays on Poetry* (New York: Farrar, Straus and Giroux, 2017), pp. 88–96 (p. 88).
7 Johan Huizinga, *The Waning of the Middle Ages: A Study of the Forms of Life, Thought and Art in France and the Netherlands in the Fourteenth and Fifteenth Centuries*, trans. F. Hopman (Harmondsworth: Penguin, [1924] 1955), p. 25.
8 J. F. C. Hecker, *The Black Death and the Dancing Mania*, trans. B. G. Babington (London: Cassell & Company, 1888), p. 50. Another example of this anachronistic fear is Barbara W. Tuchman's *A Distant Mirror: The Calamitous 14th Century* (New York: Ballantine Books, 1978), in which the war-torn Middle Ages become a mirror-image of twentieth-century violence.
9 '10 killed in 2 blasts in Jalalabad as Ghaffar is buried', *Frontier Post* (23 January 1988); I appear in the article as 'a London-based freelance journalist' who, along with my travelling companions in the *Frontier Post* vehicle, 'had a narrow escape'.
10 Robert Burton, *The Anatomy of Melancholy*, ed. Angus Gowland (London: Penguin, [1621] 2021), pp. 258–9 (p. 258); C. S. Lewis, *A Grief Observed* (New York: HarperCollins, [1961] 1996), p. 3.
11 An experience of panic similar to that described by the French philosopher Maurice Blanchot; see his observations in 'The most profound question', in *The Infinite Conversation*, trans. Susan Hanson (Minneapolis, MN: University of Minnesota Press, 1993), pp. 11–24 (p. 22); see also Emmanuel Levinas's notion of 'the horror of being' discussed in his essay 'There is: Existence without existents', in Seán Hand, ed., *The Levinas Reader* (Oxford: Blackwell, 1989), pp. 29–36.
12 Canetti's wider recognition in 1981 came after race riots in Miami, Florida, the previous year and coincided with inner-city riots in Britain, giving added significance to his insights on crowd behaviour.
13 Elias Canetti, *Crowds and Power*, trans. Carol Stewart (New York: Seabury Press, [1962] 1978), p. 26.
14 *The Recollections of Alexis de Tocqueville*, trans. Alexander Teixeira de Mattos (London: H. Henry & Co., 1896), p. 116.
15 Susan Sontag, 'On courage and resistance' [2003], in *At the Same Time: Essays and Speeches*, ed. Paolo Dilonardo and Anne Jump; fwd David Rieff (New York: Farrar, Straus and Giroux, 2007), pp. 180–91 (p. 181).

16 Canetti, *Crowds*, p. 27.
17 William McDougall, *The Group Mind: A Sketch of the Principles of Collective Psychology with Some Attempt to Apply Them to the Interpretation of National Life and Character* (Cambridge: Cambridge University Press, 1920), p. 24.
18 Frans de Waal, *Our Inner Ape: A Leading Primatologist Explains Why We Are Who We Are* (New York: Riverhead Books, 2005), pp. 19–21.
19 https://georgewbush-whitehouse.archives.gov/news/releases/2002/01/20020129-11.html
20 Richard M. Weintraub, 'Bombs kill 8 at funeral in Afghanistan', *Washington Post* (23 January 1988), p. 18; 'Terrorists in Jalalabad', *Frontier Post* (23 January 1988).
21 W. Brian Arthur, *The Nature of Technology: What It Is and How It Evolves* (New York: Free Press, 2009), pp. 18–23 (p. 21).

Prologue: Is This Fear We're Feeling?

1 Peter Hermann and John D. Harden, 'Thousands of bullets have been fired in this D.C. neighborhood. Fear is part of everyday life', *Washington Post* (23 July 2021).
2 'Hong Kong: Jimmy Lai sentenced to 14 months for pro-democracy protests', *BBC News* (16 April 2021); Ai Weiwei, 'To live your life in fear is worse than losing your freedom', *Guardian* (21 June 2012).
3 Veronika Melkozerova, 'I'm in Kyiv, and it is terrifying', *New York Times* (25 February 2022).
4 Alisha Arora, Amrit Kumar Jha, Priya Alat and Sitanshu Sekhar Das, 'Understanding coronaphobia', *Asian Journal of Psychiatry*, vol. 54 (2020), p. 102384; also Gordon J. G. Asmundson and Steven Taylor, 'Coronaphobia: Fear and the 2019-nCoV outbreak', *Journal of Anxiety Disorders*, vol. 70 (2020), p. 102196.
5 Robyn Rapoport and Christian Kline, *Methodology Report 2022: American Fears Survey* (Orange, CA: Chapman University, 2022). For an analysis of fear in the United States based on data from the Chapman Survey, see Christopher D. Bader, Joseph O. Baker, L. Edward Day and Ann Gordon, *Fear Itself: The Causes and Consequences of Fear in America* (New York: Near York University Press, 2020). Fear of a pandemic has dropped off the list from 2021.
6 Brian Massumi, 'Preface', in Brian Massumi, ed., *The Politics of Everyday Fear* (Minneapolis, MN: University of Minnesota Press, 1993), pp. vii–x (p. viii).
7 On the drivers of contemporary US fear, see Peter N. Stearns,

American Fear: The Causes and Consequences of High Anxiety (New York: Routledge, 2006); Barry Glassner, *The Culture of Fear: Why Americans Are Afraid of the Wrong Things: Crime, Drugs, Minorities, Teen Moms, Killer Kids, Mutant Microbes, Plane Crashes, Road Rage, & So Much More* (New York: Basic Books [1999], 2009); Bader et al., *Fear Itself*.

8 The term 'probability neglect' was coined by the Harvard legal scholar Cass R. Sunstein to describe a 'cognitive bias' towards exaggerated fear: see his 'Probability neglect: Emotions, worst cases, and law', *Yale Law Journal*, vol. 112 (2002), pp. 61–107, and 'The cognitive bias that makes us panic about coronavirus', *Bloomberg* (28 February 2020); Daniel Kahneman and Amos Tversky, 'Prospect theory: An analysis of decision under risk', *Econometrica*, vol. 47, no. 2 (1979), pp. 263–91. For a sociological account of fear and 'the growth of risk consciousness' in the 1980s and 1990s, see Frank Furedi, *Culture of Fear: Risk-taking and the Morality of Low Expectation* (London: Continuum, [1997] 2006), p. 146.

9 An argument made by the psychologist Steven Pinker in *Enlightenment Now: The Case for Reason, Science, Humanism, and Progress* (New York: Viking, 2018); see also Daniel Gardner, *The Science of Fear: How the Culture of Fear Manipulates Your Brain* (New York: Plume, 2009), pp. 8–10.

10 *Poverty and Shared Prosperity 2022: Correcting Course* (Washington, DC: World Bank, 2022).

11 For a sociological analysis of fear-for-profit that focuses on contemporary America, see Glassner, *Culture of Fear*.

12 Aristotle, *Rhetoric*, trans. W. Rhys Roberts (Mineola, NY: Dover Publications, [1924] 2004), p. 69.

13 Granville Stanley Hall, 'A study of fears', *American Journal of Psychology*, vol. 8, no. 2 (1897), pp. 147–249 (p. 242).

14 Gavin de Becker, *The Gift of Fear: And Other Survival Signals That Protect Us from Violence* (New York: Dell Publishing, 1997).

15 Charles Darwin, *The Expression of the Emotions in Man and Animals* (London: John Murray, 1872); see Lisa Feldman Barrett, 'Was Darwin wrong about emotional expressions?', *Current Directions in Psychological Science*, vol. 20, no. 6 (2011), pp. 400–406.

16 Matthew Cobb, *The Idea of the Brain: A History* (London: Profile Books, 2021), pp. 329–30; Justin S. Feinstein et al., 'Fear and panic in humans with bilateral amygdala damage', *Nature Neuroscience*, vol. 16, no. 3 (2013), pp. 270–72.

17 William James, 'What is an emotion?', *Mind*, vol. 9, no. 34 (April 1884), pp. 188–205 (pp. 189–90).

18 For an incisive overview of fear in relation to cognition and consciousness, which also discusses the implications for mental health that stem from 'the conflation of the neural basis of conscious feelings with body responses', see Joseph E. LeDoux, 'Thoughtful feelings', *Current Biology*, vol. 30, no. 11 (June 2020), pp. R619–R623.

19 Joseph LeDoux, *Anxious: Using the Brain to Understand and Treat Fear and Anxiety* (New York: Viking, 2015), pp. 19, x.

20 LeDoux, *Anxious*, pp. 10–11.

21 Vincent Taschereau-Dumouchel, Matthias Michel, Hakwan Lau, Stefan G. Hofmann and Joseph E. LeDoux, 'Putting the "mental" back in "mental disorders": A perspective from research on fear and anxiety', *Molecular Psychiatry*, vol. 27, no. 3 (2022), pp. 1322–30.

22 Ludwig Wittgenstein, *Philosophical Investigations*, trans. G. E. M. Anscombe (Oxford: Basil Blackwell, [1953] 1958), p. 32. As the anthropologist David L. Scruton has noted, perhaps the crucial task isn't to focus on what causes an emotion, so much as to question what role it plays in our lives; see 'The anthropology of an emotion', in David L. Scruton, ed., *Sociophobics: The Anthropology of Fear* (Boulder, CO: Westview Press, 1986), pp. 7–49 (p. 27).

23 Karl A. Menninger, *The Human Mind* (Garden City, NY: Garden City Publishing Company, 1927), p. 200.

24 'Neuroscientist Joseph LeDoux on anxiety and fear', lecture delivered at the New York State Writers Institute (27 September 2016).

25 Francis Bacon, *The Advancement of Learning*, ed. G. W. Kitchin (London and New York: Dent and Dutton, [1861] 1915), p. 172.

26 Burton, *Anatomy*, p. 999.

27 Michael Lewis, 'Has anyone seen the President?', *Bloomberg Opinion* (9 February 2018). For a compelling argument about how autocrats are using 'populism, polarization, and post-truth' to obtain power, see Naím, *Revenge of Power*, pp. xv–xix.

28 Søren Kierkegaard, *The Concept of Anxiety: A Simple Psychologically Orienting Deliberation on the Dogmatic Problem of Hereditary Sin*, trans. and intro. Alastair Hannay (New York: Liveright, 2014), p. 75. The metaphor of 'vertigo' was later developed by the philosopher Jean-Paul Sartre (1943); see *Being and Nothingness: An Essay on*

Phenomenological Ontology, trans. Sarah Richmond; fwd Richard Moran (New York: Routledge, 2018), pp. 66–7.

29 '"The mastery of fear": Sermon outline' [21 July 1957], in Clayborne Carson, Susan Carson, Susan Englander, Troy Jackson and Gerald L. Smith, eds., *The Papers of Martin Luther King, Jr.*, vol. 6, *Advocate of the Social Gospel, September 1948–March 1963* (Berkeley, CA: University of California Press, 2007), p. 318.

30 For an insightful cultural history of fear, however, see Joanna Bourke, *Fear: A Cultural History* (Emeryville, CA: Shoemaker & Hoard, [2005] 2006); and for an interdisciplinary perspective, see Jan Plamper and Benjamin Lazier, eds., *Fear: Across the Disciplines* (Pittsburgh, PA: University of Pittsburgh Press, 2012).

31 bell hooks, *All About Love: New Visions* (New York: William Morrow, 2000), p. 93; see also Sara Ahmed's discussion of 'the affective politics of fear' in *The Cultural Politics of Emotion* (London and New York: Routledge, [2004] 2014), pp. 62–81; Bauman, *Liquid Fear*; Martha C. Nussbaum, *The Monarchy of Fear: A Philosopher Looks at Our Political Crisis* (New York: Simon & Schuster, 2018).

32 Arthur M. Schlesinger, Jr, *The Vital Center: The Politics of Freedom* (New Brunswick, NJ: Transaction, [1949] 1998), p. 3; 'Communism: A clear-eyed view', *New York Times* (1 February 1948), BR Section, pp. 1, 25.

33 Erich H. Fromm, *Escape from Freedom* (New York: Henry Holt, [1941] 1969), pp. 239–40; published in Britain as *The Fear of Freedom* (1942).

34 Gandhi's presidential address delivered in Bhavnagar, Gujarat, 8 January 1925, in *Indian Quarterly Register*, vol. 1, nos. 1–2 (January–June 1925), pp. 410–18 (p. 417); Martha C. Nussbaum makes a persuasive case for love in *Political Emotions: Why Love Matters for Justice* (Cambridge, MA: Belknap/Harvard University Press, 2015).

35 Michael Ignatieff, *The Warrior Honor: Ethnic War and the Modern Conscience* (New York: Henry Holt, 1997), p. 18.

36 Corey Robin, *Fear: The History of a Political Idea* (Oxford and New York: Oxford University Press, 2004), pp. 3, 251. Robin's political history excludes 'private fears', which he describes as 'artifacts of our own psychologies and experiences' that 'have limited impact beyond ourselves'; also excluded are environmental fears, on the grounds that 'natural disaster seldom provokes citizens to embrace or enact specific political principles' (pp. 2, 4). As Deborah R. Coen has argued, 'A decade later, this statement is no longer plausible' given the politics of global warming; see 'The nature of fear and the fear

of nature from Hobbes to the hydrogen bomb', in Katrina Forrester and Sophie Smith, eds., *Nature, Action and the Future: Political Thought and the Environment* (Cambridge: Cambridge University Press, 2018), pp. 115–32 (pp. 118–19).

37 Judith N. Shklar, 'The liberalism of fear', in Nancy L. Rosenblum, ed., *Liberalism and the Moral Life* (Cambridge, MA: Harvard University Press, 1989), pp. 21–38; Hannah Arendt, *The Origins of Totalitarianism* (New York: Harcourt, [1951] 1985).

38 http://www.fdrlibrary.marist.edu/archives/collections/franklin/ [;] Ira Katznelson, *Fear Itself: The New Deal and the Origins of Our Time* (New York: Liveright, 2013), p. 122; Ira Katznelson and Samuel Issacharoff, 'Fear and democracy: Reflections on security and freedom', *Bulletin of the American Academy of Arts & Sciences*, vol. 69, no. 3 (Spring 2016), pp. 19–24.

39 On this state of exception, in which the rule of law is transcended for the public good, see Carl Schmitt, *Dictatorship*, trans. Michael Hoelzl and Graham Ward (Cambridge and Malden, MA: Polity, 2014).

40 Annelien de Dijn, *Freedom: An Unruly History* (Cambridge, MA: Harvard University Press, 2020), p. 4.

41 Fromm, *Escape*, p. 4.

42 Isaiah Berlin, 'Two concepts of liberty', in *Four Essays on Liberty* (Oxford: Oxford University Press, 1969), pp. 118–72.

43 Quentin Skinner, *Liberty before Liberalism* (Cambridge: Cambridge University Press, 1998).

44 Alexis de Tocqueville, *Democracy in America*, trans. Harvey C. Mansfield and Delba Winthrop (Chicago, IL: University of Chicago Press, 2000), pp. 3, 516, 672, 673. Tocqueville had travelled across America in 1831–2 to study the prison system.

45 Benedict [Baruch] de Spinoza, *The Ethics*, trans. R. H. M. Elwes (Mineola, NY: Dover Publications, [1883] 2018), p. 115; on fear, hope and the 'ethics of security', see Scott Bader-Saye, 'Thomas Aquinas and the culture of fear', *Journal of the Society of Christian Ethics*, vol. 25, no. 2 (2005), pp. 95–108.

46 Aung San Suu Kyi, *Freedom from Fear and Other Writings*, ed. Michael Aris; fwd Václav Havel (London: Penguin, 1991), pp. 180, 184.

1: The Great Pestilence

1 As Gordon H. Orians notes, 'Recent investigations show that behavioral patterns can persist long after natural selection no longer

favors them.' *Snakes, Sunrises, and Shakespeare: How Evolution Shapes Our Loves and Fears* (Chicago, IL: University of Chicago Press, 2014), pp. 20–21 (p. 21), 57–8; Gardner, *Science of Fear*, pp. 15–17.

2 Darwin, *Expression*, pp. 367, 362.

3 Paul Ekman, *Emotions Revealed: Recognizing Faces and Feelings to Improve Communication and Emotional Life* (New York: Owl Books, [2003] 2007). For a critique of Ekman's theory, see Ruth Leys, 'How did fear become a scientific object and what kind of object is it?', *Representations*, vol. 110, no. 1 (2010), pp. 66–104; also Lisa Feldman Barrett and James A. Russell, eds., *The Psychological Construction of Emotion* (New York: Guilford Press, 2015); Joshua Conrad Jackson et al., 'Emotion semantics show both cultural variation and universal structure', *Science*, vol. 366, no. 6472 (2019), pp. 1517–22; and Hazel Rose Markus and Shinobu Kitayama, 'Culture and the self: Implications for cognition, emotion, and motivation', *Psychological Review*, vol. 98, no. 2 (1991), pp. 224–53.

4 Adam Brumm, Adhi Agus Oktaviana, Basran Burhan et al., 'Oldest cave art found in Sulawesi', *Science Advances*, vol. 7, no. 3 (2021).

5 Jared Diamond, 'The worst mistake in the history of the human race', *Discover Magazine* (May 1987), pp. 64–6.

6 Ian Hodder, *The Domestication of Europe: Structure and Contingency in Neolithic Societies* (Oxford: Basil Blackwell, 1990), p. 11.

7 Karl Jaspers, *The Origin and Goal of History*, trans. Michael Bullock (New Haven, CT: Yale University Press, 1953), pp. 2, 4. Originally published in German in 1949.

8 Robert N. Bellah and Hans Joas, eds., *The Axial Age and Its Consequences* (Cambridge, MA: Belknap/Harvard University Press, 2012); Merlin Donald, *Origins of the Modern Mind: Three Stages in the Evolution of Culture and Cognition* (Cambridge, MA: Harvard University Press, 1991).

9 For a discussion of the etymology of these fear words, see Gregory Nagy, 'The subjectivity of fear as reflected in ancient Greek wording', *Dialogues*, vol. 5 (2010), pp. 29–45; also David Konstan, 'Fear', in *The Emotions of the Ancient Greeks: Studies in Aristotle and Classical Literature* (Toronto: University of Toronto Press, 2006), pp. 129–55.

10 Thucydides, *History of the Peloponnesian War*, trans. Rex Warner; intro. M. I. Finley (New York: Penguin, [1954] 1972), p. 49 (Book I, 23); in contrast, the Athenian representatives at Sparta claimed it was fear of Persian aggression that had motivated Athens to build up

its power: p. 80 (Book I, 75). See William Desmond, 'Lessons of fear: A reading of Thucydides', *Classical Philology*, vol. 101, no. 4 (2006), pp. 359–79.

11 Philippe Borgeaud examines the relationship between Pan and panic, beginning with a discussion of Aeneas Tacticus' military treatise *Poliorketika*, or 'Siegecraft', written in the fourth century BCE. Pan, he writes, is associated with 'an irrational terror involving noise and confused disturbance'; see 'Panic and possession', in *The Cult of Pan in Ancient Greece*, trans. Kathleen Atlass and James Redfield (Chicago, IL: University of Chicago Press, 1988), pp. 88–116 (pp. 88–9).

12 Michael Nylan and Trenton Wilson, 'Circle of fear in early China', *Religions*, vol. 12, no. 1 (2021).

13 Erika Kuijpers, 'Fear, indignation, grief and relief: Emotional narratives in war chronicles from the Netherlands (1568–1648)', in Jennifer Spinks and Charles Zika, eds., *Disaster, Death and the Emotions in the Shadow of the Apocalypse, 1400–1700* (London: Palgrave Macmillan, 2016), pp. 93–111 (p. 97). The Triumph of Death was a popular theme in late medieval and early modern art, a well-known example being the fresco from the 1440s now displayed in the Palazzo Abatellis in Palermo, Sicily. The innovation of Bruegel's art is the way it infuses this religious convention with a new realism, along with a concern for contemporary social and political worlds.

14 Erwin Panofsky, *Early Netherlandish Painting: Its Origins and Character*, 2 vols (Cambridge, MA: Harvard University Press, [1953] 1966), vol. 1, pp. 67–8 (p. 67).

15 Lynn White, Jr, *Medieval Technology and Social Change* (Oxford: Oxford University Press, 1962), pp. 39–78 (pp. 43–4). However, the great French medievalist Marc Bloch, whose work on the history of the plough White draws on, cautioned against tracing 'the whole chain of causation back to a single technological innovation'; see *French Rural History: An Essay on its Basic Characteristics*, trans. Janet Sondheimer; fwd Bryce Lyon (Berkeley, CA: University of California Press, 1966), pp. 48–56 (p. 54).

16 Thomas A. Fudgé, *Medieval Religion and Its Anxieties: History and Mystery in the Other Middle Ages* (New York: Palgrave Macmillan, 2016), p. 8; Jean Delumeau, *Sin and Fear: The Emergence of a Western Guilt Culture, 13th–18th Centuries*, trans. Eric A. Nicholson (New York: St. Martin's Press, 1990). The book was originally published in French in 1983.

17 María Cruz Cardete del Olmo, 'Entre Pan y el Diablo: el proceso de demonización del dios Pan', *Dialogues d'histoire ancienne*, vol. 41, no. 1 (2015), pp. 47–72. Patricia Merivale emphasises Pan's dual 'benevolent' and 'sinister' or 'terrifying' aspect from the early modern period, the first linked to the pastoral, Arcadian tradition, the second to the malignant spirits of the wild; see *Pan the Goat-God: His Myth in Modern Times* (Cambridge, MA: Harvard University Press, 1969), pp. 134, 154–5.

18 Dante Alighieri, *The Divine Comedy*, trans. John Ciardi (New York: New American Library, [1954] 2003), The Inferno, Canto 1, lines 1–63 (pp. 16–18).

19 Norman Cohn, *Europe's Inner Demons: The Demonization of Christians in Medieval Christendom* (Chicago, IL: University of Chicago Press, [1973] 1993), pp. 27–8 (p. 27).

20 St Thomas Aquinas, *Summa Theologiae* (London: Burns, Oates & Washbourne, 1920), Part II [Secunda Secundæ Partis]: Q. 125, Q. 126 and Q. 19. Available at: https://www.newadvent.org/summa/[.] On Aquinas's 'rehabilitation' of fear as a 'seemingly negative emotion', see Stephen Loughlin, 'The complexity and importance of *timor* in Aquinas's *Summa Theologiae*', in Anne Scott and Cynthia Kosso, eds., *Fear and Its Representations in the Middle Ages and Renaissance* (Turnhout: Brepols, 2002), pp. 1–16; also Bader-Saye, 'Thomas Aquinas', p. 100.

21 Anne Scott and Cynthia Kosso, 'Introduction', in Scott and Kosso, eds., *Fear*, pp. xi–xxxvii (pp. xxii–xxiii).

22 William of Auvergne, 'Fear', in *On Morals*, trans. and intro. Roland J. Teske (Toronto: Pontifical Institute of Medieval Studies, 2013), pp. 8–18 (pp. 11–14). The treatise is part of an encyclopaedic work entitled *The Teaching on God in the Mode of Wisdom*, or the *Magisterium Divinale et Sapientiale*.

23 Innocent III, 'On the misery of man', in Bernard Murchland, trans. and ed., *Two Views of Man* (New York: Frederick Ungar, 1966), pp. 3–60 (p. 14).

24 William Chester Jordan, 'The Great Famine, 1315–1322 revisited', in Scott G. Bruce, ed., *Ecologies and Economies in Medieval and Early Modern Europe* (Boston, MA: Brill, 2010), pp. 45–62 (p. 58).

25 Ian Kershaw, 'The Great Famine and agrarian crisis in England, 1315–1322', *Past & Present*, vol. 59, no. 1 (1973), pp. 3–50 (p. 11).

26 Barbara Hanawalt, *Crime and Conflict in English Communities, 1300–1348* (Cambridge, MA: Harvard University Press, 1979), pp. 243,

269; for an evocative summary of the famine, see Henry S. Lucas, 'The Great European Famine of 1315, 1316, and 1317', *Speculum*, vol. 5, no. 4 (1930), pp. 343–77 (p. 376).

27 Norman F. Cantor, *In the Wake of the Plague: The Black Death and the World It Made* (New York: Free Press, 2001), p. 173; John Aberth, *From the Brink of the Apocalypse: Confronting Famine, War, Plague, and Death in the Later Middle Ages* (Abingdon: Routledge, [2000] 2010), pp. 1–2.

28 Vincent J. Derbes, 'De Mussis and the Great Plague of 1348', *Journal of the American Medical Association*, vol. 196, no. 1 (1966), pp. 59–62.

29 Samuel K. Cohn, Jr, 'The Black Death: End of a paradigm', *American Historical Review*, vol. 107, no. 3 (2002), pp. 703–38 (p. 737); Kirsten I. Bos et al., 'A draft genome of *Yersinia pestis* from victims of the Black Death', *Nature*, vol. 478, no. 7370 (2011), pp. 506–10; Ewen Callaway, 'Plague genome: The Black Death decoded', *Nature*, vol. 478, no. 7370 (2011), pp. 444–6. More recent research has suggested that the plague may have spread via human ectoparasites, namely body lice and human fleas: see Katharine R. Dean, Fabienne Krauer, Lars Walløe and Boris V. Schmid, 'Human ectoparasites and the spread of plague in Europe during the Second Pandemic', *Proceedings of the National Academy of Sciences*, vol. 115, no. 6 (2018), pp. 1304–9.

30 Monica H. Green, 'The four Black Deaths', *American Historical Review*, vol. 125, no. 5 (2020), pp. 1601–31.

31 Rosemary Horrox, trans. and ed., *The Black Death* (Manchester: Manchester University Press, 1994), pp. 35–41.

32 Michael Walters Dols, 'Ibn al-Wardī's *Risālah al-naba' 'an al-waba'*, a translation of a major source for the history of the Black Death in the Middle East', in Dickran K. Kouymijan, ed., *Near Eastern Numismatics, Iconography, Epigraphy, and History: Studies in Honor of George C. Miles* (Beirut: American University of Beirut, 1974), pp. 443–55. For a later account of the plague in the Islamic world, see Ibn Hajar al-Asqalani, *Merits of the Plague*, trans. and ed. Joel Blecher and Mairaj Syed (New York: Penguin, 2023).

33 Francesco Petrarch, *Letters on Familiar Matters* [*Rerum Familiarium Libri*], trans. Aldo S. Bernardo, 3 vols (New York: Italica, [1972–1985] 2005), vol. 1, p. 356 (VII, 10), pp. 415, 417 (VIII, 7); vol. 2, p. 55 (X, 2).

34 Giovanni Boccaccio, *The Decameron*, trans. and intro. Wayne A. Rebhorn (New York: W. W. Norton, 2003), pp. 6, 13.

35 Agnolo di Tura del Grasso, 'The plague in Siena: An Italian chronicle', in William M. Bowsky, ed., *The Black Death: A Turning*

Point in History? (New York: Holt, Rinehart and Winston, 1971), pp. 12–14.

36 Shona Kelly Wray, 'Tracking families and flight in Bologna during the Black Death', *Medieval Prosopography*, vol. 25 (2004), pp. 145–60; and *Communities and Crisis: Bologna during the Black Death* (Leiden and Boston, MA: Brill, 2009).

37 Samuel Cohn, Jr, 'Plague violence and abandonment from the Black Death to the early modern period', *Annales de démographie historique*, vol. 134, no. 2 (2017), pp. 39–61.

38 Bonaiuti was also known as Marchionne di Coppo Stefani; Aberth, *From the Brink*, p. 199.

39 The Norwegian historian Ole J. Benedictow has estimated on the basis of existing data that some 50 million may have died out of a population of 80 million; see 'Part four: Mortality in the Black Death', in *The Black Death, 1346–1353: The Complete History* (Woodbridge: Boydell Press, 2004), pp. 245–386 (pp. 380–86).

40 M. L. Duran-Reynals and C.-E. A. Winslow, 'Texts and documents: "Regiment de preservació a epidèmia o pestilència e mortaldats"', *Bulletin of the History of Medicine*, vol. 23 (1949), pp. 57–89 (p. 57).

41 'D'una mortalitá la quale fu nella cittá di Firenze, dove morirono molte persone', in Roberto Palmarocchi, ed., *Cronisti del Trecento* (Milan: Rizzoli, 1935), pp. 647–52 (p. 648): 'Fu di tanta paura che niuno non sapea che si fare.'

42 Jean Delumeau, *La peur en occident: XIVe–XVIIIe siècles* (Paris: Fayard, 1978), pp. 132–87, 38–46 (p. 39); Western civilisation, he notes in *Sin and Fear*, imagined itself besieged 'by a multitude of enemies – Turks, idolaters, Jews, heretics, witches, and so on' (p. 1).

43 Cohn, 'Black Death', p. 707.

44 Boccaccio, *Decameron*, pp. 8, 7, 12.

45 'Consultation sur l'épidémie faite par le Collège de la Faculté de Médecine de Paris', in H. Émile Rébouis, *Étude historique et critique sur la peste* (Paris: Alphonse Picard, Croville-Morant et Foucart, 1888), pp. 70–145 (pp. 77, 79, 97, 99).

46 Boccaccio, *Decameron*, pp. 7–9 (p. 7).

47 William M. Bowsky, 'The medieval commune and internal violence: Police, power, and public safety in Siena, 1287–1355', *American Historical Review*, vol. 73, no. 1 (1967), pp. 1–17 (pp. 15–17); and 'The impact of the Black Death upon Sienese government and society', *Speculum*, vol. 39 (1964), pp. 1–34 (pp. 27, 34).

48 Daniel Lord Smail, 'Telling tales in Angevin courts', *French Historical Studies*, vol. 20, no. 2 (1997), pp. 183–215.
49 Colin Platt, 'Revisionism in castle studies: A caution', *Medieval Archaeology*, vol. 51, no. 1 (2007), pp. 83–102 (p. 101).
50 Richard J. Evans, 'Introduction: "The dangerous classes" in Germany from the Middle Ages to the twentieth century', in Richard J. Evans, ed., *The German Underworld: Deviants and Outcasts in German History* (Abingdon and New York: Routledge, [1988] 2015), pp. 1–28 (pp. 5–6, 9).
51 Scott and Kosso, 'Introduction', in Scott and Kosso, eds., *Fear*, pp. xxi–xxii.
52 Tzafrir Barzilay, *Poisoned Wells: Accusations, Persecution, and Minorities in Medieval Europe, 1321–1422* (Philadelphia, PA: University of Pennsylvania Press, 2022).
53 David Nirenberg, *Communities of Violence: Persecution of Minorities in the Middle Ages* (Princeton, NJ: Princeton University Press, [1996] 2015), pp. 231–50.
54 Aberth, *From the Brink*, pp. 158–9; Jacob R. Marcus, 'The Black Death and the Jews, 1348–1349', in *The Jew in the Medieval World: A Source Book, 315–1791*, rev. with intro. Marc Saperstein (Cincinnati, OH: Hebrew Union College Press, [1938] 1999), pp. 49–55 (pp. 51–3).
55 Carlo Ginzburg, 'Jews, heretics, witches', in *Ecstasies: Deciphering the Witches Sabbath*, trans. Raymond Rosenthal (Chicago, IL: University of Chicago Press, [1991] 2004), pp. 63–86 (p. 68).
56 Samuel Cohn, Jr, 'The Black Death and the burning of Jews', *Past & Present*, vol. 196, no. 1 (2007), pp. 3–36.
57 Cohn, 'Plague violence', p. 39.
58 Aberth, *From the Brink*, p. 180; Horrox, *Black Death*, pp. 221–2.
59 Samuel Cohn, 'After the Black Death: Labour legislation and attitudes towards labour in late medieval western Europe', *Economic History Review*, vol. 60, no. 3 (2007), pp. 457–85 (p. 480).
60 Samuel K. Cohn, Jr, 'Popular insurrection and the Black Death: A comparative view', *Past & Present*, vol. 195, supplement 2 (2007), pp. 188–204 (pp. 195–204).
61 Norman Cohn, *The Pursuit of the Millennium: Revolutionary Millenarians and Mystical Anarchists of the Middle Ages* (New York: Oxford University Press, [1957] 1970), pp. 127–47.

2: A New Age of Fear

1 See James M. Estes's commentary on 'To the Christian nobility of

the German nation concerning the improvement of the Christian estate, 1520', in Timothy J. Wengert, ed., *The Annotated Luther*, vol. 1, *The Roots of Reform* (Minneapolis, MN: Fortress Press, 2015), pp. 369–466.

2 Philip S. Gorski, *The Disciplinary Revolution: Calvinism and the Rise of the State in Early Modern Europe* (Chicago, IL: University of Chicago Press, 2003).

3 Jarrett A. Carty, *God and Government: Martin Luther's Political Thought* (Montreal and Kingston: McGill-Queen's University Press, 2017).

4 Martin Luther, 'Preface to Luther's German writings: The Wittenberg edition (1539)', in *The Ninety-Five Theses and Other Writings*, trans. and ed. William R. Russell (New York: Penguin, 2017), pp. 194–9 (p. 197).

5 Catherine Fletcher, *The Beauty and the Terror: An Alternative History of the Italian Renaissance* (London: Bodley Head, 2020); Alexander Lee, *The Ugly Renaissance: Sex, Greed, Violence and Depravity in an Age of Beauty* (New York: Anchor, [2013] 2015).

6 Jacob Burckhardt, *The Civilization of the Renaissance in Italy*, trans. S. G. C. Middlemore; intro. Peter Burke; notes Peter Murray (London: Penguin, 1990), pp. 70, 344–52, 20; Jean Delumeau, 'Part I: Pessimism and the macabre in the Renaissance', in *Sin and Fear*, pp. 9–185; also 'Conclusion', pp. 555–7 (p. 556).

7 This period saw a 'boom in compendia of portentous phenomena', which coincided with the dissemination of broadsheets and pamphlets. Religious conflict 'fostered special concern for signs of God's wrath and the coming end of days': see Joshua P. Waterman, 'Miraculous signs from antiquity to the Renaissance: Context and source materials of the Augsburg manuscript', in Till-Holger Borchert and Joshua P. Waterman, eds., *The Book of Miracles* (Cologne: Taschen, 2017), pp. 6–46 (p. 10).

8 Leonardo da Vinci, *Notebooks*, pref. Martin Kemp; sel. Irma A. Richter; ed. and intro. Thereza Wells (Oxford: Oxford University Press, 2008), pp. 275–7.

9 Da Vinci, *Notebooks*, p. 262.

10 Gorski, *Disciplinary Revolution*, pp. xv–xvii (p. xvi).

11 Lisa Jardine, ed. and trans. [with Neil M. Cheshire and Michael J. Heath], *Erasmus: 'The Education of a Christian Prince' with the 'Panegyric for Archduke Philip of Austria'* (Cambridge: Cambridge University Press, 1997), p. 28. While Erasmus took a broadly pacifist

view, he did argue that under certain circumstances defensive wars were admissible; see John C. Olin, 'The pacifism of Erasmus', *Thought*, vol. 50, no. 4 (1975), pp. 418–31 (p. 421).

12 Miles J. Unger, *Machiavelli: A Biography* (New York: Simon & Schuster, 2011), pp. 199–214 (pp. 204–5).

13 Niccolò Machiavelli, *The Prince*, trans. George Bull; intro. Anthony Grafton (New York: Penguin, [1961] 2003), pp. 52–6 (p. 54). The historian John Pocock has called Machiavelli's awareness of the Florentine republic's impermanence 'the Machiavellian moment'; see *The Machiavellian Moment: Florentine Political Thought and the Atlantic Republican Tradition*, intro. Richard Whatmore (Princeton, NJ: Princeton University Press, [1975] 2016).

14 Machiavelli, *Prince*, pp. 56–8 (p. 57).

15 Thomas More, *Utopia*, trans. and intro. Paul Turner (London: Penguin, [1965] 2003), pp. 62, 82, 65.

16 More, *Utopia*, p. 101.

17 Alec Ryrie, *Protestants: The Faith That Made the Modern World* (New York: Viking, 2017).

18 *The Correspondence of Erasmus: Letters 2204–2356 (August 1529–July 1530)*, trans. Alexander Dalzell; annot. James M. Estes (Toronto: University of Toronto Press, 2015), pp. 47, 165.

19 Martin Luther, *The Small Catechism, 1529*, ed. Timothy J. Wengert and Mary Jane Haemig (Minneapolis, MN: Fortress Press, 2015), p. 217; on Luther, the printing press and the Reformation, see Andrew Pettegree, *Brand Luther: 1517, Printing, and the Making of the Reformation* (New York: Penguin, 2015).

20 On Luther's thunderstorm experience and his early fears, see Lyndal Roper, *Martin Luther: Renegade and Prophet* (New York: Random House, 2016), pp. 33–4, 43–4, 53–4; on the ambiguity of fear in Luther, see Pekka Antero Kärkkäinen, 'Emotions and experience in Martin Luther', in Derek R. Nelson and Paul R. Hinlicky, eds., *The Oxford Encyclopedia of Martin Luther*, vol. 1 (Oxford: Oxford University Press, 2017), pp. 436–48.

21 Hans J. Hillerbrand, *The Reformation: A Narrative History Related by Contemporary Observers and Participants* (New York: Harper & Row, 1964), pp. 42–3.

22 Thomas Kaufmann, *Luther's Jews: A Journey into Anti-Semitism*, trans. Lesley Sharpe and Jeremy Noakes (Oxford: Oxford University Press, 2017).

23 'Article IV: Justification', in Theodore G. Tappert, ed. and trans.,

The Book of Concord: The Confessions of the Evangelical Lutheran Church (Philadelphia, PA: Fortress Press, 1959), p. 30. Fromm drew extensively on the ideas of the German sociologist Max Weber, author of *The Protestant Ethic and the Spirit of Capitalism* (1905), arguing that Luther's theology mirrored the individual's powerlessness in the face of new economic and social forces: see *Escape*, pp. 39–102 (pp. 80–81).

24 Malcolm Gaskill, *Witchcraft: A Very Short Introduction* (Oxford: Oxford University Press, 2010), p. 13.

25 P. G. Maxwell-Stuart, 'The fear of the king is death: James VI and the witches of East Lothian', in William G. Naphy and Penny Roberts, eds., *Fear in Early Modern Society* (Manchester: Manchester University Press, 1997), pp. 209–25.

26 Malcolm Gaskill, *The Ruin of All Witches: Life and Death in the New World* (London: Penguin, 2021).

27 Jason Philip Coy, *The Devil's Art: Divination and Discipline in Early Modern Germany* (Charlottesville, VA: University of Virginia Press, 2020).

28 'The bull of Innocent VIII', in *Malleus Maleficarum*, trans. and intro. Montague Summers (London: John Rodker, 1928), pp. xliii–xlv.

29 Rosemary Ellen Guiley, *The Encyclopedia of Witches, Witchcraft and Wicca* (New York: Facts on File, [1989] 2008), p. 223. The Carolina code of the Holy Roman Empire probably had a greater impact on jurists and judges than the *Malleus Maleficarum*. As Gaskill notes, it was 'never as influential in its own era as it would be in the antagonistic climate of the Reformation and Counter-Reformation'; *Witchcraft*, pp. 22–5 (p. 23).

30 H. Trevor-Roper, 'The persecution of witches', *Horizon*, vol. 2. no. 2 (1959), pp. 57–63 (p. 59); Gary K. Waite, *Heresy, Magic, and Witchcraft in Early Modern Europe* (Basingstoke: Palgrave Macmillan, 2003), p. 134.

31 Peter T. Leeson and Jacob W. Russ, 'Witch trials', *Economic Journal*, vol. 128, no. 613 (2018), pp. 2066–105 (p. 2075).

32 Brian P. Levack, 'State-building and witch hunting in early modern Europe', in Jonathan Barry, Marianne Hester and Gareth Roberts, eds., *Witchcraft in Early Modern Europe: Studies in Culture and Belief* (Cambridge: Cambridge University Press, 1996), pp. 96–116; this is the argument made in Christina Larner's *Enemies of God: The Witch-hunt in Scotland* (Baltimore, MD: Johns Hopkins University

Press, 1981), where witch-hunts are viewed as attempts by an elite to impose their Calvinist beliefs on the populace.

33 On witchcraft's 'emotional dimension', see Malcolm Gaskill, 'Fear made flesh: The English witch-panic of 1645–7', in David Lemmings and Claire Walker, eds., *Moral Panics, the Media and the Law in Early Modern England* (Basingstoke: Palgrave Macmillan, 2009), pp. 78–96.

34 'Galileo's abjuration (22 June 1633)', in Maurice A. Finocchiaro, ed., *The Trial of Galileo: Essential Documents* (Indianapolis, IN: Hackett, 2014), pp. 138–9 (p. 138).

35 On the book as a force for change, see Lucien Febvre and Henri-Jean Martin, *The Coming of the Book: The Impact of Printing, 1450–1800*, trans. David Gerard; eds. Geoffrey Nowell-Smith and David Wootton (London: Verso, [1976] 2010), pp. 248–332.

36 Quoted in Gary K. Waite, 'Fear and loathing in the radical Reformation: David Joris as the prophet of emotional tranquillity, 1525–1556', in Charles Zika and Giovanni Tarantino, eds., *Feeling Exclusion: Religious Conflict, Exile and Emotions in Early Modern Europe* (Abingdon: Routledge, 2019), pp. 100–125 (p. 101).

37 Susan James, *Passion and Action: The Emotions in Seventeenth-Century Philosophy* (Oxford: Clarendon Press, 1997), pp. 2–4.

38 Erasmus, *A Handbook on Good Manners for Children: De Civilitate Morum Puerilium Libellus*, trans. Eleanor Merchant (London: Preface Publishing, 2008), p. 3; 'A declamation on the subject of early liberal education for children: *De pueris statim ac liberaliter instituendis declamatio*', trans. Beert C. Verstraete, in *Collected Works of Erasmus: Literary and Educational Writings*, vol. 4, ed. J. K. Sowards (Toronto: University of Toronto, 1985), pp. 291–346 (pp. 324–5, 332). On the 'civilising' of manners and centralised power of the state, see Norbert Elias, *The Civilizing Process: Sociogenetic and Psychogenetic Investigations*, trans. Edmund Jephcott; ed. Eric Dunning, Johan Goudsblom and Stephen Mennell (Oxford: Blackwell, [1994] 2000) [originally published in German in 1939].

39 Michel de Montaigne, *The Complete Works: Essays, Travel Journal, Letters*, trans. Donald M. Frame; intro. Stuart Hampshire (New York: Alfred A. Knopf, [1948] 2003), Book I, Essay 18, pp. 62–4. The first two books were published in 1580, followed by the third book in 1588.

40 Delumeau, *Sin and Fear*, p. 1.

41 Montaigne, Book III, Essay 13, pp. 992–1045 (p. 1023).

42 Seneca, *Letters from a Stoic [Epistulae Morales ad Lucilium]*, trans.

Robin Campbell (London: Penguin, [1969] 2004), p. 38; Montaigne, *Essays*, Book I, Essay 26, p. 129; Book II, Essay 10, p. 364; Book II, Essay 32, p. 662.

43 Burton, *Anatomy*, p. 171; specifically on fear as a cause of melancholy, pp. 258–9 and 330–33.

44 Burton, *Anatomy*, pp. 33, 673.

45 Burton, *Anatomy*, pp. 253, 393.

46 Burton, *Anatomy*, pp. 333, 20.

47 'More than just dramatizing fear as malady,' Hobgood writes, '*Macbeth* exposed audiences to fear's dangerous infectiousness. Anticipating spectators who feared fear itself, early modern performances of *Macbeth* both staged the physiological effects of fear and summoned those effects in Renaissance playgoers.' See Allison P. Hobgood, 'Feeling fear in *Macbeth*', in Katharine A. Craik and Tanya Pollard, eds., *Shakespearean Sensations: Experiencing Literature in Early Modern England* (Cambridge: Cambridge University Press, 2013), pp. 29–46 (p. 30).

48 Burton, *Anatomy*, p. 408.

49 William Shakespeare, *Macbeth*, Act V, scene iii, 9–10.

50 Miguel de Cervantes, *Don Quixote*, trans. Edith Grossman; intro. Harold Bloom (New York: HarperCollins, 2003), pp. 8, 142.

51 Cervantes, *Quixote*, pp. 45–52.

52 Cervantes, *Quixote*, p. 129.

53 Bacon, *Advancement*, p. 147; Thomas Wright, *The Passions of the Minde in Generall* (London: Printed by Valentine Simmes [and Adam Islip] for Walter Burre [and Thomas Thorpe], 1604), p. 70; Burton, *Anatomy*, p. 999; J. F. Senault, *The Use of Passions*, trans. Henry, Earl of Monmouth (London: Printed for J. L. and Humphrey Moseley, 1649). On the emergence of the 'emotions' as a modern psychological category that replaced previous terms such as 'passions', 'sentiments' and 'affections', see Thomas Dixon, *From Passions to Emotions: The Creation of a Secular Psychological Category* (Cambridge: Cambridge University Press, 2003). However, on the ambiguity of this terminology, see Kirk Essary, 'Passions, affections, or emotions? On the ambiguity of 16th-century terminology', *Emotion Review*, vol. 9, no. 4 (2017), pp. 367–74.

54 Benedict Anderson, *Imagined Communities: Reflections on the Origin and Spread of Nationalism* (London and New York: Verso, [1983] 2006), pp. 37–46; Nina Lamal, Jamie Cumby and Helmer J. Helmers,

eds., *Print and Power in Early Modern Europe (1500–1800)* (Leiden: Brill, 2021).

55 As Richard Rex notes, Luther's theology implied 'a profound individualism'; *The Making of Martin Luther* (Princeton, NJ: Princeton University Press, 2017), p. 140.

56 Ann Blair, *Too Much to Know: Managing Scholarly Information before the Modern Age* (New Haven, CT: Yale University Press, 2010), p. 56.

57 Paul M. Dover, *The Information Revolution in Early Modern Europe* (Cambridge: Cambridge University Press, 2021), pp. 262–83.

58 Blair, *Too Much*, p. 58.

3: Theatre of Power

1 Peter H. Wilson, *Europe's Tragedy: A History of the Thirty Years War* (London: Allen Lane, 2009), p. 787; David Lederer, 'Fear of the Thirty Years War', in Michael Laffan and Max Weiss, eds., *Facing Fear: The History of an Emotion in Global Perspective* (Princeton, NJ: Princeton University Press, 2012), pp. 10–30 (p. 10); Hans Medick, 'Historical event and contemporary experience: The capture and destruction of Magdeburg in 1631', *History Workshop Journal*, vol. 52, no. 1 (2001), pp. 23–48 (p. 37).

2 Medick, 'Historical event', p. 30.

3 Jean Bodin, *Les six livres de la république* (Paris: Chez Jacques du Puys, 1576), Book I, Chapter IX, p. 152; Book V, Chapter V, p. 588; Book II, Chapter III, p. 239; Book IV, Chapter I, p. 410; Book I, Chapter IV, p. 247; Book IV, Chapter VII, p. 482. On 'salutary terror', see Ronald Schechter, *A Genealogy of Terror in Eighteenth-Century France* (Chicago, IL: University of Chicago Press, 2018), p. 17.

4 Jacques-Bénigne Bossuet, *Politique tirée des propres paroles de l'écriture sainte* (Paris: Pierre Cot, 1709), pp. 81–2, 127, 87.

5 *The Life of Mr. Thomas Hobbes of Malmesbury, Written by Himself in a Latine Poem and Now Translated into English* (London: Printed for A. C., 1680), p. 2.

6 Thomas Hobbes, *Leviathan*, ed. and intro. C. B. Macpherson (London: Penguin, [1651] 1968), Part 1, Chapter XII, pp. 168–70 (p. 169), 177 [the original spelling has been modernised for the convenience of the reader]; Samuel I. Mintz, *The Hunting of Leviathan: Seventeenth-Century Reactions to the Materialism and Moral Philosophy of Thomas Hobbes* (Cambridge: Cambridge University Press, 1962), p. 62; *'Brief Lives,' chiefly of Contemporaries, set down by John Aubrey, between the Years 1669 & 1696*, ed. Andrew

Clark [with facsimiles], 2 vols (Oxford: Clarendon Press, 1898), vol. 1, p. 339.

7 Hobbes, *Leviathan*, Part 1, Chapter XIV, p. 189; Part 1, Chapter XI, p. 167; see Coen, 'The nature of fear', p. 119.

8 Thomas Hobbes, *On the Citizen*, ed. and trans. Richard Tuck and Michael Silverthorne (Cambridge: Cambridge University Press, 1998), p. 25.

9 John Locke, 'Some thoughts concerning education', in *Works of John Locke*, vol. 3 (London: Printed for Awnsham Churchill, 1722), pp. 1–98 (pp. 50–51). Locke's 1693 treatise contains one of his best-known pronouncements on fear: 'But since the great Foundation of Fear in Children, is Pain, the way to harden, and fortify Children against Fear and Danger, is to accustom them to suffer Pain' (p. 52).

10 Hobbes, *Leviathan*, Part 1, Chapter XIII, pp. 186, 185; Part II, XVII, p. 227; Part II, Chapter XXI, p. 272; Psalms 74:14; Isaiah 27:1. Hobbes did, though, entertain the possibility of sovereignty residing 'in an Assembly of more than one', Part II, Chapter XIX, p. 239. As Robin notes, Hobbes wrestled with the question 'How can a polity or society survive when its members disagree, often quite radically, about basic moral principles?', *Fear*, pp. 31–50 (pp. 31–2). For an interpretation of the 'monstrosity' of the Leviathan and claims that it has a 'theoretical and political purpose pertaining to fear', see Magnus Kristiansson and Johan Tralau, 'Hobbes's hidden monster: A new interpretation of the frontispiece of *Leviathan*', *European Journal of Political Theory*, vol. 13, no. 3 (2014), pp. 299–320.

11 Jan H. Blits, 'Hobbesian fear', *Political Theory*, vol. 17, no. 3 (1989), pp. 417–31 (p. 417).

12 Quentin Skinner, 'Thomas Hobbes and his disciples in France and England', *Comparative Studies in Society and History*, vol. 8, no. 2 (1966), pp. 153–67.

13 Ruth Scurr, *John Aubrey: My Own Life* (New York: New York Review Books, 2015), p. 78.

14 A heliocentric model of the universe, postulated by the astronomer Nicolaus Copernicus, was by then widely accepted in France and reinforced Louis's centralised model of kingship: see Lucía Ayala, 'Cosmology after Copernicus: Decentralisation of the sun and the plurality of worlds in French engravings', in Wolfgang Neuber, Thomas Rahn and Claus Zittel, eds., *The Making of Copernicus: Early Modern Transformations of a Scientist and his Science* (Leiden: Brill, 2015), pp. 201–26 (p. 209).

15 Chandra Mukerji, *Territorial Ambitions and the Gardens of Versailles* (Cambridge: Cambridge University Press, 1997).
16 Helen Jacobsen, 'Magnificent display: European ambassadorial visitors', in Daniëlle O. Kisluk-Grosheide and Bertrand Rondot, eds., *Visitors to Versailles: From Louis XIV to the French Revolution* (New York: Metropolitan Museum of Art, 2018), pp. 94–107 (pp. 100–101).
17 *Saint-Simon at Versailles*, trans. Lucy Norton; pref. Nancy Mitford (New York: Harper & Brothers, 1958), pp. 252, 260.
18 Volker Ullrich, *Hitler: Ascent, 1889–1939*, trans. Jefferson Chase (New York: Alfred A. Knopf, 2016), p. 607.
19 Charles Dreyss, ed., *Mémoires de Louis XIV pour l'instruction du Dauphin*, 2 vols (Paris: Didier, 1860), vol. 2, p. 441.
20 Robert Muchembled, *La société policée: Politique et politesse en France du XVIe au XXe siècle* (Paris: Éditions du Seuil, 1998).
21 Jean-Marie Apostolidès, *Le roi-machine: Spectacle et politique au temps de Louis XIV* (Paris: Éditions de Minuit, 1981).
22 *Mémoires de Louis XIV*, vol. 2, p. 15.
23 Machiavelli, *Prince*, p. 58.
24 Alan Sikes, *Representation and Identity from Versailles to the Present: The Performing Subject* (Basingstoke and New York: Palgrave Macmillan, 2007), pp. 23–56; Julia Prest, 'The politics of ballet at the court of Louis XIV', in Jennifer Nevile, ed., *Dance, Spectacle, and the Body Politick, 1250–1750* (Bloomington and Indianapolis, IN: Indiana University Press, 2008), pp. 229–40.
25 Philip Mansel, *King of the World: The Life of Louis XIV* (London: Allen Lane, 2019), pp. 119–20.
26 Maureen Needham, 'Louis XIV and the Académie Royale de Danse, 1661: A commentary and translation', *Dance Chronicle*, vol. 20, no. 2 (1997), pp. 173–90 (p. 176).
27 'Declaration of the king against usurpers of nobility', in Roger Mettam, ed., *Government and Society in Louis XIV's France* (Basingstoke: Macmillan, 1977), p. 116. However, Saint-Simon would rage against the 'shameless usurpation' of titles later in Louis's reign: see *Saint-Simon at Versailles*, p. 289.
28 Bossuet, *Politique*, p. 237.
29 Peter Burke, *The Fabrication of Louis XIV* (New Haven, CT: Yale University Press, 1994), pp. 58–9.
30 Burke, *Fabrication*, pp. 91–7.
31 Jacob Soll, *The Information Master: Jean-Baptiste Colbert's Secret State*

Intelligence System (Ann Arbor, MI: University of Michigan Press 2009), p. 130.

32 Robert Justin Goldstein, *Censorship of Political Caricature in Nineteenth-Century France* (Kent, OH: Kent State University Press, 1989), p. 90.

33 William M. Reddy, *The Navigation of Feeling: A Framework for the History of Emotions* (Cambridge: Cambridge University Press, 2001), p. 145.

34 Colin Jones, *The Great Nation: France from Louis XV to Napoleon* (London and New York: Penguin, 2003), p. 485.

35 Mansel, *King*, p. 311. The Oxford English Dictionary identifies the first use of the word in English in 1628, when French Protestants were referred to as 'poore Refugees' who had been forced to settle in England.

36 *Journal de Jean Migault, ou, malheurs d'une famille protestante du Poitou a l'époque de la révocation de l'Édit de Nantes* (Paris: Chez Henry Servier, 1825), p. 17.

37 W. Gregory Monahan, *Let God Arise: The War and Rebellion of the Camisards* (Oxford: Oxford University Press, 2014).

38 *Code noir, ou recueil d'édits, déclarations et arrêts concernant les esclaves nègres de l'Amérique* (Paris: Chez les Libraires Associez, 1743), pp. 1–29 (p. 27). The first article of the code required that all Jews leave the colonies in three months or face imprisonment and the confiscation of their property.

39 Mansel, *King*, p. 173.

40 John Evelyn, *Europe a Slave, Unless England Break Her Chains: Discovering the Grand Designs of the French-Popish Party in England for Several Years Past* (London: Printed for W. D., 1681), p. 13. Translated from a book in French attributed to Jean-Paul de Cerdan.

41 Kirsten L. Cooper, 'Political fear during the wars of Louis XIV: The danger of becoming French', in Thomas J. Kehoe and Michael G. Pickering, eds., *Fear in the German-Speaking World, 1600–2000* (London: Bloomsbury, 2020), pp. 15–40.

42 Gottfried Leibniz, *Mars Christianissimus Autore Germano Gallo-Græco: Or, an Apology for the Most Christian King's Taking up Arms against the Christians* (London: Printed for R. Bentley and S. Magnes, 1684), p. 74.

43 Burke, *Fabrication*, p. 136.

44 [Attributed to Pierre Jurieu and to Michel Le Vassor] *The Sighs*

of France in Slavery, Breathing after Liberty by Way of Memorial (London: Printed for D. Newman, 1689), pp. 4–6.

45 François Fénelon, *Directions pour la conscience d'un Roi, ou examen de conscience sur les devoirs de la Royauté* (Paris: Chez Antoine-Augustin Renouard, 1825), pp. 121–44 (pp. 132, 133). Although undated, the letter is thought to have been written in 1693 or early 1694: see Ryan Patrick Hanley, *Fénelon: Moral and Political Writings* (Oxford: Oxford University Press, 2020), p. 8.

46 'Les aventures de Télémaque', in *Fénelon: Oeuvres*, ed. Jacques Le Brun, 2 vols (Paris: Pléiade, 1983 and 1997), vol. 2, p. 16.

47 Montesquieu, *De l'esprit des lois*, 2 vols (Geneva: Chez Barillot et fils, 1748), vol. 1, Livre II, Chapitre I, p. 12; Livre VI, Chapitre IX, p. 130; Livre III, Chapitre IX, p. 41; on despotism see also Roger Boesche, *Theories of Tyranny: From Plato to Arendt* (University Park, PA: Pennsylvania State University Press, 1996), pp. 167–99 (p. 169).

48 Mansel, *King*, p. 232.

49 *Francis Bacon's Essays*, intro. Oliphant Smeaton (London: J. M. Dent & Sons, 1906), pp. 57–61 (p. 57).

50 Georges Lefebvre, *The Great Fear of 1789: Rural Panic in Revolutionary France*, trans. Joan White; intro. George Rudé (Princeton, NJ: Princeton University Press, [1973] 1982).

51 Historians have written extensively on the performative aspects of royal power under Louis XIV; on the complexities of image-making during his reign, see Georgia J. Cowart, *The Triumph of Pleasure: Louis XIV and the Politics of Spectacle* (Chicago, IL: University of Chicago Press, 2008). On the importance of theatre at court, see Philippe Beaussant with Patricia Bouchenot-Déchin, *Les plaisirs de Versailles: Théâtre et musique* (Paris: Fayard, 1996); also Burke, *Fabrication*, pp. 7–8.

52 On how pamphleteers contested royal authority by 'rescripting sovereignty' and challenging 'the narratives that commemorated the Sun King's triumphs at home and abroad', see Kathrina Ann LaPorta, *Performative Polemic: Anti-Absolutist Pamphlets and Their Readers in Late Seventeenth-Century France* (Newark, DE: University of Delaware Press, 2021), pp. 16, 85, 15. On treasonous literature and the creation of a Revolutionary political culture, see Robert Darnton, *The Forbidden Best-Sellers of Pre-Revolutionary France* (London: HarperCollins, 1996), and *The Devil in the Holy Water, or the Art of Slander from Louis XIV to Napoleon* (Philadelphia, PA: University of Pennsylvania Press, 2010).

53 Claire Tomalin, *The Life and Death of Mary Wollstonecraft* (New York: Harcourt Brace Jovanovich, 1974), p. 167; Mary Wollstonecraft, *An Historical and Moral View of the Origin and Progress of the French Revolution; and the Effect It Has Produced in Europe* (London: Printed for J. Johnson, 1794), p. 252.

54 Wollstonecraft, *Historical*, pp. 24, 26–7; Tom Furniss, 'Mary Wollstonecraft's French Revolution', in Claudia L. Johnson, ed., *The Cambridge Companion to Mary Wollstonecraft* (Cambridge: Cambridge University Press, 2002), pp. 59–79. On revolutionary politics as theatre, see the review essay by Yann Robert, '"La politique spectacle": A legacy of the French Revolution?', *French Politics, Culture & Society*, vol. 27, no. 3 (2009), pp. 104–15, and his *Dramatic Justice: Trial by Theater in the Age of the French Revolution* (Philadelphia, PA: University of Pennsylvania Press, 2018).

4: Colonising Panic

1 José Antonio Chávez, 'Las investigaciones arqueológicas de Alta Montaña en el sur del Perú', *Chungará: Revista Chilena de Antropología*, vol. 33, no. 2 (2001), pp. 283–8.

2 Mario Vargas Llosa, 'A Maiden', in *The Language of Passion: Selected Commentary*, trans. Natasha Wimmer (New York: Farrar, Straus and Giroux, 2003), pp. 172–6 (p. 175).

3 Andrew S. Wilson et al., 'Stable isotope and DNA evidence for ritual sequences in Inca child sacrifice', *Proceedings of the National Academy of Sciences*, vol. 104, no. 42 (2007), pp. 16456–61 (p. 16460).

4 Joseph Watts, Oliver Sheehan, Quentin D. Atkinson, Joseph Bulbulia and Russell D. Gray, 'Ritual human sacrifice promoted and sustained the evolution of stratified societies', *Nature*, vol. 532, no. 7598 (2016), pp. 228–31 (p. 228). On sacrifice, cannibalism and ritual violence as a means of social control, see Christy G. Turner II and Jacqueline A. Turner, *Man Corn: Cannibalism and Violence in the Prehistoric American Southwest* (Salt Lake City, UT: University of Utah Press, 1999), p. 484.

5 Kim MacQuarrie, *Last Days of the Incas* (New York: Simon & Schuster, 2007), pp. 40, 46.

6 Camilla Townsend, *Fifth Sun: A New History of the Aztecs* (Oxford: Oxford University Press, 2019), pp. 3, 7.

7 Francis Augustus MacNutt, ed., *Fernando Cortés: His Five Letters of Relation to the Emperor Charles V*, 2 vols (Cleveland, OH: Arthur H. Clark Company, 1908), vol. 1, pp. 30–31, 333.

8 Peter Silver, *Our Savage Neighbors: How Indian War Transformed Early America* (New York: W. W. Norton, 2009).
9 Bartolomé de las Casas, *The Devastation of the Indies: A Brief Account*, trans. Herma Briffault; intro Bill M. Donovan (Baltimore, MD: Johns Hopkins University Press, [1974] 1992), pp. 122, 85, 62–3.
10 Sherburne F. Cook and Lesley Byrd Simpson, *The Population of Central Mexico in the Sixteenth Century* (Berkeley, CA: University of California Press, 1948); Alfred W. Crosby, *The Columbian Exchange: Biological and Cultural Consequences of 1492* (Westport, CT: Greenwood, 1972). For an important reassessment of the 'theory of virgin soil epidemics', however, see David S. Jones, 'Virgin soils revisited', *William and Mary Quarterly*, vol. 60, no. 4 (October 2003), pp. 703–42.
11 *Motolinia's History of the Indians of New Spain*, trans. and ed. Elizabeth Andros Foster (Westport, CT: Greenwood Press, [1950] 1973), p. 38.
12 Peter Gordon and Juan José Morales, *The Silver Way: China, Spanish America and the Birth of Globalisation, 1565–1815* (London: Penguin, 2017).
13 W. E. Cheong, 'The decline of Manila as the Spanish entrepôt in the Far East, 1785–1826: Its impact on the pattern of Southeast Asian trade', *Journal of Southeast Asian Studies*, vol. 2, no. 2 (1971), pp. 142–58.
14 Robert Peckham, 'Symptoms of empire: Cholera in Southeast Asia, 1820–1850', in Mark Jackson, ed., *The Routledge History of Disease* (London: Routlege, 2016), pp. 183–201; *Epidemics in Modern Asia* (Cambridge: Cambridge University Press, 2016), pp. 54–63.
15 Alexandre Moreau de Jonnès, *Rapport au Conseil Supérieur de Santé sur le choléra-morbus pestilentiel* (Paris: Imprimerie de Cosson, 1831), p. 150; Carlos Luis Benoit, *Observaciones sobre el cólera-morbo espasmódico, ó mordechi de las Indias Orientales: recogidas en las Islas Filipinas, y publicadas con su método curativo* (Madrid: Imprenta de D. L. Amarita, 1832), p. 10.
16 Paul de la Gironière, *Aventures d'un gentilhomme Breton aux îles Philippines* (Paris: Au Comptoir des Imprimeurs-Unis, Lacroix-Comon, 1855), p. 26.
17 Benoit, *Observaciones*, p. 55; José P. Bantug, *A Short History of Medicine in the Philippines during the Spanish Regime, 1565–1898* (Quezon City: Colegio Médico-Farmacéutico de Filipinas, 1953), p. 30.

18 Paul de la Gironière, *Twenty Years in the Philippines* (New York: Harper & Brothers, 1854), p. 20.
19 Gironière, *Twenty Years*, p. 27.
20 Gironière, *Aventures*, pp. 25–44 (p. 27); 'Îles Philippines, Manille, nécrologie, Godefroy, massacre des étrangers', *Revue Encyclopédique*, vol. 11 (July 1821), pp. 405–9; 'Massacre at Manilla', in *The Annual Register, or, A View of the History, Politics, and Literature of the Year 1821* (London: Baldwin, Cradock, and Joy, 1822), pp. 314–24.
21 'Îles Philippines', p. 407.
22 Gironière, *Aventures*, pp. 26–9; Emma Helen Blair and James Alexander Robertson, eds., *The Philippine Islands, 1493–1898*, vol. 51, *1801–1840* (Cleveland, OH: Arthur H. Clark Company, 1907), p. 44; 'Îles Philippines', p. 407. On Godefroy's mission as a naturalist for the French government, see Richard W. Burkhardt, Jr, 'Naturalists' practices and nature's empire: Paris and the platypus, 1815–1833', *Pacific Science*, vol. 55, no. 4 (2001), pp. 327–41 (p. 334).
23 'Philippines: Massacre at Manilla', *Asiatic Journal and Monthly Register*, vol. 11 (May 1821), pp. 528–32.
24 Blair and Robertson, *Philippine Islands*, p. 41; 'Peter Dobell on the massacre of foreigners in Manila, 1820', *Bulletin* (New York Public Library), vol. 7, no. 6 (June 1903), pp. 198–200.
25 Blair and Robertson, *Philippine Islands*, p. 45.
26 *Calcutta Annual Register, for the Year 1821* (Calcutta: Government Gazette Press, 1823), pp. 256–7 (p. 257).
27 'History of the rise, progress, ravages, &c. of the blue cholera of India', *Lancet*, vol. 17, no. 429 (19 November 1831), pp. 241–81 (p. 245). On the stereotyping of the panicked native crowd, see Robert Peckham, 'Critical mass: Colonial crowds and contagious panics in 1890s Hong Kong and Bombay', in Harald Fischer-Tiné, ed., *Anxieties, Fear and Panic in Colonial Settings: Empires on the Verge of a Nervous Breakdown* (Cham, Switzerland: Palgrave, 2016), pp. 369–92.
28 Daniel Defoe, *A Journal of the Plague Year* (London: Printed for E. Nutt, J. Roberts, A. Dodd and J. Graves, 1722), p. 118.
29 Gabriel Lafond, *Quinze ans de voyages autour du monde*, 2 vols (Paris and Leipzig: Société des Publications Cosmopolites/Brockhaus et Avenarius, 1840), vol. 2, p. 303.
30 Andrew Jervise, *Epitaphs and Inscriptions from Burial Grounds & Old Buildings in the North East of Scotland*, 2 vols (Edinburgh: David Douglas, 1879), vol. 2, p. 361.
31 Dean C. Worcester, *A History of Asiatic Cholera in the Philippine*

Islands (Manila: Bureau of Printing, 1908), p. 3; *Appendix to A History of Asiatic Cholera in the Philippine Islands* (Manila: Bureau of Printing, 1909), p. 47.

32 Lafond, *Quinze ans*, vol. 2, p. 308.

33 William Wilson Hunter, *A Brief History of the Indian People* (London: Trübner & Co., 1882), p. 204.

5: Despotism of Liberty

1 Schechter, *Genealogy*, p. 42.

2 *Memoirs of Bertrand Barère*, trans. De V. Payen-Payne, 4 vols (London: H. S. Nichols, 1896), vol. 2, p. 305; Timothy Tackett, *The Coming of the Terror in the French Revolution* (Cambridge, MA: Belknap/ Harvard University Press, 2015), pp. 299–302.

3 The historians Michel Biard and Marisa Linton have argued that 'The Terror' was the retrospective invention of deputies in the National Assembly who blamed others for the regime's violence in order to exonerate themselves; see *Terror: The French Revolution and Its Demons* (Cambridge and Medford, MA: Polity, 2021), p. 4.

4 See the definitions of 'terreur' and 'tragédie' in Denis Diderot and Jean Le Rond d'Alembert, eds., *Encyclopédie, ou, dictionnaire raisonné des sciences, des arts et des métiers*, vol. 16 (Neuchâtel: Chez Samuel Faulche, 1765), pp. 184–5, 513–22.

5 Schechter, *Genealogy*, pp. 100–123.

6 Edmund Burke, *A Philosophical Enquiry into the Origin of Our Ideas of the Sublime and Beautiful* (London: Printed for R. and J. Dodsley, 1757), pp. 42–3 (p. 42).

7 Burke, *Philosophical*, pp. 42, 14.

8 Burke, *Philosophical*, pp. 43–4 (p. 44).

9 Edmund Burke, *Reflections on the Revolution in France* (London: Printed for J. Dodsley, 1790), p. 121.

10 Lefebvre, *Great Fear*.

11 Timothy Tackett, *Becoming a Revolutionary: The Deputies of the French National Assembly and the Emergence of a Revolutionary Culture (1789–1790)* (Princeton, NJ: Princeton University Press, 1996), pp. 152–4; Barry M. Shapiro, *Traumatic Politics: The Deputies and the King in the Early French Revolution* (University Park, PA: Pennsylvania State University Press, 2009), pp. 11, 18.

12 Tackett, *Coming of the Terror*, p. 7; Biard and Linton, *Terror*.

13 Marisa Linton, *Choosing Terror: Virtue, Friendship, and Authenticity*

in the French Revolution (Oxford: Oxford University Press, 2013), pp. 19–20 (p. 20).

14 Camille Desmoulins, *Le Vieux Cordelier*, no. 4 (20 December 1793), p. 62.

15 Desmoulins, 'Le Pour et le contre, ou conversation de deux vieux cordeliers', *Le Vieux Cordelier*, no. 7 (3 February 1794), pp. 123, 124, 131–2 (p. 132).

16 David P. Jordan, 'Rumor, fear, and paranoia in the French Revolution', in Charles B. Strozier, David M. Terman and James W. Jones, with Katharine A. Boyd, eds., *The Fundamentalist Mindset* (Oxford and New York: Oxford University Press, 2010), pp. 175–94 (p. 175).

17 Marisa Linton, 'Fatal friendships: The politics of Jacobin friendship', *French Historical Studies*, vol. 31, no. 1 (Winter 2008), pp. 51–76.

18 Maximilien Robespierre, *Rapport sur les principes de morale politique qui doivent guider la Convention nationale dans l'administration intérieure de la République, fait au nom du Comité de salut public, le 18 pluviôse, l'an 2e de la République* (Paris: Chez G. Le Roy, 1794), p. 13.

19 'Séance du II Germinal An II (31 Mars 1794). Contre la comparution à la barre de Danton, détenu', in Marc Bouloiseau and Albert Soboul, eds., *Oeuvres de Maximilien Robespierre*, vol. 10, *Discours, 27 juillet 1793–27 juillet 1794* (Paris: Presses Universitaires de France, 1967), pp. 412–18 (p. 414); Slavoj Zizek, 'Robespierre, or, the "divine violence" of terror', in *Robespierre: Virtue and Terror* (London and New York: Verso, 2007), pp. vii–xxxix (pp. xi–xii).

20 Robespierre, 'Séance du 5 Novembre 1792: Réponse à l'accusation de Louvet', in Marc Bouloiseau, Georges Lefebvre, Jean Dautry and Albert Soboul, eds., *Oeuvres de Maximilien Robespierre*, vol. 9, *Discours, septembre 1792–27 juillet 1793* (Paris: Presses Universitaires de France, 1957), pp. 77–104 (p. 89).

21 Robespierre, 'Séance du II Germinal An II (31 Mars 1794)', p. 414.

22 Ruth Scurr, *Fatal Purity: Robespierre and the French Revolution* (New York: Henry Holt, 2006), p. 321.

23 For other dissenting views, see Marilyn Butler, ed., *Burke, Paine, Godwin, and the Revolution Controversy* (Cambridge: Cambridge University Press, 1984).

24 Richard Price, *A Discourse on the Love of Our Country* (London: Printed for T. Cadell, 1789), pp. 6–7, 13.

25 *Substance of the Speech of the Right Honourable Edmund Burke, in thr* [sic] *Debate on the Army Estimates, in the House of Commons· on*

Tuesday, the 9th Day of February, 1790. Comprehending a Discussion of the Present Situation of Affairs in France (London: Printed for J. Debrett, 1790), p. 12.

26 *Burke: Selected Works: Four Letters on the Proposals for Peace with the Regicide Directory of France*, ed. E. J. Payne (Oxford: Clarendon Press, [1796] 1892), pp. 7, 315.

27 As Dan Edelstein argues, Jacobin leaders 'drew on natural right to authorize and draft the laws underpinning the Terror': see *The Terror of Natural Right: Republicanism, the Cult of Nature, and the French Revolution* (Chicago, IL: University of Chicago Press, 2009), p. 4.

28 Thomas Paine, *Rights of Man: Being an Answer to Mr Burke's Attack on the French Revolution* (London: Printed for J. S. Jordan, 1791), pp. 32–4; *Rights of Man: Part the Second* (London: Printed for J. S. Jordan, 1792), p. 2.

29 David Hume, *A Treatise of Human Nature*, 2 vols, ed. David Fate Norton and Mary J. Norton (Oxford: Oxford University Press, 2007), vol. 1, p. 266. Although, as Susan James has argued in her study of seventeenth-century philosophy, the role that the emotions were understood to play 'in rational thought and action' tends to be neglected; *Passion and Action*, pp. 16–18.

30 Originally published in Latin but translated into French in 1772 by M. Gouvion; François Boissier de Sauvages, *Nosologie méthodique, ou distribution des maladies, en genres et en espèces* (Lyon: Chez Jean-Marie Bruyset, 1772), vol. 7, pp. 242–7.

31 Jean-Jacques Rousseau, *Emile or On Education*, trans. and intro. Allan Bloom (New York: Basic Books, 1979), p. 37.

32 Rousseau, *Emile*, pp. 54–5.

33 William M. Reddy, 'Sentimentalism and its erasure: The role of emotions in the era of the French Revolution', *Journal of Modern History*, vol. 72, no. 1 (2000), pp. 109–52; see also Rachel Hewitt, *A Revolution of Feeling: The Decade That Forged the Modern Mind* (London: Granta, 2017).

34 Rousseau, *Emile*, p. 40; Allan Bloom, 'Introduction', pp. 3–29 (pp. 4–5) and note 6, p. 482; see Karl Löwith, 'The problem of bourgeois society', in *From Hegel to Nietzsche: The Revolution in Nineteenth-Century Thought*, fwd Hans-Georg Gadamer; trans. David F. Green (New York: Columbia University Press, [1964] 1991), pp. 235–62 (pp. 235–9).

35 Burke, *Reflections*, pp. 164, 119.

36 Dena Goodman, *The Republic of Letters: A Cultural History of the French Enlightenment* (Ithaca, NY: Cornell University Press, 1994).
37 Antoine Lilti, *The World of the Salons: Sociability and Worldliness in Eighteenth-Century Paris*, trans. Lydia G. Cochrane (Oxford: Oxford University Press, 2015), p. 233; see also Steven Kale, *French Salons: High Society and Political Sociability from the Old Regime to the Revolution of 1848* (Baltimore, MD: Johns Hopkins University Press, 2004).
38 David J. Denby, *Sentimental Narrative and the Social Order in France, 1760–1820* (Cambridge: Cambridge University Press, 1994).
39 Colin Jones, *The Smile Revolution in Eighteenth Century Paris* (Oxford: Oxford University Press, 2014).
40 Jean-Jacques Rousseau, *Discours sur l'origine et les fondements de l'inégalité parmi les hommes* (Amsterdam: Chez Marc Michel Rey, 1755), p. lxv.
41 Rousseau, *Emile*, p. 221; Rousseau distinguishes between a self-centred form of love, *amour de soi*, and a kind of self-love that he calls *amour-propre*, pp. 213–14.
42 Sarah Maza, *The Myth of the French Bourgeoisie: An Essay on the Social Imaginary, 1750–1850* (Cambridge, MA: Harvard University Press, 2003), pp. 61–8.
43 David A. Bell, *The Cult of the Nation in France: Inventing Nationalism, 1680–1800* (Cambridge, MA: Harvard University Press, 2001), p. 67; Tackett, *Becoming*, p. 102.
44 On the rise of the 'good father', see Lynn Hunt, *The Family Romance of the French Revolution* (Berkeley, CA: University of California Press, 1992), pp. 17–52.
45 Thomas E. Kaiser, 'Louis *le bien-aimé* and the rhetoric of the royal body', in Sara E. Melzer and Kathryn Norberg, eds., *From the Royal to the Republican Body: Incorporating the Political in Seventeenth- and Eighteenth-Century France* (Berkeley, CA: University of California Press, 1998), pp. 131–61 (pp. 133, 136–7).
46 Dena Goodman, 'Introduction: Not another biography of Marie-Antoinette!', in Dena Goodman, ed., *Marie-Antoinette: Writings on the Body of a Queen* (New York and London: Routledge, 2003), pp. 1–15 (pp. 4–5).
47 Joseph Baillio, Katharine Baetjer and Paul Lang, *Vigée Le Brun* (New York: Metropolitan Museum of Art, 2016), pp. 86–9 (pp. 87, 88); Mary D. Sheriff, 'The portrait of the queen', in Goodman, ed., *Marie-Antoinette*, pp. 45–72; *The Exceptional Woman: Elisabeth*

Vigée-Lebrun and the Cultural Politics of Art (Chicago, IL: University of Chicago Press, 1996), pp. 165–8; also Antoine de Baecque, ed., *Marie-Antoinette: Métamorphoses d'une image* (Paris: Patrimoine, 2019).

48 Arlette Farge and Jacques Revel, *The Vanishing Children of Paris: Rumor and Politics before the French Revolution*, trans. Claudia Miéville (Cambridge, MA: Harvard University Press, 1991).

49 Lynn Hunt, 'The many bodies of Marie-Antoinette: Political pornography and the problem of the feminine in the French Revolution', in Goodman, ed., *Marie-Antoinette*, pp. 117–38; Simon Schama, *Citizens: A Chronicle of the French Revolution* (New York: Vintage, 1989), pp. 203–27.

50 Remo Bodei, 'The despotism of liberty', in *Geometry of the Passions: Fear, Hope, Happiness: Philosophy and Political Use*, trans. Gianpiero W. Doebler (Toronto: University of Toronto Press, 2018), p. 337.

51 The sketch, which is in the Louvre, is now thought to be the work of the artist Dominique-Vivant Denon; see Alain Chevalier, 'Le peintre David dessinant Marie-Antoinette conduit au supplice', in de Baecque, ed., *Marie-Antoinette*, pp. 112–13.

52 These issues were to be central to debates about the relative merits of direct and representative democracy. The deputies elected to the National Assembly didn't claim, after all, to embody the nation as the king did, but simply to speak on behalf of their constituencies; Paul Friedland, *Political Actors: Representative Bodies and Theatricality in the Age of the French Revolution* (Ithaca, NY: Cornell University Press, 2002), p. 12.

53 Burke, *Reflections*, pp. 121, 58, 54.

54 Burke, *Reflections*, pp. 105–6.

55 Burke, *Reflections*, pp. 121, 143.

56 François A. Mignet, *Histoire de la révolution française, depuis 1789 jusqu'en 1814*, 2 vols (Paris: Firmin Didot, père et fils, [1824] 1827), vol. 1, p. 350.

57 Mark McDonald, *Goya's Graphic Imagination* (New Haven, CT, and London: Metropolitan Museum of Art/Yale University Press, 2021), p. 146.

58 McDonald, *Goya's Graphic Imagination*, p. 27.

59 Gilles Deleuze, *Desert Islands and Other Texts, 1953–1974*, ed. David Lapoujade; trans. Michael Taormina (Cambridge, MA: MIT Press, 2003), p. 262.

60 Max Horkheimer and Theodor W. Adorno, *Dialectic of Enlightenment:*

Philosophical Fragments, ed. Gunzelin Schmid Noerr; trans. Edmund Jephcott (Stanford, CA: Stanford University Press, 2002), p. 1.

61 *A Letter from Mr Burke, to a Member of the National Assembly* (Paris and London: Reprinted for J. Dodsley, 1791), p. 28; on 'irrational fear' see *Burke: Selected Works*, p. 9. In her scathing repudiation of Burke's *Reflections* in 1790, however, Mary Wollstonecraft had accused Burke of letting his passions get the better of his reason, despite his claims to be pushing back against 'irrational fear'; *A Vindication of the Rights of Men, in a Letter to the Right Honourable Edmund Burke; Occasioned by his Reflections on the Revolution in France* (London: Printed for J. Johnson, 1790), pp. 63, 4.

62 Hannah Arendt, *On Revolution*, intro. Jonathan Schell (New York: Penguin, [1963] 2006), p. 70.

63 Arendt, *Revolution*, pp. 70–71.

64 Arendt, *Revolution*, p. 80, also pp. 39–48.

65 *Burke: Selected Works*, p. 7; *A Letter from the Right Honourable Edmund Burke to a Noble Lord* (London: Printed for J. Owen and F. and C. Rivington, 1796), p. 21.

66 De Dijn, *Freedom*, p. 236.

67 Adam Zamoyski, *Phantom Terror: Political Paranoia and the Creation of the Modern State, 1789–1848* (New York: Basic Books, 2015), pp. 10–21.

68 *Journey for Our Time: The Journals of the Marquis de Custine*, ed. and trans. Phyllis Penn Kohler; intro. Simon Sebag Montefiore (London: Phoenix Press, 2001), p. 111.

69 Henri [Heinrich] Heine, *Lutèce. Lettres sur la vie politique, artistique et sociale de la France* (Paris: Michel Lévy Frères, 1855), p. 272.

6: The Slave Matrix

1 Rediker quotes the novelist Barry Unsworth's description of the slave trade's 'violence of abstraction': see Marcus Rediker, *The Slave Ship: A Human History* (New York: Penguin, 2007), p. 12. For data on the transatlantic slave trade, see https://www.slavevoyages.org/

2 See Jennifer L. Morgan, *Reckoning with Slavery: Gender, Kinship, and Capitalism in the Early Black Atlantic* (Durham, NC: Duke University Press, 2021).

3 Trevor Burnard, 'Terror, horror and the British Atlantic slave trade in the eighteenth century', in Robert Antony, Stuart Carroll and Caroline Dodds Pennock, eds., *The Cambridge World History of Violence* (Cambridge: Cambridge University Press, 2020), pp. 17–35.

4 Thomas Clarkson, *The History of the Rise, Progress, and Accomplishment of the Abolition of the African Slave-Trade by the British Parliament*, 2 vols (London: Longman, Hurst, Rees, and Orme, 1808), vol. 1, p. 14; see also Clarkson's dissertation *An Essay on the Slavery and Commerce of the Human Species, Particularly the African* (London: Printed by J. Phillips, 1786).
5 Alexander Falconbridge, *An Account of the Slave Trade on the Coast of Africa* (London: Printed by J. Phillips, 1788), pp. 35, 25.
6 Slavery, as an institution, would not be abolished until the passing of the Slavery Abolition Act, 1833.
7 Manuel Barcia, *The Yellow Demon of Fever: Fighting Disease in the Nineteenth-Century Transatlantic Slave Trade* (New Haven, CT: Yale University Press, 2020), p. 153.
8 *Correspondence with Spain, Portugal, Brazil, The Netherlands, Sweden, and the Argentine Federation Relative to the Slave Trade: From January 1 to December 31, 1841* [General Report of the Emigration Commissioners: Great Britain. Emigration Commission] (London: William Clowes and Sons, 1842), pp. 76–7, 80.
9 Clarkson, *History*, vol. 1, p. 16.
10 Sowande' M. Mustakeem, *Slavery at Sea: Terror, Sex, and Sickness in the Middle Passage* (Urbana, IL: University of Illinois Press, 2016); John Savage, '"Black magic" and white terror: Slave poisoning and colonial society in early 19th century Martinique', *Journal of Social History*, vol. 40, no. 3 (2007), pp. 635–62.
11 Eric Robert Taylor, *If We Must Die: Shipboard Insurrections in the Era of the Atlantic Slave Trade* (Baton Rouge, LA: Louisiana State University Press, 2006).
12 John Newton, *Thoughts upon the Africa Trade* (London: Printed for J. Buckland and J. Johnson, 1788), p. 12.
13 John Newton, *The Journal of a Slave Trader, 1750–1754*, ed. and intro. Bernard Martin and Mark Spurrell (London: Epworth Press, 1962), p. 56; Rediker, *Slave Ship*, pp. 163–74.
14 On the working life of sailors aboard slave ships, see Emma Christopher, *Slave Ship Sailors and Their Captive Cargoes, 1730–1807* (Cambridge: Cambridge University Press, 2006).
15 Clarkson, *History*, vol. 1, pp. 338–9 (p. 339).
16 Clarkson, *History*, vol. 2, pp. 19–20.
17 *Report of the Lords of the Committee of Council Appointed for the Consideration of all Matters Relating to Trade and Foreign Plantations*

(1789), Part I, 'Some particulars of a voyage to Guinea'; Part II, 'Evidence with respect to carrying slaves to the West Indies'.

18 Newton, *Thoughts*, p. 17; Robert Isaac Wilberforce and Samuel Wilberforce, *Life of Wilberforce*, 5 vols (London: John Murray, 1838), vol. 2, p. 84.

19 The Scottish poet James Thomson described in 1727 how the 'direful shark', lured by the scent of 'rank disease' and death on the slave ships, waited to attack and dyed the sea with gore: see *The Seasons* (London: Printed for A. Hamilton, 1793), pp. 87–8; see also Marcus Rediker, 'History from below the water line: Sharks and the Atlantic slave trade', *Atlantic Studies*, vol. 5, no. 2 (2008), pp. 285–97; *Slave Ship*, pp. 37–40.

20 Another ten slaves committed suicide by jumping into the ocean.

21 Jane Webster, 'The *Zong* in the context of the eighteenth-century slave trade', *Journal of Legal History*, vol. 28, no. 3 (2007), pp. 285–98. In the end, the insurers were forced to pay up.

22 For a nuanced reading of Turner's painting, see Ian Baucom, *Specters of the Atlantic: Finance Capital, Slavery, and the Philosophy of History* (Durham, NC: Duke University Press, 2005), pp. 247–8, 274–5, 288–9, 291–2.

23 Rediker, *Slave Ship*, p. 9; John Coffey, '"Tremble, Britannia!": Fear, providence and the abolition of the slave trade, 1758–1807', *English Historical Review*, vol. 127, no. 527 (2012), pp. 844–81. As Mustakeem observes, slave ships were also 'mobile battlefields'; see *Slavery at Sea*, p. 77.

24 Judith Jennings, *The Business of Abolishing the British Slave Trade, 1783–1807* (Abingdon and New York: Routledge, 1997), p. 8.

25 Clarkson, *History*, vol. 2, p. 11.

26 John R. Spears, *The American Slave-Trade: An Account of Its Origin, Growth and Suppression* (New York: Charles Scribner's Sons, 1900), p. 71.

27 Newton, *Thoughts*, p. 33. On the crowded conditions on slave ships, see Nicholas Radburn and David Eltis, 'Visualizing the Middle Passage: The *Brooks* and the reality of ship crowding in the transatlantic slave trade', *Journal of Interdisciplinary History*, vol. 49, no. 4 (2019), pp. 533–65.

28 Marcus Wood, *Blind Memory: Visual Representations of Slavery in England and America, 1780–1865* (Manchester: Manchester University Press, 2000), p. 7.

29 Ramesh Mallipeddi, *Spectacular Suffering: Witnessing Slavery in the*

Eighteenth-Century British Atlantic (Charlottesville, VA: University of Virginia Press, 2016).

30 Based on cultural information contained in the narrative, including details of facial markings (*ichi*), the Canadian historian Paul E. Lovejoy has argued that Olaudah Equiano must have had first-hand experience of his Igbo homeland; see 'Autobiography and memory: Gustavus Vassa, alias Olaudah Equiano, the African', *Slavery & Abolition*, vol. 27, no. 3 (2006), pp. 317–47.

31 *The Interesting Narrative of the Life of Olaudah Equiano, or Gustavus Vassa, the African, Written by Himself*, 2 vols (London: Printed by T. Wilkins, 1789), vol. 1, pp. 79, 132.

32 On which, see Mallipeddi, *Spectacular Suffering*.

33 Newton, *Thoughts*, p. 8; *Interesting Narrative*, vol. 1, p. 227.

34 Newton, *Thoughts*, p. 2.

35 As the historian Karen Halttunen expresses it, 'The emergent pornography of pain became a troubling moral dilemma within the literature of humanitarian reform.' She also notes 'a heightened awareness of the close relationship between the revulsion and the excitement aroused by pain': see 'Humanitarianism and the pornography of pain in Anglo-American culture', *American Historical Review*, vol. 100, no. 2 (April 1995), pp. 303–34 (pp. 307, 318–19).

36 Rediker, *Slave Ship*, p. 8.

37 Paul Gilroy, *The Black Atlantic: Modernity and Double Consciousness* (London and New York: Verso, 1993), pp. 16–17.

38 C. L. R. James, *The Black Jacobins: Toussaint L'Ouverture and the San Domingo Revolution* (New York: Vintage, [1938] 1989), p. 12.

39 *The Secret Diary of William Byrd of Westover, 1709–1712*, ed. Louis B. Wright and Marion Tinling (Richmond, VA: The Dietz Press, 1941), p. 46.

40 Trevor Burnard, *Mastery, Tyranny, and Desire: Thomas Thistlewood and His Slaves in the Anglo-Jamaican World* (Chapel Hill, NC: University of North Carolina Press, 2004), pp. 184, 31, 104, 156.

41 *American Slavery as It Is: Testimony of a Thousand Witnesses* (New York: American Anti-Slavery Society, 1839), pp. 7, 109. The 1840 US census reports just under 2.5 million slaves out of a total population of 17 million; see *Compendium of the Enumeration of the Inhabitants and Statistics of the United States as Obtained at the Department of State, from the Returns of the Sixth Census* (Washington, DC: Thomas Allen, 1841), pp. 363–4.

42 Frederick Douglass, *Narrative of the Life of Frederick Douglass, an American Slave* (Boston, MA: Published at the Anti-Slavery Office, 1845).
43 Douglass, *Narrative*, pp. 74, 75.
44 Savage, '"Black magic" and white terror'; Carolyn E. Fick, *The Making of Haiti: The Saint Domingue Revolution from Below* (Knoxville, TN: University of Tennessee Press, 1990), p. 66.
45 Vincent Brown, *Tacky's Revolt: The Story of an Atlantic Slave War* (Cambridge, MA: Belknap/Harvard University Press, 2020).
46 Harriet Jacobs, *Incidents in the Life of a Slave Girl*, ed. L. Maria Child (Boston, MA: Published for the Author, 1861), pp. 97, 98, 99.
47 Jason T. Sharples, *The World That Fear Made: Slave Revolts and Conspiracy Scares in Early America* (Philadelphia, PA: University of Pennsylvania Press, 2020), pp. 13–14.
48 Michael Craton, *Testing the Chains: Resistance to Slavery in the British West Indies* (Ithaca, NY: Cornell University Press, 1982).
49 Sharples, *World That Fear Made*, p. 7.
50 Douglass, *Narrative*, pp. 33, 36.
51 Douglass, *Narrative*, p. 46.
52 David W. Blight, *Frederick Douglass: Prophet of Freedom* (New York: Simon & Schuster, 2018).
53 William L. Andrews, 'Introduction', in William L. Andrews, ed., *The Oxford Frederick Douglass Reader* (New York and Oxford: Oxford University Press, 1996), pp. 1–19 (p. 12).
54 *The Life and Times of Frederick Douglass* (Hartford, CT: Park Publishing Co., 1881), p. 269.
55 Jacobs, *Incidents*, pp. 154, 175, 186, 224.
56 Douglass, *Narrative*, pp. 36, 82.
57 Frederick Douglass, 'Letter to his old master', in *My Bondage and My Freedom*, intro. James McCune Smith (New York and Auburn: Miller, Orton & Mulligan, 1855), pp. 421–8 (p. 421); 'The color line', *North American Review*, vol. 132, no. 295 (1881), pp. 567–77 (pp. 568, 567).
58 Douglass, 'Letter to his old master', p. 427.
59 Bernard R. Boxill, 'Fear and shame as forms of moral suasion in the thought of Frederick Douglass', *Transactions of the Charles S. Peirce Society*, vol. 31, no. 4 (1995), pp. 713–44.
60 Thomas C. Holt, *The Problem of Freedom: Race, Labor, and Politics in Jamaica and Britain, 1832–1938* (Baltimore, MD: Johns Hopkins University Press, 1992); also Padraic X. Scanlan, *Freedom's Debtors:*

British Antislavery in Sierra Leone in the Age of Revolution (New Haven, CT: Yale University Press, 2017).

61 This is part of a larger project entitled *Workers: An Archaeology of the Industrial Age*, completed between 1986 and 1992.

62 Parvati Nair, *A Different Light: The Photography of Sebastião Salgado* (Durham, NC: Duke University Press, 2011), pp. 71–3, 234–7, 244–6, 262–3 (p. 72).

63 Herbert S. Klein and Francisco Vidal Luna, *Slavery in Brazil* (Cambridge: Cambridge University Press, 2009), pp. 151–2.

64 Klein and Luna, *Slavery*, pp. 55, 120.

65 Auguste de Saint-Hilaire, *Voyage dans le district des diamans et sur le littoral du Brésil*, 2 vols (Paris: Librairie Gide, 1833), vol. 1, pp. 11–12.

66 For a discussion of how an anti-slavery ideology shaped Britain's imperial mission, even as indentured, slave-wage labour underpinned that mission, see Richard Huzzey, *Freedom Burning: Anti-Slavery and Empire in Victorian Britain* (Ithaca, NY: Cornell University Press, 2012).

67 Karl Marx, *Capital: A Critique of Political Economy*, vol. 1, intro. Ernest Mandel; trans. Ben Fowkes (London: Penguin/New Left Review, [1976] 1990), p. 925.

68 Eric Williams, *Capitalism and Slavery*, fwd William A. Darity, Jr; intro. Colin A. Palmer (Chapel Hill, NC: University of North Carolina Press, [1944] 1994), pp. 14, 4, 13.

69 Williams, *Capitalism*, p. 21.

70 Williams, *Capitalism*, p. 169, 25.

71 Adam Hochschild, *King Leopold's Ghost: A Story of Greed, Terror, and Heroism in Colonial Africa* (Boston, MA, and New York: Houghton Mifflin Harcourt, 1998).

72 Robert Harms, *Land of Tears: The Exploration and Exploitation of Equatorial Africa* (New York: Basic Books, 2019).

73 Joseph Conrad, *Heart of Darkness and Other Tales*, ed. Cedric Watts (Oxford: Oxford University Press, 2008), p. 151.

74 As the British philosopher Mark Fisher has suggested, today there is a 'widespread sense that not only is capitalism the only viable political and economic system, but also that it is now impossible even to imagine a coherent alternative to it'; *Capitalist Realism: Is There No Alternative?* (Winchester and Washington, DC: Zero Books, 2009), p. 2.

75 Clair MacDougall and James Harding Giahyue, 'Liberia troops

fire on protesters as West Africa's Ebola toll hits 1,350', *Reuters* (27 August 2014).

76 Which lent an irony to the name 'Liberia', meaning 'free land'.

77 Alan Huffman, *Mississippi in Africa: The Saga of the Slaves of Prospect Hill Plantation and Their Legacy in Liberia Today* (Jackson, MS: University Press of Mississippi, 2010).

78 Helene Cooper, *The House at Sugar Beach: In Search of a Lost African Childhood* (New York: Simon & Schuster, 2008).

79 Leo Cendrowicz, 'Warlord convicted: Liberia's Charles Taylor found guilty of war crimes', *Time* (26 April 2012).

80 Benjamin G. Dennis and Anita K. Dennis, *Slaves to Racism: An Unbroken Chain from America to Liberia* (New York: Algora Publishing, 2008).

7: Lost in the Crowd

1 Thirty-four per cent of the population of England, Wales and Scotland lived in cities of 20,000 or larger; *The Census of Great Britain in 1851* (London: Longman, Brown, Green and Longmans, 1854), pp. 13–14.

2 'Article VIII. The Moral and Physical Condition of the Working Classes in Manchester; An Address to the Higher Classes on the Present State of Public Feeling among the Working Classes', *Westminster Review*, vol. 18 (April 1833), pp. 380–404 (p. 382).

3 John Morley, 'Young England and the political future', *Fortnightly Review*, vol. 7, no. 4 (1 April, 1867), pp. 491–6 (p. 493). On fear of the revolutionary poor, see Gareth Stedman Jones, *Outcast London: A Study in the Relationship Between Classes in Victorian Society* (London: Verso, [1971] 2013), p. 290.

4 On the political exploitation of these panics, see Rob Sindall, *Street Violence in the Nineteenth Century: Media Panic or Real Danger?* (Leicester: Leicester University Press, 1990).

5 By this time the 'masses' had become synonymous with the 'working classes'; Asa Briggs, 'The language of mass and masses in nineteenth-century England', in *The Collected Essays of Asa Briggs*, vol. 1, *Words, Numbers, Places, People* (Urbana, IL: University of Illinois Press, 1985), pp. 34–54.

6 'Article VIII', p. 381.

7 Rousseau, *Emile*, p. 59.

8 John Stuart Mill, 'Civilization' [1836], in *Dissertations and*

Discussions: Political, Philosophical, and Historical, 2 vols (London: John W. Parker and Son, 1859), vol. 1, pp. 160–205 (pp. 182–3).

9 John Stuart Mill, *On Liberty* (London: John W. Parker, 1859), p. 118.

10 Émile Durkheim, *Suicide: étude de sociologie* (Paris: Félix Alcan, 1897).

11 'Summary of politics', *Cobbett's Weekly Political Register*, vol. 8, no. 15 (12 October 1805), p. 549. The same idea was expressed by Cobbett in the 1790s: see Craig Nelson, *Thomas Paine: Enlightenment, Revolution, and the Birth of Modern Nations* (New York: Viking, 2006), pp. 2–3.

12 Edmund Burke letter to Thomas Mercer (26 February 1790), in *Correspondence of the Right Honourable Edmund Burke, between the Year 1744, and the Period of His Decease in 1797*, 4 vols (London: Francis & John Rivington, 1844), vol. 3, p. 147; *A Letter from Mr Burke*, p. 28.

13 On the modern processes that 'tended to render every subject of the state functionally equivalent', see Mary Poovey, *Making a Social Body: British Cultural Formation, 1830–1864* (Chicago, IL: Chicago University Press, 1995), p. 29.

14 Tocqueville, *Democracy*, p. 663.

15 Mill, 'Civilization', pp. 187, 163; also *Liberty*, pp. 12–13.

16 Newspapers had been crucial to the 'energetic demonstration of determined will' that had enabled the extension of voting rights secured by the 1832 Reform Act; Mill, 'Civilization', p. 170.

17 Mill, *Liberty*, pp. 131–3, 129, 13.

18 John Carey, *The Intellectuals and the Masses: Pride and Prejudice among the Literary Intelligentsia, 1880–1939* (London: Faber and Faber, 1992), p. 5.

19 Hippolyte Taine, *Les origines de la France contemporaine: la Révolution*, 3 vols (Paris: Librairie Hachette, 1878), vol. 1, p. 137.

20 Carey, *Intellectuals*, pp. 4–5.

21 Sigmund Freud, 'My contact with Josef Popper-Lynkeus (1932)', *International Journal of Psycho-Analysis*, vol. 23, part 2 (1942), pp. 85–7 (p. 86).

22 Friedrich Engels, *The Condition of the Working Class in England in 1844* (New York: John W. Lovell Company, 1887), p. 18.

23 Walter Benjamin, 'On some motifs in Baudelaire', *Selected Writings*, vol. 4, *1938–1940*, trans. Edmund Jephcott et al.; ed. Howard Eiland and Michael W. Jennings (Cambridge, MA: Belknap/Harvard University Press, 2003), pp. 313–55 (p. 327).

24 *The Collected Tales and Poems of Edgar Allan Poe* (New York: The Modern Library, 1992), pp. 475–81 (pp. 475, 476).

25 Engels, *Condition*, p. 18.
26 Karl Marx, 'Economic and philosophical manuscripts', in *Early Writings*, intro. Lucio Colletti; trans. Rodney Livingstone and Gregor Benton (London: Penguin/New Left Review, 1975), pp. 322–44; terms he borrowed but adapted from the German philosopher Georg Wilhelm Friedrich Hegel. On the history of Marx's alienation, see Marcello Musto, 'Alienation redux: Marxian perspectives', in Marcello Musto, ed., *Karl Marx's Writings on Alienation* (Cham, Switzerland: Palgrave Macmillan, 2021), pp. 3–48.
27 Engels, *Condition*, pp. 20, 37, 43, 18.
28 Karl Marx and Friedrich Engels, *The Communist Manifesto*, intro. A J. P. Taylor (London: Penguin, 1967), p. 78.
29 'Article VIII', pp. 381, 394.
30 *The Times* [London] (10 November 1856), p. 6; R. Sindall, 'The London garotting panics of 1856 and 1862', *Social History*, vol. 12, no. 3 (1987), pp. 351–9 (p. 351); for a definition of 'garrotting', see Sindall, *Street Violence*, p. 10.
31 Labrador and Queensland were apparently two other options for a penal colony; see Sindall, *Street Violence*, p. 40.
32 Sindall, *Street Violence*, p. 40.
33 Sindall, *Street Violence*, pp. 142, 146.
34 'Occasional notes', *Pall Mall Gazette* (21 January 1885), p. 3.
35 General Booth, *In Darkest England and the Way Out* (New York and London: Funk & Wagnalls, 1890), pp. 9, 12.
36 Stedman Jones, *Outcast London*, pp. 295–6 (and on the riots of February 1886, pp. 345–6); 'The defence of Trafalgar Square', *The Times* [London] (14 November 1887), p. 8.
37 Quoted in T. A. Critchley, *The Conquest of Violence: Order and Liberty in Britain* (London: Constable, 1970), p. 153.
38 *The Times* [London] (14 November 1887), p. 9.
39 Patrice de Moncan, *Le Paris d'Haussmann* (Paris: Éditions du Mécène, 2002), p. 10.
40 *Mémoires du Baron Haussmann*, vol. 3, *Grands travaux de Paris* (Paris: Victor Havard, 1893), p. 54; Jeanne Gaillard, *Paris, la ville (1852–1870): l'urbanisme parisien à l'heure d'Haussmann* (Lille and Paris: Honoré Champion, 1977), pp. 29–40.
41 Charles Baudelaire, 'A Martyr', and 'To a Woman Passing By', in *The Flowers of Evil*, trans. Keith Waldrop (Middletown, CT: Wesleyan University Press, 2006), pp. 151, 123; 'The Crowd', in *Paris Spleen:*

Little Poems in Prose, trans. Keith Waldrop (Middletown, CT: Wesleyan University Press, 2009), p. 22.

42 Gustave Le Bon, *The Crowd: A Study of the Popular Mind* (New York: Macmillan & Co., 1896), pp. xxi–xxiv (p. xxiii).

43 Le Bon, *Crowd*, pp. 128, 13, 9; see also Georges Lefebvre, 'Foules révolutionnaires', *Annales Historiques de la Révolution Française*, no. 61 (1934), pp. 1–26.

44 Le Bon, *Crowd*, pp. 7, 10.

45 J. M. Charcot and Pierre Marie, 'Hysteria, mainly hystero-epilepsy', in Daniel Hack Tuke, ed., *A Dictionary of Psychological Medicine*, 2 vols (Philadelphia, PA: P. Blakiston, Son & Co., 1892), vol. 1, pp. 627–41 (p. 628); see also Georges Guinon, *Les agents provocateurs de l'hystérie* (Paris: Aux Bureaux du Progrès/A. Delahaye et Lecrosnieb, 1889).

46 Le Bon, *Crowd*, p. 21.

47 Le Bon, *Crowd*, p. ix.

48 Le Bon, *Crowd*, pp. x, xv.

49 Le Bon, *Crowd*, p. xx.

50 Gabriel Tarde, 'Les crimes des foules', *Archives de l'Anthropologie Criminelle*, vol. 7 (1892), pp. 353–86; 'Foules et sectes au point de vue criminel', *Revue des Deux Mondes*, vol. 332 (1893), pp. 349–87.

51 Scipio Sighele, *La foule criminelle: essai de psychologie collective* (Paris: Félix Alcan, 1892), p. 2.

52 Robert E. Park and Ernest W. Burgess, *An Introduction to the Science of Sociology* (Chicago, IL: University of Chicago Press, 1921), pp. 869, 34.

53 E. Ray Lankester, *Degeneration: A Chapter in Darwinism* (London: Macmillan and Co., 1880), p. 32.

54 Miles [Sir John Frederick Maurice], 'Where to get men', *Contemporary Review*, vol. 81 (January 1902), pp. 78–82 (pp. 80, 81).

55 *Report of the Inter-Departmental Committee on Physical Deterioration* (London: HMSO, 1904), pp. 84–93 (p. 84).

56 H. G. Wells, 'Zoological retrogression', *Gentleman's Magazine*, vol. 271 (September 1891), pp. 246–53.

57 H. G. Wells, 'The extinction of man: Some speculative suggestions', *Pall Mall Gazette* (25 September 1894), p. 3.

58 George M. Beard, 'Neurasthenia, or nervous exhaustion', *Boston Medical and Surgical Journal*, vol. 3, no. 13 (29 April 1869), pp. 217–21; *Cases of Hysteria, Neurasthenia, Spinal Irritation, and Allied Affections; with Remarks* (Chicago, IL: J. J. Spalding & Co., 1874).

59 P. Pichot, 'The semantics of anxiety', *Human Psychopharmacology: Clinical and Experimental*, vol. 14, no. S1 (1999), pp. 22–8 (p. 26).
60 Henry Maudsley, *The Pathology of Mind* (London: Macmillan and Co., 1879), pp. 365, 362, 392.
61 Sigmund Freud, 'Lecture 25: Anxiety', in *Introductory Lectures on Psychoanalysis*, vol. 1, trans. James Strachey; ed. James Strachey and Angela Richards (London: Penguin, 1976), pp. 440–60 (pp. 441, 449); 'On the grounds for detaching a particular syndrome from neurasthenia under the description "anxiety neurosis"' [1895], in James Strachey, Anna Freud, Alex Strachey and Alan Tyson, eds., *The Standard Edition of the Complete Psychological Works of Sigmund Freud*, vol. 3, *1893–1899: Early Psycho-Analytic Publications* (London: The Hogarth Press, 1962), pp. 85–115 (p. 92); 'Draft E: How anxieties originate' [1894], in Marie Bonaparte, Anna Freud and Ernst Kris, eds., *The Origins of Psycho-Analysis: Letters to Wilhelm Fliess, Drafts and Notes: 1887–1902*, trans. Eric Mosbacher and James Strachey (New York: Basic Books, 1954), pp. 88–93 (p. 90); *Three Essays on the Theory of Sexuality*, trans. James Strachey; intro. Steven Marcus (New York: Basic Books, 1962), p. 90.
62 Sigmund Freud, 'Group psychology and the analysis of the ego', in *Complete Psychological Works (1920–1922)*, vol. 18 (1955), pp. 69–143. Note that the original German refers to the analysis of 'mass' psychology – *Massenpsychologie* – not 'group' psychology.
63 Georg Simmel, 'The metropolis and mental life', in Kurt H. Wolff, trans. and ed., *The Sociology of Georg Simmel* (Glencoe, IL: Free Press, 1950), pp. 409–24 (p. 414).
64 Simmel, 'Metropolis', p. 410.
65 David Trotter, 'The invention of agoraphobia', *Victorian Literature and Culture*, vol. 32, no. 2 (2004), pp. 463–74 (p. 463).
66 Camillo Sitte, *City Planning According to Artistic Principles*, trans. George R. Collins and Christiane Crasemann Collins (New York: Random House, 1965), pp. 45–6.
67 Carl E. Schorske, 'The Ringstrasse, its critics, and the birth of urban modernism', in *Fin-de-Siècle Vienna: Politics and Culture* (New York: Alfred A. Knopf, 1980), pp. 24–115 (p. 24).
68 Schorske, 'Ringstrasse', pp. 63–4 (p. 64).
69 Trotter, 'Invention', p. 464.
70 Henri Legrand du Saulle, *Étude clinique sur la peur des espaces (agoraphobie des Allemands), névrose émotive* (Paris: V. Adrien Dalahaye 1878), pp. 5–10; Trotter, 'Invention', p. 464; Anthony Vidler,

Warped Space: Art, Architecture and Anxiety in Modern Culture (Cambridge, MA: MIT Press, 2000), pp. 30–31.

71 'Dr Andrea Verga', *British Medical Journal*, vol. 2, no. 1824 (14 December 1895), p. 1531; Stefano Zago and Chiara Randazzo, 'Andrea Verga (1811–1895)', *Journal of Neurology*, vol. 253, no. 8 (2006), pp. 1115–16.

72 B. Ball, 'On claustrophobia', *British Medical Journal*, vol. 2, no. 975 (6 September 1879), p. 371.

73 Robert Jones, 'A case of agoraphobia, with remarks upon obsessions', *Lancet*, vol. 151, no. 3887 (26 February 1898), pp. 568–70. Darwin, it has been claimed, was also agoraphobic; see Thomas J. Barloon and Russell Noyes, Jr, 'Charles Darwin and panic disorder', *Journal of the American Medical Association*, vol. 277, no. 2 (1997), pp. 138–41.

74 J. Headley Neale, 'Agoraphobia', *Lancet*, vol. 152, no. 3925 (19 November 1898), pp. 1322–3; Trotter, 'Invention', p. 464. Perhaps it was the umbrella's therapeutic and talismanic properties in the face of the condition that made it such a feature of late nineteenth-century art.

75 Théodule Ribot, *The Psychology of the Emotions* (London: Walter Scott, 1897), pp. v–ix (p. v).

76 Le Bon had dedicated his book to the psychologist.

77 Ribot, *Psychology*, pp. 213–14. 'Panphobia', according to Ribot, was 'a state in which a patient fears everything or nothing, where anxiety, instead of being riveted on one object, floats as in a dream' (p. 214).

78 Max Nordau, *Degeneration* (London: William Heinemann, 1895), pp. 242–3.

79 Evangelos Vassos, Carsten B. Pedersen, Robin M. Murray, David A. Collier and Cathryn M. Lewis, 'Meta-analysis of the association of urbanicity with schizophrenia', *Schizophrenia Bulletin*, vol. 38, no. 6 (2012), pp. 1118–23.

80 Andreas Heinz, Lorenz Deserno and Ulrich Reininghaus, 'Urbanicity, social adversity and psychosis', *World Psychiatry*, vol. 12, no. 3 (2013), pp. 187–97; Florian Lederbogen, Peter Kirsch, Leila Haddad et al., 'City living and urban upbringing affect neural social stress processing in humans', *Nature*, vol. 474, no. 7352 (2011), pp. 498–501.

81 Elaine Tyler May, *Fortress America: How We Embraced Fear and Abandoned Democracy* (New York: Basic Books, 2017).

82 Kyle Riismandel, *Neighborhood of Fear: The Suburban Crisis in*

American Culture, 1975–2001 (Baltimore, MD: Johns Hopkins University Press, 2020).

8: Diabolus ex Machina

1 'The Great Exhibition', *The Times* [London] (2 May 1851), p. 6.

2 Klaus Schwab, *The Fourth Industrial Revolution*, fwd Marc R. Benioff (London: Penguin, [2016] 2017), p. 2.

3 The term 'technology', resurrected from the ancient Greek by the German economist Johann Beckmann in the 1770s, would come to describe this assemblage, although it wasn't until the twentieth century that the word gained wider traction. The tech futurist Kevin Kelly has called this 'global, massively interconnected system of technology' the *technium*, in contradistinction to 'technology', which refers to a specific technology such as the spinning jenny or the locomotive; see *What Technology Wants* (London: Penguin, 2010), pp. 8, 11–12 (p. 11).

4 John Brown, *A Memoir of Robert Blincoe, an Orphan Boy* (Manchester: J. Doherty, 1832), p. 26.

5 'The factory accident at Stockport', *The Times* [London] (21 March 1851), p. 8.

6 Mark Seltzer, *Bodies and Machines* (London and New York: Routledge, 1992), pp. 18–20.

7 As the cultural historian and theorist Paul Virilio observed, 'To invent the train is to invent the rail accident of derailment'; see *The Original Accident*, trans. Julie Rose (Cambridge: Polity, 2007), p. 10. Or as he put it elsewhere, 'Every technology carries its own negativity, which is invented at the same time as technical progress'; see *Politics of the Very Worst: An Interview by Philippe Petit*, trans. Michael Cavaliere; ed. Sylvère Lotringer (New York: Semiotext(e), 1999), p. 89.

8 Amy Milne-Smith, 'Shattered minds: Madmen on the railways, 1860–80', *Journal of Victorian Culture*, vol. 21, no. 1 (2016), pp. 21–39.

9 John Eric Erichsen, *On Railway and Other Injuries of the Nervous System* (Philadelphia, PA: Henry C. Lea, 1867), p. 17; also Herbert William Page, *Injuries of the Spine and Spinal Cord without Apparent Mechanical Lesion, and Nervous Shock* (London: J. & A. Churchill, 1883).

10 *A Week at the Fair, Illustrating the Exhibits and Wonders of the World's Columbian Exposition, with Special Descriptive Articles* (Chicago, IL: Rand, McNally & Company, 1893); William E. Cameron, ed., *The*

World's Fair, Being a Pictorial History of the Columbian Exposition (Philadelphia, PA: National Publishing Company, 1893).

11 Denton J. Snider, *World's Fair Studies* (Chicago, IL: Sigma Publishing Co., 1895), p. 16.

12 Snider, *World's Fair*, p. 6.

13 'The castle of a modern bluebeard', *The World* (11 August 1895), p. 1.

14 Many details of these 'mysterious machines' found in Holmes's building, including the 'elasticity determinator', were first mentioned in Herbert Asbury's *Gem of the Prairie: An Informal History of the Chicago Underworld* (New York: Alfred A. Knopf, 1940), pp. 181–9 (p. 184); see Adam Selzer, *H. H. Holmes: The True History of the White City Devil* (New York: Skyhorse, 2017), p. 364.

15 Mark Seltzer, *Serial Killers: Death and Life in America's Wound Culture* (New York: Routledge, 1998), p. 206.

16 'Touched the golden key: President Cleveland sets world's fair wheels in motion', *Washington Post* (2 May 1893), p. 1.

17 'Modern bluebeard: H. H. Holmes' castles [*sic*] reveals his true character', *Chicago Tribune* (18 August 1895), p. 40.

18 'Holmes confesses 27 murders. The most awful story of modern times told by the fiend in human shape', *Philadelphia Inquirer* (12 April 1896), p. 1.

19 Upton Sinclair, *The Jungle* (New York: Doubleday, Page & Company, 1906), pp. 38, 23, 5, 66, 161–2, 117.

20 Sinclair, *Jungle*, p. 40.

21 'The meat strike', *New York Times* (15 July 1904), p. 6; 'Man killed in riot at Chicago stock yards', *New York Times* (21 August 1904), p. 1.

22 'Wilson makes public new meat regulations', *New York Times* (28 July 1906), p. 3.

23 Henry Ford [with Samuel Crowther], *My Life and Work* (Garden City, NY: Doubleday, Page & Company, 1922), p. 81.

24 David A. Hounshell, *From the American System to Mass Production, 1800–1932: The Development of Manufacturing Technology in the United States* (Baltimore, MD: Johns Hopkins University Press, 1984), pp. 1, 228.

25 Frederick Winslow Taylor, *The Principles of Scientific Management* (New York: Harper & Brothers, [1911] 1913), p. 83.

26 Thomas Carlyle, 'Signs of the times', *Edinburgh Review*, vol. 49 (June 1829), pp. 439–59 (pp. 442, 444).

27 Marx, 'Economic and philosophical manuscripts', pp. 323–4.

28 Marx, *Capital*, p. 554.

29 Andrew Ure, *The Philosophy of Manufactures: Or, an Exposition of the Scientific, Moral, and Commercial Economy of the Factory System of Great Britain* (London: Charles Knight, 1835), pp. 18, 13–14.
30 Marx, *Capital*, pp. 544–5; Ure, *Philosophy*, p. 147.
31 Marx, *Capital*, p. 503.
32 Samuel Butler, *Erewhon, or Over the Range* (London: Trübner & Co., 1872), pp. 191–2; the title of the novel almost spells 'nowhere' backwards.
33 Sir Henry Thompson, *Modern Cremation: Its History and Practice* (London: Kegan Paul, Trench, Trübner & Co., 1891), pp. 2, 8, 14.
34 Park Benjamin, 'The infliction of the death penalty', *Forum*, vol. 3 (July 1887), pp. 503–12 (p. 512).
35 'Far worse than hanging; Kemmler's death proves an awful spectacle', *New York Times* (7 August 1890), p. 1.
36 For other words mooted to describe execution by electricity, see *American Notes and Queries*, vol. 3 (25 May and 1 June 1889), pp. 45–7, 57.
37 W. E. Steavenson and H. Lewis Jones, *Medical Electricity: A Practical Handbook for Students and Practitioners* (London: H. K. Lewis, 1892), p. 347.
38 Antonio Perciaccante, Alessia Coralli, Luca Cambioli and Michele Augusto Riva, 'Nonconvulsive electrotherapy in psychiatry: The treatment of the mental disorders of the Norwegian painter Edvard Munch', *Bipolar Disorders*, vol. 19, no. 2 (2017), pp. 72–3. Scrawled across the top left-hand corner of the 1893 version of *The Scream* is the sentence 'Could only have been painted by a madman!', now confirmed to have been written by Munch, probably in 1895.
39 John E. Finding and Kimberly D. Pelle, *Encyclopedia of World's Fairs and Expositions* (Jefferson, NC: McFarland & Co., 2008), p. 103.
40 Pierre Vidal Senèze and Jean Noctzli, 'Sur les momies découvertes dans le haut Pérou', *Bulletins de la Société d'Anthropologie de Paris*, vol. 12 (1877), pp. 640–41; Robert Rosenblum, 'Introduction. Edvard Munch: Some changing contexts', in *Symbols and Images of Edvard Munch* (Washington, DC: National Gallery of Art, 1978), pp. 1–9 (p. 8).
41 A possible inspiration for Munch's painting identified in Kelly Grovier, *A New Way of Seeing: The History of Art in 57 Works* (London: Thames & Hudson, 2018), pp. 176–9.
42 Mary W. Shelley, *Frankenstein: Or, the Modern Prometheus* (London: Henry Colburn and Richard Bentley, 1831), pp. 43, x.

43 John [Giovanni] Aldini, *General Views on the Application of Galvanism to Medical Purposes: Principally in Cases of Suspended Animation* (London: J. Callow, 1819).
44 Thomas Commerford Martin, 'Tesla's oscillator and other inventions', *Century Magazine*, vol. 49, no. 6 (April 1895), pp. 916–33 (pp. 916, 917).
45 Martin, 'Tesla's oscillator', p. 933; Grovier, *New Way of Seeing*, p. 179.
46 *The Private Journals of Edvard Munch: We Are Flames Which Pour Out of the Earth*, trans. and ed. Gill Holland; fwd Frank Høifødt (Madison, WI: University of Wisconsin Press, 2005), pp. 155–6, 151, 62; see also Grovier, *New Way of Seeing*, p. 176.
47 Thomas Edison, 'The phonograph and its future', *North American Review*, vol. 126, no. 262 (1878), pp. 527–36 (p. 527).
48 'The aerophone', *New York Times* (25 March 1878), p. 4.
49 'The aerophone', *New York Times*, p. 4.
50 'The aerophone', *London Figaro* (13 April 1878), pp. 557, 559.
51 James W. Carey, 'Technology and ideology: The case of the telegraph', in *Communication as Culture: Essays on Media and Society* (New York and London: Routledge, [1989] 2009), pp. 155–77 (p. 157).
52 'The ocean telegraph – relative benefits and evils', *New York Times* (19 August 1858), p. 4.
53 'Forecasts for 1907', *Punch, or the London Charivari* (26 December 1906), p. 451.
54 Brian Hochman, *The Listeners: A History of Wiretapping in the United States* (Cambridge, MA: Harvard University Press, 2022); *All About the Telephone and Phonograph* (London: Ward, Lock and Co., 1878), pp. 81–6 (p. 81).
55 See Deep Kanta Lahiri Choudhury, *Telegraphic Imperialism: Crisis and Panic in the Indian Empire, c.1830–1920* (Basingstoke: Palgrave Macmillan, 2010); Robert Peckham, 'Panic encabled: Epidemics and the telegraphic world', in Robert Peckham, ed., *Empires of Panic: Epidemics and Colonial Anxieties* (Hong Kong: Hong Kong University Press, 2015), pp. 131–54.
56 Gabriele Balbi, '"I will answer you, my friend, but I am afraid": Telephones and the fear of a new medium in nineteenth and early twentieth-century Italy', in Siân Nicholas and Tom O'Malley, eds., *Moral Panics, Social Fears, and the Media: Historical Perspectives* (New York: Routledge, 2013), pp. 59–75; 'Left-earedness and the telephone', *New York Times* (20 April 1904), p. 8.

57 'The public telephone call office as a factor in the spread of disease', *Lancet*, vol. 171, no. 4411 (14 March 1908), p. 829.
58 Clarence Day, 'Father lets in the telephone', *New Yorker* (13 May 1933), pp. 18–20 (p. 19).
59 Nancy Tomes, *The Gospel of Germs: Men, Women, and the Microbe in American Life* (Cambridge, MA: Harvard University Press, 1998), p. 133.
60 On the fears associated with early cinema, see Francesco Casetti, 'Why fears matter: Cinephobia in early film culture', *Screen*, vol. 59, no. 2 (2018), pp. 145–57.
61 In October 1895 there had in fact been a spectacular derailment in Paris when a train overran the terminus at Montparnasse, crashing into a street below.
62 Jay Leyda, *Kino: A History of the Russian and Soviet Film, with a New Postscript and a Filmography Brought Up to the Present* (Princeton, NJ: Princeton University Press, 1983), pp. 407–9 (p. 408); on the 'legend' of the film panic and the complex history of the film's screening, see Martin Loiperdinger, 'Lumière's "Arrival of the Train": Cinema's founding myth', *Moving Image*, vol. 4, no. 1 (2004), pp. 89–118.
63 A scene of panic pictured in dramatic form on the front of an illustrated supplement to the Paris newspaper *Le Petit Journal* (16 May 1897). The journalist Jules Huret wrote a detailed and dramatic account, which includes photographs: see *La catastrophe du Bazar de la Charité (4 Mai 1897)* (Paris: J. Juven, 1897); the tragedy forms the subject of the 2019 Netflix series *The Bonfire of Destiny* (*Le Bazar de la Charité*).
64 'Tribunaux. L'incendie du bazar de la Charité', *Journal des Débats* (20 August 1897), p. 3.
65 T. R. P. Ollivier, *Les victimes de la Charité: discours prononcé à Notre-Dame-de-Paris le 8 Mai 1897* (Paris: P. Lethielleux, 1897), p. 7; see Casetti, 'Why fears matter', pp. 151–2; also Jacqueline Lalouette, 'Parler de Dieu après une catastrophe: l'exemple de prédicateurs catholiques après l'incendie du Bazar de la Charité (4 mai 1897)', *Histoire Urbaine*, vol. 2, no. 34 (2012), pp. 93–110.
66 Casetti, 'Why fears matter', p. 145; Leyda, *Kino*, pp. 407–9.
67 Casetti, 'Why fears matter', pp. 146, 150; Tom Gunning, 'Flickers: On cinema's power for evil', in Murray Pomerance, ed., *Bad: Infamy, Darkness, Evil and Slime on Screen* (Albany, NY: State University of New York Press, 2004), pp. 21–38; Thierry Lefebvre, 'Une "maladie"

au tournant du siècle: la "cinématophtalmie"', *Revue d'Histoire de la Pharmacie*, no. 297 (1993), pp. 225–30.

68 William Healy, *The Individual Delinquent* (Boston, MA: Little, Brown, 1915), p. 308; quoted in Casetti, 'Why fears matter', p. 146.

9: Crash

1 The degree to which financial institutions were driving economic growth and industrialisation, or vice versa, is still debated; see Geoffrey M. Hodgson, 'Financial institutions and the British Industrial Revolution: Did financial underdevelopment hold back growth?', *Journal of Institutional Economics*, vol. 17, no. 3 (2021), pp. 429–48.

2 Thomas W. Lawson, *Friday, the Thirteenth: A Novel* (New York: Doubleday, Page & Company, 1907), p. 193.

3 Halford Mackinder, 'The great trade routes: Lecture V', *Journal of the Institute of Bankers*, vol. 21, no. 5 (1900), pp. 266–73 (p. 271).

4 Charles Mackay, *Memoirs of Extraordinary Popular Delusions and the Madness of Crowds*, 3 vols (London: Richard Bentley, 1841), vol. 1, pp. v–vi, 1–3.

5 The economic environment darkened further in 1845 with the failure of the potato crop in Ireland and the prospect of famine.

6 S. A. Broadbridge, 'The sources of railway share capital', in M. C. Reed, ed., *Railways in the Victorian Economy: Studies in Finance and Economic Growth* (Newton Abbot: David & Charles, 1969), pp. 184–211; William Quinn and John D. Turner, 'Democratising speculation: The great railway mania', in *Boom and Bust: A Global History of Financial Bubbles* (Cambridge: Cambridge University Press, 2020), pp. 58–76. Gareth Campbell and John D. Turner, however, challenge the idea of the inexperienced investor, in 'Dispelling the myth of the naive investor during the British Railway Mania, 1845–1846', *Business History Review*, vol. 86, no. 1 (2012), pp. 3–41.

7 Tamara S. Wagner, *Financial Speculation in Victorian Fiction: Plotting Money and the Novel Genre, 1815–1901* (Columbus, OH: Ohio State University Press, 2010), p. 3; Charles Dickens, *Little Dorrit* (London: Bradbury & Evans, 1857), p. 534.

8 Anne Goldgar, *Tulipmania: Money, Honor, and Knowledge in the Dutch Golden Age* (Chicago, IL: University of Chicago Press, 2007), pp. 6, 3; Karl Marx, *Capital: A Critique of Political Economy*, vol. 3, intro. Ernest Mandel; trans. David Fernbach (London: Penguin/New Left Review, 1981), pp. 525–42.

9 Formally the United Dutch Chartered East India Company, or Vereenigde Nederlandsche Geoctroyeerde Oostindische Compagnie, otherwise known as the VOC.
10 Joseph de la Vega, *Confusión de Confusiones*, trans. Hermann Kellenbenz (Cambridge, MA: Kress Library of Business and Economics, Harvard University, 1957), pp. vii–xx, 31, 40; see also Hervé Dumez, 'The description of the first financial market: Looking back on *Confusion of Confusions* by Joseph de la Vega', *Annales des Mines: Gérer et Comprendre*, vol. 1, no. 119 (2015), pp. 7–12.
11 On the 'unsocial sociability' of the markets, as the philosopher Immanuel Kant put it, see István Hont, *Politics in Commercial Society: Jean-Jacques Rousseau and Adam Smith*, ed. Béla Kapossy and Michael Sonenscher (Cambridge, MA: Harvard University Press, 2015), pp. xiv, 11, 13.
12 Adam Anderson, *An Historical and Chronological Deduction of the Origin of Commerce*, 4 vols (London: Printed by J. Walter, [1764] 1787), vol. 3, p. 103.
13 Richard Dale, *The First Crash: Lessons from the South Sea Bubble* (Princeton, NJ: Princeton University Press, 2004), p. 137.
14 Anderson, *Historical and Chronological Deduction*, vol. 3, p. 103.
15 [A. B. Gent] Daniel Defoe, *Curious and Diverting Journies, thro' the Whole Island of Great-Britain* (London: Printed by G. Parker, 1734); see also *Villainy of Stock Jobbers Detected; and the Causes of the Late Run upon the Bank and Bankers Discovered and Considered* (London: 1701).
16 Quoted in Jonathan Sheehan and Dror Wahrman, *Invisible Hands: Self-Organization and the Eighteenth Century* (Chicago, IL: University of Chicago Press, 2015), p. 105.
17 Joseph Harris, *An Essay upon Money and Coins*, 3 vols (London: G. Hawkins, 1757–8), vol. 1, pp. 31, 108–9.
18 An argument made by economic historian Michael Perelman, who holds that 'the dispossession of the majority of the small-scale producers and the construction of laissez-faire are closely connected' – an expropriation summed up in the notion of 'primitive accumulation': see Michael Perelman, *The Invention of Capitalism: Classical Political Economy and the Secret History of Primitive Accumulation* (Durham, NC: Duke University Press, 2000), pp. 2–3.
19 Ricardo had gambled on a British victory at Waterloo; see David

Weatherall, *David Ricardo: A Biography* (The Hague: Martinus Nijhoff, 1976), pp. 70–71.

20 David Ricardo, *On the Principles of Political Economy, and Taxation* (London: John Murray, [1817] 1821), p. 430.

21 Adam Smith, *An Inquiry into the Nature and Causes of the Wealth of Nations*, 2 vols (London: Printed for W. Strahan and T. Cadell, 1776), vol. 2, pp. 388, 42, 119.

22 Smith, *Inquiry*, vol. 1, pp. 161, 133–4, 485.

23 *The Works of Adam Smith*, 5 vols (London: T. Cadell and W. Davies, 1811), vol. 5, p. 59.

24 Michael J. Cullen, *The Statistical Movement in Early Victorian Britain: The Foundations of Empirical Social Research* (Hassocks: Harvester Press, 1975), p. 36; quoted in Elaine Freedgood, 'Banishing panic: Harriet Martineau and the popularization of political economy', *Victorian Studies*, vol. 39, no. 1 (1995), pp. 33–53 (p. 33).

25 Harriet Martineau, *Autobiography*, 2 vols (Boston, MA: James R. Osgood and Company, 1877), vol. 1, p. 10; quoted in Freedgood, 'Banishing', p. 37.

26 Freedgood, 'Banishing', pp. 36–7, 50.

27 Arthur Crump, *The Theory of Stock Exchange Speculation* (London: Longmans, Green, Reader & Dyer, 1874), p. 1.

28 'New publications', *New York Times* (14 November 1874), p. 6.

29 Crump, *Theory*, pp. 1–2, 30–31.

30 Crump, *Theory*, pp. 2, 40–41, 47, 50.

31 Daniele Besomi, 'The periodicity of crises: A survey of the literature before 1850', *Journal of the History of Economic Thought*, vol. 32, no. 1 (2010), pp. 85–132.

32 Baker Library Special Collections, Harvard Business School, Harvard University. The associations of commerce with health and sickness pre-date the eighteenth century: see Jonathan Gil Harris, *Sick Economies: Drama, Mercantilism, and Disease in Shakespeare's England* (Philadelphia, PA: University of Pennsylvania Press, 2004), who examines the use of bodily metaphors in early modern economic thinking, particularly in relation to infectious diseases and worries about the contagious risks posed by global trade.

33 Walter Bagehot, *Lombard Street: A Description of the Money Market* (New York: Scribner, Armstrong & Co., 1873), pp. 51, 56–7.

34 Daniele Besomi, 'Crises as a disease of the body politick: A metaphor in the history of nineteenth-century economics', *Journal of the History of Economic Thought*, vol. 33, no. 1 (2011), pp. 67–118.

35 'Danger from panic germs', *New York Times* (27 June 1907), p. 7.
36 Nouriel Roubini and Stephen Mihm, *Crisis Economics: A Crash Course in the Future of Finance* (New York: Penguin, 2010), p. 8; see Robert Peckham, 'Economies of contagion: Financial crisis and pandemic', *Economy and Society*, vol. 42. no. 2 (2013), pp. 226–48.
37 Andrew Dawson, 'Reassessing Henry Carey (1793–1879): The problems of writing political economy in nineteenth-century America', *Journal of American Studies*, vol. 34, no. 3 (2000), pp. 465–85 (p. 465).
38 Jessica M. Lepler, *The Many Panics of 1837: People, Politics, and the Creation of a Transatlantic Financial Crisis* (New York: Cambridge University Press, 2013).
39 Dawson, 'Reassessing', pp. 476, 479.
40 Henry C. Carey, *Financial Crises: Their Causes and Effects* (Philadelphia, PA: Henry Carey Baird, 1864), p. 3.
41 The home of Drexel, Morgan & Company, the bank that would become J. P. Morgan in 1895.
42 Karl Marx, 'The economic crisis in Europe', *New-York Daily Tribune* (9 October 1856).
43 John Dennis Brown, *Panic Profits: How to Make Money When the Market Takes a Dive* (New York: McGraw-Hill, 1993).
44 Naomi Klein, *The Shock Doctrine: The Rise of Disaster Capitalism* (New York: Henry Holt, 2007).
45 David A. Zimmerman, *Panic!: Markets, Crises, and Crowds in American Fiction* (Chapel Hill, NC: University of North Carolina Press, 2006), p. 1.
46 Lawson's book was in large part responsible for popularising the ominous associations of the date.
47 Upton Sinclair, *The Moneychangers* (New York: B. W. Dodge, 1908), pp. 262, 260, 311.
48 Frank Norris, *The Pit: A Story of Chicago* (New York: Doubleday, Page & Co., 1903), pp. 79, 80.
49 Thorstein Veblen, *The Theory of the Leisure Class* (New York: Macmillan, 1899), pp. 68–101; see also Clare Virginia Eby, *Dreiser and Veblen, Saboteurs of the Status Quo* (Columbia, MO: University of Missouri Press, 1998).
50 Richard Bach Jensen, *The Battle against Anarchist Terrorism: An International History, 1878–1934* (Cambridge: Cambridge University Press, 2014), pp. 22, 28. The writer Fyodor Dostoevsky describes this world of terror in his novel *Demons* (1871–2), where the misdirected

idealism of a revolutionary group becomes a vehicle for demonic violence. Joseph Conrad's novel *The Secret Agent* (1907), set in 1886, focuses on an anarchist plot to bomb the Greenwich Observatory.

51 Quoted in Bennett Lowenthal, 'The jumpers of '29', *Washington Post* (25 October 1987), p. 5.

52 'New York banker's death', *The Times* [London] (11 November 1929), p. 14.

53 F. Scott Fitzgerald, *The Great Gatsby* (New York: Charles Scribner's Sons, 1925), pp. 39, 91.

54 H. G. Wells, *The War in the Air* (New York: Macmillan, 1908), pp. 253–4.

55 'Wall-Street panic', *The Times* [London] (25 October 1929), p. 14.

56 'Fisher says stock slump is only temporary', *New York Times* (24 October 1929), p. 2; 'Fisher says prices of stocks are low', *New York Times* (22 October 1929), p. 24.

57 'Fisher sees stocks permanently high', *New York Times* (16 October 1929), p. 8.

58 'Fisher denies crash is due', *New York Times* (5 September 1929), p. 12.

59 'The break in Wall Street', *Economist*, vol. 109, no. 4497 (2 November 1929), p. 824.

60 'Investigating the panic of 1929', *New York Times* (6 December 1931), p. 63; 'American panic of 1929 blamed for the present world depression', *New York Times* (1 June 1931), p. 27.

61 Archibald MacLeish, *Panic: A Play in Verse* (Boston, MA: Houghton Mifflin, 1935), pp. 9, 51, 3; Scott Donaldson, *Archibald MacLeish: An American Life* (Boston, MA: Houghton Mifflin, 1992), p. 239; see 'MacLeish's "Panic"', *New York Times* (16 March 1935), p. 18. The part of J. P. McGafferty was played by Orson Welles in the original New York production.

62 John Kenneth Galbraith, *The Great Crash, 1929* (Boston, MA: Houghton Mifflin, [1955] 1997), p. 146.

63 Quoted in Frederick Lewis Allen, *Only Yesterday: An Informal History of the Nineteen Twenties* (New York: Harper & Brothers, 1931), pp. 345–6.

10: Horror in the Trenches

1 H. G. Wells, *The War That Will End War* (London: Frank & Cecil Palmer, 1914), p. 37.

2 Wells, *War in the Air*, p. 355.

3 https://www.getty.edu/art/collection/object/104GXR

4 Gabriel Chevallier, *Fear*, trans. Malcolm Imrie; intro. John Berger (London: Serpent's Tail, 2011), p. 117.
5 'If you could hear, at every jolt, the blood / Come gargling from the froth-corrupted lungs': 'Dulce et Decorum Est', in *The Collected Poems of Wilfred Owen*, ed. and intro. C. Day Lewis (New York: New Directions, 1965), pp. 55–6.
6 'IV – the United States an undefended treasure land', *Scientific American*, vol. 112, no. 9 (27 February 1915), pp. 198–9, 204–5.
7 John Berger, 'Introduction: The imperative need', in Chevallier, *Fear*, pp. v–viii (p. vi).
8 Erich Maria Remarque, *All Quiet on the Western Front*, trans. A. W. Wheen (New York: Little, Brown and Company, 1929), p. 140.
9 Stratis Myrivilis, *Life in the Tomb*, trans. Peter Bien (London and New York: Quartet Books, 1987), p. 1.
10 Paul Nash, *Outline: An Autobiography and Other Writings* (London: Faber and Faber, 1949), p. 210.
11 Anthony Slide, ed., *D. W. Griffith: Interviews* (Jackson, MS: University Press of Mississippi, 2012), p. 94.
12 William Philpott, *Three Armies on the Somme: The First Battle of the Twentieth Century* (New York: Vintage, [2009] 2011), p. 92.
13 Owen, 'The Show', *Collected Poems*, pp. 50–51; Remarque, *All Quiet*, pp. 279–80.
14 Mary Borden, *The Forbidden Zone: A Nurse's Impressions of the First World War*, ed. Hazel Hutchison; fwd Malcolm Brown (London: Hesperus Press, [1929] 2008), pp. xv, 74–5.
15 Elizabeth Bowen, 'Postscript by the author', in *The Demon Lover and Other Stories* (London: Jonathan Cape, 1945), pp. 216–24 (p. 217).
16 Henri Barbusse, *Under Fire: The Story of a Squad* (London and Toronto: J. M. Dent & Sons, 1917), pp. 4, 343, 320.
17 C. S. Lewis, *The Pilgrim's Regress* (London: J. M. Dent & Sons, 1933), p. 58. You can hear Palmer today on the Imperial War Museum's 'Voices of the First World War' podcast: https://www.iwm.org.uk/history/voices-of-the-first-world-war-passchendaele
18 Borden, *Forbidden*, pp. 11–13 (p. 11).
19 Remarque, *All Quiet*, p. 128.
20 A. D. Gristwood, *The Somme, including also The Coward*, pref. H. G. Wells; intro. Hugh Cecil (Columbia, SC: University of South Carolina Press, [1927] 2006), p. 19.
21 C. Stanford Read, *Military Psychiatry in Peace and War* (London: H. K. Lewis & Co., 1920), p. 11.

22 *Report of the War Office Committee of Enquiry into 'Shell-Shock'* (London: HMSO, 1922), p. 138.
23 W. H. R. Rivers, *Instinct and the Unconscious: A Contribution to a Biological Theory of the Psycho-Neuroses* (Cambridge: Cambridge University Press, 1920), p. 210.
24 Jan Plamper, 'Fear: Soldiers and emotion in early twentieth-century Russian military psychology', *Slavic Review*, vol. 68, no. 2 (2009), pp. 259–83 (pp. 269–71).
25 'The psychology of panic in war', *American Review of Reviews*, vol. 50 (October 1914), pp. 628–9 (p. 629); cited in Joanna Bourke, 'The experience of combat', in Antonio Monegal and Francesc Torres, eds., *At War* (Barcelona: Centre de Cultura Contemporània de Barcelona, 2004), pp. 108–18 (p. 110).
26 Ana Carden-Coyne, *The Politics of Wounds: Military Patients and Medical Power in the First World War* (Oxford: Oxford University Press, 2014), p. 48; on hope as a counter-strategy to fear, see Roger Petersen and Evangelos Liaras, 'Countering fear in war: The strategic use of emotion', *Journal of Military Ethics*, vol. 5, no. 4 (2006), pp. 317–33.
27 Robert W. Mackenna, *The Adventure of Death* (London: John Murray, 1916), pp. 29, xi; C. S. Lewis, *Surprised by Joy: The Shape of My Early Life* (New York: Harcourt, Brace & World, 1955), pp. 196–7.
28 Charles S. Myers, 'A contribution to the study of shell shock', *Lancet*, vol. 185, no. 4772 (13 February 1915), pp. 316–20.
29 Myers, 'Contribution'.
30 Sir William Grant Macpherson, Sir Wilmot Parker Herringham, Thomas Renton Elliott and Andrew Balfour, eds., *History of the Great War (Based on Official Documents)*, vol. 2, *Medical Services: Diseases of the War* (London: HMSO, 1923), p. 10.
31 A. F. Hurst and J. L. M. Symns, 'The rapid cure of hysterical symptoms in soldiers', *Lancet*, vol. 192, no. 4953 (3 August 1918), pp. 139–41 (p. 139).
32 See https://catalogue.wellcomelibrary.org/record=b1667864~S8
33 'Moulding new faces: Nose and chin making', *Daily Mail* (15 September 1916); quoted in Reginald Pound, *Gillies, Surgeon Extraordinary: A Biography* (London: Michael Joseph, 1964), p. 39.
34 Ward Muir, *The Happy Hospital* (London: Simpkin, Marshall, Hamilton, Kent & Co., 1918), pp. 143–4.
35 Joseph Hone, *The Life of Henry Tonks* (London: Heinemann, 1939), p. 127.

36 Muir, *Happy Hospital*, pp. 143–4.
37 Siegfried Sassoon, *Sherston's Progress* (London: Faber and Faber, 1936), p. 71.
38 Hurst and Symns, 'Rapid cure', p. 140.
39 Stefanie C. Linden, Edgar Jones and Andrew J. Lees, 'Shell shock at Queen Square: Lewis Yealland 100 years on', *Brain*, vol. 136, no. 6 (June 2013), pp. 1976–88. Adrian later distanced himself from this treatment and went on to win the Nobel Prize in Physiology in 1932 for his research on the function of neurons.
40 E. D. Adrian and L. R. Yealland, 'The treatment of some common war neuroses', *Lancet*, vol. 189, no. 4893 (1917), pp. 867–72 (p. 869).
41 Lewis R. Yealland, *Hysterical Disorders of Warfare* (London: Macmillan and Co., 1918), pp. 27, 9.
42 Paul Lerner, 'Psychiatry and casualties of war in Germany, 1914–18', *Journal of Contemporary History*, vol. 35, no. 1 (2000), pp. 13–28.
43 George L. Mosse, 'Shell-shock as a social disease', *Journal of Contemporary History*, vol. 35, no. 1 (2000), pp. 101–8.
44 Laurent Tatu, Julien Bogousslavsky, Thierry Moulin and Jean-Luc Chopard, 'The "torpillage" neurologists of World War I: Electric therapy to send hysterics back to the front', *Neurology*, vol. 75, no. 3 (2010), pp. 279–83.
45 Ben Shephard, '"The early treatment of mental disorders": R. G. Rows and Maghull, 1914–1918', in Hugh Freeman and G. E. Berrios, eds., *150 Years of British Psychiatry*, vol. 2, *The Aftermath* (London: Athlone, 1996), pp. 434–64.
46 G. Elliot Smith and T. H. Pear, *Shell Shock and Its Lessons*, 2nd edn (Manchester and London: Manchester University Press and Longmans, Green & Co., 1917), p. xiv.
47 Edgar Jones, 'Shell shock at Maghull and the Maudsley: Models of psychological medicine in the UK', *Journal of the History of Medicine and Allied Sciences*, vol. 65, no. 3 (2010), pp. 368–95; Elliot Smith and Pear, *Shell Shock*, pp. 36–43, 63, 73.
48 Rivers, *Instinct*, pp. 2, 123, 203; W. H. R. Rivers, 'The repression of war experience', *Proceedings of the Royal Society of Medicine*, vol. 11 (1918), pp. 1–20 (pp. 2–3).
49 W. H. R. Rivers, 'Psychiatry and the war', *Science*, vol. 49, no. 1268 (1919), pp. 367–9 (p. 367); 'Freud's psychology of the unconscious', *Lancet*, vol. 189, no. 4894 (16 June 1917), pp. 912–14 (p. 913). However, Rivers had reservations about some of Freud's ideas and their benefits for clinical practice.

50 Sassoon, *Sherston's Progress*, pp. 12, 70–71.
51 Hugh Crichton Miller, *Hypnotism and Disease: A Plea for Rational Psychotherapy* (London: T. Fisher Unwin, 1912).
52 Elliot Smith and Pear, *Shell Shock*, p. 108; H. Crichton Miller, *The New Psychology and the Parent* (London: Jarrolds, 1922).
53 Sir Robert Armstrong-Jones, 'The psychology of fear: The effects of panic fear in wartime', *The Hospital*, vol. 61 (24 March 1917), pp. 493–4 (p. 494).
54 Armstrong-Jones, 'Psychology', pp. 493, 494.
55 Walter B. Cannon, *Traumatic Shock* (New York and London: D. Appleton and Company, 1923), pp. 53–62; *Bodily Changes in Pain, Hunger, Fear and Rage: An Account of Recent Researches into the Function of Emotional Excitement* (New York and London: D. Appleton and Company, [1915] 1925), p. 187.
56 F. W. Mott, 'The Chadwick lecture on mental hygiene and shell shock during and after the war', *British Medical Journal*, vol. 2, no. 2950 (1917), pp. 39–42 (p. 40); 'The Lettsomian lectures on the effects of high explosives upon the central nervous system', *Lancet*, vol. 1, nos. 4824, 2846, 2848 (1916), pp. 331–8, 441–9, 546–53; 'Special discussion on shell shock without visible signs of injury', *Proceedings of the Royal Society of Medicine*, vol. 9 (1916), pp. i–xxiv.
57 Mott, 'Mental hygiene', p. 41.
58 Edgar Jones, '"An atmosphere of cure": Frederick Mott, shell shock and the Maudsley', *History of Psychiatry*, vol. 25, no. 4 (2014), pp. 412–21; Ben Shephard, *A War of Nerves: Soldiers and Psychiatrists, 1914–1994* (London: Jonathan Cape, 2000).
59 Mott, 'Mental hygiene', p. 39.
60 W. H. R. Rivers, *Conflict and Dream*, pref. G. Elliot Smith (London: Kegan Paul, Trench, Trubner & Co., 1923), p. 26; Ted Bogacz, 'War neurosis and cultural change in England, 1914–1922: The work of the War Office Committee of Enquiry into "shell-shock"', *Journal of Contemporary History*, vol. 24, no. 2 (April 1989), pp. 227–56.
61 *Report of the War Office*, p. 139.
62 *Report of the War Office*, pp. 192–3.
63 Ana Carden-Coyne, 'Soldiers' bodies in the war machine: Triage, propaganda and military medical bureaucracy, 1914–1918', in M. Larner, J. Peto and N. Monem, eds., *War and Medicine* (London: Wellcome, 2008), pp. 67–83 (pp. 67, 81).
64 Chevallier, *Fear*, pp. 28–9.
65 Umberto Boccioni, 'Futurist painting: Technical manifesto' [11 April

1910], in Herschel B. Chipp, ed., *Theories of Modern Art: A Source Book by Artists and Critics* (Berkeley, CA: University of California Press, 1968), pp. 289–93 (p. 290).

66 Filippo Tommaso Marinetti, *Critical Writings*, ed. Günter Berghaus; trans. Doug Thompson (New York: Farrar, Straus and Giroux, 2006), p. 87.

67 Marinetti, *Critical Writings*, p. 97.

68 Lucia Re, 'Maria Ginanni vs. F. T. Marinetti: Women, speed, and war in Futurist Italy', *Annali d'Italianistica*, vol. 27 (2009), pp. 103–24; quoted in Selena Daly, *Italian Futurism and the First World War* (Toronto: University of Toronto Press, 2016), pp. 104, 134.

69 Daly, *Italian Futurism*, p. 120.

70 Paul Virilio, *Art and Fear*, trans. Julie Rose (London: Continuum, [2003] 2006).

71 'The mental factors in modern war: Shell shock and nervous injuries', in *The Times History of the War*, vol. 7 (London: The Times, 1916), pp. 313–48 (p. 314); Lewis, *Surprised*, p. 196.

72 W. Scott Poole, *Wasteland: The Great War and the Origins of Modern Horror* (Berkeley, CA: Counterpoint, 2018), pp. 3–4.

73 Remarque, *All Quiet*, pp. 100, 123. Max Schreck, the actor who played the role of the vampire Count Orlok in *Nosferatu*, was a veteran of the trenches; Murnau and the producer Albin Grau had also seen action in the First World War.

11: Death Camps and Dictators

1 *Fear: A German State of Mind?* (*Angst – Eine deutsche Gefühlslage?*), held at the German History Museum (Haus der Geschichte) in Bonn from 10 October 2018 to 19 May 2019.

2 John Borneman and Parvis Ghassem-Fachandi, 'The concept of *Stimmung*: From indifference to xenophobia in Germany's refugee crisis', *Journal of Ethnographic Theory*, vol. 7, no. 3 (2017), pp. 105–35 (pp. 123–4).

3 Götz Aly and Karl Heinz Roth, *The Nazi Census: Identification and Control in the Third Reich*, trans. Edwin Black and Assenka Oksiloff (Philadelphia, PA: Temple University Press, [2000] 2004); Matthew G. Hannah, *Dark Territory in the Information Age: Learning from the West German Census Controversies of the 1980s* (Abingdon and New York: Routledge, [2010] 2016).

4 Edwin Black, *IBM and the Holocaust: The Strategic Alliance*

between Nazi Germany and America's Most Powerful Corporation (Washington, DC: Dialog Press, [2001] 2012).

5 *The Collected Poems of Bertolt Brecht*, trans. and ed. Tom Kuhn and David Constantine (New York: Liveright, [2015] 2019), pp. 716–19.

6 Robert Gellately, *The Gestapo and German Society: Enforcing Racial Policy, 1933–1945* (Oxford: Clarendon Press, 1990), pp. 130–58.

7 *Collected Poems*, p. 717.

8 Bertolt Brecht, *Fear and Misery of the Third Reich*, in *Collected Plays: Four*, ed. Tom Kuhn and John Willett; trans John Willett with M. Steffin (London: Bloomsbury, [2001] 2003), pp. 119–206 (pp. 119–20).

9 Winston Churchill, 'The defence of freedom and peace: Address to the people of the United States of America, October 16, 1938', in *Into Battle: Winston Churchill's War Speeches* (London: Cassell, 1941), pp. 83–91.

10 Joseph Brodsky, *On Grief and Reason: Essays* (New York: Farrar, Straus and Giroux, 1995), pp. 223–66.

11 Carl Schmitt, *The Crisis of Parliamentary Democracy*, trans. Ellen Kennedy (Cambridge, MA: MIT Press, 1985), p. 17; *The Concept of the Political*, trans. George Schwab (New Brunswick, NJ: Rutgers University Press, 1976), pp. 26, 32.

12 Peter Fritzsche, *Life and Death in the Third Reich* (Cambridge, MA: Belknap/Harvard University Press, 2008), p. 4.

13 Timothy Snyder, *Black Earth: The Holocaust as History and Warning* (New York: Tim Duggan Books, 2015).

14 Gustave M. Gilbert, *Nuremberg Diary* (New York: Signet, 1947), pp. 255–6 (p. 256).

15 Sergei Khrushchev, ed., *Memoirs of Nikita Khrushchev*, vol. 2, *Reformer* (Philadelphia, PA: Pennsylvania State University Press, 2006), pp. 167–8.

16 Laurence Rees, *Auschwitz: The Nazis and the 'Final Solution'* (London: BBC Books, 2005), p. 10.

17 'Fears', *Index on Censorship*, vol. 27, no. 6 (1998), pp. 44.

18 Robert Conquest, *The Great Terror: A Reassessment* (New York and Oxford: Oxford University Press, [1968] 2007), p. 3.

19 Jan Plamper, *The Stalin Cult: A Study in the Alchemy of Power* (New Haven, CT: Yale University Press, 2012).

20 Stalin had been born Joseph Dzhugashvili.

21 *Complete Poetry of Osip Emilevich Mandelstam*, trans. Burton Raffel and Alla Burago; intro. Sidney Monas (Albany, NY: State University of New York Press, 1973), p. 228. The description of

Stalin as 'Genghis Khan with a telephone' was used of him by the *New York Times* in an article on his death: see 'Stalin rose from Czarist oppression to transform Russia into a mighty socialist state' (6 March 1953), p. 9; Robert Service, *A History of Twentieth-Century Russia* (London: Allen Lane, 1997), p. 226.

22 Hannah Arendt, *Eichmann in Jerusalem: A Report on the Banality of Evil* (London and New York: Penguin, [1963] 2006), p. 252.

23 James Harris, *The Great Fear: Stalin's Terror of the 1930s* (Oxford: Oxford University Press, 2016).

24 *The Gulag Archipelago* was first published in three volumes in Paris by Éditions du Seuil in 1973, 1974 and 1976; it appeared in English as *The Gulag Archipelago, 1918–1956: An Experiment in Literary Investigation*, 3 vols, trans. Thomas P. Whitney and Harry Willetts (New York: Harper and Row, 1973); within the USSR it circulated in samizdat format ('self-publishing' in Russian) to avoid state censorship, until excerpts were published in the literary magazine *Novy Mir* in 1989.

25 Anne Applebaum, *Gulag: A History* (New York: Anchor, 2004), pp. 3–4, 40–58; Service, *History*, p. 227.

26 Quoted in Kevin McDermott, '"To the final destruction of all enemies!": Rethinking Stalin's terror', in Brett Bowden and Michael T. Davis, eds., *Terror: From Tyrannicide to Terrorism* (St Lucia: University of Queensland Press, 2008), pp. 175–89 (p. 188).

27 Robert Conquest, *The Harvest of Sorrow: Soviet Collectivization and the Terror-Famine* (Oxford and New York: Oxford University Press, 1986), p. 117.

28 Anne Applebaum, *Red Famine: Stalin's War on Ukraine* (New York: Doubleday, 2017).

29 Paul Hagenloh, '"Socially harmful elements" and the Great Terror', in Sheila Fitzpatrick, ed., *Stalinism: New Directions* (London: Routledge, 2000), pp. 286–307; David Shearer, 'Social disorder, mass repression and the NKVD during the 1930s', in Barry McLaughlin and Kevin McDermott, eds., *Stalin's Terror: High Politics and Mass Repression in the Soviet Union* (Basingstoke: Palgrave Macmillan, 2003), pp. 85–117.

30 Service, *History*, p. 227.

31 Harris, *Great Fear*, p. 177.

32 Julius Margolin, *Journey into the Land of the Zeks and Back: A Memoir of the Gulag*, fwd Timothy Snyder (Oxford: Oxford University Press, 2020), p. 246.

33 Gustaw Herling, 'Nightfall', in *A World Apart*, trans. Andrzej Ciołkosz; pref. Bertrand Russell (London: Penguin, [1951] 1986), pp. 143–51 (pp. 147, 151).
34 Christopher S. Wren, 'Solzhenitsyn asserts fear motivates Soviet attacks', *New York Times* (19 January 1974), p. 4.
35 Oleg V. Khlevniuk, *Stalin: New Biography of a Dictator*, trans. Nora Seligman Favorov (New Haven, CT: Yale University Press, 2015), p. 328.
36 Anatoli Rybakov, *Fear*, trans. Antonina W. Bouis (New York: Little, Brown and Company, 1992), pp. 164–5.
37 'Less a state policy than a state of mind' is how the historian Igal Halfin describes the terror in *Terror in My Soul: Communist Autobiographies on Trial* (Cambridge, MA: Harvard University Press, 2003), p. 4. Georgi Plekhanov, who fell out with Lenin, was to change his views on terror and the French Revolution: see Jay Bergman, *The French Revolutionary Tradition in Russian and Soviet Politics, Political Thought, and Culture* (Oxford: Oxford University Press, 2019), p. 97.
38 Arendt, *Origins*, p. 325.
39 Vasily Grossman, *Life and Fate*, trans. and intro. Robert Chandler (London: Harvill, 1985), pp. 528, 569, 837.
40 Halfin, *Terror*, p. 4.
41 Robert Chandler, Boris Dralyuk and Irina Mashinski, eds., *The Penguin Book of Russian Poetry* (London: Penguin, 2015), p. xiv.
42 Vasily Grossman, *Everything Flows*, trans. Robert Chandler and Elizabeth Chandler with Anna Aslanyan (New York: New York Review of Books, 2009), p. 192.
43 On the economic rationale for the Gulag, see the essays in Paul R. Gregory and Valery Lazarev, eds., *The Economics of Forced Labor: The Soviet Gulag* (Stanford, CA: Hoover Institution Press, 2003); on the continuing debates about the origins of the camps and their place in Stalin's breakneck industrialisation programme, see Applebaum, *Gulag*, pp. 59–72.
44 Sarah Kovner, *Prisoners of the Empire: Inside Japanese POW Camps* (Cambridge, MA: Harvard University Press, 2020); Nicole Kempton, ed., *Laogai: The Machinery of Repression in China* (Brooklyn, NY: Umbrage Editions, 2009).
45 Primo Levi, *If This Is a Man*, in *The Complete Works of Primo Levi*, ed. Ann Goldstein; trans. Stuart Woolf, 3 vols (New York: Liveright, 2015), vol. 1, p. 18.

46 Paul R. Gregory, *Terror by Quota: State Security from Lenin to Stalin* (New Haven, CT: Yale University Press, 2009); see Garry Pierre-Pierre, 'Ex-P.O.W.'s sue 5 big Japanese companies over forced labor', *New York Times* (15 September 1999), Section A, p. 7.
47 Christopher Hitchens, 'On *Animal Farm*', in *Arguably* (London: Atlantic Books, 2011), pp. 228–36 (pp. 234–5). The CIA funded the 1954 film version of Orwell's novella: see Daniel J. Leab, *Orwell Subverted: The CIA and the Filming of Animal Farm*, fwd Peter Davison (University Park, PA: Pennsylvania State University Press, 2007).
48 'The Alexandria Ocasio-Cortez "concentration camp" debate, explained', *Times of Israel* (19 June 2019).
49 Ruth Klüger, *Still Alive: A Holocaust Girlhood Remembered* (New York: Feminist Press of the City University of New York, 2001), p. 71.
50 David Rousset, *L'univers concentrationnaire* (Paris: Éditions de Minuit, [1946] 1965), p. 253.
51 One of the satellite camps in the Neuengamme network.
52 David Rousset, 'Au secours des déportés dans les camps soviétiques: un appel de David Rousset aux anciens déportés des camps nazis', *Lignes*, no. 2 [1949] (2000/2), pp. 143–60; see also Emma Kuby, 'David Rousset's Cold War call to arms', in *Political Survivors: The Resistance, the Cold War, and the Fight against Concentration Camps after 1945* (Ithaca, NY: Cornell University Press, 2019), pp. 46–77; and Philip Nord, 'The concentrationary universe', in *After the Deportation: Memory Battles in Postwar France* (Cambridge: Cambridge University Press, 2020), pp. 53–87.
53 Margolin, *Journey*, p. 507.
54 Timothy Barney, '"Gulag" – Slavery, Inc.: The power of place and the rhetorical life of a Cold War map', *Rhetoric and Public Affairs*, vol. 16, no. 2 (2013), pp. 317–54.
55 Applebaum, *Gulag*, pp. 5–6.
56 Levi, *If This Is a Man*, pp. 12, 14.
57 Viktor E. Frankl, *Man's Search for Meaning*, trans. Ilse Lasch, pref. Gordon W. Allport (London: Penguin, [1959] 2004), pp. 22–3.
58 Klüger, *Still Alive*, pp. 94–5.
59 Frankl, *Man's Search*, pp. 23–32 (p. 23).
60 Edgar C. Trautman, 'Fear and panic in Nazi concentration camps: A biosocial evaluation of the chronic anxiety syndrome', *International Journal of Social Psychiatry*, vol. 10, no. 2 (1964), pp. 134–41 (p. 136). The Dutch-Jewish doctor Elie A. Cohen, who was sent to Auschwitz

in 1943, wrote an early account of the psychology of camp prisoners and their SS guards, which includes discussions of the role of fear and panic: see Elie Aron Cohen, *Human Behavior in the Concentration Camp* (Westport, CT: Greenwood, [1953] 1984), pp. 115–210, 211–76.

61 Margolin, *Journey*, p. 352.

62 Levi, *If This Is a Man*, pp. 117–18.

63 Frankl, *Man's Search*, p. 100.

64 Primo Levi, *The Periodic Table*, in *Complete Works of Primo Levi*, trans. Ann Goldstein, vol. 2, pp. 927–38.

65 Quoted in Berel Lang, *Primo Levi: The Matter of a Life* (New Haven, CT: Yale University Press, 2013), p. 4.

66 Arendt, *Origins*, pp. viii-ix, 443.

67 Robert Capa, *Slightly Out of Focus*, intro. Richard Whelan; fwd Cornell Capa (New York: Modern Library, [1947] 1999), p. 226.

68 Theodor W. Adorno, 'Cultural criticism and society', in *Prisms*, trans. Samuel and Shierry Weber (Cambridge, MA: MIT Press, [1981] 1983), pp. 17–34 (p. 34).

69 Levi, *If This Is a Man*, pp. 19, 30.

70 Rachel Donadio, 'Preserving the ghastly inventory of Auschwitz', *New York Times* (15 April 2015), Section A, p. 1.

71 Tadeusz Borowski, *This Way for the Gas, Ladies and Gentlemen*, intro. Jan Kott, trans. Barbara Vedder (London: Penguin, [1967], 1976), pp. 48–9.

12: A Contest of Nightmares

1 George Orwell, 'You and the atom bomb', *Tribune* (19 October 1945), reprinted in *The Collected Essays, Journalism and Letters of George Orwell*, vol. 4, *In Front of Your Nose, 1945–1950*, ed. Sonia Orwell and Ian Angus (New York: Harcourt Brace Jovanovich, 1968), pp. 6–10.

2 Walter Lippmann, *The Cold War: A Study in US Foreign Policy*, intro. Ronald Steel (New York: Harper & Row, [1947] 1972), pp. 23–4. The book was a collection of Lippmann's articles previously published in the *New York Herald Tribune* and *Foreign Affairs*.

3 'Mr. Baruch's address to the South Carolina legislature', in *Congressional Record: Proceedings and Debates of the 80th Congress: First Session. Appendix. Volume 93, Part 11, April 2, 1947, to June 12, 1947* (Washington, DC: US Government Printing Office, 1947), A1761–A1762. Baruch's speech had apparently been written by the Pulitzer Prize-winning journalist Herbert Bayard Swope, who had used the term 'cold war' in a document the previous year: see James L. Grant,

Bernard M. Baruch: The Adventures of a Wall Street Legend (New York and Chichester: John Wiley & Sons, 1997), pp. 308–9.

4 'Inaugural Address' (20 January 1953); '"Atoms for Peace" Address before the General Assembly of the United Nations on Peaceful Uses of Atomic Energy' (8 December 1953); '"The Chance for Peace" delivered before the American Society of Newspaper Editors' (16 April 1953): https://www.eisenhowerlibrary.gov/eisenhowers/speeches

5 Blanche Wiesen Cook, *The Declassified Eisenhower: A Divided Legacy* (Garden City, NY: Doubleday, 1981), p. 121.

6 'George Tooker', *Arts Digest*, vol. 29, no. 3 (1955), p. 28.

7 Albert Camus, 'Neither victims nor executioners: The century of fear' (19 November 1946), in Jacqueline Lévi-Valensi, ed., *Camus at Combat: Writing, 1944–1947*, fwd David Carroll; trans. Arthur Goldhammer (Princeton, NJ: Princeton University Press, 2002), pp. 257–60.

8 Arendt, 'Preface to the first edition', *Origins of Totalitarianism*, pp. vii–ix. Despite the end of the war, many Europeans felt in limbo, trapped in 'the gap between past and future', a theme explored by Arendt in *Between Past and Future: Eight Exercises in Political Thought* (New York: Viking, [1954] 1968), pp. 3–15.

9 Bowen, 'Postscript', pp. 221, 217.

10 Eric Hobsbawm, *The Age of Extremes: A History of the World, 1914–1991* (London: Abacus, 1994), p. 83.

11 'The sinews of peace, March 5, Missouri', in *Churchill Speaks: Winston S. Churchill in Peace and War. Collected Speeches, 1897–1963*, ed., Robert Rhodes James (Leicester: W. H. Smith & Son, 1981), pp. 876–84 (pp. 881, 877, 882).

12 Aleksandr Fursenko and Timothy Naftali, *Khrushchev's Cold War: The Inside Story of an American Adversary* (New York: W. W. Norton, 2006), p. 211.

13 Hua-yu Li, *Mao and the Economic Stalinization of China, 1948–1953* (Lanham, MD: Rowman & Littlefield, 2006).

14 Ruth Rogaski, 'Nature, annihilation, and modernity: China's Korean War germ-warfare experience reconsidered', *Journal of Asian Studies*, vol. 61, no. 2 (May 2002), pp. 381–415.

15 Frank Dikötter, *Mao's Great Famine: The History of China's Most Devastating Catastrophe, 1958–1962* (London: Bloomsbury, 2010), pp. 292, 219, 220.

16 *Nightwaves*, BBC Radio 3 (25 May 2005). Quoted in Jonathan Mirsky,

'China: The uses of fear', *China File* (6 October 2005). Even today fear of possible reprisals makes it difficult for Chinese people to openly discuss the Cultural Revolution, as Tania Branigan shows in *Red Memory: The Afterlives of China's Cultural Revolution* (London: Faber and Faber, 2023).

17 Francis MacDonnell, *Insidious Foes: The Axis Fifth Column and the American Home Front* (Oxford: Oxford University Press, 1995).

18 Schlesinger, *Vital Center*, p. 97.

19 Thomas G. Paterson, *Meeting the Communist Threat: Truman to Reagan* (Oxford: Oxford University Press, 1988), p. 10.

20 David Caute, *The Great Fear: The Anti-Communist Purge under Truman and Eisenhower* (New York: Simon & Schuster, 1978).

21 'McCarthy sees a plot; he will attack Marshall', *New York Times* (13 June 1951), p. 12.

22 Attributed to Senator Arthur Vandenberg and quoted in Robert L. Ivie, 'Fire, flood, and red fever: Motivating metaphors of global emergency in the Truman doctrine speech', *Presidential Studies Quarterly*, vol. 29, no. 3 (1999), pp. 570–91; Ted Morgan, *Reds: McCarthyism in Twentieth-Century America* (New York: Random House, 2004).

23 https://www.trumanlibrary.gov/library/public-papers/56/special-message-congress-greece-and-turkey-truman-doctrine

24 https://www.trumanlibrary.gov/library/public-papers/19/inaugural-address

25 Larry Ceplair, 'The film industry's battle against left-wing influences, from the Russian Revolution to the blacklist', *Film History*, vol. 20, no. 4 (2008), pp. 399–411.

26 See Zachary Smith, *Age of Fear: Othering and American Identity during World War I* (Baltimore, MD: Johns Hopkins University Press, 2019).

27 Morgan, *Reds*, p. 61.

28 'Red Stockings become Redlegs in Cincinnati', *New York Times* (10 April 1953), p. 26.

29 'The Communist Control Act of 1954', *Yale Law Journal*, vol. 64, no. 5 (April 1955), pp. 712–65 (pp. 715, 745).

30 'The Reds have a standard plan for taking over a new country', *Life* (7 June 1948), pp. 36–7 (p. 36).

31 William Safire, *Before the Fall: An Inside View of the Pre-Watergate White House* (New Brunswick, NJ: Transaction Publishers, [1975] 2005), p. 8.

32 See David J. Hogan, ed., *Invasion USA: Essays on Anti-Communist Movies of the 1950s and 1960s* (Jefferson, NC: McFarland and Company, 2017).

33 Gerson Legman, 'The comic books and the public', an abstract featured among the proceedings of a symposium entitled 'The Psychopathology of Comic Books', introduced by Fredric Wertham and held under the auspices of the Association for the Advancement of Psychotherapy on 19 March 1948, *American Journal of Psychotherapy*, vol. 2. no. 3 (July 1948), pp. 473–7 (p. 473).

34 Walter J. Ong, 'The comics and the super state: Glimpses down the back alleys of the mind', *Arizona Quarterly*, vol. 1, no. 3 (Autumn 1945), pp. 34–48.

35 See David Hajdu, *The Ten-Cent Plague: The Great Comic-Book Scare and How It Changed America* (New York: Farrar, Straus and Giroux, 2008); Chris York and Rafiel York, eds., *Comic Books and the Cold War, 1946–1962: Essays on Graphic Treatment of Communism, the Code and Social Concerns* (Jefferson, NC: McFarland and Company, 2012).

36 'Catholic students burn up comic books', *New York Times* (11 December 1948), p. 18.

37 'Burning of comic books avoided', *New York Times* (16 January 1949), p. 59.

38 Fredric Wertham, *Seduction of the Innocent* (New York: Rinehart & Company, 1954), p. 107, 185, 230, 193, 33, 217. On Wertham and the comic scare, see Jeremy Dauber, *American Comics: A History* (New York: W. W. Norton, 2022), pp. 92–137.

39 *Interim Report of the New York State Joint Legislative Committee to Study the Publication of Comics* (Albany, NY: Williams Press, 1950), p. 7; 'Psychiatrist asks crime comics ban', *New York Times* (14 December 1950), p. 50.

40 Nona Brown, 'Reform of comic books is spurred by hearings', *New York Times* (13 June 1954), Section E, p. 7; see also 'Are comics horrible?', *Newsweek* (3 May 1954), p. 60; Wolcott Gibbs, 'Keep those paws to yourself, space rat!', *New Yorker* (8 May 1954), pp. 134–41; *Report of the Select Committee on Current Pornographic Materials* (Washington, DC: Government Printing Office, 1952), p. 27.

41 Frances Stonor Saunders, *The Cultural Cold War: The CIA and the World of Arts and Letters* (New York: The New Press, 1999).

42 https://www.jfklibrary.org/archives/other-resources/john-f-kennedy-speeches/united-nations-19610925

43 Val Peterson, 'Panic: The ultimate weapon?', *Collier's Weekly* (21 August 1953), pp. 99–109 (p. 101).

44 Enrico L. Quarantelli, 'The nature and conditions of panic', *American Journal of Sociology*, vol. 60, no. 3 (November 1954), pp. 267–75 (p. 275); also his later article 'Conventional beliefs and counterintuitive realities', *Social Research*, vol. 75, no. 3 (Fall 2008), pp. 873–904. Similar arguments critiquing the myth of a panic-prone public continue to be made: see Ben Sheppard, G. James Rubin, Jamie K. Wardman and Simon Wessely, 'Terrorism and dispelling the myth of a panic prone public', *Journal of Public Health Policy*, vol. 27, no. 3 (2006), pp. 21–45; Lee Clarke and Caron Chess, 'Elites and panic: More to fear than fear itself', *Social Forces*, vol. 87, no. 2 (2008), pp. 993–1014.

45 Laura McEnaney, *Civil Defense Begins at Home: Militarization Meets Everyday Life in the Fifties* (Princeton, NJ: Princeton University Press, 2000), p. 53.

46 Melvin E. Matthews, Jr, *Duck and Cover: Civil Defense Images in Film and Television from the Cold War to 9/11* (Jefferson, NC: McFarland, 2012), p. 17. The philosopher Guy Oakes has suggested that the purpose of this civil defence propaganda was to promote a 'program of emotional management designed to control American fears of nuclear attack and put them to work in fighting the Cold War': see *The Imaginary War: Civil Defense and American Cold War Culture* (Oxford: Oxford University Press, 1995), p. 8.

47 Tracy C. Davis, *Stages of Emergency: Cold War Nuclear Civil Defense* (Durham, NC: Duke University Press, 2007), p. 24.

48 C. McKim Norton, 'Report on Project East River', *Journal of the American Institute of Planners*, vol. 19, no. 2 (1953), pp. 87–94; 'Report on Project East River Part II: Development of standards', *Journal of the American Institute of Planners*, vol. 19, no. 3 (1953), pp. 159–67.

49 '2 "atomic bombs," one in harbor, keep 50,000 busy in raid drill', *New York Times* (4 April 1952), pp. 1, 12.

50 Peterson, 'Panic', pp. 100, 105, 107, 108.

51 '"The mastery of fear": Sermon outline', pp. 318, 320.

52 https://www.jfklibrary.org/archives/other-resources/john-f-kennedy-speeches/cuba-radio-and-television-report-19621022

53 https://www.jfklibrary.org/archives/other-resources/john-f-kennedy-speeches/inaugural-address-19610120

54 *Fallout Protection: What to Know and Do About Nuclear Attack* (Arlington, VA: US Department of Defense, 1961), p. 6.

55 Robert S. McNamara, *Out of the Cold: New Thinking for American Foreign and Defense Policy in the 21st Century* (New York: Simon & Schuster, 1989), p. 101.
56 James G. Blight, *The Shattered Crystal Ball: Fear and Learning in the Cuban Missile Crisis* (Savage, MD: Rowman & Littlefield, 1990).
57 Serhii Plokhy, *Nuclear Folly: A History of the Cuban Missile Crisis* (New York: W. W. Norton, 2021), p. xvii.
58 Quoted in Norman Cousins, *The Improbable Triumvirate: John F. Kennedy, Pope John, Nikita Khrushchev* (New York: W. W. Norton, 1972), p. 46.
59 The BBC, however, rejected suggestions of collusion with the government; see the government's draft reply to the parliamentary question asked about the film in the House of Commons by William Hamilton MP in December 1965, UK National Archives, Kew, CAB 21/5808: https://www.nationalarchives.gov.uk/education/resources/sixties-britain/bbc-film-censored/
60 Robert Mann, *Daisy Petals and Mushroom Clouds: LBJ, Barry Goldwater, and the Ad That Changed American Politics* (Baton Rouge, LA: Louisiana State University Press, 2011).
61 George Orwell, *Nineteen Eighty-Four* (New York: Harcourt, Brace and Company, 1949), p. 193. Earlier examples of novels that deal with dystopian tech futures are the Russian writer Yevgeny Zamyatin's *We*, written in 1920–21, and Aldous Huxley's *Brave New World*, published in 1932.
62 On the promotion of the 'People Machine' as 'a hacky publicity stunt', see Seth Mnookin, 'The bumbling 1960s data scientists who anticipated Facebook and Google', *New York Times* (15 September 2020).
63 Thomas Bruce Morgan, 'The people-machine', *Harper's* (January 1961), pp. 53–7 (p. 57); discussed in Jill Lepore, *If Then: How the Simulmatics Corporation Invented the Future* (New York: Liveright, 2020), pp. 126–7.
64 Quoted in Lepore, *If Then*, p. 126.
65 Lepore, *If Then*, p. 5.
66 Daniel Crevier, *AI: The Tumultuous History of the Search for Artificial Intelligence* (New York: Basic Books, 1993), pp. 44–6 (p. 44).
67 John McCarthy, Marvin L. Minsky, Nathaniel Rochester and Claude E. Shannon, *A Proposal for the Dartmouth Summer Research Project on Artificial Intelligence* (31 August 1955), reprinted in *AI Magazine*, vol. 27, no. 4 (2006), pp. 12–14 (p. 12).

68 Manfred E. Clynes and Nathan S. Kline, 'Cyborgs and space', *Astronautics* (September 1960), pp. 26–7, 74–6.
69 Norbert Wiener, *God & Golem, Inc.: A Comment on Certain Points Where Cybernetics Impinges on Religion* (Cambridge, MA: MIT Press, 1964), p. vii.
70 Norbert Wiener, 'Some moral and technical consequences of automation', *Science*, vol. 131 (6 May 1960), pp. 1355–8 (p. 1355).
71 Wiener, *God & Golem*, p. 60.
72 Ida Russakoff Hoos, 'When the computer takes over the office', *Harvard Business Review*, vol. 38, no. 4 (1 July 1960), pp. 102–12 (p. 102).
73 Erich Fromm, 'The present human condition', *American Scholar*, vol. 25, no. 1 (Winter 1955/6), pp. 29–35 (p. 31).
74 Herbert Marcuse, *One-Dimensional Man: Studies in the Ideology of Advanced Industrial Society* (Abingdon and New York: Routledge, [1964] 2002), p. 7.
75 Timothy Melley, *Empire of Conspiracy: The Culture of Paranoia in Postwar America* (Ithaca, NY: Cornell University Press, 2000), p. 7.
76 Philip K. Dick, *Do Androids Dream of Electric Sheep?* (New York: Del Rey, [1968] 2017), p. 121.
77 Hunter S. Thompson, *Fear and Loathing in Las Vegas: A Savage Journey to the Heart of the American Dream* (London: HarperCollins, [1971] 2005), pp. 38, 23; 'Fear and loathing at the Super Bowl' [1974], in *Fear and Loathing at Rolling Stone: The Essential Writing of Hunter S. Thompson*, ed. and intro. Jann S. Wenner (New York: Simon & Schuster, 2011), pp. 294–319 (p. 297).
78 Douglas Murphy, *Last Futures: Nature, Technology and the End of Architecture* (London: Verso, 2016).

13: Break-Up, Breakdown

1 James M. Scott, *Deciding to Intervene: The Reagan Doctrine and American Foreign Policy* (Durham, NC: Duke University Press, 1996).
2 Eliot A. Cohen, 'Ronald Reagan and American defense', in Jeffrey L. Chidester and Paul Kengor, eds., *Reagan's Legacy in a World Transformed* (Cambridge, MA: Harvard University Press, 2015), pp. 124–38 (p. 126).
3 Frank Biess, *German Angst: Fear and Democracy in the Federal Republic of Germany* (Oxford: Oxford University Press, 2020), p. vii.
4 Michael Dobbs, 'Chernobyl: Symbol of Soviet failure', *Washington Post* (26 April 1991), p. 1; Stephen Weeks, 'The Chernobyl disaster

was the fatal blow to the USSR', in David Erik Nelson, ed., *Chernobyl: Perspectives on Modern World History* (Farmington Hills, MI: Greenhaven Press, 2010), pp. 113–18 (p. 116).

5 *Ten Years after Chernobyl: What Do We Really Know?*, Proceedings of the IAEA/WHO/EC International Conference, Vienna, April 1996, p. 8.

6 Dobbs, 'Chernobyl'.

7 https://www.icty.org/x/cases/krstic/tjug/en/krs-tj010802e-1.htm

8 Francis Fukuyama, 'The end of history?', *National Interest*, no. 16 (Summer 1989), pp. 3–18 (p. 4). The essay was later expanded into a book, *The End of History and the Last Man* (New York: Free Press, 1992).

9 https://www.reaganlibrary.gov/archives/speech/inaugural-address-1981

10 Susan Strange, *Casino Capitalism* (Oxford: Blackwell, 1986).

11 Philip Jenkins, *Decade of Nightmares: The End of the Sixties and the Making of Eighties America* (Oxford: Oxford University Press, 2006).

12 Marc Levinson, 'End of a golden age', *Aeon* (22 February 2017); also, *An Extraordinary Time: The End of the Postwar Boom and the Return of the Ordinary Economy* (New York: Basic Books, 2016).

13 Steven Brill, *Tailspin: The People and Forces Behind America's Fifty-Year Fall – and Those Fighting to Reverse It* (New York: Alfred A. Knopf, 2018).

14 Patrick Hutber, *The Decline and Fall of the Middle Class and How It Can Fight Back* (Harmondsworth: Penguin, [1976] 1977), p. 9.

15 Robert Moss, *The Collapse of Democracy* (London: Temple Smith, 1975), pp. 12, 38, 55, 76.

16 Stanley Cohen, *Folk Devils and Moral Panics: The Creation of the Mods and Rockers* (New York: Routledge, [1972] 2002).

17 Stuart Hall, Chas Critcher, Tony Jefferson, John Clarke and Brian Roberts, *Policing the Crisis: Mugging, the State and Law and Order* (London: Macmillan and Red Globe Press, [1978] 2013), pp. 2, 111, 121, 123, 323.

18 *Welcome to Fear City: A Survival Guide for Visitors to the City of New York* (New York: NYPD, 1975); Kevin Baker, '"Welcome to fear city": The inside story of New York's civil war, 40 years on', *Guardian* (18 May 2015); Kim Phillips-Fein, *Fear City: New York's Fiscal Crisis and the Rise of Austerity Politics* (New York: Metropolitan Books, 2017), pp. 129–44.

19 'Transcript of President's talk on city crisis, questions asked and his responses', *New York Times* (30 October 1975), p. 46.
20 Frank Van Riper, 'Ford to city: Drop dead', *New York Daily News* (30 October 1975), p. 1.
21 Phillips-Fein, *Fear City*, p. 257.
22 Richard Krause, 'Foreword', in Stephen S. Morse, ed., *Emerging Viruses* (Oxford: Oxford University Press, 1993), pp. xvii–xix (p. xvii).
23 Stephen Jay Gould, 'The terrifying normalcy of AIDS', *New York Times Magazine* (19 April 1987), p. 33.
24 Jeffrey Weeks, 'AIDS: The intellectual agenda', in Peter Aggleton, Graham Hart and Peter Davies, eds., *AIDS: Social Representations, Social Practices* (Abingdon: Routledge, 1989), pp. 1–20 (p. 3).
25 Jeffrey Weeks, *Sexuality* (London: Tavistock, 1986), p. 95.
26 Simon Watney, 'AIDS, "moral panic" theory, and homophobia', in *Practices of Freedom: Selected Writings on HIV/AIDS* (Durham, NC: Duke University Press, 1994), pp. 3–16.
27 Robert Peckham, 'Polio, terror and the immunological worldview', *Global Public Health*, vol. 13, no. 2 (2018), pp. 189–210 (p. 190).
28 https://www.cdc.gov/mmwr/preview/mmwrhtml/june_5.htm
29 Randy Shilts, *And the Band Played On: Politics, People, and the AIDS Epidemic* (New York: St. Martin's Griffin, [1987] 2007), p. 44.
30 Margaret Engel, 'AIDS and prejudice: One reporter's account of the nation's response', *Washington Post* (1 December 1987), p. 10.
31 Quoted in David Shaw, 'Anti-gay bias? Coverage of AIDS story: A slow start', *Los Angeles Times* (20 December 1987), p. 1.
32 Gina M. Bright, *Plague-Making and the AIDS Epidemic: A Story of Discrimination* (New York: Palgrave Macmillan, 2012).
33 Robert Pear, 'Health chief calls AIDS battle "no. 1 priority"', *New York Times* (25 May 1983), Section A, pp. 1, 19. Brandt had established the Executive Task Force on AIDS in 1983.
34 Philip M. Boffey, 'Reagan urges wide AIDS testing but does not call for compulsion', *New York Times* (1 June 1987), Section A, pp. 1, 15 (p. 1).
35 'Surgeon general's report on acquired immune deficiency syndrome', *Public Health Reports*, vol. 102, no. 1 (1987), pp. 1–3. Koop was an evangelical who supported the pro-life cause; on his role in shaping the moral politics of AIDS, see Anthony M. Petro, 'Governing authority: The surgeon general and the moral politics of public

health', in *After the Wrath of God: AIDS, Sexuality, and American Religion* (Oxford: Oxford University Press, 2015), pp. 53–90.

36 Janet Holland, Caroline Ramazanoglu and Sue Scott, 'AIDS: From panic stations to power relations – sociological perspectives and problems', *Sociology*, vol. 24, no. 3 (1990), pp. 499–518 (p. 499). 'The AIDS epidemic,' they wrote, 'has brought together sex, deviance and death in ways which have provoked both widespread fear of infection and also horror of the infected' (p. 499).

37 Charles Krauthammer, 'AIDS hysteria', *New Republic* (5 October 1987), pp. 18–20.

38 Justin McCarthy, 'Fear and anxiety during the 1980s AIDS crisis', *Gallup Vault* (28 June 2019): https://news.gallup.com/vault/259643/gallup-vault-fear-anxiety-during-1980s-aids-crisis.aspx

39 William J. Buckley, 'Crucial steps in combating the AIDS epidemic; identify all the carriers', *New York Times* (18 March 1986), p. 27.

40 Joel Zizik, 'Pneumocystis', in Michael Klein and Richard McCann, eds., *Things Shaped in Passing: More 'Poets for Life' Writing from the AIDS Pandemic* (New York: Persea Books, 1997), pp. 195–206 (p. 199).

41 Thom Gunn, 'Lament', in *Collected Poems* (London: Faber and Faber, 1993), p. 465.

42 Mark Doty, *Heaven's Coast: A Memoir* (New York: HarperCollins, 1997), p. 204.

43 Christine Doyle, 'AIDS: It does affect us all', *Daily Telegraph* (16 September 1986), p. 11.

44 Watney, 'AIDS', p. 5; Holland et al., 'AIDS', p. 505.

45 'AIDS: It does affect us all', p. 11, discussed in Watney, 'AIDS', p. 5; Richard Evans, 'AIDS', *Financial Times* (22 November 1986), p. 6.

46 'The panic spreads', *Economist* (15 November 1986), p. 28.

47 'Panic stations', *Daily Telegraph* (16 September 1986), p. 11.

48 Evans, 'AIDS'.

49 Tim Jonze, '"It was a life-and-death situation. Wards were full of young men dying": How we made the Don't Die of Ignorance Aids campaign', *Guardian* (4 September 2017).

50 On the use of fear in HIV public health campaigns, as well as arguments against fear on the grounds that it stigmatises, see Amy Lauren Fairchild et al., 'The two faces of fear: A history of hard-hitting public health campaigns against tobacco and AIDS', *American Journal of Public Health*, vol. 108, no. 9 (2018), pp. 1180–86 (p. 1184).

51 Holland et al., 'AIDS', p. 499.

52 Holland et al., 'AIDS', pp. 500–501; Robert Peckham, 'The crisis of crisis: Rethinking epidemics from Hong Kong', *Bulletin of the History of Medicine*, vol. 94, no. 4 (2020), pp. 658–69 (p. 658).
53 'The time bomb', *Daily Telegraph* (16 September 1986), p. 11.
54 Evans, 'AIDS'.
55 Jacqueline Foertsch, *Enemies Within: The Cold War and the AIDS Crisis in Literature, Film, and Culture* (Urbana, IL: University of Illinois Press, 2001).
56 Susan Sontag, *Illness as Metaphor and AIDS and Its Metaphors* (London: Penguin, 2013); Roger Cooter and Claudia Stein, 'Coming into focus: Posters, power, and visual culture in the history of medicine', in *Writing History in the Age of Biomedicine* (New Haven, CT: Yale University Press, 2013), pp. 112–37 (pp. 120–23); and John O'Neill, 'AIDS as a globalizing panic', *Theory, Culture & Society*, vol. 7, nos. 2/3 (1990), pp. 493–508.
57 Quoted in Holland et al., 'AIDS', p. 501.
58 'A premium for panic', *Financial Times* (19 November 1986), p. 48.
59 John Mullin, 'Journals ban dying AIDS victim advertisement', *Guardian* (24 January 1992), p. 22; Helen Fielding, 'Pulling the woollies over our eyes', *Sunday Times* (26 January 1992), Section 4, p. 3.
60 Paula Span, 'Colored with controversy', *Washington Post* (13 February 1992), Section D, p. 1; McKenzie Wark, 'Still life today: The Benetton campaign', *Photofile*, no. 36 (August 1992), pp. 33–6 (p. 33); Barbara Browning, *Infectious Rhythm: Metaphors of Contagion and the Spread of African Culture* (New York and London: Routledge, 1998), pp. 149–50.
61 Ann S. Anagnost, 'Strange circulations: The blood economy in rural China', *Economy and Society*, vol. 35, no. 4 (2006), pp. 509–29 (p. 516).
62 Shilts, *And the Band*, p. 4.
63 Joshua Lederberg, Robert E. Shope and Stanley C. Oaks, eds., *Emerging Infections: Microbial Threats to Health in the United States* (Washington, DC: National Academies Press, 1992), p. v.
64 Lederberg et al., *Emerging Infections*, pp. 1–15.
65 'Don't panic, yet, over AIDS', *New York Times* (7 November 1986), Section A, p. 34.
66 'A global disaster', *Economist* (2 January 1999), pp. 50–52 (p. 50).
67 Elizabeth Pisani et al., *Report on the Global HIV/AIDS Epidemic* (Geneva: UNAIDS, June 2000), p. 6.
68 Jonny Steinberg, *Sizwe's Test: A Young Man's Journey through Africa's*

AIDS Epidemic (New York: Simon & Schuster, 2008); Quang Nguyen and Kearsley Stewart, 'AIDS denialism: Conspiratorial ideation and the internet', *Journal of Global Health*, vol. 5, no. 2 (2015), pp. 44–7.

69 https://www.cdc.gov/tuskegee/timeline.htm

70 Cristine Russell, 'Map of AIDS' deadly march evolves from hepatitis study', *Washington Post* (1 February 1987), p. 1.

71 Seth C. Kalichman, 'Peter Duesberg and the origins of HIV/AIDS denialism', in *Denying AIDS: Conspiracy Theories, Pseudoscience, and Human Tragedy*, fwd Nicoli Nattrass (New York: Springer, 2009), pp. 25–56; Peter H. Duesberg, *Inventing the AIDS Virus*, fwd Kary Mullis (Washington, DC: Regnery Publishing, 1996), p. vii.

72 Milton William Cooper, *Behold a Pale Horse* (Flagstaff, AZ: Light Technology Publishing, 1991), p. 214.

73 Didier Fassin, 'The politics of conspiracy theories: On AIDS in South Africa and a few other global plots', *Brown Journal of World Affairs*, vol. 17, no. 2 (2011), pp. 39–50 (p. 40).

74 Fassin, 'Politics', p. 41.

75 Luise White, *Speaking with Vampires: Rumor and History in Colonial Africa* (Berkeley, CA: University of California Press, 2000).

76 Elizabeth B. van Heyningen, 'The social evil in the Cape Colony, 1868–1902: Prostitution and the Contagious Diseases Acts', *Journal of Southern African Studies*, vol. 10, no. 2 (1984), pp. 170–97 (p. 178); Karen Jochelson, *The Colour of Disease: Syphilis and Racism in South Africa, 1880–1950* (Basingstoke: Palgrave, 2001); Maynard W. Swanson, 'The sanitation syndrome: Bubonic plague and urban native policy in the Cape Colony, 1900-1909', *Journal of African History*, vol. 18, no. 3 (1977), pp. 387–410 (p. 393).

77 Jacques Pépin et al., 'Risk factors for hepatitis C virus transmission in colonial Cameroon', *Clinical Infectious Diseases*, vol. 51, no. 7 (2010), pp. 768–76.

78 Jacques Pépin, *The Origins of AIDS* (Cambridge: Cambridge University Press, [2011] 2021).

79 Léopoldville became Kinshasa in 1966.

80 Pépin, *Origins*, pp. 124–52.

81 Fassin, 'Politics', p. 47.

82 Edward Hooper, *The River: A Journey to the Source of HIV and AIDS* (Boston, MA: Little, Brown and Company, 1999).

83 Peckham, 'Polio', pp. 198–9. Save the Children denied any involvement in the plot.

84 Doug Rossinow, 'Days of fear', in *The Reagan Era: A History of the*

1980s (New York: Columbia University Press, 2015), pp. 139–60 (p. 139).
85 Michelle Alexander, *The New Jim Crow: Mass Incarceration in the Age of Colorblindness* (New York: The New Press, [2010] 2012).
86 Centers for Disease Control and Prevention, 'Mortality attributable to HIV infection/AIDS – United States, 1981–1990', *Morbidity & Mortality Weekly Report*, vol. 40, no. 3 (25 January 1991), pp. 41–4.
87 https://www.reaganlibrary.gov/archives/speech/farewell-address-nation

14: War on Terror

1 Wayman C. Mullins, 'Terrorism in the '90s: Predictions for the United States', *Police Chief*, vol. 57, no. 9 (September 1990), pp. 44–6.
2 Bryan Burrough, *Days of Rage: America's Radical Underground, the FBI, and the Forgotten Age of Revolutionary Violence* (New York: Penguin, 2015).
3 https://www.fbi.gov/history/famous-cases/weather-underground-bombings
4 *Prairie Fire: The Politics of Revolutionary Anti-Imperialism – The Political Statement of the Weather Underground* (Brooklyn, NY, and San Francisco, CA: Communications Co., 1974), pp. 11, 107, 113, 115.
5 Leroy E. Aarons, 'Symbionese Army: Beyond fantasy', *Washington Post* (11 February 1974), Section A, pp. 1, 6 (p. 1).
6 See Les Payne and Tim Findley, with Carolyn Craven, *The Life and Death of the SLA: A True Story of Revolutionary Terror* (New York: Ballantine Books, 1976).
7 Aarons, 'Symbionese Army', p. 6.
8 Brendan I. Koerner, *The Skies Belong to Us: Love and Terror in the Golden Age of Hijacking* (New York: Broadway Books, 2013).
9 Maud Ellmann, *The Hunger Artists: Starving, Writing, and Imprisonment* (Cambridge, MA: Harvard University Press, 1993), p. 23.
10 Claims persist that they were murdered.
11 Hans Magnus Enzensberger, *Civil Wars: From LA to Bosnia* (New York: The New Press, 1994), pp. 20, 30.
12 https://georgewbush-whitehouse.archives.gov/news/releases/2001/09/20010920-8.html
13 David Rieff, 'Fear and fragility sound a wake-up call', *Los Angeles Times* (12 September 2001); Stearns, *American Fear*, p. 36.
14 Douglas Kellner, '9/11, spectacles of terror, and media manipulation:

A critique of Jihadist and Bush media politics', *Critical Discourse Studies*, vol. 1, no. 1 (2004), pp. 41–64 (p. 43).

15 Rieff, 'Fear'; for a celebration of the towers, see David Lehman's poem 'The World Trade Center', *Paris Review*, no. 136 (1995), p. 74.

16 Frank J. Prial, 'Governors dedicate Trade Center here; world role is cited', *New York Times* (5 April 1973), pp. 1, 34.

17 Philippe Petit, 'In search of fear: Notes from a high-wire artist', *Lapham's Quarterly* (Summer 2017), pp. 214–19 (p. 214).

18 Samuel P. Huntington, *The Clash of Civilizations and the Remaking of World Order* (New York: Simon & Schuster, 1996).

19 'Altman says Hollywood "created atmosphere" for September 11', *Guardian* (18 October 2001).

20 Michael McCaul, *Failures of Imagination: The Deadliest Threats to Our Homeland – and How to Thwart Them* (New York: Crown Forum, 2016).

21 Richard N. Haass, 'The Bush administration's response to September 11th – and beyond. Remarks to the Council of Foreign Relations, New York' (15 October 2001): https://2001-2009.state.gov/s/p/rem/5505.htm

22 https://georgewbush-whitehouse.archives.gov/news/releases/2002/01/20020129-11.html

23 Ronnie Lippens, 'Viral contagion and anti-terrorism: Notes on medical emergency, legality and diplomacy', *International Journal for the Semiotics of Law*, vol. 17, no. 2 (2004), pp. 125–39 (p. 126).

24 As the historian Philipp Sarasin has argued, after 9/11 'epidemiology and epidemic control become one: terrorism, infectious diseases, bioterror, and border control' merged into a single security threat; see 'Vapors, viruses, resistance(s): The trace of infection in the work of Michel Foucault', in S. Harris Ali and R. Keil, eds., *Networked Disease: Emerging Infections in the Global City* (Oxford: Wiley-Blackwell, 2008), pp. 267–80 (p. 268); Scott Shane, 'FBI, laying out evidence, closes anthrax case', *New York Times* (19 February 2010).

25 Barry S. Levy and Victor W. Sidel, 'Challenges that terrorism poses to public health', in Barry S. Levy and Victor W. Sidel, eds., *Terrorism and Public Health: A Balanced Approach to Strengthening Systems and Protecting People* (Oxford: Oxford University Press), pp. 3–18 (pp. 7–9).

26 Nick Muntean, 'Viral terrorism and terrifying viruses: The homological construction of the war on terror and the avian flu

pandemic', *International Journal of Media & Cultural Politics*, vol. 5, no. 3 (October 2009), pp. 199–216 (p. 199).

27 Derek Gregory, 'The everywhere war', *Geographical Journal*, vol. 177, no. 3 (2011), pp. 238–50; Christopher Drew, 'Drones are weapons of choice in fighting Qaeda', *New York Times* (16 March 2009), Section A, p. 1.

28 James Der Derian, 'Imaging terror: Logos, pathos, and ethos', *Third World Quarterly*, vol. 26, no. 1 (2005), pp. 23–37 (p. 26).

29 Jane Mayer, *The Dark Side: The Inside Story of How the War on Terror Turned into a War on American Ideals* (New York: Anchor, 2009), pp. 9–10.

30 https://georgewbush-whitehouse.archives.gov/news/releases/2002/09/20020912-1.html

31 https://georgewbush-whitehouse.archives.gov/news/releases/2001/09/20010920-8.html

32 https://www.un.org/press/en/2003/sc7658.doc.htm

33 https://www.inigomanglano-ovalle.com/

34 'What was the 45-minute claim?', *Guardian* (5 February 2004); Andrew Sparrow, '45-minute WMD claim "may have come from an Iraqi taxi driver"', *Guardian* (8 December 2009).

35 Barry Buzan, 'Will the "global war on terrorism" be the new Cold War?', *International Affairs*, vol. 82, no. 6 (2006), pp. 1101–18 (p. 1101).

36 Quoted in Rick Weiss, 'Gore criticizes Bush approach to security', *Washington Post* (10 November 2003), Section A, p. 2.

37 Zbigniew Brzezinski, 'Terrorized by "war on terror"', *Washington Post* (25 March 2007), Section B, p. 1.

38 'Authorization for Use of Military Force' (2001): https://www.congress.gov/bill/107th-congress/senate-joint-resolution/23/text

39 Ken Ballen and Peter Bergen, 'The worst of the worst?', *Foreign Policy* (20 October 2008); Michael Ratner, 'Guantánamo at 10: The defeat of liberty by fear', *Guardian* (11 January 2012).

40 Rodney C. Roberts, 'The American value of fear and the indefinite detention of terrorist suspects', *Public Affairs Quarterly*, vol. 21, no. 4 (2007), pp. 405–19.

41 Robin, *Fear*, p. 25.

42 Brigitte L. Nacos, Yaeli Bloch-Elkon and Robert Y. Shapiro, *Selling Fear: Counterterrorism, the Media, and Public Opinion* (Chicago, IL: University of Chicago Press, 2011); Susan Faludi, *The Terror Dream: Fear and Fantasy in Post-9/11 America* (New York: Metropolitan Books, 2007); Dawn Rothe and Stephen L. Muzzatti, 'Enemies

everywhere: Terrorism, moral panic, and US civil society', *Critical Criminology*, vol. 12 (2004), pp. 327–50. At the same time, 'large parts of the progressive side of the political spectrum got spooked', leaving an opportunity for populist movements to exploit. As Naomi Klein has expressed it, 'Politics hates a vacuum. If it isn't filled with hope, someone will fill it with fear.' See *No Is Not Enough: Resisting Trump's Shock Politics and Winning the World We Need* (Chicago, IL: Haymarket Books, 2017), p. 113.

43 John Mueller, *Overblown: How Politicians and the Terrorism Industry Inflate National Security Threats, and Why We Believe Them* (New York: Free Press, 2006), p. 2.

44 Thomas K. Duncan and Christopher J. Coyne, 'The origins of the permanent war economy', *Independent Review*, vol. 18, no. 2 (2013), pp. 219–40 (pp. 219, 234). The term 'permanent war economy' was coined by Walter J. Oakes in 1944; see 'Toward a permanent war economy?', *Politics* (February 1944), pp. 11–16.

45 The memorial had been erected in 1884 to commemorate the life of Colonel E. C. Hastings.

46 'Katrina, 9/11 and disaster capitalism', Naomi Klein interview with Lenora Todaro, *Salon.com* (21 September 2007); Klein, *Shock Doctrine*.

47 Charles Bremner, 'Dawn raids on Islamists in Paris as Emmanuel Macron vows to get tough', *The Times* [London] (20 October 2020).

48 Ewen MacAskill and Dominic Rushe, 'Snowden document reveals key role of companies in NSA data collection', *Guardian* (1 November 2013).

49 Raphael Satter, 'US court: Mass surveillance program exposed by Snowden was illegal', *Reuters* (2 September 2020).

15: Eco-Panic

1 Timothy Morton, *Hyperobjects: Philosophy and Ecology after the End of the World* (Minneapolis, MN: Minnesota University Press, 2013); *The Ecological Thought* (Cambridge, MA: Harvard University Press, 2010), pp. 19, 130–31.

2 Amitav Ghosh, *The Great Derangement: Climate Change and the Unthinkable* (Chicago, IL: University of Chicago Press, 2016).

3 Paul J. Crutzen and Eugene F. Stoermer, 'The Anthropocene', *International Geosphere-Biosphere Programme Newsletter*, no. 41 (2000), pp. 17–18.

4 Anthony Giddens, 'Risk and responsibility', *Modern Law Review*, vol. 62, no. 1 (1999), pp. 1–10 (p. 4); Ulrich Beck, *Risk Society: Towards a*

New Modernity, trans. Scott Lash and Brian Wynne (London: Sage, 1992); for an insightful discussion of 'hazard' in relation to fear, science and a Cold War sociology of disaster, see Coen, 'The nature of fear'.

5 John McPhee, *Basin and Range* (New York: Farrar, Straus and Giroux, 1981), p. 77.

6 https://www.rightlivelihoodaward.org/speech/acceptance-speech-bill-mckibben-350-org/

7 Greta Thunberg, speech delivered on 30 October 2022 at the Climate Event, Southbank Centre, London, to launch *The Climate Book: The Facts and the Solutions* (London: Allen Lane, 2022).

8 Jonathan Franzen, *The End of the End of the Earth* (New York: Farrar, Straus and Giroux, 2018), pp. 16–21; see also 'Carbon capture: Has climate change made it harder for people to care about conservation?', *New Yorker* (6 April 2015), pp. 56–65.

9 Gladwin Hill, 'Nation set to observe Earth Day', *New York Times* (21 April 1970), p. 36.

10 In 1973 the Endangered Species Act came into operation to protect species facing extinction due to untrammelled 'economic growth and development'.

11 'The end of civilization feared by biochemist', *New York Times* (19 November 1970), p. 24.

12 Paul R. Ehrlich, *The Population Bomb* (New York: Ballantine Books, 1968), p. 13.

13 Paul Ehrlich, 'Eco-catastrophe!', *Ramparts Magazine*, vol. 8, no. 3 (September 1969), pp. 24–8 (pp. 24–5, 28).

14 Bernard Dixon, 'In praise of prophets', *New Scientist* (16 September 1971), p. 606.

15 Paul R. Ehrlich, 'Looking back from 2000 AD', in *The Crisis of Survival*, intro. Eugene P. Odum and Benjamin DeMott (Madison, WI: The Progressive, 1970), pp. 235–45 (pp. 239, 245).

16 Frederik Pohl, ed., *Nightmare Age* (New York: Ballantine Books, 1970).

17 See the report co-authored by the microbiologist René Dubos and the economist Barbara Ward for the 1972 Stockholm conference, *Only One Earth: The Care and Maintenance of a Small Planet* (New York: W. W. Norton, 1972), p. xviii. The term 'spaceship earth' was coined in 1969 by the architect and systems theorist Richard Buckminster Fuller: see *Operating Manual for Spaceship Earth* (Carbondale, IL: Southern Illinois University Press, 1969).

18 Holly Henry and Amanda Taylor, 'Re-thinking Apollo: Envisioning environmentalism in space', *Sociological Review*, vol. 57, no. 1 (2009), pp. 190–203; Robert Poole, *Earthrise: How Man First Saw the Earth* (New Haven, CT: Yale University Press, 2010).
19 http://www.un-documents.net/ocf-ov.htm
20 Donella H. Meadows, Dennis L. Meadows, Jørgen Randers and William W. Behrens III, *The Limits to Growth* (New York: Universe Books, 1972), p. 23.
21 Margaret Hunt Gram, '*Freedom*'s limits: Jonathan Franzen, the realist novel, and the problem of growth', *American Literary History*, vol. 26, no. 2 (2014), pp. 295–316 (p. 306).
22 Ehrlich, *Population Bomb*, p. 15.
23 Gram, '*Freedom*'s limits', p. 306.
24 Peter Gwynne, 'The cooling world', *Newsweek* (28 April 1975), p. 64.
25 Lowell Ponte, *The Cooling: Has the Next Ice Age Already Begun?* (New York: Prentice-Hall, 1976), p. xv.
26 Meg Jacobs, *Panic at the Pump: The Energy Crisis and the Transformation of American Politics in the 1970s* (New York: Farrar, Straus and Giroux, 2016).
27 Amanda Rohloff, *Climate Change, Moral Panics and Civilization* (New York: Routledge, 2020). For an argument about the 'ecological panic' that shaped the environmental revolution, see Rael Jean Isaac and Erich Isaac, *The Coercive Utopians: Social Deception by America's Power Players* (Chicago, IL: Regnery Gateway, 1983), pp. 45–8.
28 Mike Tidwell, 'A climate of change: Activist prepares for the worst', *Washington Post* (25 February 2011); cited in Alex Chambers, 'A panicky atmosphere: On the coloniality of climate change', in Micol Seigel, ed., *Panic, Transnational Cultural Studies, and the Affective Contours of Power* (New York: Routledge, 2018), pp. 87–107 (p. 87).
29 David Wallace-Wells, 'The uninhabitable Earth: Famine, economic collapse, a sun that cooks us: What climate change could wreak – sooner than you think', *New York Magazine* (10 July 2017).
30 David Wallace-Wells, 'Time to panic', *New York Times* (16 February 2019).
31 Intergovernmental Panel on Climate Change [IPCC], *Global Warming of 1.5* °C (Switzerland, 2018); Jonathan Watts, 'We have 12 years to limit climate change catastrophe, warns UN', *Guardian* (8 October 2018).
32 Greta Thunberg, 'Our house is on fire', *Guardian* (25 January 2019).

33 Marie-Hélène Huet, *The Culture of Disaster* (Chicago, IL: University of Chicago Press, 2012), p. 4.

34 Oliver Milman, 'How the global climate fight could be lost if Trump is re-elected', *Guardian* (27 July 2020). As Bjørn Lomborg agues, although climate change is real, it isn't 'like a huge asteroid hurtling toward earth': *False Alarm: How Climate Change Panic Costs Us Trillions, Hurts the Poor, and Fails to Fix the Planet* (New York: Basic Books, 2020), p. 17.

35 Melvin J. Grayson and Thomas R. Shepard, Jr, *The Disaster Lobby: Prophets of Ecological Doom and Other Absurdities* (Chicago, IL: Follett Publishing Company, 1973), pp. 4, 21–43.

36 Petr Beckmann, *Eco-Hysterics and the Technophobes* (Boulder, CO: Golem Press, 1973), pp. 8, 78, 202.

37 Michael Crichton, *State of Fear: A Novel* (New York: HarperCollins, 2004).

38 Greta Thunberg, Svante Thunberg, Malena Ernman and Beata Ernman, *Our House Is on Fire: Scenes of a Family and a Planet in Crisis*, trans. Paul Norlen and Saskia Vogel (New York: Penguin, 2020), pp. 74, 67.

39 Emily Witt, 'How Greta Thunberg transformed existential dread into a movement', *New Yorker* (6 April 2020).

40 https://languages.oup.com/word-of-the-year/2019/

41 Molly S. Castelloe, 'Coming to terms with ecoanxiety', *Psychology Today* (9 January 2018).

42 Jared Diamond, *Collapse: How Societies Choose to Fail or Succeed* (New York: Viking, [2005] 2011); Laurie Laybourn, Henry Throp and Suzannah Sherman, *1.5 °C: Dead or Alive?* (London: Chatham House/Institute for Public Policy Research, 2023), p. 5.

43 Susan Clayton, Christie Manning, Kirra Krygsman and Meighen Speiser, *Mental Health and Our Changing Climate: Impacts, Implications, and Guidance* (Washington, DC: American Psychological Association and ecoAmerica, 2017), p. 27.

44 https://www.climatepsychiatry.org/[;] https://www.goodgriefnetwork.org

45 David Sobel, *Beyond Ecophobia: Reclaiming the Heart in Nature Education* (Great Barrington, MA: Orion Society, 1996), p. 5. The political commentator George F. Will used the term in 1988, writing that 'the mood of the moment is ecophobia, the fear that the planet is increasingly inhospitable': see 'Who's the real environmentalist?', *Washington Post* (18 September 1988), Section C, p. 7.

46 Wai Chee Dimock, 'Planet and America, set and subset', in Wai Chee Dimock and Lawrence Buell, eds., *Shades of the Planet: American Literature as World Literature* (Princeton, NJ: Princeton University Press, 2007), pp. 1–16 (p. 1); also Simon C. Estok, *The Ecophobia Hypothesis* (New York: Routledge, 2018), p. 35.
47 Roy Scranton, *Learning to Die in the Anthropocene: Reflections on the End of a Civilization* (San Francisco, CA: City Lights, 2015); 'I've said goodbye to "normal." You should, too', *New York Times* (25 January 2021).
48 Sabrina V. Helm et al., 'Differentiating environmental concern in the context of psychological adaption to climate change', *Global Environmental Change*, no. 48 (2018), pp. 158–67.
49 Michael Shellenberger, 'Sorry, but I cried wolf on climate change', *Australian* (2 July 2020); Graham Readfearn, 'The environmentalist's apology: How Michael Shellenberger unsettled some of his prominent supporters', *Guardian* (4 July 2020).
50 Michael Shellenberger, *Apocalypse Never: Why Environmental Alarmism Hurts Us All* (New York: HarperCollins, 2020), pp. 21–2, 24–5, 272–3.
51 Bjørn Lomborg, *The Skeptical Environmentalist: Measuring the Real State of the World* (Cambridge: Cambridge University Press, 2021); *False Alarm*; 'An evening with Bjørn Lomborg: Putting global warming into perspective', lecture at the London School of Economics (16 February 2011).
52 Daniel Smith, 'It's the end of the world as we know it . . . and he feels fine', *New York Times Magazine* (17 April 2014).
53 Alex Steffen, 'The transapocalyptic now: It's not the end of the world, but it is the end of the world as we've known it', *The Snap Forward* (4 November 2021): https://alexsteffen.substack.com/p/the-transapocalyptic-now[;] 'Editor's introduction', in Alex Steffen, ed., *Worldchanging: A User's Guide for the 21st Century*, intro. Bill McKibben; rev. ed. (New York: Abrams, 2011), pp. 17–26 (pp. 17, 19).
54 Jennie King, *Deny, Deceive, Delay*, vol. 2, *Exposing New Trends in Climate Mis- and Disinformation at COP27* (London: Institute for Strategic Dialogue, 2023); for the report's key findings discussed here, see pp. 4–7.
55 Rebecca Solnit and Thelma Young Lutunatabua, eds., *Not Too Late: Changing the Climate Story from Despair to Possibility* (Chicago, IL: Haymarket Books, 2023); also https://www.nottoolateclimate.com
56 Edward Burtynsky, *China* (Göttingen: Steidl, 2005). For an analysis

of Burtynsky's 'manufactured landscapes', climate change, and US 'cultural anxieties about the geopolitical rise of China', see Michael Ziser and Julie Sze, 'Climate change, environmental aesthetics, and global environmental justice cultural studies', *Discourse*, vol. 29, nos. 2/3 (2007), pp. 384–410 (pp. 396–404); see also: https://www.edwardburtynsky.com/projects/photographs/china

57 Ziser and Sze, 'Climate change', pp. 396–400.

58 Alastair Marsh, 'Gore says climate crisis is like "hike through Book of Revelation"', *Bloomberg* (20 September 2022).

59 Damian Carrington, 'Rising seas threaten "mass exodus on a biblical scale", UN chief warns', *Guardian* (14 February 2023).

60 Pascal Bruckner, 'Against environmental panic', *Chronicle of Higher Education* (17 June 2013); see also *The Fanaticism of the Apocalypse: Save the Earth, Punish Human Beings*, trans. Steven Rendall (Cambridge: Polity, 2013).

61 http://www.hawaiifreepress.com/Articles-Main/ID/2818/Crichton-Environmentalism-is-a-religion

62 'Fact check: Video presents climate change statements that lack key context', *Reuters* (16 October 2020); King, *Deny, Deceive, Delay*, p. 15; https://www.prageru.com/religion-of-green

Epilogue: Pandemic and the Rule of Fear

1 Tocqueville, *Democracy*, p. 673.

2 Tocqueville, *Democracy*, p. 663.

3 This is a central theme in Furedi, *Culture of Fear*.

4 Salman Rushdie, *Joseph Anton: A Memoir* (New York: Random House, 2012), p. 175.

5 Nicole Perlroth, Mark Scott and Sheera Frenkel, 'Cyberattack hits Ukraine then spreads internationally', *New York Times* (27 June 2017); it was later understood that this malware, which appeared to be ransomware, was actually a cover for a subsequent Russian-orchestrated attack by the NotPetya virus, which permanently erased data; see Ellen Nakashima, 'Russian military was behind "NotPetya" cyberattack in Ukraine, CIA concludes', *Washington Post* (12 January 2018); Josephine Wolff, 'The Colonial Pipeline shutdown says we're in a scary new world', *Washington Post* (13 May 2021).

6 David Baltimore, 'SAMS – severe acute media syndrome?', *Wall Street Journal* (28 April 2003), p. 12.

7 David J. Rothkopf, 'When the buzz bites back', *Washington Post* (11 May 2003), Section B, pp. 1, 5.

8 Richard Orange, 'Coronavirus: Norway wonders if it should have been more like Sweden', *Daily Telegraph* (30 May 2020).
9 Lewis, 'Has anyone seen the President?'
10 Patrick Boucheron, '"Real power is fear": What Machiavelli tells us about Trump in 2020', *Guardian* (8 February 2020); also *Machiavelli: The Art of Teaching People What to Fear*, trans. Willard Wood (New York: Other Press, 2020), p. 1.
11 Bob Woodward, *Rage* (New York: Simon & Schuster, 2020), p. xviii.
12 Mike Pence, 'There isn't a coronavirus "second wave"', *Wall Street Journal* (16 June 2020).
13 Megan Greene, 'Fear is a more potent weapon than we know in the fight against Covid', *Financial Times* (11 November 2020).
14 Steve Holland and Michael Martina, 'In split-screen town halls, Trump and Biden squabble over coronavirus response', *Reuters* (15 October 2020).
15 https://www.whitehouse.gov/briefing-room/speeches-remarks/2021/01/20/inaugural-address-by-president-joseph-r-biden-jr/
16 Robert Peckham, 'The chronopolitics of COVID-19', *American Literature*, vol. 92, no. 4 (December 2020), pp. 767–79 (p. 770).
17 https://www.who.int/director-general/speeches/detail/who-director-general-s-opening-remarks-at-the-media-briefing-on-covid-19---11-march-2020
18 'De Blasio scares, Cuomo soothes', *Wall Street Journal* (19 March 2020).
19 Damian R. Murray and Mark Schaller, 'The behavioral immune system: Implications for social cognition, social interaction, and social influence', in James M. Olson and Mark P. Zann, eds., *Advances in Experimental Social Psychology* (Cambridge, MA: Academic Press, 2016), pp. 75–129.
20 David Robson, 'The fear of coronavirus is changing our psychology', *BBC Future* (2 April 2020).
21 Mark McDonald, *United States of Fear: How America Fell Victim to a Mass Delusional Psychosis* (New York and Nashville: Post Hill Press, 2021); *Freedom from Fear: A 12 Step Guide to Personal and National Recovery* (New York and Nashville: Post Hill Press, 2022), p. 8. The term 'mass formation psychosis' was used by Robert Malone – a controversial doctor and infectious disease researcher who has claimed that Covid-19 vaccines are ineffective and opposed coronavirus mandates – on Joe Rogan's Spotify podcast, *The Joe Rogan Experience*. Malone likened the hysterical response

to Covid-19 to Germany in the 1920s and 1930s, where 'they had a highly intelligent, highly educated population, and they went barking mad'; see Linda Qiu, 'Fact-checking Joe Rogan's interview with Robert Malone that caused an uproar', *New York Times* (8 February 2022).

22 https://www.who.int/dg/speeches/detail/munich-security-conference

23 Rothkopf, 'When the buzz bites back', p. 5.

24 Robert Peckham, 'Covid-19 infodemic: To stem the tide of panic, we need to understand people's fears, not condemn them', *South China Morning Post* (1 March 2020); '"This is a time for facts, not fear," says WHO chief as COVID-19 virus spreads', *UN News* (15 February 2020).

25 https://reports.weforum.org/global-risks-2013/

26 https://counterhate.com/research/the-disinformation-dozen/

27 See Stuart Russell, *Human Compatible: Artificial Intelligence and the Problem of Control* (New York: Viking, 2019).

28 https://openai.com/product/gpt-4

29 https://futureoflife.org/open-letter/pause-giant-ai-experiments/[.] This warning was pre-empted by an earlier open letter published in 2015. 'Because of the great potential of AI, it is important to research how to reap its benefits while avoiding potential pitfalls': https://futureoflife.org/open-letter/ai-open-letter/

30 Flora Carmichael and Jack Goodman, 'Vaccine rumours debunked: Microchips, "altered DNA" and more', *BBC News* (2 December 2020).

31 https://www.weforum.org/agenda/2020/06/great-reset-launch-prince-charles-guterres-georgieva-burrow/[;] Klaus Schwab, 'Now is the time for a "great reset"', *World Economic Forum* (3 June 2020); Klaus Schwab and Thierry Malleret, *Covid-19: The Great Reset* (Geneva: Forum Publishing/World Economic Forum, 2020), p. 3; see also Jack Goodman and Flora Carmichael, 'The coronavirus pandemic "Great Reset" theory and a false vaccine claim debunked', *BBC News* (22 November 2020).

32 Seth Mnookin, *The Panic Virus: A True Story of Medicine, Science, and Fear* (New York: Simon & Schuster, 2011).

33 Christie Aschwanden, 'Five reasons why COVID herd immunity is probably impossible', *Nature*, vol. 591, no. 7851 (March 2021), pp. 520–22.

34 For an account of how '"Plandemic" went from a niche conspiracy video to a mainstream phenomenon', see Sheera Frenkel, Ben

Decker and Davey Alba, 'How the "Plandemic" movie and its falsehoods spread widely online', *New York Times* (20 May 2020).

35 Ahmar Khan, 'Trudeau says he "won't back down" from anti-vaxx protesters', *Global News* (6 September 2021).

36 Paul Kingsnorth, *The Vaccine Moment: Covid, Control and the Machine* (2022); also 'How fear fuels the vaccine wars', *UnHerd* (30 November 2021).

37 Lewis, 'Has anyone seen the President?'

38 Elon Musk, who acquired Twitter in October 2022, has ended lifetime suspensions from the platform and in November 2022 reinstated Donald Trump's account.

39 Timothy Snyder, *The Road to Unfreedom: Russia, Europe, America* (New York: Tim Duggan Books, 2018), pp. 10–12, 162–6; Naím, *Revenge of Power*, pp. 158–60.

40 Fang Fang, *Wuhan Diary: Dispatches from a Quarantined City*, trans. Michael Berry (New York: HarperCollins, 2020), pp. 13, 44, 171–2, 7, 4, 177, 53, 90, 91.

41 'China: National security law must not become a weapon of fear', *Amnesty International* (30 June 2020).

42 'Amnesty to close Hong Kong offices over national security law', *BBC News* (25 October 2021).

43 'Dragon strike: China has launched rule by fear in Hong Kong', *Economist* (28 May 2020).

44 Isabel Hilton, 'Beijing's Hong Kong takeover is a masterclass in creating fear', *Financial Times* (3 July 2020).

45 Kimmy Chung, 'Hong Kong leader Carrie Lam slams Trump administration's "double standard" for city, points to force used at US protests', *South China Morning Post* (2 June 2020); Jennifer Creery, 'Not doom and gloom: Hong Kong's Carrie Lam says "mild" security law "removes fear"', *Hong Kong Free Press* (7 July 2020).

46 Vivian Wang, 'As Hong Kong law goes after "black sheep," fear clouds universities', *New York Times* (7 November 2020).

47 Wang, 'Hong Kong law'.

48 Emma Graham-Harrison, 'Hong Kong police launch hotline for residents to inform on each other', *Guardian* (5 November 2020).

49 Michael Bristow, 'Hong Kong's new security law: Why it scares people', *BBC News* (1 July 2020).

50 Paul Mozur, 'TikTok to withdraw from Hong Kong as tech giants halt data requests', *New York Times* (6 July 2020); Christy Leung, 'Hong Kong police to launch national security hotline for public to

help specialist officers enforce Beijing-imposed law', *South China Morning Post* (28 October 2020); Graham-Harrison, 'Hong Kong police'.

51 Eric Baculinao and Yuliya Talmazan, 'Chinese citizen journalist Zhang Zhan jailed for "provoking trouble" with Wuhan reporting', *NBC News* (28 December 2020).

52 Wang, 'Hong Kong law'.

53 'Pillar of shame: Hong Kong's Tiananmen Square statue removed', *BBC News* (23 December 2021).

54 Elaine Showalter, *Hystories: Hysterical Epidemics and Modern Media* (New York: Columbia University Press, 1997). On the rise of a culture of victimhood in the 1980s linked to risk aversion and to fears of harassment and abuse, see Furedi, *Culture of Fear*, pp. 45–106.

55 Jenkins, *Decade of Nightmares*, pp. 14, 108–33.

56 Robby Soave, *Panic Attack: Young Radicals in the Age of Trump* (New York: St. Martin's Press, 2019), p. 11.

57 Chimamanda Ngozi Adichie, 'The four freedoms: Freedom of speech', The Reith Lectures, *BBC Radio 4* (30 November 2022).

58 https://www.amnesty.org/en/petition/julian-assange-usa-justice/

59 Evgeny Morozov, *The Net Delusion: The Dark Side of Internet Freedom* (New York: Public Affairs, 2011); see also his 'Critique of techno-feudal reason', *New Left Review*, nos. 133/134 (2022), pp. 89–126.

60 *China: Country Climate and Development Report* [CCDR] (Washington, DC: World Bank, 2022), p. 2.

61 Mark Stevenson, 'In Mexico, "green gold" brings both riches and violence', *AP News* (23 October 2019).

62 Olaf Scholz, 'The global *Zeitenwende*: How to avoid a new Cold War in a multipolar era', *Foreign Affairs*, vol. 102, no. 1 (January/February 2023), pp. 22–38.

Index

Note: The index covers the main text but not the Illustrations, Acknowledgements or Notes. Entries beginning with numbers, like '9/11' and '2001: A Space Odyssey' are alphabetised as though spelled out, in this case at 'nine' and 'two'. The English-language titles of literary works, movies and paintings, are alphabetised ignoring initial articles (A, An and The).

Index

Index

Index

Index

Index

Index

Index

Index